GLACIER NATIONAL PARK

BECKY LOMAX

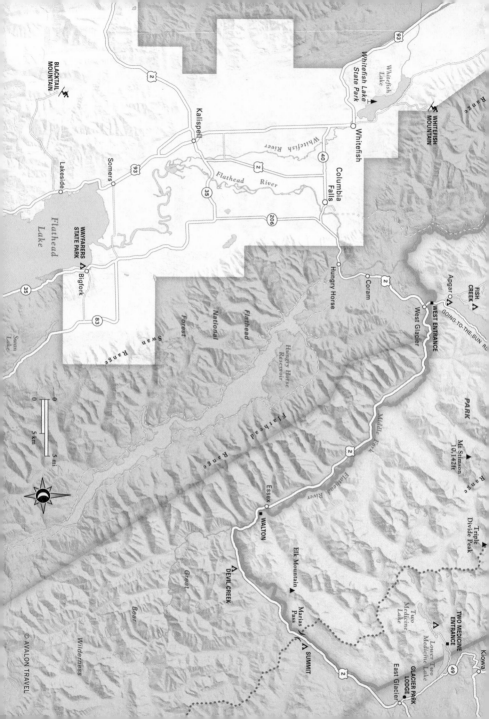

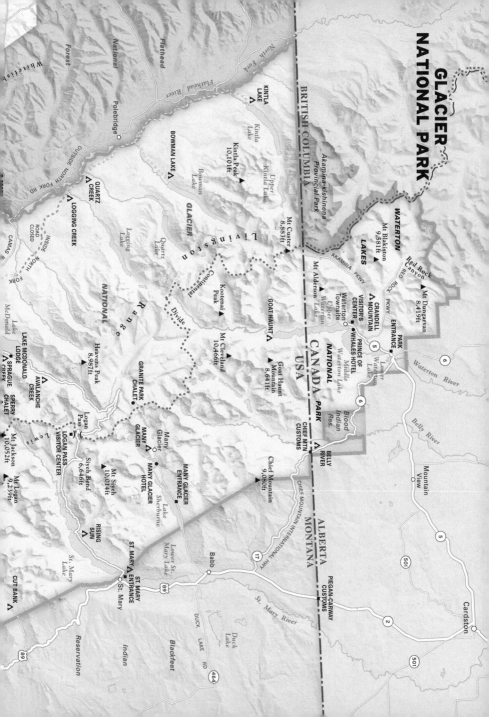

Contents

Glacier National Park

Glacier National Park is the undisputed "Crown of the Continent." It's a place where the earth's forces have left their imprints on the landscape with jagged arêtes, red pinnacles, and glacier-carved basins. Acres of lush green parkland plunge from jagged summits. Waterfalls roar, ice cracks, and rockfall echoes in scenery still under the paintbrush of change.

In this rugged one million acres, indigenous grizzly bears and wolves top the food chain. Mountain goats prance on precarious ledges. Wolverines romp in high glacial cirques. Bighorn sheep graze in alpine meadows while pikas shriek nearby. Only two animals present in Lewis and Clark's day are missing: the woodland caribou and bison.

The Continental Divide splits Glacier into the west side and the east side. They differ in character, yet are wrought from the same geologic building blocks. Two Wild and Scenic Rivers splash along park boundaries, converging at 3,150 feet in elevation, while six peaks surpass 10,000 feet. Mount Cleveland is the tallest, its north face one of the highest vertical walls in the United States.

Slicing through the park's heart, the historic Going-to-the-Sun Road twists and turns on a narrow cliff climb. Tunnels, arches, and bridges lead sightseers

Clockwise from top left: a hanging valley; Trail of the Cedars; mountain goat; bear grass; crossing a creek; kayaking Lake McDonald.

over precipices where seemingly no road could go. Visitors overlook ice-abraded valleys, thundering cascades, mammoth lakes, and serrated peaks.

More than 700 miles of trails wind through Glacier's remote wilderness. Hikers walk up verdant valleys, beneath frigid waterfalls, and over high passes. Peak panoramas and blue-green lakes are strung like pearls along trails in places of solitude.

Designated a Biosphere Reserve by the United Nations Educational, Scientific, and Cultural Organization (UNESCO), Glacier hosts a rich diversity of wildlife and has a wealth of natural attributes, boasting a tremendous geological heritage, as well as a cultural history as sacred Native American land. Glacier National Park, combined with Canada's Waterton Lakes National Park, is the world's first International Peace Park and has also been declared a World Heritage Site by UNESCO.

As the Crown of the Continent, the park's glaciers fuel North America's major rivers, with crystal-clear water tumbling to Hudson Bay, the Gulf of Mexico, and the Pacific. But those glaciers will soon meet their demise. That change will repaint the scenery once again.

Glacier preserves some of the nation's wildest country. Welcome to this rugged slice of nature's best.

Clockwise from top left: bicycling Going-to-the-Sun Road; hiking through Preston Park wildflowers; St. Mary Falls; black bear.

Planning Your Trip

Where to Go

West Glacier and Apgar

West Glacier and Apgar form the park's western portal. Divided by a nationally designated **Wild and Scenic River,** the pair attracts a frenzy of visitors with **white-water rafting, horseback riding, fishing, kayaking, boating, and hiking.**

North Fork

Escape the crowds in the remote North Fork on Glacier's west side. It has real rusticity, not just the look of it. **Polebridge Mercantile** and **Northern Lights Saloon** attract travelers who relish bumpy dirt roads, solitude at **Bowman** and **Kintla Lakes,** and wolf serenades.

Going-to-the-Sun Road

Glacier's biggest attraction and the only road

bisecting the park leads drivers on a skinny cliff shimmy into the craggy alpine. The National Historic Landmark crosses the **Continental Divide** at **Logan Pass** and accesses top-of-the-world trails.

St. Mary and Many Glacier

Small, seasonal **St. Mary** bustles as a hub of campgrounds, lodges, cabins, cafés, shops, and Going-to-the-Sun Road's eastern portal. Just north, the grizzly bear haven at **Many Glacier** holds the historic **Many Glacier Hotel** and trails to sapphire lakes and high passes.

Two Medicine and East Glacier

In Glacier's southeast corner, the historic **Glacier Park Lodge** greets travelers with its flowered walkway and huge lobby. **Two Medicine Lake**

hiking Scenic Point Trail in Two Medicine

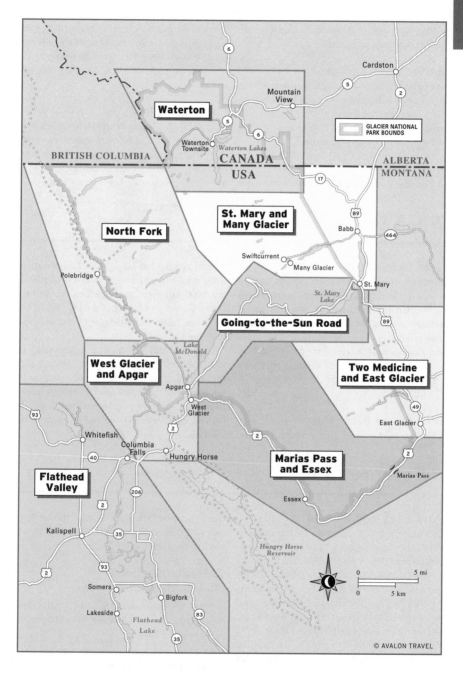

Cardston

Mountain View

Waterton

Waterton Townsite · Waterton Lakes

BRITISH COLUMBIA · CANADA · USA · ALBERTA · MONTANA

GLACIER NATIONAL PARK BOUNDS

North Fork

St. Mary and Many Glacier

Babb

Swiftcurrent · Many Glacier

Polebridge

St. Mary Lake · St. Mary

Lake McDonald

Going-to-the-Sun Road

West Glacier and Apgar

Apgar

Two Medicine and East Glacier

West Glacier

East Glacier

Whitefish

Columbia Falls · Hungry Horse

Flathead Valley

Marias Pass and Essex

Marias Pass

Kalispell

Essex

Somers · Bigfork

Lakeside · Flathead Lake

Hungry Horse Reservoir

0 5 mi
0 5 km

© AVALON TRAVEL

yields a quiet contrast for hikers, boaters, anglers, wildlife-watchers, and campers.

Marias Pass and Essex

Pale next to Going-to-the-Sun Road's drama, U.S. 2 crosses mile-high **Marias Pass** in the fastest route over the **Continental Divide**. The scenic drive squeezes between Glacier and the **Bob Marshall Wilderness Complex.**

Waterton

In Canada, **Waterton Lakes National Park** provides access to Glacier's remote north end via boat across the international boundary to **Goat Haunt, USA.** Waterton Townsite bustles with boat tours, hiking, shopping, bicycling, dining, and camping.

Flathead Valley

Flathead Valley towns **Whitefish, Columbia Falls, Kalispell,** and **Bigfork** draw visitors for their unique personalities. They are outdoor towns with boating, fishing, rafting, camping, biking, golf, swimming, hiking, and skiing.

When to Go

High Season (June-Sept.)

Summer attracts crowds when **lodges, campgrounds, and trails are open.** Barring deep snows, **Going-to-the-Sun Road is open mid-June-mid-October,** with peak visitation and the best weather crammed into July and August. Snow buries some trails into July. Mosquitoes descend in early summer, wildflowers peak in late July, and huckleberries ripen in August.

Off-Season (Oct.-May)

Although saddled with unpredictable weather, off-season offers less-hectic visits. Low-elevation trails are usually snow-free May-October, but **minimal commercial services are open.** When **Going-to-the-Sun Road is closed to vehicles,** bikers and hikers tour it without cars in spring and fall.

In **spring,** May-June rains intersperse with cobalt-blue skies. In **fall,** warm bug-free days and cool nights usher in the larch and aspen turning gold. Peak-top snows descend in September. In **winter,** snow closes most park roads, which become quiet snowshoeing and cross-country ski trails.

Before You Go

Park Fees and Passes

Entrance passes are valid for seven days. Vehicle entrance costs $30 ($20 winter), motorcyclists pay $25 ($15 winter), hikers and bicyclists pay $15 ($10 winter). **Annual passes** include the Glacier National Park Annual Pass ($50) or the America the Beautiful National Parks and Federal Recreational Lands Passes ($80, free for military and fourth graders). Lifetime passes are available for U.S. seniors ($10, increasing to $80 in 2017). Free admission is on Martin Luther King Day (Jan.), National Park Week (Apr.), National Park Service Birthday (Aug.), Public Lands Day (Sept.), and Veterans Day (Nov. 11).

Entrance Stations

Glacier has eight entrance stations:

- **West Glacier** from U.S. 2; west portal for Going-to-the-Sun Road and Lake McDonald (open year-round)

- **St. Mary** on U.S. 89; east portal for Going-to-the-Sun Road (open May-Oct.)

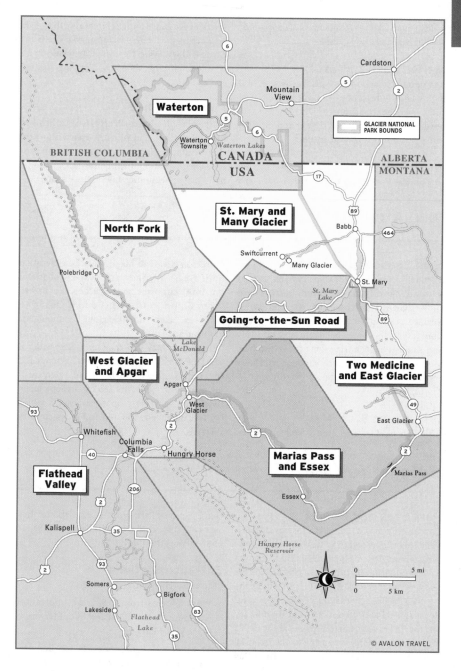

GLACIER NATIONAL PARK BOUNDS

Waterton

St. Mary and Many Glacier

North Fork

Going-to-the-Sun Road

West Glacier and Apgar

Two Medicine and East Glacier

Marias Pass and Essex

Flathead Valley

Cardston

Mountain View

Waterton Townsite

Waterton Lakes

BRITISH COLUMBIA

CANADA
USA

ALBERTA
MONTANA

Babb

Swiftcurrent

Many Glacier

St. Mary

St. Mary Lake

Polebridge

Lake McDonald

Apgar

West Glacier

Whitefish

Columbia Falls

Hungry Horse

East Glacier

Marias Pass

Essex

Kalispell

Hungry Horse Reservoir

Somers

Bigfork

Lakeside

Flathead Lake

0   5 mi

0   5 km

© AVALON TRAVEL

yields a quiet contrast for hikers, boaters, anglers, wildlife-watchers, and campers.

Marias Pass and Essex

Pale next to Going-to-the-Sun Road's drama, U.S. 2 crosses mile-high **Marias Pass** in the fastest route over the **Continental Divide.** The scenic drive squeezes between Glacier and the **Bob Marshall Wilderness Complex.**

Waterton

In Canada, **Waterton Lakes National Park** provides access to Glacier's remote north end via boat across the international boundary to **Goat Haunt, USA.** Waterton Townsite bustles with boat tours, hiking, shopping, bicycling, dining, and camping.

Flathead Valley

Flathead Valley towns **Whitefish, Columbia Falls, Kalispell,** and **Bigfork** draw visitors for their unique personalities. They are outdoor towns with boating, fishing, rafting, camping, biking, golf, swimming, hiking, and skiing.

When to Go

High Season (June-Sept.)

Summer attracts crowds when **lodges, campgrounds, and trails are open.** Barring deep snows, **Going-to-the-Sun Road is open mid-June-mid-October,** with peak visitation and the best weather crammed into July and August. Snow buries some trails into July. Mosquitoes descend in early summer, wildflowers peak in late July, and huckleberries ripen in August.

Off-Season (Oct.-May)

Although saddled with unpredictable weather, off-season offers less-hectic visits. Low-elevation trails are usually snow-free May-October, but **minimal commercial services are open.** When **Going-to-the-Sun Road is closed to vehicles,** bikers and hikers tour it without cars in spring and fall.

In **spring,** May-June rains intersperse with cobalt-blue skies. In **fall,** warm bug-free days and cool nights usher in the larch and aspen turning gold. Peak-top snows descend in September. In **winter,** snow closes most park roads, which become quiet snowshoeing and cross-country ski trails.

Before You Go

Park Fees and Passes

Entrance passes are valid for seven days. Vehicle entrance costs $30 ($20 winter), motorcyclists pay $25 ($15 winter), hikers and bicyclists pay $15 ($10 winter). **Annual passes** include the Glacier National Park Annual Pass ($50) or the America the Beautiful National Parks and Federal Recreational Lands Passes ($80, free for military and fourth graders). Lifetime passes are available for U.S. seniors ($10, increasing to $80 in 2017). Free admission is on Martin Luther King Day (Jan.), National Park Week (Apr.), National Park Service Birthday (Aug.), Public Lands Day (Sept.), and Veterans Day (Nov. 11).

Entrance Stations

Glacier has eight entrance stations:

- **West Glacier** from U.S. 2; west portal for Going-to-the-Sun Road and Lake McDonald (open year-round)
- **St. Mary** on U.S. 89; east portal for Going-to-the-Sun Road (open May-Oct.)

If You Want...

- **Bicycling:** For road cyclists, the coup is the demanding, but scenic climb of **Going-to-the-Sun Road.**

- **Backpacking:** Reserve a backcountry permit for the 52-mile **North Circle** loop from Many Glacier, 33-mile **Boulder Pass,** or 28-mile **Gunsight Pass.**

- **Fishing:** Cast a line for wild trout into the **North Fork** or **Middle Fork of the Flathead River,** which form boundaries of the park.

- **Hiking:** In summer, the most popular and crowded trails are located in Many Glacier (**Iceberg Lake, Grinnell Lake,** and **Grinnell Glacier**) and at Logan Pass (**Hidden Lake Overlook** and **Highline Trail**). Two Medicine offers more solitude on the **Dawson-Pitamakin Loop** or **Cobalt Lake** trails.

- **Horseback Riding:** Hop on guided horse rides in **Many Glacier, Apgar, West Glacier, East Glacier,** and **Lake McDonald.**

- **Lakes:** Going-to-the-Sun Road flanks **Lake McDonald** and **St. Mary Lake,** the park's two largest lakes. Paved roads also terminate at smaller subalpine lakes at **Two Medicine** or **Many Glacier,** but to avoid crowds, head up the North Fork to the solitude of **Kintla Lake** or **Bowman Lake.**

rafting the Middle Fork of the Flathead River

- **River Rafting:** Four rafting companies based out of West Glacier guide white-water, scenic float, or overnight trips on the **North Fork** and **Middle Fork of the Flathead River.**

- **Wildflowers:** Alpine wildflowers burst into bloom on the meadows at **Logan Pass** in July and early August. They bloom earlier in July in lower elevations and on **Many Glacier Road** or **Two Medicine Road.**

- **Many Glacier** from U.S. 89; leads to Many Glacier and Swiftcurrent (open mid-May-early Nov.)

- **Two Medicine** from MT 49; leads to Two Medicine Lake (open late May-Oct.)

- **Polebridge** via Outside North Fork Road; access to Bowman and Kintla Lakes (open late May-Oct.)

- **Camas** via Outside North Fork Road; connects to Apgar and West Glacier (open mid-May-Oct.)

- **Cut Bank** from U.S. 89; dirt road leads to Cut Bank Campground and trailheads (open June-Sept.)

- **Goat Haunt** by boat or trail from Waterton Lakes National Park (open late May-mid-Sept.)

Reservations

Advance reservations for all in-park lodgings are **imperative,** especially for July and August. Contact **Xanterra** (855/733-4522, www.glacier-nationalparklodges.com) 13 months in advance

Granite Park Chalet

for Many Glacier Hotel, Lake McDonald Lodge, Rising Sun Motor Inn, Swiftcurrent Motor Inn, and Apgar Village Inn. Make reservations a year ahead with **Glacier Park, Inc.** (406/892-2525, www.glacierparkinc.com) for Apgar Village Lodge and Motel Lake McDonald. For the Granite or Sperry backcountry chalets, make reservations in early January through **Belton Chalets** (406/387-5654 or 888/345-2649, www. sperrychalet.com, www.graniteparkchalet.com).

Most of Glacier's 13 campgrounds are **first-come, first-served.** Reservations (877/444-6777, www.recreation.gov) are accepted for **Fish Creek** (176 sites), **St. Mary** (146 sites), and **Many Glacier** (41 sites) starting six months in advance. Reserve group campsites 12 months in advance. If you want to backpack, secure an advance reservation ($40) for a **backcountry permit** ($7 pp per day) starting mid-March, or pick up a permit one day before your departure.

In the Park

Visitors Centers

Glacier National Park has tiny visitors centers. On Going-to-the-Sun Road, **Apgar Visitor Center** (year-round, weekends only in winter) sits at the west entrance and **St. Mary Visitor Center** (late May-early Oct.) at the east entrance, while **Logan Pass Visitor Center** (mid-June-mid-Sept.) perches at the apex.

Campgrounds

The park houses 13 campgrounds. **Apgar, Fish Creek, Sprague Creek,** and **Avalanche** flank the Lake McDonald Valley on the west side of Going-to-the-Sun Road, while **Rising Sun** and **St. Mary** anchor the east side. On the park's east side, three separate entrance roads terminate at **Two Medicine, Cut Bank,** and **Many**

Tips for Beating the Crowds

In recent years, Glacier has seen record-breaking crowds in summer. Parking fills up at Logan Pass and some trailheads, a few overcrowded trails see long lines of hikers, and shuttles pack out with riders. So what can you do to have a more enjoyable trip?

- **Visit in June or September.** Avoid the crowd season between July 4 and Labor Day. Because June still has snow in the high country, precluding access to Logan Pass and some trails, plan for potential limitations pending road plowing and weather. September brings more breathing space with access to Logan Pass and high-elevation trails. But be ready for schizophrenic weather bouncing between warm weather and snow.

- **Drive Going-to-the-Sun Road early or late.** Once open for the season, you can drive Going-to-the-Sun Road 24/7. Drive it to catch the sunrise or sunset, and you'll encounter fewer people. Plus, early morning and evening yield better lighting for photography.

- **Spend the Evening at Logan Pass.** Instead of spending the day at Logan Pass, arrive around 5pm to hike Hidden Lake Overlook with a picnic dinner. Due to bears, be off the trail by dusk. Then, stay in the parking lot after dark to soak up the Milky Way from this location with minimal light pollution.

- **Hike off the beaten path.** Avoid the heavily used trails along the Going-to-the-Sun Road corridor and in Many Glacier. Instead, hike trails in Two Medicine (Scenic Point, Cobalt Lake, Dawson-Pitamakin), Cut Bank (Triple Divide, Medicine Grizzly Lake), or the North Fork (Glacier View, Numa Lookout).

- **Plan ahead for backpacking.** Apply in mid-March for an advance reservation for a summer backpacking permit to get to those idyllic backcountry havens.

- **Camp and stay put.** Rather than fighting for a new campsite in a new campground every morning, select a campground to use as home base. Then, drive to other locations as day trips. Make reservations six months ahead for campgrounds at St. Mary, Fish Creek, and Many Glacier.

Glacier. In the remote North Fork Valley, smaller campgrounds are at **Kintla Lake, Bowman Lake, Quartz Creek,** and **Logging Creek.** Check fill times online (www.nps.gov/glac).

Getting Around

The **free Going-to-the-Sun Road shuttles** (www.nps.gov/glac, July-early Sept.) transport visitors to 17 locations on Going-to-the-Sun Road, including Logan Pass, trailheads, campgrounds, and lodges. Shuttles outside the park are run for a fee by **Glacier Park, Inc.** (406/892-2525, www.glacierparkinc.com) and **Xanterra** (855/733-4522, www.glaciernationalparklodges.com). Historic **red buses** (855/733-4522, www.glaciernationalparklodges.com) and large-windowed **Sun Tours** coaches (406/226-9220, http://glaciersuntours.com) tour Going-to-the-Sun Road in summer.

Weather, rockfall, fire, snow, floods, and construction can close the Sun Road. Check on current conditions for driving all park roads (406/888-7800, www.nps.gov/glac).

Glacier In-Park Lodging

	Location	Price	Season	Amenities
Apgar Campground	Apgar	$20	Apr.–Oct.	tent sites, unserviced RV sites
Fish Creek Campground	Apgar	$23	June–early Sept.	tent sites, unserviced RV sites
Apgar Village Lodge	Apgar	$100-400	late May–late Sept.	motel rooms, cabins
Apgar Village Inn	Apgar	$160-290	late May–mid-Sept.	motel rooms
Logging Creek Campground	North Fork	$10	July–mid-Sept.	tent sites
Quartz Creek Campground	North Fork	$10	July–Oct.	tent sites
Bowman Lake Campground	North Fork	$15	late May–Oct.	tent sites
Kintla Lake Campground	North Fork	$15	mid-June–Oct.	tent sites
Avalanche Campground	Going-to-the-Sun Road	$20	mid-June–mid- Sept.	tent sites, unserviced RV sites
Rising Sun Campground	Going-to-the-Sun Road	$20	mid-June–mid-Sept.	tent sites, unserviced RV sites
Sprague Creek Campground	Going-to-the-Sun Road	$20	early May–mid-Sept.	tent sites, unserviced RV sites
Lake McDonald Lodge	Going-to-the-Sun Road	$105-360	late May–late Sept.	hostel rooms, main lodge rooms, cottage rooms, suites, restaurants
Motel Lake McDonald	Going-to-the-Sun Road	$130-170	early June–mid- Sept.	motel rooms
Rising Sun Motor Inn	Going-to-the-Sun Road	$155-175	mid-June–mid-Sept.	cabins, motel rooms, restaurant
Sperry Chalet	Going-to-the-Sun Road	$150-220 pp	early July–early Sept.	Full-service backcountry lodge
Granite Park Chalet	Going-to-the-Sun Road	$80-105 pp	July–early Sept.	Backcountry hostel
St. Mary Campground	St. Mary	$23	Apr.–Oct.	tent sites, unserviced RV sites
Many Glacier Campground	Many Glacier	$23	late May–Oct.	tent sites, unserviced RV sites
Swiftcurrent Motor Inn	Many Glacier	$95-175	mid-June–mid-Sept.	cabins, motel rooms, restaurant
Many Glacier Hotel	Many Glacier	$186-528	mid-June–mid-Sept.	hotel rooms, suites, restaurant
Cut Bank Campground	Two Medicine	$10	early June–late Sept.	tent sites, unserviced RV sites
Two Medicine Campground	Two Medicine	$20	late May–Oct.	tent sites, unserviced RV sites

Lake McDonald Lodge

Siyeh Pass

Best of Glacier National Park

Exploring Glacier National Park, along with Waterton Lakes National Park—collectively the Waterton-Glacier International Peace Park—yields indelible memories. Enjoy a two-nation vacation by staying in historic lodges. Plan ahead; you'll need lodging reservations inside the park a year in advance.

Day 1

Meet Glacier by starting at **Lake McDonald.** Settle into the historic **Lake McDonald Lodge** for two nights and enjoy the lake with an hour of paddling, motorboating, or swimming. Dine early in **Russell's Fireside Dining Room** in time to take the evening **red bus tour** to **Logan Pass.**

Day 2

In the morning, hike **Trail of the Cedars and Avalanche Lake** to revel in the western forest environment. In the afternoon, don a life jacket for splashing down the **Middle Fork of the**

Flathead River with one of West Glacier's raft companies. A photographer captures your paddling in frothy Bonecrusher Rapid.

Day 3

Get an early departure up **Going-to-the-Sun Road** to hike through the wildflowers of **Preston Park** to **Siyeh Pass.** Take in views of peaks and glaciers, too. Descending eastward on the Sun Road, stop at scenic pullouts and **St. Mary Visitor Center.** Head to historic **Many Glacier Hotel** for three nights.

Day 4

In the morning while the water is calm, rent a canoe or kayak to paddle around **Swiftcurrent Lake,** listening for loons. At noon, saddle up to **ride horseback** with Swan Mountain Outfitters. Relax on the hotel deck, watch for **bears** on Mount Altyn, **moose** in Swiftcurrent Lake, and the sunset over the Continental Divide.

horse at Swan Mountain Outfitters at Many Glacier

Day 5

Hop the first boat across **Swiftcurrent Lake** and **Lake Josephine** to hike to **Grinnell Glacier** with a park naturalist for a close-up view of one of the park's remaining glaciers. The trail climbs above turquoise **Grinnell Lake** and along cliffs. Steep switchbacks ascend moraine to overlook **Upper Grinnell Lake** and the shrinking ice.

Day 6

Head out early to cross the international border into **Waterton.** Drive **Akamina Parkway** to **Cameron Lake** for a short paddle or lakeshore walk. In the afternoon, drive **Red Rock Parkway** to tour the interpretive trail around **Red Rock Canyon.** Settle into a lakeside room in the historic **Prince of Wales Hotel** and, by surrey bike, explore the **Waterton Townsite.**

Day 7

Take the **Upper Waterton Lake** tour boat across the border to **Goat Haunt** in Glacier. Afterwards, end your week on a high note by climbing **Bear's Hump.** The two-nation view takes in the peaks of Waterton and Glacier.

Best in One Day

Hidden Lake Overlook Trail

Without a doubt, Glacier's biggest attraction is the 50-mile **Going-to-the-Sun Road.** A tour of the road over Logan Pass yields a small taste of the park's grandeur, with waterfalls, immense glacier-carved valleys, and serrated peaks. Depart by 7am; the Logan Pass parking lot often fills by 8:30am. Plan to drive over and back for different views.

ST. MARY

From the east entrance to Going-to-the-Sun Road in St. Mary, enjoy the scenery of **St. Mary Lake,** the second-longest lake in the park. Save the scenic stops in the 18 miles to Logan Pass for the return. After rounding **Going-to-the-Sun Mountain,** you'll burst through the **East Side Tunnel** looking straight at **Logan Pass.**

LOGAN PASS

At **Logan Pass,** nab a photo of the Continental Divide sign, tour the small visitors center and self-guided paved interpretive trails. Climb the board-walk and trail to **Hidden Lake Overlook** for views of Hidden Lake.

LAKE MCDONALD

Descend the west side of the Sun Road 20 miles to **Lake McDonald,** largest of the park's lakes. Save

the sightseeing stops for your return—they're easier to access on the uphill drive. Aim for the historic **Lake McDonald Lodge** for a late lunch. Stroll the grounds and hotel after lunch before beginning your return trip over Logan Pass.

WEST SIDE CLIMB

After driving through the **West Side Tunnel,** stop at **The Loop** to photograph **Heavens Peak.** Between The Loop and Logan Pass, use pullouts to admire the scenery, especially to see **Haystack Falls** and **Bird Woman Falls.** Just before reaching Logan Pass, pull over at **Oberlin Bend Overlook.** Views extend north along the Continental Divide to **Mount Cleveland,** the tallest peak in the park.

EAST SIDE DESCENT

After crossing Logan Pass, descend back into St. Mary Valley. Stop at **Jackson Glacier Overlook** to see **Jackson Glacier** (binoculars will help) and **Sun Point** to take in the Continental Divide to the west. If time permits, finish your day with the late afternoon or evening tour boat ride from **Rising Sun** around **Wild Goose Island.** The tour on **St. Mary Lake** will leave you wanting more.

Best Hikes

Waterton-Glacier International Peace Park is a hiker's paradise, with more than 900 miles of trails. Summer shuttles accommodate point-to-point hiking on Going-to-the-Sun Road and in Waterton.

Trail of the Cedars and Avalanche Lake

In McDonald Valley, a popular trail tours a boardwalk through ancient cedars, from which you can link up with a 1.9-mile trail that cuts up a red-rock side canyon to an idyllic lake. Fed by unseen Sperry Glacier, waterfalls spew down cliffs rimming the lake. A rougher trail continues up-lake to better fishing and thinner crowds.

Highline Trail and Granite Park Chalet

Beginning at Logan Pass, the stunning 11.4-mile point-to-point goat walk tiptoes along the Continental Divide to historic Granite Park Chalet. Hikers often see mountain goats, bighorn sheep, bears, or wolverines.

Siyeh Pass

From Siyeh Bend on Going-to-the-Sun Road, this point-to-point trail circles 10 miles around Going-to-the-Sun Mountain. View glaciers and the colorful wildflowers in Preston Park en route.

Scenic Point

Three miles of switchbacks ascend a rocky slope with sparse vegetation to crest a windswept knoll. Views plummet down to Two Medicine Lake and shoot miles across the plains.

Dawson-Pitamakin Loop

This 17.6-mile loop crosses three passes on a narrow top-of-the-world trek. Subalpine lakes glisten like gems below this bighorn sheep summering range.

Iceberg Lake

Fun for Kids

For a successful Glacier trip with kids, be prepared on hikes and drives. Bring water and snacks; places to fuel kids up are few and far between. Take along layers to don in case the weather sours. Have kids, even little ones, carry their own packs even if they only tote a sweatshirt.

LEARNING

- Stop at a ranger station or visitors center to pick up the Junior Ranger booklet, and complete five activities to receive a badge.

- Visit the Apgar Nature Center for hands-on learning about wildlife, plants, and rocks.

- Hone in on wildlife through the ranger spotting scope in the Swiftcurrent parking lot at Many Glacier.

- Drive through the Bison Paddock in Waterton to see remnants of the herds that once filled the grasslands.

Rent a double kayak to paddle with kids.

ENGAGING

- Take older kids for a trail ride on horseback in Apgar, West Glacier, East Glacier, Many Glacier, or Lake McDonald.

- Rent a canoe or kayak for paddle fun on Lake McDonald, Swiftcurrent Lake in Many Glacier, Two Medicine Lake, or at Cameron Lake in Waterton.

- Pedal through the Waterton Townsite on a two-person surrey bike.

- Raft the Middle Fork of the Flathead River with one of the companies in West Glacier. Older kids will love the white water, but do a scenic float with young children.

- Fish Lower McDonald Creek.

- Go stargazing at Logan Pass.

HIKING

After hitting one of these trails, reward young hikers with ice cream at Eddie's in Apgar.

- Hike from Logan Pass to Hidden Lake Overlook to walk across the Continental Divide. Sturdy hikers can extend the trail to swim in Hidden Lake.

- Hop the double boat ride across Swiftcurrent Lake and Lake Josephine in Many Glacier to hike to Grinnell Lake, crossing a river on a swinging bridge.

- Hike to Avalanche Lake to wade at its foot or fish at its head.

Iceberg Lake

To see icebergs in August, a 5.2-mile ascent in Many Glacier leads to one of the park's most popular lakes tucked into a toothy cirque. The brave dive in for an icy swim.

Grinnell Glacier

The 5.5-mile path delights with wildflowers, bighorn sheep, grizzly bears, waterfalls, and turquoise Grinnell Lake. At the top, the glacier basin fills with crevassed ice and icebergs floating in Upper Grinnell Lake.

Ptarmigan Tunnel

From Swiftcurrent, the 5.7-mile trail climbs to a tunnel chiseled through a cliff wall. Creep through the dark, 183-foot-long tunnel to burst out its north side into a blaze of red.

Sperry Glacier

Accessible from Sperry Chalet, climb 3.5 miles through an upper basin of wildflowers, alpine lakes, and rock cairns to a stairway carved through the cliff entrance into the ice-scoured rock of Sperry Glacier basin.

Carthew-Alderson

In Waterton, catch a shuttle for the 18-kilometer (11.2-mile) point-to-point path that crawls over the high, windswept Carthew Pass. The trail dips past Alderson Lake before finishing at the Waterton Townsite.

Flathead-Glacier Road Trip

From popular stops to remote places of solitude, this road loop stitches together touring with iconic scenery. Enjoy this seven-day tour by staying in motels, park lodges, or camping.

Day 1
Kalispell to Whitefish
29 MILES; 1 HOUR

From the gateway town of Kalispell, drive to **Whitefish.** Hop the chairlift at **Whitefish Mountain Resort** for a ride to the summit of **Big Mountain.** Clear days yield your first expansive views of Glacier's peaks. Walk trails around the summit, and visit the **Forest Service Summit Nature Center.** Return to the base to ride the alpine slide, or challenge yourself in the aerial park. Then return to town to stroll through shops and dine. Stay in Whitefish for two nights.

Day 2
Whitefish to Bigfork
64 MILES; 2 HOURS

Drive to **Bigfork** on Flathead Lake. Check out the shops in town. Rent a kayak to paddle **Flathead Lake.** Dine and take in a live performance at the **Bigfork Summer Playhouse.** Return to Whitefish for the night.

Day 3
Whitefish to East Glacier
81 MILES; 2 HOURS

From Whitefish, aim for **West Glacier.** Explore the tiny burg and the historic **Belton Bridge.** Cruise Glacier's southern boundary on U.S. 2 following the **Middle Fork of the Flathead River** as it careens through **John F. Stevens Canyon.** Lunch at the historic **Izaak Walton Inn.** Stop to see the white goats at the **Goat Lick** and the interpretive site at **Marias Pass.** In East Glacier, visit the historic **Glacier Park Lodge** and stay in town for two nights.

Day 4
East Glacier to Browning
66 MILES; 2 HOURS

Pack a lunch for a loop drive in the land of the Blackfeet. From **East Glacier,** head toward **Two Medicine Lake.** Stop to see **Running Eagle Falls** en route and then tour the lake by boat.

Afterwards, drive the curvy Highway 49 and U.S. 89 to reach **Browning,** the center of Blackfeet culture. Tour the small **Museum of the Plains Indian** to get a glimpse into Blackfeet history. Return to East Glacier to dine and spend the night.

Day 5
East Glacier to St. Mary
51 MILES; 2 HOURS

In the morning, aim for **St. Mary,** exploring the mountain front falling away into plains. Stop at the **St. Mary Scenic Overlook and Blackfeet Interpretive Loop** for a panoramic view of peaks and the St. Mary Valley before dropping to the **St. Mary Visitor Center** to tour the Native American exhibit. After lunch, continue north to **Many Glacier.** Visit the historic **Many Glacier Hotel,** stroll the nature trail around **Swiftcurrent Lake** to look for moose, and dine in the hotel. Drive slowly on the **Many Glacier Road** to look for **bears** en route back to St. Mary for the night.

Day 6
St. Mary to Apgar
50 MILES; 2 HOURS

With an early start to beat the crowds and a picnic lunch, drive up **Going-to-the-Sun Road.** Stop at scenic spots: **Wild Goose Island Overlook, Sun Point,** and **Sunrift Gorge.** Walk to **St. Mary Falls.** At **Logan Pass,** take a selfie at the **Continental Divide** sign and hike across the cliff walk on the **Highline Trail.** On the western descent, stop at scenery-laden spots: **Oberlin Bend Overlook, Haystack Falls,** and **The Loop.** Walk into the rainforest of **Trail of the Cedars** before overnighting in Apgar for two nights on **Lake McDonald.**

Day 7
Apgar to Bowman Lake
65 MILES; 4 HOURS

See Glacier's backwoods where fewer people trek. Pack a picnic lunch to drive up the rugged **North Fork Road.** Stop at the **Polebridge Mercantile** for fresh-baked cookies before

Bowman Lake

bouncing to **Bowman Lake** to enjoy a picnic on its idyllic beach. Tour part of the **Inside Road** south toward Logging Ranger Station before returning to Polebridge for dinner at the **Northern Lights Saloon.** Finish your tour back on the beach at Apgar on Lake McDonald watching the setting sun cast alpenglow across Glacier's peaks.

Geologic Wonders

With some of North America's oldest exposed rock, a landscape created from moving earth, and the carving action of ice, Glacier National Park fills one million acres with captivating scenery. Enjoy sinking into iconic Glacier landscapes by touring roads, but then don your hiking boots, for the best of Glacier's features are seen up close from trails.

Rock Features

The geologic landscape of Glacier National Park is like no other. Tremendous forces shaped the scenery. Here's where to see the handiwork of these earth forces.

ANCIENT SEABED LAYERS

An ancient, shallow, inland sea gave Glacier its multicolored rocks. At **Logan Pass,** hike 1.3 miles to **Hidden Lake Overlook,** examining the rocks along the trail. Ripple marks and mud cracks show evidence of the **Belt Sea.** Look for layers of many colors on **Clements Peak,** created from various sediments deposited in the sea.

SHIFTING PLATES

Drive to **Marias Pass** to see where geologists discovered the **Lewis Overthrust Fault,** a shifting of the earth's plates where the Pacific Plate's older rock slid over the Continental Plate's younger rock. Hike to **Firebrand Pass** to see the older mountains drop to the younger plains as you gain elevation.

ICE-SCULPTED ROCK

Ancient rivers of ice followed by a smaller, shorter ice age shaped mountains and valleys throughout Glacier. Even though **Two Medicine** no longer has glaciers, find their footprints in the **U-shaped valley,** Pumpelly Pillar **arête,** and Flinsch Peak **horn.**

Glacial Features

Glacier National Park's ice is melting. The glaciers are predicted to disappear by 2030. So where can you see them before extinction?

BLACKFOOT AND JACKSON GLACIERS

From Going-to-the-Sun Road, **Jackson Glacier Overlook** and the next two pullouts east offer the best views of glaciers. Use binoculars to scope out the glacial basin across the valley or hike eight miles to get a closer look.

SPERRY GLACIER

From **Sperry Chalet,** climb up through tranquil lake shelves and the rock-hewn stairway at **Comeau Pass** into the scoured basin that houses **Sperry Glacier.** Follow rock cairns to an overlook of the ice, now reduced to less than 200 acres.

PIEGAN AND SEXTON GLACIERS

From Siyeh Bend on Going-to-the-Sun Road, hike the **Siyeh Pass Trail.** The route offers views of **Piegan Glacier** while climbing to the pass and **Sexton Glacier** while descending to Sunrift Gorge.

GRINNELL GLACIER

In Many Glacier, hike to **Grinnell Glacier,** the most accessible glacier. Sit on the shore of the frigid iceberg-filled lake at the toe of the melting glacier. On the jagged wall above the lake perch the tiny **Salamander Glacier** and **Gem Glacier,** both of which have shrunk to static snowfields.

Glacier has 60 mammal species and more than 260 species of birds; bring the binoculars to aid in watching wildlife.

INSIDE ROAD

Spot elusive gray wolves on this uncrowded dirt road at dawn or dusk.

MCGEE MEADOWS

The North Fork Valley houses 196 bird species. McGee Meadows bustles with snipes, soras, and red-tailed hawks.

AVALANCHE PATHS

In early spring, grizzly bears prowl for carcasses on avalanche slopes on Mount Cannon and the Glacier Wall on Going-to-the-Sun Road.

LOGAN PASS

Mountain goats and bighorn sheep circle the Logan Pass parking lot and frequent the Hidden Lake Overlook trail.

TWO DOG FLATS

In spring and late fall, elk feed in early morning at Two Dog Flats near Rising Sun while aspens attract woodpeckers, flickers, and owls.

ST. MARY AND VIRGINIA FALLS

These two waterfalls create perfect habitat for dark, bobbing American dippers.

MOUNTS ALTYN AND HENKEL

Grizzly and black bears feed on huckleberries on these two peaks in Many Glacier in late summer.

SWIFTCURRENT VALLEY

A gentle hike runs through moose country to Red Rock and Bullhead Lakes. Listen for white-crowned sparrows, loons, Clark's nutcrackers, and golden eagles.

bighorn sheep ram

GOAT LICK

On U.S. 2, the natural mineral lick attracts mountain goats in early summer.

WATERTON LAKES

Waterton's Maskinonge and Linnet Lakes wetlands abound with ospreys, swans, and kingfishers.

BISON PADDOCK

The Waterton bison paddock houses a small herd of shaggy bovines that once roamed wild.

KOOTENAI LAKES

Hop the Waterton tour boat and hike to Glacier's Kootenai Lakes to see moose and trumpeter swans.

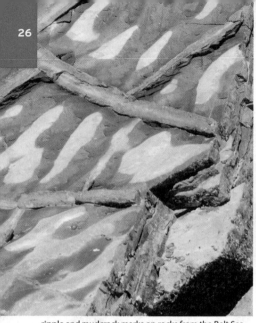

ripple and mudcrack marks on rocks from the Belt Sea

Jackson Glacier

Water Features

Glacier is one of the most water-filled parks in the nation, due to depressions left from glaciers. Experience a few of the park's most notable 762 lakes, all the footprints of glaciers.

LAKES TO TOUR

Take a boat tour on park lakes: **Lake McDonald, Two Medicine,** or **St. Mary.** In Many Glacier, a double boat ride crosses **Swiftcurrent Lake** and **Lake Josephine.** In **Waterton Lakes National Park,** take a two-nation tour that crosses from Canada into the United States on **Waterton Lake.**

LAKES TO PADDLE

For quiet paddling in solitude, escape up the North Fork to remote **Bowman Lake** or **Kintla Lake** for day paddles or overnights in wilderness.

LAKES TO HIKE AND FISH

To see milky turquoise waters produced from glacial melt, hike to **Grinnell Lake** or **Cracker Lake.** To fish for native cutthroat, go to **Red Eagle Lake.** For arctic grayling and rainbow trout, backpack to **Elizabeth Lake.**

West Glacier and Apgar

Look for ★ to find recommended
sights, activities, dining, and lodging.

Highlights

★ **Belton Chalet:** Enjoy a tribute to a bygone era of tourism in a chalet as old as the park. On chillier days, cuddle up at the stone fireplace; on warmer days, lounge at sunset on the deck with a local brew (page 35).

★ **Lake McDonald:** Leap into the park's largest lake for a refreshing swim, or catch the sunset over the water. The clear waters lure paddlers, boaters, anglers, scuba divers, photographers, and rock skippers (page 36).

★ **Apgar Lookout:** Climb to where you can look down at Lake McDonald, West Glacier, and the North Fork. You'll see a huge panorama of peaks from Canada to the park's southern tip (page 38).

★ **Huckleberry Lookout:** Walk along a top-of-the-world ridge where views stretch from Flathead Lake to Canada (page 39).

★ **Rafting Middle Fork of the Flathead River:** A ride on this Wild and Scenic River drops through rapids such as Screaming Right Turn, Bonecrusher, Jaws, and Could Be Trouble. The names say it all (page 42).

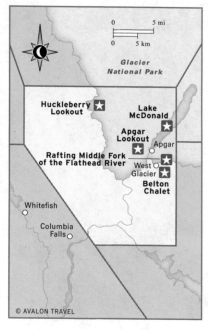

Sitting two miles apart, West Glacier and Apgar span Glacier National Park's southwestern boundary, marked by the Middle Fork of the Flathead River.

While West Glacier sprouted up outside the park along Great Northern Railway tracks, early trapper and logger homesteads dug in a foothold at Apgar on Lake McDonald as the port to the park's wild interior before Going-to-the-Sun Road was built. Connected by the "new bridge," the park entrance road, and a two-mile paved bicycling and walking path, the pair are doorways for exploring Glacier. As such, they throng with cars and visitors in summer; 60 percent of visitors access the park via this west entrance. The communities also launch sightseers in two different directions: to the untrammeled North Fork Valley and to Glacier's crowning highway, Going-to-the-Sun Road.

Today, many concessionaires are headquartered in West Glacier, just outside the national park boundaries. The small town has evolved into a seasonal mecca for rafting, guided hiking and backpacking, guided fishing trips, horseback rides, and helicopter tours. Along with the train station, campgrounds, restaurants, motels, and shops, West

Glacier is a place to gas up the car one last time before seeking the park's interior. On Lake McDonald's shores and inside the park, Apgar swarms in high season, too. Its restaurant, lodging, camping, shopping, boat ramp, and tiny west-side visitors center add to miles of lake sprawling with blue waters and enough shoreline to find a niche for solitude.

HISTORY
Native Americans

For the Ksanka or Standing Arrow people, known today as the Salish and Kootenai, whose lands are at Flathead Lake's south end, Glacier's Lake McDonald area held special significance. Ten thousand generations ago, legend says, the Ksanka were first given a ceremonial dance by the spirits at their winter camp near Apgar. Originally called the Blacktail Deer Dance, the ceremony became an annual event for the Ksanka, and the area became known as "the place where people dance." Today, the annual dance, now called the Jump Dance, takes place on the Flathead

Previous: swimming in Lake McDonald; horseback riding. **Above:** Apgar on Lake McDonald.

West Glacier and Apgar

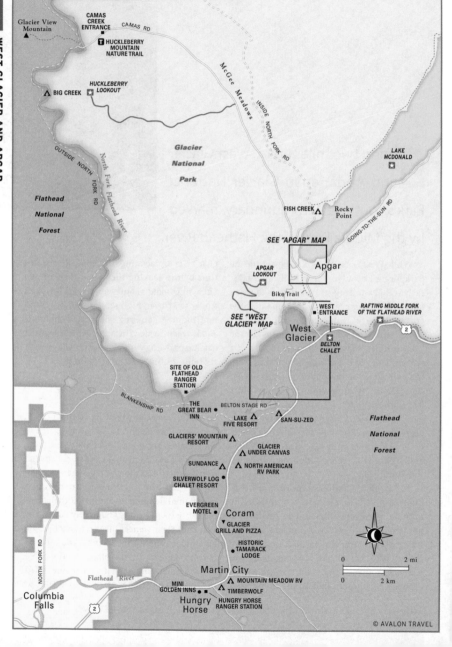

© AVALON TRAVEL

Reservation, but rapids on McDonald Creek still hold the original name, Sacred Dancing Cascade.

Early Tourism

When the Great Northern Railway completed its westbound track in 1891, early visitors jumped off the train in Belton (now West Glacier) to see the area. With no bridge across the Middle Fork of the Flathead, visitors rowed across the river and then saddled up for a horseback ride to Apgar. Finally, in 1895 a rough dirt road eased the two-mile journey, followed two years later by a bridge across the river.

As the railroad dropped visitors in Belton, Lake McDonald homesteaders leaped into the tourism business, offering cabins, meals, pack trips, boat rides, and guided tours. To coincide with Glacier's first summer as a national park, the Great Northern Railway opened Belton Chalet in 1910 across from the depot. After Glacier parkhood, local landowners along Lake McDonald retained their property as inholdings. Some of these are still the property of private families.

Exploring West Glacier and Apgar

VISITORS CENTERS
Apgar Visitor Center

Tucked in the woods at the four-way intersection one mile north of Glacier's west entrance station, **Apgar Visitor Center** (Going-to-the-Sun Rd., 406/888-7940, daily mid-May-early Oct., 8am-6pm daily mid-June-Aug., spring and fall hours shorten, weekends only in winter) is the place to find maps, kids Junior Ranger Program activity guides, ranger-guided walk schedules, astronomy programs, evening naturalist presentation schedules, trail and road conditions, fishing and boating information, and a few shelves that serve as the Glacier National Park Conservancy **bookstore** (406/892-3250, http://glacier.org). The building reflects green standards: restrooms with low-flow toilets, automatic lights, and indigenous flora landscaping. Outdoor interpretive signage highlights information for all major park regions. Paved biking and walking trails from Apgar

Get permits for backpacking at the Apgar Backcountry Permit Office.

West Glacier

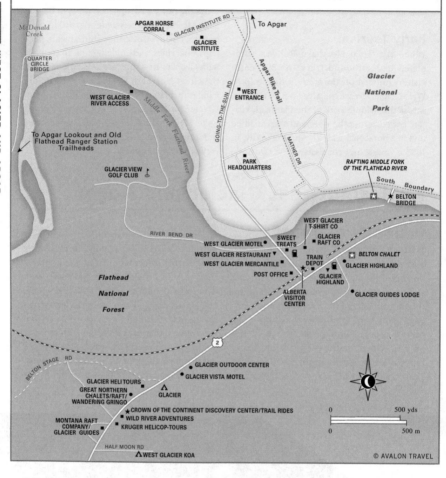

McDonald Creek

APGAR HORSE CORRAL

GLACIER INSTITUTE RD

To Apgar

GLACIER INSTITUTE

QUARTER CIRCLE BRIDGE

Apgar Bike Trail

GOING-TO-THE-SUN RD

Glacier

WEST ENTRANCE

National

Park

WEST GLACIER RIVER ACCESS

Middle Fork Flathead River

To Apgar Lookout and Old Flathead Ranger Station Trailheads

MATHER DR

GLACIER VIEW GOLF CLUB

PARK HEADQUARTERS

RAFTING MIDDLE FORK OF THE FLATHEAD RIVER

South Boundary

BELTON BRIDGE

RIVER BEND DR

WEST GLACIER T-SHIRT CO

WEST GLACIER MOTEL

SWEET TREATS

GLACIER RAFT CO

WEST GLACIER RESTAURANT

TRAIN DEPOT

BELTON CHALET

WEST GLACIER MERCANTILE

GLACIER HIGHLAND

POST OFFICE

GLACIER HIGHLAND

Flathead

National

Forest

ALBERTA VISITOR CENTER

GLACIER GUIDES LODGE

2

BELTON STAGE RD

GLACIER OUTDOOR CENTER

GLACIER VISTA MOTEL

GLACIER HELI TOURS

GREAT NORTHERN CHALETS/RAFT/ WANDERING GRINGO

GLACIER

CROWN OF THE CONTINENT DISCOVERY CENTER/TRAIL RIDES

WILD RIVER ADVENTURES

MONTANA RAFT COMPANY/ GLACIER GUIDES

KRUGER HELICOP-TOURS

HALF MOON RD

WEST GLACIER KOA

0   500 yds

0   500 m

© AVALON TRAVEL

Village and Apgar Campground connect with the visitors center, and an expanded parking area accommodates big RVs. The center serves as a shuttle stop and pickup for concession-operated tours.

For some free, fun, hands-on activities for kids, stop by the **Apgar Nature Center** (10am-4pm daily mid-June-Aug.), in the woods across the street from Eddie's Cafe & Mercantile. With the help of interpretive rangers, learning stations teach about wildlife, geology, and natural history. Rangers also hold Junior Ranger talks and walks.

The **Apgar Backcountry Permit Office** (406/888-7859 May-Oct., 406/888-7800 Nov.-Apr., 7am-4:30pm daily May-Sept., 8am-4pm daily Oct.) is opposite the old red schoolhouse in Apgar. This is the main office for acquiring permits for overnight backpacking or boating trips. Rush hour is the first 2-3 hours of each morning in July and August; lines begin forming at 6am.

Alberta Visitor Information Center

Located in West Glacier, the **Alberta Visitor Information Center** (125 Going-to-the-Sun Rd., 800/252-3782, www.travelalberta.com, 8am-7pm daily late May-early Sept., 8am-5pm daily early-late Sept.) is a building-size advertisement for Alberta, complete with dinosaur bones. For those heading on to Canada, the center is worth a stop to help with travel planning and pick up brochures and maps.

West Glacier Visitor Information Center

Located in Belton Train Depot in West Glacier, the **West Glacier Visitor Information Center** (junction of Going-to-the-Sun Rd. and Hwy. 2, 406/892-3250, http://glacier.org, 1pm-5pm daily summer) is the main Glacier Conservancy bookstore. It also serves as a visitors information center, especially for Flathead Valley.

Crown of the Continent Discovery Center

The **Crown of the Continent Discovery Center** (12000 U.S. 2 E., 406/387-4405, www.crowndiscoverycenter.com, 10am-7pm daily early May-mid-Oct.) is primarily used for booking horseback riding trips with Swan Mountain Outfitters, which operates the adjacent corral and three corrals in Glacier. It also has information on geotourism activities across 18 million acres that includes Glacier National Park, surrounding national forests and wilderness areas, World Heritage Sites, and Canadian national parks.

ENTRANCE STATIONS

Crossing the West Glacier Bridge over the Middle Fork of the Flathead River officially is the entry to Glacier National Park. After the bridge, a parking pullout allows for photo-documenting your travel with the park sign. Be prepared for lines in July and August. In 2016, this entrance station saw more than 11,000 people per day.

The **West Glacier entrance station** is usually staffed during daylight hours in summer and on weekends off-season. When unstaffed, use the self-pay cash-only kiosk to purchase a pass. If you don't have an annual pass, seven-day passes cost $30 per vehicle, $25 for motorcyclists, and $15 for hikers and bikers. Winter rates drop to $20, $15, and $10. The entrance station hands out a map and the summer or winter edition of the *Waterton-Glacier Guide,* the park's newspaper.

From the rough, dirt Outside North Fork Road, the Camas Road connects with Apgar. The **Camas entrance** has a self-pay cash-only kiosk.

SHUTTLES AND TOURS
Shuttles

Seasonal shuttles in summer operate around West Glacier and Apgar. The shuttles do not come with interpretive guides, and rates do not include park entrance fees.

From the Apgar Visitor Center, **free shuttle buses** depart for destinations along the Going-to-the-Sun Road (7am-7pm July-Labor Day). Some early morning shuttles go directly to Logan Pass; others go only to Avalanche or Lake McDonald Lodge. Check the shuttle destination before boarding to be sure it is going where you want to go. The last shuttle departs for Logan Pass at 4:15pm. Apgar has three places to catch the shuttles: the visitors center, village, and campground. Look for the interpretive signs marking the shuttle stops. Shuttles run every 15-30 minutes. The no-reservations, no-tickets shuttles are popular, so you may have to wait an hour for a seat during the peak season. If you are heading toward Logan Pass, be sure to take a day pack with water, snacks, and extra clothing for fast-changing weather. In 2016, a pilot program extended limited shuttles on the west side into September. Check with the park on status.

Meeting all train arrivals and departures, **Xanterra** (855/733-4522, www.glaciernationalparklodges.com, daily late May-late

Sept., adults $5-10, kids half price) shuttles rail passengers between West Glacier's Belton Depot and Apgar Village Inn or Lake McDonald Lodge. Reservations are mandatory.

For connections to or from Flathead Valley, **Glacier Charters** (406/892-3390, http://glaciertransportation.com) runs shuttle vans and small buses by reservation between Glacier Park International Airport and West Glacier or Apgar ($50-80 one-way). The **Glacier Express** (406/892-3390, http://big-mtncommercial.org, July-early Sept., adults $10, kids half price) takes riders between Apgar Visitor Center and Whitefish with four trips each way daily. Buy tickets with cash only in advance at Apgar Visitor Center or Whitefish outlets.

Bus Tours

Two companies offer the easiest way to tour Going-to-the-Sun Road to Logan Pass when it is open. For visitors in RVs, which are not permitted on the road, these are the way to go. Both companies have pickups in West Glacier or Apgar. Rates do not include park entrance fees, meals, taxes, or driver tips. Make reservations at least a day in advance, especially in midsummer.

Glacier Park's fleet of **red buses** (855/733-4522, www.glaciernationalparklodges.com, daily mid-June-mid-Sept., adults $40-98, kids half price) are the best way to tour in historic style, with roll-back tops allowing for unobstructed peak views and au naturel air-conditioning. Half-day, full-day, and evening tours have pickups at West Glacier KOA and Apgar Visitor Center. Before Logan Pass opens, the red buses tour late May-mid June around Huckleberry Mountain.

From the Apgar Visitor Center, **Sun Tours** (406/732-9220 or 800/786-9220, http://glacier-suntours.com, 9am-1pm daily June-Sept., adults $50, kids 6-12 $30) goes to Logan Pass and back. The air-conditioned 25-passenger coaches are comfortable, with extra-big windows enhancing the views. Native American guides give insight into the park's rich Native American heritage from the days of the buffalo to modern spirituality.

Helicopter Tours

Two helicopter tour companies located less than one mile west of the West Glacier train depot fly tours over Glacier National Park daily mid-May-September. Rates range $250-1,100 per person per hour, based on the number of passengers. Since tours are weather dependent, storms may force rescheduling. Make reservations in advance, especially if you want to keep the cost down by sharing the ride with other passengers. **Glacier Heli Tours** (12205 U.S. 2 E., 406/387-4141 or 800/879-9310, www.glacierhelitours.com) flies two helicopters seating four or six passengers for one-hour tours. **Kruger Helicopter Tours** (11892 U.S. 2 E., 406/387-4565 or 800/220-6565, www.krugerhelicopters.com) carries four passengers per bird for 30- or 60-minute tours.

Driving Tour
CAMAS ROAD

From Apgar, the 11.3-mile Camas Road (officially the Camas Creek Cutoff Road, open May-Oct.) goes from Lower McDonald Creek to the North Fork of the Flathead River. In 2015, it was added to the National Register of Historic Places. Climbing along the base of the Apgar Range, the road traverses through the **2003 Robert Fire** and the **2001 Moose Fire**, which offer a contrast in post-burn forest succession. Several pullouts are worth a stop: If you can stand the mosquitoes, grab binoculars to peruse **McGee Meadows** (at 5.5 miles) for moose, deer, and bear. Just west of the Camas entrance station, at 11.1 miles, a turnoff leads to **Huckleberry Mountain Nature Trail**, a 0.9-mile self-guided loop in a thick lodgepole forest regrowing from the 2001 Moose Fire. After crossing the park boundary at the North Fork River, the Camas Road terminates at Outside North Fork Road. Bears frequent the Camas Road in spring; rangers haze them away from the roadway to prevent them from becoming conditioned to people and cars.

Sights

Most visitors head straight to Lake McDonald, the biggest attraction. But smaller noteworthy sights sprinkle through the area.

WEST GLACIER

The town of West Glacier, originally known as Belton, was historically centered around the Belton Train Depot and Belton Chalet. Today, U.S. 2 divides the two, and West Glacier now has recreational concessions such as rafting, backpacking, hiking, helicopter tours, and fishing. To leave the highway rush, drive through the railroad tunnel and enter a historic world of vintage, brown 1938 buildings that house a bar, a restaurant, gift shops, a grocery, and a motel. Fall finds birch leaves covering the ground as shops board their windows, leaving the town's 224 year-round residents to themselves.

★ BELTON CHALET

In 1910, Glacier became a national park, and the Belton Chalet opened its doors to guests arriving via the Great Northern Railway. The first in a series of Swiss-themed railroad-company chalets built in the park, the Belton featured milkmaid-attired hostesses and flowered walkways to greet guests. In the Taproom, a photo of that bygone era includes the trellised walkway from the train depot to the chalet. Over the years, the chalet changed hands, serving as housing for Civilian Conservation Corps crews building Going-to-the-Sun Road as well as a pizza parlor and a bakery. After heavy snows destroyed roofs and floors in the late 1990s, owners from Bigfork restored the lodge and cabins. Belton Chalet is on the National Register of Historic Places.

BELTON BRIDGE

Belton Bridge opened in 1920, allowing park visitors to drive across the Middle Fork of the Flathead River instead of rowing a boat. Ironically, this wood and cement bridge remained standing during the 1964 flood while torrents of water destroyed the new bridge downstream. For a time, this bridge was used again while the new bridge was being repaired. The National Park Service recently fixed up the "old bridge," as locals call it, open now for foot traffic only. It accesses the Boundary Trail, Middle Fork fishing spots, and calm but deep, chilly pools for swimming. To find it in West Glacier, turn east onto Old Bridge Road and drive to the end to a small turnaround and minimal parking (no RVs).

MIDDLE FORK OF THE FLATHEAD RIVER

The Middle Fork of the Flathead River collects its waters from deep within the Bob Marshall Wilderness Complex and Glacier National Park. Its north-shore high-water mark denotes the national park boundary.

historic Belton Chalet

Designated a Wild and Scenic River, the Middle Fork (the shortened moniker favored by locals) vacillates between raging rapids and mesmerizing meanders. Anglers and swimmers gravitate to its blue-green pools. Rafters and kayakers splash through rapids known as Bonecrusher and Jaws. Hikers tootle along its Boundary Trail.

APGAR

Two miles from West Glacier, Apgar is on the shore of the park's largest body of water, Lake McDonald. With Apgar Campground within walking distance and Fish Creek Campground a couple of miles away, Apgar crowds in summer but is still less harried than the West Glacier highway hubbub. It's a quintessential national park community. A restaurant, camp store, two inns, the lake's only boat ramp, swimming beaches, visitors center, campground, and picnic area all cluster here at Lake McDonald's foot. Apgar's historic red schoolhouse now houses a gift shop. Like West Glacier, most of Apgar shuts down by October and opens again in May.

ROBERT FIRE REBIRTH

Summer 2003 unleashed some of the biggest fires in Glacier National Park's history. Raging winds shoved the Robert Fire over Apgar Mountain, burning 7,000 acres in four hours. Campers, motel guests, and park personnel evacuated from West Glacier and Apgar while helicopters doused the fire with water scooped from Lake McDonald. The fire burned 39,000 acres, 29 percent of the park's forests. See postfire forest regeneration on the Camas Road, the Lake McDonald Trail starting at Fish Creek Campground, or from

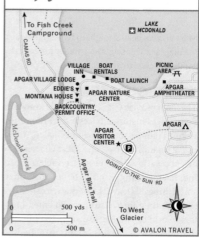

Apgar Lookout. Fast-growing new vegetation thriving on the fire's ash and nutrient-rich soils prompted prolific flower blooms, and lodgepoles that require fire to sprout are gaining height.

★ LAKE MCDONALD

Catching water from Glacier's longest river, Lake McDonald is 10 miles long, 1.5 miles wide, and 472 feet deep. It is the park's largest and deepest lake. Squeezed between Howe and Snyder Ridges, both lateral moraines, the 6,823-acre lake sits where an ancient glacier gouged out a trough. Larch forests that turn gold in fall rim the shores. On the lake, visitors fish, boat, paddle, and swim in its cold blue; Jet Skis are not allowed, but waterskiing attracts a few wetsuited diehards. Access the lakeshore via Fish Creek or Apgar Picnic Areas, the Apgar boat ramp, or the many pullouts along Going-to-the-Sun Road.

Recreation

If Glacier has a recreation center, it's West Glacier and Apgar. The communities offer hiking, biking, rafting, horseback riding, paddling, boating, fishing, swimming, and golfing. West Glacier is the unofficial park headquarters for white-water rafting, with two Wild and Scenic Rivers (nationally designated rivers protected for their wilderness and beauty) marking park boundaries.

DAY HIKES

Apgar has the only park trail that permits dogs. The two-mile paved Apgar Bike Trail connecting West Glacier and Apgar is open to walkers, leashed dogs, and bicyclists.

Most of the Apgar trails are accessible year-round, except for Huckleberry Lookout. In winter, you will need snowshoes or skis, and for a few trails, expect to add on 1-2 miles across snow-buried roads to reach trailheads.

Rocky Point
Distance: 1.4-1.6 miles round-trip
Duration: 1 hour
Elevation gain: none
Effort: easy
Trailhead: Fish Creek Campground Loop D or the start of the Inside North Fork Road (see map p. 40)
Rocky Point is a short interpretive romp

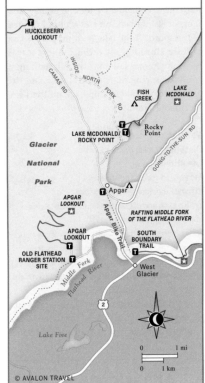

West Glacier and Apgar Hikes

© AVALON TRAVEL

West Glacier and Apgar Hikes

Trail	Effort	Distance	Duration
Rocky Point	easy	1.4-1.6 mi rt	1 hr
Apgar Lookout	moderate	7 mi rt	4 hr
Huckleberry Lookout	strenuous	12 mi rt	6 hr
Lake McDonald	easy	7 mi one-way	3.5 hr
South Boundary Trail	easy	11.6 mi rt	5 hr

along Lake McDonald's north shore through the 2003 Robert Fire and up a promontory. Places of heavy burn with slow regrowth alternate with lighter burn now clogged with lush greenery. Don't forget your camera: The view from Rocky Point looks up the lake toward the Continental Divide and grabs grand shots of Mount Jackson and Mount Edwards to the south. If the lake is calm, photos can capture stunning reflections. Snow leaves early and comes late to this trail, making it good for spring and fall hiking. From the promontory, make a loop back on the Lake McDonald Trail.

★ Apgar Lookout

Distance: 7 miles round-trip
Duration: 4 hours
Elevation gain: 1,868 feet
Effort: moderate
Trailhead: end of Glacier Institute Road, 1.9 miles from Going-to-the-Sun Road
Directions: Take the first left after the west entrance station at the Glacier Institute sign. At the first fork, follow the sign to the horse barn and veer left, crossing over Quarter Circle Bridge. Drive to the road's terminus at the trailhead (see map p. 38).

Beginning with a gentle walk, the trail soon climbs steeply uphill toward the first of three long switchbacks. As the trail ascends, some

Apgar Lookout

large burned sentinels stand as relics from the 2003 Robert Fire, though many of the burned trees have blown down in the time since, opening up views of the Middle Fork, Rubideau Basin, the railroad tracks, and West Glacier. But in 2016, thick lodgepoles

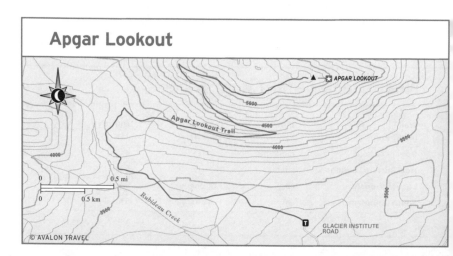

are starting to limit views again. Following the third switchback, the trail traverses the ridge, which has snow in June, to the rebuilt lookout. From this 5,236-foot aerie, a panoramic view unfolds from Canada to the park's southern sector, including all six of the park's peaks that are higher than 10,000 feet and Lake McDonald below.

A tree canopy no longer shades the southwest-facing slope; hike in the morning on hot days. Park communication radio antennas clutter the summit, but at least they are clustered in one location.

★ Huckleberry Lookout

Distance: 12 miles round-trip
Duration: 6 hours
Elevation gain: 2,725 feet
Effort: strenuous
Trailhead: six miles up Camas Road from Apgar, just past McGee Meadows (see map p. 39)

Huckleberry Lookout Trail is aptly named, for huckleberries do abound in this area. Due to a heavy concentration of huckleberries attracting a significant bruin population in fall, check with the park service for closure information. Snow often packs the upper trail until early July.

The trail begins with a gentle walk through lodgepole forest. Soon the path climbs, steadily gaining elevation among larches until it emerges on steep-sloped meadows and reaches a saddle at 4.5 miles. In a reprieve from the climb, the trail traverses two bowls until it crests the Apgar Range for the final scenery-laden ascent to the lookout at 6,593 feet. A spectacular view of the North Fork Valley and the park's Livingston Range unfolds. Glacier's six highest peaks are visible, as is Flathead Lake, Swan Peak, and Great Northern. During summer, the lookout is staffed. Evidence of the 2001 Moose Fire clings to Huckleberry Mountain as well as Demers Ridge below and the North Fork Valley.

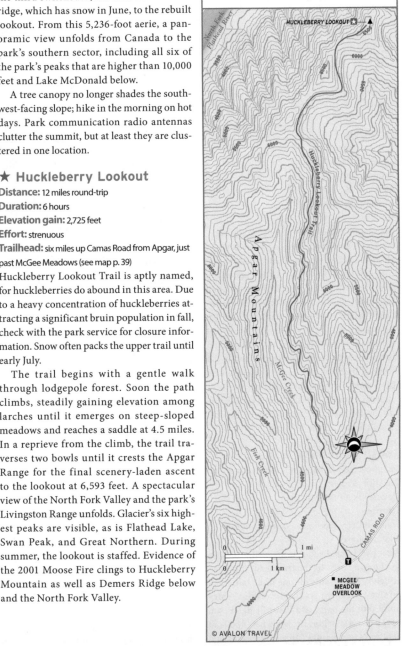

Huckleberry Lookout

Lake McDonald

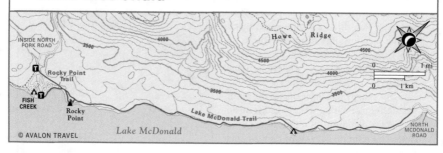

Lake McDonald

Distance: 7 miles one-way
Duration: 3.5 hours
Elevation gain: none
Effort: easy
Trailhead: Fish Creek Campground Loop D or Inside North Fork Road southern entrance (see map p. 40)

While this year-round trail (use skis or snowshoes in winter) wanders mostly back in the trees paralleling the north shore of Lake McDonald, you can garner views of the peak-flanked lake when it pops out to the shoreline. The brushy trail also shows postfire forest succession. Burned by the 2003 Robert Fire, the trail passes through lush new growth and stands of black or gray trunks. Most hikers opt to saunter out for a few miles to the backcountry campsite, perhaps drop a fishing line into the lake, and turn around again. Set up a car shuttle to hike the full length.

South Boundary Trail

Distance: 11.6 miles round-trip to Lincoln Creek
Duration: 5 hours
Elevation gain: 400 feet
Effort: easy
Trailhead: behind park headquarters on Mather Drive's south end

After parking at headquarters, walk through the housing area to the trailhead. (Starting at Belton Bridge cuts off one mile, but offers minimal parking.) Follow the original entry point into the park, Old River Bridge Road, to the historic Belton Bridge, where the trail continues upstream. With gentle ascents and descents, the path hugs the north-shore hillside above the Wild and Scenic Middle Fork of the Flathead River.

This year-round trail won't feel like wilderness: Noise from the railroad and highway competes with the river's roaring white water. But it's a great place to watch rafters shoot rapids, swim in deep pools, or fish. The trail descends to a fine rocky beach at Lincoln Creek, a stopping point for rafters before they hit the white water. Backpackers can continue another 15 miles upriver to Coal Creek or turn 10.5 miles up Lincoln Creek to Lincoln Lake.

Guided Hikes

National Park Service naturalists guide hikes and walks around Apgar mid-June-mid-September. Days and times vary, and the hikes range from easy to strenuous. In winter, naturalists lead snowshoe trips to look for animal tracks. Grab a current *Ranger-led Activity Guide* at visitors centers to check the schedule. These guided hikes are the best price of all: free.

Glacier Guides (11970 U.S. 2 E., West Glacier, 406/387-5555 or 800/521-7238, www.glacierguides.com, mid-May-Sept.) leads day hikes, backpacking, and overnight chalet trips, but most destinations are outside the West Glacier-Apgar area. For day hiking, reservations are required, and rates include the guide service, a deli lunch, and transportation to the trailhead. Solo travelers can hook up with the daily group day hikes (July-early Sept., $98 pp), scheduled to a different destination each day and meeting at 8am at its West Glacier office. Custom day hikes cost $560 for 1-5 people. Backpacking trips depart every week for 3-6-day adventures; rates run around $190 per day and include the guide service, transportation to and from the trailhead, meals, and snacks. Overnight hikes to backcountry chalets run multiple times each summer for three days ($960-1,290) or six days ($2,350). With higher price tags, customized day hikes and backpacking trips tailor routes to your liking. The company also offers a five-day camping and hiking trip, backpacking trips designed for seniors, and combination hike-raft trips. Plan to tip your guide at least 15 percent for day hikes and 20 percent for overnights.

Rentals

From a yurt in Apgar, **Glacier Outfitters** (196 Apgar Loop Rd., 406/219-7466, www. goglacieroutfitters.com, 9am-8pm daily mid-May-late Sept., shorter hours in shoulder seasons) rents the biggest selection of gear for hikers and backpackers. Find pepper spray, ice axes, crampons, backpacks and backpack baby carriers, trekking poles, tents, sleeping bags and pads, mess kits, water filters, and stoves for $3-14 per item per day. Pack rafts run $65. **Glacier Outdoor Center** (11957 U.S. 2 E., West Glacier, 406/888-5454 or 800/235-6781, www.glacierraftco.com) and **Glacier Guides** (11970 U.S. 2 E., West Glacier, 406/387-5555 or 800/521-7238, www.glacierguides.com) also rent hiking and backpacking gear, but with more limited inventory.

BIKING

Bicycling Glacier National Park is not for everyone. Narrow, shoulderless roads are packed with curves, and most trails prohibit bikes. However, the West Glacier-Apgar area does provide off-road options.

Bicycle Trails

Especially good for families, a level, paved bicycle trail connects West Glacier with Apgar. Approximately two miles long, the **Apgar Bike Trail** begins on the north side of the West Glacier Bridge. After dropping through the woods, it crosses through the National Park Service employee housing area before entering the forest again, where it continues on to Apgar, connecting the village, visitors center, and campground. Be cautious at two road crossings en route. The dirt **Fish Creek Bike Trail** provides a shortcut between Apgar and Fish Creek. These two bike trails permit dogs on leashes.

The 10-mile round-trip **Old Flathead Ranger Station** ride tours a combination of dirt road and trail that was once a road. It terminates at the confluence of the Flathead River's North and Middle Forks. Access the route from midway between West Glacier and Apgar on the Apgar Bike Trail, turning west onto the dirt Glacier Institute Road. At the first junction, follow the sign to the horse barn; at the second, hang a left toward Quarter Circle Bridge. About 0.5 mile past the bridge, the Old Flathead Ranger Station Trail begins. Turn left, biking 3.4 miles to the confluence and the site of the old ranger station.

The most challenging ride is the **Inside North Fork Road** north of Fish Creek. From Camas Creek, an 11-mile segment of road is closed to vehicles due to flood damage. The 6.5-mile portion from Camas Creek to Anaconda Creek climbs and drops through regrowing fire zones until reaching the steep drop down Anaconda Hill. Flooding has eroded the roadbed at Anaconda Creek; only bikers capable of carrying their bikes while fording multiple creek cuts should cross the area to continue on. Early summer rides may need to contend with downed trees. Check with the park for current conditions (406/888-7800).

The 10-mile, paved **Gateway to Glacier** Trail (www.gatewaytoglaciertrail.com), built in 2016, parallels U.S. 2 from Hungry Horse to West Glacier.

Cycling Road Tours

Several roads offer bike-tour options. From Apgar, all bikes can climb the paved **Camas**

Road, but mountain bikes are needed to explore the dirt **Inside North Fork Road** departing from Fish Creek Campground. Apgar is also the launch point for those cycling **Going-to-the-Sun Road.**

For a longer bike tour (about 37 miles, 4 hours) on a mix of dirt and paved roads best for hybrid or mountain bikes, the **Apgar Mountain Loop** starts in West Glacier and heads west over Belton Stage and Blankenship Roads to connect with Outside North Fork Road. From here, ride north, parallel with the North Fork River to the Camas Road entrance and back into the park. Follow the rolling, paved Camas Road back to the Apgar Bike Trail. The scenic loop is well worth a ride, especially in late spring before Going-to-the-Sun Road is open, but be prepared to suck serious dust on the dirt sections during dry spells and to battle mosquitoes and dodge bears along Camas Road.

Rentals

In Apgar, **Glacier Outfitters** (196 Apgar Loop Rd., 406/219-7466, www.goglacieroutfitters.com, 9am-8pm daily mid-May-late Sept., shorter hours in shoulder seasons, $10-17 for 2 hours, $25-45 for 24 hours) rents cruisers, hybrids, tandems, and kids bikes. Helmets are included, and for wee ones, you can tow a kiddie trailer ($7-20). **Eddie's Café & Mercantile** (236 Apgar Loop Rd., 406/888-5361, www.eddiescafegifts.com, 8am-10pm daily May-Sept.) in Apgar and **Glacier Village Sweet Treats** (205 Going-to-the-Sun Road, 406/888-5662) in West Glacier rent adult and kids bikes.

HORSEBACK RIDING

Swan Mountain Outfitters (406/387-4405 or 877/888-5557, www.swanmountainoutfitters.com/glacier, daily late May-early Sept.) operates two corral locations: one in Apgar and one in West Glacier. Reservations are strongly advised. For trail riding, be sure to wear long pants; you'll be a lot less sore afterward. For safety, wear sturdy shoes or hiking boots, not sandals. The outfitters do not take

children under age seven or riders weighing over 250 pounds.

Located on Glacier Institute Road northeast of the park entrance station, the **Apgar Corral** (summer 406/888-5010, $45-115) leads daily trail rides to three destinations in Glacier. An easy one-hour saunter to McDonald Meadows and a popular two-hour ride along the C. M. Russell Trail depart several times each day. The half-day ride to Apgar Lookout, which requires a minimum of four people, departs at 7:45am.

At the Crown of the Continent Discovery Center, the **West Glacier Corral** (12000 U.S. 2 E., 406/387-5005, $40-300) offers horseback tours through the lodgepole foothills of Flathead National Forest. One- and two-hour tours amble through the forest while the half-day and full-day rides climb to viewpoints. It also offers combination saddle-paddles, ride-and-dine, and cowboy cookout trips plus overnight trips for more time in the saddle.

RAFTING

Two Wild and Scenic-designated rivers form the west and southwest boundaries of Glacier National Park. The Middle Fork and North Fork of the Flathead River offer scenery, wilderness, flat-water float sections, and white water. Together the rivers provide 219 miles of recreation. The rafting season runs May-September, with high water usually peaking in late May. By late August, both rivers run at their lowest levels.

★ Middle Fork of the Flathead River

Bordering Glacier's southern boundary, the Middle Fork of the Flathead has scenic float sections interrupted by raging white water. The river's headwaters are deep within the Bob Marshall Wilderness Complex and Glacier's immense southern valleys.

While the white water cannot compete with the Grand Canyon's monster rapids, the Middle Fork is a splashy place where rapids named Screaming Right Turn, Jaws, and Pinball provide the fun. It's a good introductory paddle for a first-time river trip and kids. White-water trips begin at Moccasin Creek and end in West Glacier; scenic float trips begin in West Glacier and end at Blankenship.

For launching or taking out, the Middle Fork has several river access points easily reached along U.S. 2. Different sections are appropriate for overnights, day trips, fishing, and short floats. While a few rapids at certain water levels are rated Class IV, the river along Glacier's boundary is primarily Class II and III. No permits are required. However, all camping must be done on the south shore; no camping is permitted on Glacier's shoreline. Since private property abuts some of the south shore, you'll need to be knowledgeable about where you can camp.

Mountain Photography (www.mountainphotography.net) shoots photos of commercial and private rafts in Bonecrusher Rapid.

North Fork of the Flathead River

From Canada, the North Fork of the Flathead flows 59 miles through the remote North Fork Valley. As the river enters the United States, it forms the western boundary of Glacier.

Accessed via the bumpy, dirt Outside North Fork Road, the Class II-III river provides multiday float trips, day rafting, and fishing. Those looking for tamer water can take out at Big Creek before the Upper Fool Hen rapids. River accesses flank the North Fork Road. No permits are required, but all campsites must be set up on the western shore; no camping is permitted on Glacier's bank except by permit at Round Prairie. The river ends at the confluence with the Middle Fork at the Blankenship River Access, a 10-minute drive west of West Glacier.

Guides

The commercial rafting season runs May-September, with the biggest water in early summer. Four West Glacier rafting companies lead half-day and full-day trips on the Middle Fork as well as scenic, dinner, barbecue, and evening floats. They also do saddle-paddle combinations that put you on a horse and a boat the same day. Each company launches 4-6 half-day raft trips daily through the white-water section and guides overnight and multiday trips. Children should be at least six years old for white water, but younger ones can enjoy scenic float trips.

To compare companies (they're all very similar in cost), ask three questions: Is the

West Glacier is the rafting capital of Glacier.

7 percent service fee included in the rate or added on, what size are the rafts and how many people do they carry (smaller rafts and fewer paddlers have a more exciting ride), and are wetsuits and booties included. Per adult, expect to pay about $58 for half-day trips or $95 for full day; kids run about $10-25 cheaper. For more fun, tackle the white water in a small sport raft with more kick or on an inflatable kayak, otherwise known as a rubber ducky ($62-82 pp half day, includes helmets). Paddles and life jackets are included in all rates, but some companies charge additional fees for wetsuits and booties. Plan on tipping the guide about 15 percent.

Overnight rafting trips range 2-5 days; longer trips are usually paired with hiking, horseback riding, or backpacking. Expect to pay around $190 per adult per day for overnight rafting trips; rates for children run less. Specialty trips with cabin stays, horseback riding, or flights will cost more. Plan to tip guides 20 percent. When making reservations, clarify what you'll need to bring for your overnight. The companies can provide tents, sleeping bags, sleeping pads, and dry bags for your gear.

Glacier Raft Company (6 Going-to-the-Sun Rd., West Glacier, 406/888-5454 or 800/235-6781, www.glacierraftco.com) is right in West Glacier village adjacent to the river. White-water rafters debark at the Middle Fork Bridge to walk two blocks back to the office. In addition to standard rafting options, Glacier Raft has combo packages pairing up half-day white-water rafting with half-day horseback riding or fly-fishing. Overnights go out for 2-4 days. This is the only local company permitted to guide trips on the Class III-IV upper Middle Fork of the Flathead River in the Great Bear Wilderness. Access requires a flight to a remote put-in near the headwaters for the four-day trip ($1,600).

Great Northern Whitewater (12127 U.S. 2 E., 406/387-5340 or 800/735-7897, www.greatnorthernresort.com) has the standard trips, plus it is the one company that offers river instruction through Glacier River School

courses. Find them one mile west of downtown West Glacier.

Montana Raft Company (11970 U.S. 2 E., 406/387-5555 or 800/521-7238, www.glacierguides.com) is the only company that can combine guided hiking in Glacier National Park with raft trips. In addition to standard raft trips, an extensive menu of hike-raft or backpack-raft combos can fill a day or a week. Overnight river trips float the Middle Fork or the North Fork of the Flathead River. Two-day North Fork overnight trips can include a cabin stay ($500). Find MRC/Glacier Guides off the north side of the highway 1.5 miles west of West Glacier.

Wild River Adventures (11900 U.S. 2 E., 406/387-9453 or 800/700-7056, www.riverwild.com), the smallest company, runs all the standard trips plus adds several paddle-saddle combos. One is a four-day campout adventure. Find Wild River on the south side of the highway 1.5 miles west of West Glacier.

DIY Float Trips

Got the river savvy and the gear to guide yourself? For locations of rapids and public lands for camping on overnight trips, purchase the waterproof *Three Forks of the Flathead Float Guide* ($13) from **Hungry Horse Ranger Station** (10 Hungry Horse Dr., Hungry Horse, 406/387-3800, www.fs.fed.us/r1/flathead). It can also be downloaded online (free, but not in waterproof flip-book format). Flathead National Forest manages both rivers. Stop in the ranger station, located nine miles west of West Glacier, for assistance in planning a self-guided overnight trip. Depending on where you camp, toilet systems and fire pans are required or recommended.

Rentals and Shuttles

Glacier Raft Company (6 Going-to-the-Sun Rd., West Glacier, 406/888-5454 or 800/235-6781, www.glacierraftco.com) caters to self-guided floaters from West Glacier down 10 miles of Class I-II river. Departing twice a day, the package includes rafts or inflatable froth between Moccasin Creek and West Glacier, surfing Tunnel Rapids. Some eliminate the flat water before and after the rapids by hiking down railroad accesses. Bring your own kayak; no rentals are available in West Glacier. To locate rapids and ascertain their difficulty on the Middle Fork and North Fork, consult **Hungry Horse Ranger Station** (10 Hungry Horse Dr., Hungry Horse, 406/387-3800, www.fs.fed.us/r1/flathead). The ranger station sells *Three Forks of the Flathead Float Guide* ($13), or you can download it online for free.

Glacier Kayak School (12127 U.S. 2 E., West Glacier, 406/387-5340 or 800/735-7897, www.greatnorthernresort.com, $225-600) teaches white-water kayaking to introduce beginners to paddling fundamentals and rolling. Experienced kayakers can hire a guide to lead them down the lines of the Middle Fork.

BOATING

With its vast water acreage, Lake McDonald attracts boaters, but it's never crowded, except around Apgar. Usually just a few quiet anglers start out the early morning followed by a few die-hard water-skiers, sightseers, and kayakers touring the shoreline. Because the frigid waters inhibit most water-skiers and Jet Skis are not permitted, the lake never has a frenzied hubbub of noise. In fact, national park regulations enforce a maximum noise level of 82 decibels. Similar to many of the park's lakes, you'll rarely see a sailboat or sailboard: unpredictable swirling winds on Lake McDonald make other lakes outside the park more appealing. Apgar's boat launch provides the lake's only public ramp access.

Rentals

For boating and fishing on Lake McDonald, **Glacier Park Boat Company** (406/257-2426, www.glacierparkboats.com, daily late May-Labor Day) rents rowboats and small motorboats for $10-25 per hour from the Apgar boat dock next to Apgar Village Inn. Paddles, life jackets, and fishing regulations are included in the rates.

boat dock at Lake McDonald

kayaks, paddles, helmets, life jackets, and shuttle setup. With a bit of instruction from an experienced guide, you can then float at your own pace ($65-255).

To assist DIY floaters, GRC does custom shuttles for all locations on the Middle and North Forks of the Flathead River. Use your vehicle ($20-140) or go in its rigs ($30-450).

To ensure availability to rent gear, make reservations with **Glacier Raft Company** or **Montana Raft Company** (11970 U.S. 2 E., West Glacier, 406/387-5555 or 800/521-7238, www.glacierguides.com). Per day rates for rafts, inflatable kayaks, paddleboards, oars, paddles, and frames run $45-150; dry bags, toilet systems, camping equipment, wetsuits, throw bags, pumps, and repair kits cost $3-12 per item.

WHITE-WATER KAYAKING

White-water kayakers drop into the **Middle Fork of the Flathead River,** which churns up Class II-III rapids. Kayakers play in the

Fishing in Glacier

With 27,023 acres of lakes, 563 streams, and 22 species of fish, Glacier is a place where no angler should sit with a slack line. Only a scant 10 percent of park visitors fish, so those who do typically enjoy calm vistas and a few native trout. While weather and skill variables influence success, a few tips for Glacier's waters can help.

FISHING TIPS

- Avoid a long hike to a remote lake to fish unless you go for the sake of the journey. While many anglers find more success in waters away from roads, remoteness doesn't mean good fishing. Waterfalls prevent fish from reaching some streams and lakes.

- Since arrival at a high mountain lake will most likely be midday, when fishing is lackluster, stay overnight in the backcountry or at a nearby lodge. Then fish in the morning or evening, when fish feed, for best results. Overcast days also produce better fishing than sunny days.

- During early summer runoff, when river waters cloud with sediments, fish hang out on the bottom to feed; try lures that mimic insect larvae. Alternatively, fish in lakes instead.

- When streams run clear, fly-fishing is the most productive. Try to match a prominent hatch, but traditional high-floating attractor patterns will also move fish.

- At lakes, look for inlets and outlets to fish, but be considerate of heavily trafficked areas.

- Trolling from a motorboat (where allowed) or canoe is the most effective way to fish for lake trout.

FISHING IN BEAR COUNTRY

- Bears pose special considerations. Since smells attract bears that travel waterways, lessen your bear encounter chances by keeping fishy scents away from clothing. Catch-and-release fishing minimizes attracting bears.

- For cleaning fish in the front country, dispose of the entrails in bear-resistant garbage cans. In the backcountry, do not bury or burn the innards, as that may attract bears. Instead, go at least 200 feet away from a campsite or trail, puncture the air bladder, and throw the entrails

Regulations

Boaters must get **permits** ($10 for 7-day motorized permit, $40 for annual motorized permit, free for nonmotorized boats) and show that their boats have been cleaned, drained, and dried to avoid bringing aquatic invasive species into park lakes. Permits are available at the Apgar Backcountry Permit Office or park headquarters, as directed by the orange sign at the west-side entrance station.

Two shoreline closures affect boaters: from the Apgar boat ramp north to the lake's outlet, and between the Apgar Amphitheater and Going-to-the-Sun Road. To protect swimmers, boaters must stay 300 feet off the shoreline and are not permitted to beach. Watch for additional temporary wildlife closures marked with buoys, especially where bald eagles nest at the lake's east end. For a complete list of boating regulations, check with visitors centers or Glacier's website (www.nps.gov/glac).

PADDLING

With its monstrous shoreline, **Lake McDonald** is a treat for canoeing and kayaking, but watch for winds whipping up large whitecaps. When glassy calm waters prevail, you'd be hard-pressed to beat it at sunrise or sunset. Touring the shoreline, you into deep water. Keep only what you can eat, and eat it as soon as you can.

NATIVE SPECIES

Glacier's fishing regulations enforce protection of native species through selected area closures and limits on taking native species. The park service no longer stocks fish, as many of the introduced species took a toll on native fish through competition for food and predation. Until 1972, an estimated 45-55 million fish and eggs were planted in Glacier's waters, introducing arctic grayling, rainbow trout, kokanee salmon, brook trout, and Yellowstone cutthroat trout. Lake trout and lake whitefish also invaded the park's west-side water systems through stocking in Flathead Lake.

fishing at Quarter Circle Bridge

Of Glacier's 10 sport fish and 12 nonsport fish, the **bull trout** is listed as a threatened species under the Endangered Species Act. In Montana, this predatory fish, which can grow to two feet long, now inhabits less than half of its original streams due to a number of factors, including habitat degradation. No fishing for bull trout is allowed; immediately release any that are caught incidentally. Look on the dorsal fin: no black, put it back.

Glacier is also one of the few remaining strongholds for **westslope cutthroat trout,** which now inhabit only 2.5 percent of their original range. Threatened by interbreeding with rainbow trout, genetically pure populations of cutthroat remain in 15-19 park lakes. Conscientious anglers release them after catching them.

While the law protects bull trout, anglers need to help preserve the park's native fishery. Learn to identify native and nonnative species. Follow park guidelines for harvesting or releasing fish. In general, release native fish; keep only your limit of nonnative species.

For the best fishing recommendations, grab a copy of Russ Schneider's *Fishing Glacier National Park*.

may encounter wildlife closures, especially for nesting bald eagles at the lake's head. Paddlers must pick up free permits to launch on any park lake. Get them at the Apgar Backcountry Permit Office or park headquarters, as directed by the orange sign near the west-side entrance station. Paddlers can also camp overnight at the Lake McDonald backcountry campground, a five-mile paddle from Apgar that is only accessible by trail or water. An overnight permit is required, just like for backpackers.

For paddling moving water, the scenic **Lower McDonald Creek** starts north of the Apgar boat launch on Lake McDonald and floats past beaver dams to Quarter Circle Bridge, a one-hour paddle. The **Middle Fork of the Flathead River** is gentle enough for canoeing and kayaking from West Glacier downriver to Blankenship, but the section includes one challenging rapid that can be portaged.

Find gear rentals in Apgar at three locations. All rentals ($10-20/hour) come with life jackets and paddles. From the dock on the lake, **Glacier Park Boat Company** (406/257-2426, www.glacierparkboats.com, 9am-7pm daily late May-early Sept., shorter hours in early summer) rents paddleboards, canoes, double kayaks, and rowboats. **Glacier**

Outfitters (196 Apgar Loop Rd., 406/219-7466, www.goglacieroutfitters.com, 9am-8pm daily mid-May-late Sept., shorter hours in shoulder seasons) rents paddleboards, canoes, and kayaks. It's the only rental service with a 24-hour option, so you can take the boats elsewhere in Glacier. **Eddie's Café & Mercantile** (236 Apgar Loop Rd., 406/888-5361, 8am-10pm daily May-Sept.) rents paddleboards and kayaks.

FISHING

Lake McDonald, the park's biggest lake, has a reputation for mediocre fishing. Boats work best to troll for lake trout. For catch-and-release fly-fishing, **Lower McDonald Creek** from the lake to Quarter Circle Bridge works, but it's also heavily fished because of its easy access. For several miles in both directions from West Glacier, the **Middle Fork of the Flathead** presents good fishing, but be ready to contend with rafters and fishing outfitters. Because of the concentration of visitors in the West Glacier-Apgar area during high season, you may not feel like you're off in the wilderness when you toss in a line, but you just might pull in native trout. Good fishing usually starts by early July when the water clears.

Regulations

Fishing inside Glacier National Park does not require a license, but waters here have some restrictions, such as a ban on lead lures. Lake McDonald has no limit on lake trout or whitefish. Westslope cutthroat are catch-and-release only, and endangered bull trout must be released. Lower McDonald Creek from the lake outlet to Quarter Circle Bridge has been catch-and-release only, but check with the rangers as nonnative-species rules may change. Despite its name, Fish Creek is closed to fishing. Lake McDonald is open to fishing all year, but stream fishing in and outside the park runs from the third Saturday in May through November 30.

Licenses and Rentals

Fishing outside Glacier on Flathead River drainages requires a **Montana fishing license** (Montana residents: $8-18 season, $13 adults for 2 days, free ages 1-11; nonresidents: $25 for 2 days, $44 for 10 days, $60 season, kids ages 1-14 free with adult with license for shared limit or $8 for own license). Pick up licenses at **Glacier Outdoor Center** (11957 U.S. 2 E., West Glacier, 406/888-5454 or 800/235-6781, www.glacierraftco.com). Glacier Outdoor Center also sells fishing

Lake McDonald is a paddler's paradise.

gear and rents rods ($12-15/day), waders, and float tubes. **Glacier Outfitters** (196 Apgar Loop Rd., 406/219-7466, www.goglacieroutfitters.com, 9am-8pm daily mid-May-late Sept., shorter hours in shoulder seasons, $3-20) rents spin-casting and fly rods, including smaller models for kids.

Guides

Four fly-fishing companies in West Glacier guide trips daily in drift boats on Glacier's boundary waters on the Middle Fork and the North Fork of the Flathead River, but none guide fishing adventures inside Glacier National Park. For beginners, they offer fly-fishing schools ($490 for 2 people) to teach the basics of casting, mending, and catch-and-release. Reservations are mandatory. The companies begin fishing trips in late June-early July when the waters clear and then run through mid-September.

Half-day ($390), full-day ($490), and overnight ($425-1,000/day) guided fishing trips for 1-2 people are available from all West Glacier companies. Plan on tipping the guides about 15 percent. Tip higher if you catch lots of fish or for overnight trips. It's pricey, but the guides usually get you to the good fishing holes. Rates include all equipment, such as life jackets, rods, and flies. As with rafting trips, a 7 percent service fee is added to all fishing trips, but some companies include it in the price. You'll also need to buy your own fishing license.

All West Glacier fishing companies are licensed with the state: **Glacier Guides** (11970 U.S. 2 E., 406/387-5555 or 800/521-7238, www.glacierguides.com), **Montana Fly-Fishing Guides** (Great Northern Resort, 12127 U.S. 2 E., 406/387-5340 or 800/735-7897, www.greatnorthernresort.com), **Wild River Fishing Guides** (11900 U.S. 2 E., 406/387-9453 or 800/700-7056, www.riverwild.com), and **Glacier Anglers** (Glacier Outdoor Center, 11957 U.S. 2 E., 406/888-5454 or 800/235-6781, www.glacierraftco.com), which adds on its specialty four- or five-day Great Bear Wilderness fishing trips ($720 pp/day),

half-day private pond fishing ($290), and one-hour casting school ($45).

GOLF

Glacier View Golf Club (640 River Bend Dr., West Glacier, 406/888-5471, wwww.glacierviewgolf.com, daily Apr.-Oct., snow permitting, 18 holes $33) may tax your concentration as you tee off. Moose, elk, bears, and deer wander across the fairways, and the mountain views are hard to ignore. The 18-hole course has a pro shop, restaurant, practice green, driving range, lessons, cart rentals ($28), and club rentals ($15). To locate the golf course in West Glacier, turn west onto River Bend Drive and follow signs to the clubhouse. The club has RV hookups ($40).

THRILL SPORTS AND FAMILY FUN

The **Glacier Highline** (10167 Hwy. 2 E., Coram, 406/387-5007, www.glacierhighline.com, 10am-6pm Mon.-Sat., 1pm-6pm Sun. mid-June-mid-Sept., two hours adults $50, kids 12 and under $40) packs its aerial park full of ziplines, ropes courses, and treetop challenges. The climbing wall and giant swing cost extra. The **Amazing Fun Center** (10265 Hwy. 2 E., Coram, 406/387-5902, www.glacierhighline.com, 9:30am-9:30pm daily late May-mid-Sept., closes earlier in shoulder seasons, $3-8 pp/activity, Fun Passes $15-30) has a two-level maze, go-carts, bumper boats, bank-shot basketball, and mini golf.

CROSS-COUNTRY SKIING AND SNOWSHOEING

Winter converts the roads and trails around Apgar into easy cross-country ski and snowshoe paths late November-early April. Quiet and scenic, road skiing makes for easy route-finding with little avalanche danger at lower elevations. Roads are plowed into Apgar and up Lake McDonald's south shore. Beyond plowing, popular ski tours follow roads and trails to **Fish Creek Campground, Rocky Point, McGee Meadows,** and the **Old Flathead**

A skier tours Quarter Circle Bridge.

Ranger Station near the Middle Fork and North Fork confluence. Those with stamina and skiing expertise climb to **Apgar Lookout.** For route descriptions, pick up *Skiing and Snowshoeing* in the visitors centers or online (www.nps.gov/glac). Skiers and snowshoers should be well equipped and versed in winter travel safety before venturing out.

Guides

The National Park Service guides free weekend snowshoe tours from **Apgar Visitor Center** (406/888-7939) January-mid-March. Call for departure times for the two-hour walks to look for animal tracks. Interpretive rangers point out how flora and fauna adapt to harsh winters. Hikers should wear winter footwear, dress in layers, and bring water. Rent snowshoes from the park service or at Flathead Valley shops.

Guided snowshoe, cross-country ski, and backcountry ski tours are available by reservation through **Glacier Adventure Guides** (406/892-2173 or 877/735-9514, www.glacieradventureguides.com, Dec.-Mar.). For solo travelers, it's the best way to get connected with avalanche-certified guides who know the routes and where to find pristine powder stashes. Lunch, snacks, park entrance fees, and equipment are included. Multiday trips are also available. Check online for rates; plan on tipping the guide 15-20 percent.

Entertainment and Shopping

Most park visitors take advantage of the long daylight hours (dark doesn't descend until almost 11pm in June) to explore everything they can instead of seeking nightlife. If you're looking to party, you can shoot pool in the **West Glacier Bar,** a classic dive bar nicknamed **Freda's,** (200 Going-to-the-Sun Rd., 406/888-5359, www.glacierparkinc.com, noon-1:30am daily late May-mid Sept.,). It's attached to the West Glacier Restaurant. For music on select nights, head to the **Stonefly Lounge** (10154 US 2, Coram, 406/387-5440, www.stoneflylounge.com, 2pm-2am daily).

RANGER PROGRAMS

Every night in summer, **Fish Creek Campground Amphitheater** (9pm) and **Apgar Campground Amphitheater** (7:30pm) host free 45-minute park naturalist evening programs on wildlife, fires, and natural phenomena. Schedules are posted in campgrounds and at the visitors centers. In the Apgar Visitor Center parking lot (10pm-midnight), visitors can view **stars and planets through telescopes** when weather and dark skies permit. In July and August on clear days, rangers set up a special solar viewing telescope in the afternoon at Apgar Village Green. Consult the *Ranger-led Activity Guide* or online (www.nps.gov/glac) for scheduled dates and times.

SHOPPING

West Glacier and Apgar each have several small gift shops with souvenirs, T-shirts, and books. In Apgar, stop by **Montana House of Gifts** (198 Apgar Loop Rd., 406/888-5393, year-round) for its locally made pottery, weaving, jewelry, crafts, and arts. Some is by Native Americans.

For outdoor gear, three stores in West Glacier open during the summer season with limited inventories. **Glacier Outdoor Center** (11957 U.S. 2 E., 406/888-5454 or 800/235-6781, www.glacierraftco.com) specializes in fishing, camping, and rafting gear. The **Crown of the Continent Discovery Center** (12000 U.S. 2 E., 406/387-4405, www.crowndiscoverycenter.com) carries gear for hiking, camping, and backpacking. **Montana Raft Company/Glacier Guides** (11970 U.S. 2 E., 406/387-5555 or 800/521-7238, www.glacierguides.com) sells hiking and rafting gear.

Located in the historic Belton Train Depot in West Glacier, the **Glacier National Park Conservancy** (GNPC, 406/892-3250, http://glacier.org, year-round) sells books, posters, and maps of Glacier. This is the place to go for all reference, natural history, hiking, and picture books on the park. GNPC also runs a tiny bookstore in the Apgar Visitor Center and at six other park locations. You can also order products from the GNPC website.

While you can find huckleberry products in any gift shop, the **Huckleberry Patch** (8868 Hwy. 2 E., Hungry Horse, 406/387-5000, www.huckleberrypatch.com, 7am-10pm daily May-Oct., 11am-6pm daily Nov.-Apr.) cannery specializes in local jams, jellies, syrups, pie filling, and preserves. It sells fresh-baked huckleberry pies too.

Accommodations

On Lake McDonald's shore, the limited inside-park lodging at Apgar is extremely popular, so West Glacier options often serve as backup. But given that the communities are only two miles apart and are connected by a bike and walking path, they are equally convenient to each other and their outdoor activities. Additional lodging is found in Coram and Hungry Horse. You can also find private cabins and vacation homes to rent at **VRBO** (www.vrbo.com). Montana tacks on a 7 percent bed tax, so your bill will be higher than the quoted room rate.

INSIDE THE PARK

Early reservations a year in advance are a must at the two adjacent lodges in Apgar tucked at Lake McDonald's foot. To preserve their get-away-from-it-all ambience, neither have air-conditioning, Internet access, in-room phones, or TVs. Pay phones can be found outside the lobbies. Both share a block with a restaurant, mercantile, ice cream shop, boat rentals, several gift shops, shuttle stops, and the Apgar Bike Trail. Although the area is a busy hive during the day, it quiets at night.

Apgar Village Inn

On Lake McDonald's beach, every one of the 36 guest rooms in the ★ **Apgar Village Inn** (62 Apgar Loop Rd., 0.3 mile from Camas Rd. or 0.8 mile from Going-to-the-Sun Rd., 855/733-4522, front desk 406/888-5632, www. glaciernationalparklodges.com, late May-mid-Sept., $160-290) wakes up to an unobstructed million-dollar lake view. Although the nondescript guest rooms were redecorated in 2015, not much else has changed since it was built in 1956. Some guest rooms include kitchenettes, and family units can sleep up to six people in three rooms. Stairs access the 2nd floor.

Apgar Village Lodge

Set back in huge old-growth cedars along McDonald Creek, **Apgar Village Lodge** (33 Apgar Loop Rd., 0.3 mile from Camas Rd. or 0.8 mile from Going-to-the-Sun Rd., 406/892-2525, www.glacierparkinc.com, late May-late Sept.) clusters 20 small motel rooms ($100-170) and 28 rustic cabins ($110-400) within a few steps of Lake McDonald. The creek cabins (6, 7, and 8) are particularly serene, mixed with a wonderful ambience of wildlife and the sound of the stream. Although older, the cabins have all been upgraded since the mid-1990s, and some come with kitchens. All baths contain shower stalls.

OUTSIDE THE PARK
West Glacier

Lodging in West Glacier is convenient for hopping on the train, going river rafting or fishing, and heading off on guided backpacking trips. Only two miles from Lake McDonald, West Glacier lodging works as an easy backup to booked-out in-park locations. Be prepared, however, for nightly noise. It's not from people, who are tired from packing in so much activity during the long days, but from trains on the BNSF Railway line. Bring earplugs if you're a light sleeper. During midsummer, most West Glacier lodging fills nightly; reservations are advised. Lower rates are available in spring and fall.

Apgar Village Lodge

LODGES

Located across from Belton Train Depot, the historic ★ **Belton Chalet** (12575 U.S. 2 E., 406/888-5000 or 888/235-8665, www.belton-chalet.com) saw a restoration in 2000. The cozy lobby centers around a large fireplace. Stay in the main lodge rooms (late May-Sept., $140-190) or private year-round cottages ($250-345 summer; $115-230 winter). Simple guest rooms are a slice of history: original wainscoting and wood floors, push-button lights, twig tables, and historical photos, but no phones, TVs, air-conditioning, or alarm clocks. Original closets were converted into in-room baths with showers. Stay in one of the nine balcony rooms to sit in wicker rockers with a glass of wine as the sun sets over the Apgar Range. Wireless Internet, earplugs for train noise, and day spa services are available on-site. The chalet's restaurant serves outstanding dinners.

★ **Glacier Guides Lodge** (120 Highline Blvd., 406/387-5555 or 800/521-7238, www. glacierguides.com, May-mid-Oct., $170-225), owned by Glacier Guides/Montana Raft Company, is an ecofriendly lodge that opened in 2010. It has 12 guest rooms for two people each with wireless Internet access, TVs, mini-fridges, and air-conditioning. Continental breakfast is included with stays, and two lounge areas provide places to relax outside the guest rooms. Its location tucked back in the woods under mossy cliffs makes it one of the quietest places.

Ten minutes outside the town center, ★ **The Great Bear Inn** (5672 Blankenship Rd., 406/250-4577, www.thegreatbearinn.com, late May-Sept, $230-350) offers seclusion in the woods and the most upscale lodging in West Glacier. Large lodge rooms come in four styles, with the high-end guest rooms including king beds, rock fireplaces, and balconies. All rooms have mini-fridges, televisions, and wine glasses. Two cabins with lofts and kitchens offer more privacy.

CABINS

Two cabin complexes operated by raft companies sit less than one mile west of West Glacier's shops and restaurants. Both come with fully equipped kitchens, wireless Internet access, TVs, and gas grills. ★ **Glacier Outdoor Center** (11957 U.S. 2

E., 406/888-5454 or 800/235-6781, www.glacierraftco.com, Apr.-Oct., $150-650) has one- to three-bedroom log cabins that sleep 6-14 people. Set back from the highway amid birch trees surrounding a trout pond, the cabins include log furniture, decks, and gas fireplaces. Deluxe cabins add washer and dryer. Part of the Great Northern Resort, with the rafting, fishing, and kayaking company located on-site, **Great Northern Chalets** (12127 U.S. 2 E., 406/387-5340 or 800/735-7897, www.greatnorthernresort.com, May-mid-Oct., 3-night min. summer, $150-420) rents one- to three-bedroom log chalets that can sleep 2-10 people. Set around a landscaped garden pond but in view of the highway, the cozy two-story chalets with kitchens are decorated in Glacier outdoor themes, and several have sweeping views of Glacier's peaks.

Set in forest back from the highway, the **West Glacier KOA** (355 Half Moon Flats Rd., 406/387-5341 or 800/562-3313, www.koa.com, May-Sept., $100-350) in 2016 added new deluxe cabins to its collection. Now 19 deluxe cabins that each sleep 2-8 people are available. They come with kitchens or kitchenettes, linens, and in-cabin bathrooms. Some have lofts, balconies or decks, gas grills, outdoor fire pits, or mountain views. One cabin is a log home

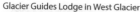

Glacier Guides Lodge in West Glacier

($600). For those on a budget, 28 bare-bones cabins have no kitchens, no bed linens (bring sleeping bags), and share communal campground bathrooms. Guests staying in cabins have access to campground amenities including a heated swimming pool, hot tubs, evening programs, an ice cream shop, Wi-Fi, and summertime breakfasts and dinners.

Located outside the town center on Lake Five, **Lake Five Resort** (540 Belton Stage Rd., 406/387-5601, www.lakefiveresort.com, early May-late Oct., $95-275) rents 12 older cabins. Over half claim lake frontage. Eight cabins have kitchens, and several can sleep up to six people. Two rustic cabins share communal bathrooms in another building with campers. Bed linens are provided, but not kitchen and eating utensils or towels and toiletries. The resort has beach access, canoe rentals, a boat dock, and Wi-Fi.

MOTELS

Basic, no-frills guest rooms sit near shopping, rafting, restaurants, the park entrance, and the train depot. Thin-walled rooms come without in-room phones or air-conditioning. Located above the Middle Fork River, **West Glacier Motel** (200 Going-to-the-Sun Rd., 406/892-2525 from U.S. or 403/236-3400 from Canada, www.glacierparkinc. com, late May-mid-Sept.) has 32 motel units ($100-160) and three kitchen-equipped cabins ($130-320). All rooms lack TVs. To have a TV and Wi-Fi, go to one of the 33 rooms in the **Glacier Highland** (12555 U.S. 2 E., 406/888-5427, www.glacierhighland.com, May-Oct., $100-220), located across from the train depot. Some rooms have been upgraded with sound-reducing walls.

About 0.5 mile west of the Belton Train Depot, **Glacier Vista Motel** (12340 U.S. 2 E., 406/888-5311 or 877/888-5311, www.glaciervistamotel.com, mid-May-Sept., $100-170) perches on a hill with Glacier views. The family-run 1950s motel has an outdoor heated swimming pool. Some rooms have kitchenettes or mini-fridges, but none of the rooms have TVs or air-conditioning. Guests have access to Wi-Fi, a gas grill, and a communal room.

Along U.S. 2

When lodging facilities in Apgar and near West Glacier's town center book up July-August, you can find alternatives lining the nine miles of U.S. 2 from West Glacier to Hungry Horse. In some locations, be prepared for trains rumbling by at night.

Two modern cabin complexes feature log furniture, wireless Internet access, and satellite TV. **Glaciers' Mountain Resort** (1385 Old U.S. 2 E., 406/387-5712 or 877/213-8001, www.glaciersmountainresort.com, $210-260 summer, $130 winter) has five air-conditioned one-bedroom knotty pine cabins with distant Glacier views. Sleeping four, the cabins come with fully equipped kitchens, Wi-Fi, and gas grills. A two-night minimum stay is required. **Silverwolf Log Chalet Resort** (Gladys Glenn Rd. and U.S. 2 E., 406/387-4448, www.silverwolfchalets.com, May-mid-Oct., $140-210) has 10 two-person log chalets plus a two-bedroom deluxe chalet on a landscaped lawn under lodgepole pines enclosed in a privacy fence. Chalets include gas fireplaces, microwaves, coffeemakers, and mini-fridges. Discounts are available for multiple-night stays.

In Coram, **Evergreen Motel** (10159 U.S. 2, 406/387-5365, http://evergreenmotelglacier.com, May-Oct., $110-180) has small cabins and motel rooms, some with kitchenettes. **Historic Tamarack Lodge** (9549 U.S. 2 E., 877/387-4420, www.historictamaracklodge.com, $225-320 summer, $90-130 winter) has 14 cabins set behind its historic lodge and motel that provide a buffer with the highway. The newest loft cabins were built in 2012. The cabins come in various configurations, with the largest sleeping six people. Most have kitchens.

In the town of Hungry Horse, **Mini Golden Inns** (8955 U.S. 2, 406/387-4313 or 800/891-6464, www.hungryhorselodging. com, May-Sept., $120-150) has 38 motel units with satellite television and wireless Internet. Some have kitchenettes and are pet friendly.

Camping

Lake McDonald is the big attraction for camping at Apgar. But if you require RV hookups and showers, you'll need to stay in commercial campgrounds outside the park near West Glacier.

INSIDE THE PARK

Two National Park Service-operated campgrounds flank Lake McDonald with sites under a forest canopy. Rustic and without hookups, they have flush toilets, fire rings with grills, disposal stations, shared hiker-biker sites ($5-8), amphitheaters for evening naturalist talks, and sites that accommodate large RVs. Due to the lakeside location inside the park, away from highway and railroad noise, they are popular. Midsummer, they fill up by 8am-9am. Bring your own firewood; collecting wood is prohibited.

Fish Creek Campground

Fish Creek Campground (end of Fish Creek Rd., 406/888-7800, June-early Sept., $23), one of two campgrounds in the park that can be reserved starting six months in advance (877/444-6777, www.recreation. gov), is one of the larger park campgrounds, with 178 sites tucked under cedars, lodgepole pines, and larches. Loops C and D have the best sites, adjacent to the lake, although Loop B has some larger, more level sites. A few lukewarm token-operated showers are available. Eighteen campsites accommodate RVs up to 35 feet long; 62 sites fit RVs up to 27 feet. To find Fish Creek, drive 1.25 miles north from Apgar on Camas Road and turn right, dropping one mile down to the campground. Lake McDonald Trail departs from the campground.

Apgar Campground

Apgar Campground (Apgar Loop Rd., 0.4 mile from Going-to-the-Sun Rd., 406/888-7800, Apr.-Nov., $20) is within a short walking distance of Apgar Village, Lake McDonald, and the shuttles. The campground has 194 sites, making it the park's largest, with group campsites too. For RVs, 25 sites fit up rigs to 40 feet. A paved trail connects with the Apgar Transit Center, the visitors center, and the Apgar Bike Trail. A separate walking path leads to Apgar Village's restaurant, gift shops, and boat dock. Primitive camping (Apr. and mid-Oct.-Nov., $10) has pit toilets available but no running water. In winter, you can camp free at the plowed Apgar Picnic Area. A pit toilet is there.

McDonald Lake Backcountry Campsite

Lake McDonald has one prime backcountry campsite on the north shore, accessible by foot, paddling, or motorboat. It perches on a point with huge views up and down the lake, plus outstanding night sky watching. It has a communal cooking site, a fire pit, a pebble beach, and two large tent sites that can sleep four people each. Pick up required overnight permits in person at the **Apgar Backcountry Permit Office** (406/888-7859 May-Oct., 406/888-7800 Nov.-Apr., adults $7 pp/night) 24 hours in advance. You can also apply online for advance reservations starting in mid-March (www.nps.gov/glac, $40).

OUTSIDE THE PARK

Commercial campgrounds in the West Glacier vicinity are convenient for rafting, fishing, biking, and trail rides, but they are located outside the park. For hookups, this is where you'll need to be. Standard amenities in these campgrounds include flush toilets, laundries, hot showers, camp stores, picnic tables, fire rings with grills, firewood, propane, disposal stations, playgrounds, hookups, and wired or wireless Internet access. Also, these campgrounds can handle the big RV rigs. If you're a light sleeper, bring earplugs; many of

Wildfires

In an average summer, 13 wildfires burn in Glacier, altering 5,000 acres of forest landscape. Most are caused by lightning; about 80 percent of strikes hit the park's heavily timbered west side. Some are small and unseen while others send huge smoke plumes thousands of feet in the air.

Several large fire seasons have ripped through Glacier since 2000. In 2001 the Moose Fire burned 71,000 acres in the North Fork area, including in Flathead National Forest. In 2003 an onslaught of lightning strikes burned nearly 150,000 acres in several separate fires, creating one of the largest fire seasons in the park's history. You can see the evidence on Apgar Mountain and the north shore of Lake McDonald. In 2006, the Red Eagle fire ate up 32,000 acres outside St. Mary. In 2015, the Reynolds Creek Fire burned 4,850 acres along the east side of Going-to-the-Sun Road between St. Mary Falls and Rising Sun. But even in these recent fire zones, plants and trees are already regenerating.

As flames eat up wood, ash falls to the ground, releasing nutrients. Similar to putting good fertilizer on a garden, the ash fosters energetic plant growth, especially with the open tree canopy permitting more sunlight to reach the ground. As a natural succession of greenery takes over, wildlife dependent on plant foraging finds improved habitat. In short, fires help maintain a natural balance. They also remove deadfall and insect infestations that can kill trees. Fires reduce the power of future fires and create forests that are more resistant to drought and nonnative plant invasions. Fire isn't the end of a forest, but an ongoing process of succession in an ever-changing landscape.

Larch and ponderosa, with thick resin-less bark and minimal low branches, survive fires. Some species even rely on fires for reproduction: The lodgepole pine's serotinous cones require high heat to release their fast-growing seeds from the sticky resin. Ceanothus, hollyhock, and morel mushrooms flourish after fires. See this regrowth from 2001 and 2003 fires along the Camas Road.

Until 1968, federal policy suppressed all fires, which resulted in excessive fuel buildup, bug infestations, and elimination of some floral species. Today, the National Park Service manages each fire individually. If fires threaten human life or structures, they are suppressed, but lightning fires ranging in the wilds are often just monitored, allowing for a natural cycle. Sometimes, park crews set intentional fires to reduce fuel buildup or protect a resource, such as a prairie, from invasion by other species.

Glacier's wildfires used to be monitored from 17 different lookouts. Today, satellite and airplane surveys have reduced the need for staffed lookouts at Huckleberry, Scalplock, Numa, and Swiftcurrent.

the campgrounds hear the rumble and screech of passing trains. Rates are for two people with additional campers costing $5-10 per person.

Although most commercial campgrounds lean toward serving RVers and car campers, bikers and backpackers should ask about special rates in shared sites, which run around $10-12 per person. Many of the campgrounds offer rustic camping cabins or yurts, which have no kitchens or baths; bring your own sleeping bags or pay extra for clean linens, blankets, and towels ($10-15 pp). Commercial campgrounds tack on a 7 percent Montana bed tax to their rates. When you make your reservations, check for deals; many give discounts for Internet registration, seniors, staying early or late in the season, and Good Sam, AAA, or military members. For July-August, make reservations in advance.

West Glacier

On 40 timbered acres 0.5 mile from West Glacier, **Glacier Campground** (12070 U.S. 2 E., 406/387-5689 or 888/387-5689, www. glaciercampground.com, May-Sept., $25-35) is one mile west of the park entrance. Lush undergrowth surrounds private sites separated by birch and fir trees. RV hookups are for water and electricity only, but the campground has a mobile pump-out service ($25). Several cabins ($40-60) share a covered outdoor cooking area with gas burners and a barbecue. Leashed pets are welcome. With the campground set back from the road, trees reduce highway and railroad noise. The open-air pavilion serves sandwiches.

Removed one mile from U.S. 2 and 2.5 miles west of the park entrance, **West Glacier KOA** (355 Half Moon Flats Rd., 406/387-5341 or 800/562-3313, www.koa. com, May-Sept., $38-95) is the only campground with a heated swimming pool (June-mid-Sept.) and a few hot tubs (all season). It also has patio campsites, full RV hookups, evening programs, horseshoes, an ice cream shop, summer barbecue dinners, and pancake breakfasts. Tucked in the forest away from the highway and railroad, this is one of the quieter campgrounds.

Just off U.S. 2, RV campsites at **Lake Five Resort** (540 Belton Stage Rd., 406/387-5601, www.lakefiveresort.com) enjoy lakefront access.

Along U.S. 2

Commercial campgrounds (tents $30-40, hookups $38-80, May-Oct.) sprawl along U.S. 2 in the nine miles between West Glacier and Hungry Horse. A few have distinctive attributes. **North American RV Park and Campground** (10784 U.S. 2 E., 406/387-5800 or 800/704-4266, www.northamericanrvpark.com) spreads RV campsites and rental yurts in a big grassy area with shorter trees for satellite reception. One of the quietest RV campgrounds, **Mountain Meadows RV Park** (9125 U.S. 2 E., 406/387-9125, www. mmrvpark.com) spans 77 acres of forested hillside with a stocked catch-and-release rainbow trout pond.

For upscale camping, **Glacier Under Canvas** (10780 U.S. 2 E., 406/219-0441, www. glacierundercanvas.com, mid-June-mid-Sept., $100-430) provides luxury tenting. Canvas tents (some with en suite hot running water and bathrooms), tepees, a treehouse, and a cabin offer the poshy experience of cots, beds, wood and carpeted floors, private bathrooms, and other amenities.

Food

Glacier is a place for good home-style cooking, where tasty fresh-baked fruit pies are still the rage, rather than upscale or international fare. Seasonal restaurants cater to summer visitors; hours can shorten in spring or fall, and only a few remain open in winter.

INSIDE THE PARK
Eddie's Café & Mercantile

As the only diner in Apgar, **Eddie's Café & Mercantile** (236 Apgar Loop Rd., 406/888-5361, www.eddiescafegifts.com, 8am-10pm daily May-mid-Sept.) has waiting lines in midsummer. It serves breakfasts and lunches ($9-16), including hiker lunches to go. Dinner ($13-26) entrées feature salads, trout, chicken, buffalo meatloaf, and burgers. Montana

microbrews or wine can accompany dinner. Dine inside or outside on the streetside deck. An outdoor stand serves ice cream cones and basic espresso drinks, and you can also buy convenience foods, drinks, camping supplies, ice, and firewood at Eddie's.

Picnic Areas

Two popular picnic areas, both with beach access, rim Lake McDonald's western shores. **Apgar Picnic Area** is just off Going-to-the-Sun Road on the lake's southwest corner, with a beautiful up-lake view to the Continental Divide. **Fish Creek Picnic Area** is next to Fish Creek Campground, where a 0.7-mile hike leads out to Rocky Point for more views. Both have picnic tables, flush toilets, and fire rings with grills, but firewood is not provided, and gathering it is prohibited; purchase firewood in Apgar or West Glacier. On weekends and holidays, plan to nab a table early.

OUTSIDE THE PARK
West Glacier
FINE DINING

At the historic ★ **Belton Chalet** (12575 U.S. 2 E., 406/888-5000 or 888/235-8665, www.beltonchalet.com, late May-early Oct.), you can dine in the intimate Belton Grill (5pm-10pm daily), by the fireplace in the Taproom (3pm-midnight daily), or on the deck watching trains and the sunset over Apgar Mountain. The Belton's restoration to its 1910 allure converted the lodge's old boiler into the kitchen's outdoor grill. Fine-dining flavors, some with fusion Asian elements, are made with fresh local ingredients. Entrées ($21-38) like the bacon-wrapped bison meatloaf or fresh veggie tart pair well with Taproom wines and Montana microbrews. The dessert tray changes nightly: If available, try those made with huckleberries or cherries from the owners' Bigfork orchard. Lighter meals and appetizers are served in the Taproom ($10-15), and box lunches are available to go. In winter (Dec.-Mar.), the Belton serves sandwiches and comfort-food entrées (3pm-8pm Fri.-Sat.) and Sunday brunch (10am-2pm).

CASUAL DINING

Two restaurants serve family café fare with breakfasts and lunches running $8-15 and dinners $10-25. Menus can pacify a variety of tastes, and both restaurants serve beer and wine. Dinner menus have lighter meals of burgers and sandwiches as well as full plated entrées. The **West Glacier Restaurant** (200 Going-to-the-Sun Rd., 406/888-5359, www.glacierparkinc.com, 7am-9pm daily mid-May-late Sept.) caters to hungry hikers with its Grizzly Bear Burger, which sates huge appetites with two 1/3-pound patties. Elk sausage puts a twist on the brats and spaghetti. The beer crowd heads to the adjacent bar, locally known as Freda's, to order saloon food. With

a larger menu, the family-owned **Glacier Highland** (12555 U.S. 2 E., 406/888-9982, www.glacierhighland.com, 7:30am-10pm daily mid-Apr.-mid-Oct.) bakes huckleberry pancakes for breakfast and serves fresh huckleberry pie for dessert. Dinner specialties include buffalo meatloaf and rainbow trout.

MEXICAN

Go for south-of-the-border cuisine in two locations. From an orange food truck surrounded by festive picnic tables, the **Wandering Gringo** (12135 U.S. 2 E., 11:30am-7:30pm Wed.-Mon. late May-early Sept., $3-12) wraps up tasty tacos and burritos. Prepare for outside dining only and mosquitoes in early summer at this locals' hangout. In the Crown of the Continent Discovery Center, **La Casita** (12000 U.S. 2 E., 406/471-2570, 11am-7pm Mon.-Sat. May-Sept., $4-14) dishes up authentic chimichangas, quesadillas, tacos, and mole with ample portions from family recipes. The salsas, guacamole, and tortillas are made fresh daily.

COFFEE AND ICE CREAM

Summer-only espresso and ice cream outlets are ubiquitous in this bustling corner of the park. In West Glacier, **Glacier Village Sweet Treats** (205 Going-to-the-Sun Rd., 406/888-5662, www.glacierparkinc.com, 7am-9pm daily mid-May-late Sept.) and the **West Glacier Restaurant** (200 Going-to-the-Sun Rd., 7am-9pm daily mid-May-late Sept.) have ice cream and espresso, both with outside seating in the parking lots. The **Crown of the Continent Discovery Center** (12000 Hwy. 2 E., West Glacier, 406/387-4405, www.crowndiscoverycenter.com, 7:30am-6:30pm) sells espresso drinks, beer, wine, craft cocktails, and Montana-made ice cream.

GROCERIES

Open daily May-September, two stores carry convenience foods, beer, wine, camping items, ice, and firewood. In West Glacier, the **West Glacier Mercantile** (0.1 mile west of U.S.

2-Going-to-the-Sun Rd. junction) adds a small selection of meats, fresh veggies, and fruits. Hikers can make lunches with pre-made sandwiches, fruit, energy bars, jerky, and snacks. Across from the Belton Train Depot, the **Glacier Highland** (12555 U.S. 2 E., 406/888-9982) has a reputation for cheaper beer and wine prices.

In summer, the **farmers market** comes to West Glacier 3:30pm-6:30pm on Friday afternoons adjacent to the West Glacier Mercantile. The nearest year-round grocery store is in Hungry Horse, on U.S. 2 nine miles west of the park entrance. Look for the "Supermarket" sign. To hit the megastores that carry huge brand selections, you'll have to drive 30 minutes into Flathead Valley.

Along U.S. 2

In Coram, 5.5 miles west of West Glacier, locals head to ★ **Glacier Grill and Pizza** (10026 U.S. 2 E., 406/387-4223, 7am-10pm daily) for any meal of the day. Café fare ($7-14) includes breakfasts, soups, salads, sandwiches, waffle-cut sweet potato fries, and nachos, but the main reason to eat here is the inexpensive beer and pizza ($12-22). Portions are generous, and you can go over the top with huckleberries in pulled pork sandwiches, lemonade, wheat beer, and pie.

WEST GLACIER AND APGAR
TRANSPORTATION AND SERVICES

Transportation and Services

DRIVING AND PARKING

Two-lane highways and roads dominate the West Glacier and Apgar area. Most roads are paved, although dirt and gravel byways reach river accesses. **Glacier Heli Tours** (12205 U.S. 2 E., 406/387-4141 or 800/879-9310, www.glacierhelitours.com) rents a selection of sedans, minivans, and SUVs.

Find public parking lots in West Glacier or at the Alberta Visitor Information Center, streetside, on commercial properties north of the railroad underpass, and at the train depot. Parking is available streetside in Apgar and in three small parking lots in the village, as well as at the picnic area, boat dock, and visitors center. The biggest parking lot that can fit RVs is Apgar Visitor Center.

SERVICES

The West Glacier KOA and West Glacier Campground have **laundries.** You can also get a **hot shower** ($5) at West Glacier Campground.

A **year-round post office** is in West Glacier opposite the Alberta Visitor Information Center. **ATMs** are located in Apgar at Eddie's Cafe & Mercantile and in West Glacier near the gas station.

The headquarters for **rental equipment** for camping, hiking, backpacking, paddling, fishing, and bicycling is **Glacier Outfitters** (196 Apgar Loop Rd., 406/219-7466, www.goglacieroutfitters.com, 9am-8pm daily mid-May-late Sept., shorter hours in shoulder seasons). Some items may be reserved online.

Gas and Repairs

Gasoline is not available inside the park, on Going-to-the-Sun Road, or on U.S. 2 between West and East Glacier. West Glacier is the last chance for gas, available year-round with a credit card at **Glacier Highland** across from the train depot or in summer at **Calumet Station** across from the West Glacier Mercantile.

Cell Phone and Internet Access

Cell phones can get reception in West Glacier and Apgar, but it is intermittent in adjacent canyons and portions of Apgar Campground. Only a few hotels, private campgrounds, and businesses between West Glacier and Hungry Horse provide Internet access. Wi-Fi is also at the coffee and spirits bar in the **Crown of the Continent Discovery Center** (12400 Hwy. 2

E., West Glacier, 406/871-0754, www.crown-discoverycenter.com, May-Sept.).

Newspapers/Magazines

Look for three daily newspapers: Kalispell's *Daily Interlake,* the *Missoulian* from Missoula, and the *Great Falls Tribune.* For the scoop on park news, the weekly *Hungry Horse News* gives a good inside look. You can also find the free weekly *Flathead Beacon* (www.flatheadbeacon.com), covering Flathead Valley and park news.

Emergencies

Call 911 for emergencies. To reach a ranger or the park service, call 406/888-7800. A seasonal **urgent-care clinic** operates in West Glacier (100 Rea Rd., 406/888-9224, 9am-4pm daily Memorial Day-Labor Day). The nearest

hospitals are in the Flathead Valley: **Kalispell Regional Medical Center** (310 Sunny View Ln., 406/752-5111) and **North Valley Hospital** (1600 Hospital Way, 406/863-3500 or 888/815-5528) in Whitefish.

The nearest ranger station inside the park is **Glacier National Park headquarters** (406/888-7800), on Going-to-the-Sun Road west of the park entrance station. Turn onto the signed side road and take the first right into the parking lot for the headquarters building. You can also get assistance at the Apgar Visitor Center.

For concerns with the Flathead River system or in Flathead National Forest, stop in **Hungry Horse Ranger Station** (10 Hungry Horse Dr., Hungry Horse, 406/387-3800, www.fs.fed.us/r1/flathead). Find it south off U.S. 2 on the east end of town.

West Glacier is home to the Alberta Visitor Information Center.

North Fork

62

Look for ★ to find recommended sights, activities, dining, and lodging.

Highlights

★ **Inside Road:** From Polebridge, this scenic backroad challenges vehicles and mountain bikes, offering close encounters with wildlife—and potholes (page 68).

★ **Polebridge:** This tiny, off-the-grid enclave is the center of the North Fork. The Polebridge Mercantile churns out baked goods, and Northern Lights Saloon serves up drinks, dinner, and music (page 69).

★ **Bowman Lake:** Paddle, boat, or hike at this remote lake. Rainbow Peak juts 4,500 feet straight up from the lakeshore, while Thunderbird Mountain scrapes the sky behind nesting bald eagles (page 69).

★ **Kintla Lake:** This remote lake is the centerpiece of some of the park's most isolated backpacking terrain, while the no-motors-allowed waters yield primo paddling (page 70).

★ **Numa Lookout:** A steep forest climb ascends almost 3,000 vertical feet to a perch with views of Bowman Lake and the Rainbow-Carter massif (page 74).

★ **Glacier View:** Climb up a short grunt with scenery galore. The route may tax your lungs, but you'll smell wild roses, and your eyes will relish Glacier's panorama from the top (page 76).

★ **Boulder Pass:** This trek is loaded with alpine meadows, glacier-carved scenery—and solitude (page 77).

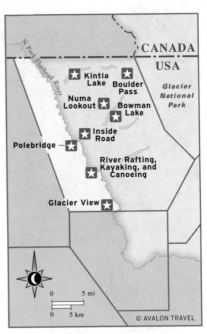

© AVALON TRAVEL

★ **River Rafting, Kayaking, and Canoeing:** Throw your watch away to let river time take over as you float the scenic North Fork of the Flathead River, which courses through remote, prime wildlife habitat (page 79).

The North Fork Valley defines rustic —and not rustic as in cute and comfortable, but backwoods. Remote and wild, it's the place to go for those who want to decompress.

A visit to the North Fork transports you back in time. No flush toilets, no electricity, and no cell-phone service. The pace of life slows with the ambience of the Polebridge Mercantile and Northern Lights Saloon.

For the average traveler, the North Fork's nasty dirt roads alone deter interest. Brutal potholes, jarring washboards, and clouds of dust launch vehement debates about paving the North Fork Road, but pavement into this remote enclave would alter its nature forever.

The North Fork Valley spans diverse habitats from grassland prairies to alpine glaciers. It's home to an immense range of wildlife from huge grizzly bears to tiny pygmy shrews. Spruce trees 300 years old root the valley in deep history. Surrounded by thick subalpine fir forests, Bowman and Kintla Lakes have miles of empty shoreline dotted with only the boats of anglers or a few kayaks. Trails from the North Fork see only a few people, even in high season. Wildlife watchers can find animals and birds at the northernmost and southernmost fringes of their habitats.

Nothing chills the soul quite like the wild call of wolves in the dead of night.

HISTORY

In the late 1800s, handfuls of homesteaders, loggers, hunters, and trappers eked out a living in the North Fork Valley, connected to each other only by a network of trails. In 1900, a Butte businessman, on a quest for oil at Kintla Lake, built the Inside North Fork Road, a 65-mile wagon track riddled with ruts, bogs, and stumps. It was sufficient for hauling drilling equipment from Belton (now West Glacier) to Kintla Lake, where sleds skidded supplies across the frozen lake to drill Montana's first oil well in 1901. The road attracted more homesteaders, but there was already talk of Glacier becoming a national park, a change the homesteaders disliked because the park would mean an end to their hunting and timber livelihoods.

When Glacier achieved national park status in 1910, construction of the rough Outside North Fork Road two years later prompted

---

Previous: backpackers climbing to Boulder Pass; fishing the North Fork of the Flathead River.
Above: Polebridge Mercantile.

North Fork

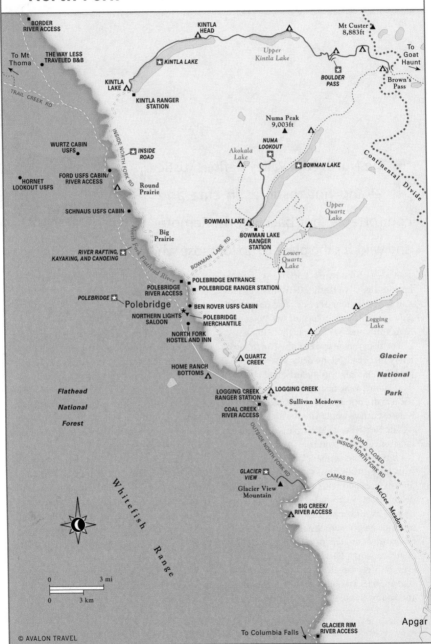

© AVALON TRAVEL

many of the 35 homesteading families within the park boundaries to move across the North Fork of the Flathead River, outside the park boundary. In 1914 near Hay Creek, resident Bill Adair built a new two-story plank building to be the mercantile. The "Merc," as locals call·it, is listed on the National Register of Historic Places. The area today is known as Polebridge, named for the funky, one-lane lodgepole North Fork River bridge that burned in the 1988 Red Bench Fire.

CULTURE

The North Fork is unique. It's a small, intimate community that prides itself on its rustic nature. Not L.L. Bean squeaky-clean cookie-cutter rustic, but real bucolic earthiness with no electricity and few phone lines. Generators and propane tanks provide lights and power, along with some solar energy. Year-round residents living off the grid and summer cabins are sprinkled around the four-mile-wide floodplain. Most residents roll their eyes at visitors who complain about the North Fork Road's dust and potholes; talk of paving raises the hackles of many, who don't want to see the North Fork changed.

The hub of valley life is **Polebridge,** where residents catch up on news, sometimes not much differentiated from gossip. Dogs run amok and lounge on the front porch. However, visiting canines must be leashed. Hand-painted signs will tell you so: "Local dogs at large." One of the warning signs at the Northern Lights Saloon claims, "Unleashed dogs will be eaten."

ECOLOGICAL SIGNIFICANCE

The North Fork area contains all five of Glacier's ecosystems: grassland prairies, aspen parklands, montane forests, subalpine, and alpine tundra. Rich floodplains teem with wildflowers, berries, shrubs, and trees. Fens abound with orchids, bladderworts, sundews, mosses, sedges, ferns, and bulrushes; McGee Meadows houses at least 50 species of flora. The valley is rife with grizzly and black bears, moose, coyotes, mountain lions, and elk. Sizes shrink down to its tiniest mammal, the pygmy shrew, which preys on 25 species of bugs, insects, and snails. Birders have documented 196 species of woodpeckers, owls, raptors, waterfowl, and songbirds, over half of which nest here. As of late 2014, the North Fork Watershed Protection Act prohibits mining and natural resource extraction to protect the sensitive region.

With the natural migration of wolves from Canada in the 1980s, Glacier saw its first wolf pack in 50 years and its first litter of pups in 1986. Numbers have since rebounded. Now wolf packs range across Montana, which has prompted the removal of the wolf as an endangered species. But don't expect to see a wolf around every tree; their numbers vary year to year, they roam up to 300 square miles, and they are elusive. But you may hear them at night. High concentrations of deer and elk make the North Fork Valley prime wolf habitat; to maintain its health, a wolf must eat 10 percent of its body weight in meat every day.

FIRES

Years of fire suppression policies led to thick lodgepole stands and bug infestations. The 38,000-acre Red Bench Fire in 1988 saw policy change when the fire was allowed to run its natural course. Silver sentinels stand as a reminder that Polebridge was nearly wiped off the map. In 2001, the Moose Fire shot over Demers Ridge, burning 71,000 acres, over one-third inside Glacier. In 2003, the Wedge Canyon Fire burned 53,315 acres, jumping the North Fork River into the park and traveling up the side of Parke Peak, while the Robert Fire burned the valley's south end. Evidence of each of these fires is obvious, but new lodgepole forests are overtaking the burns.

Exploring the North Fork

ENTRANCE STATIONS

The North Fork River is the boundary between national forest and national park. From the North Fork Valley, two roads cross the river into the park. On the south end, the paved **Camas Road** has a self-pay kiosk for entry fees. A mile northeast of Polebridge, the **Polebridge Ranger Station** serves as an entrance and is staffed during summer only, but a self-pay kiosk is also available. Backcountry permits for boaters and backpackers are available at the entrance station (9am-4:30pm daily in summer).

SHUTTLES AND TOURS

No buses or vans tour up the North Fork. Guided outdoor recreation such as river rafting or backpacking is the only "tour." However, the companies that guide these trips are based in West Glacier. Several **Glacier Institute** (406/755-1211, www.glacierinstitute.org) courses visit the North Fork for wildlife-watching.

Routine bus shuttles do not go up the North Fork. **Glacier Charters** (406/892-3390 or 800/829-7039, www.glaciertransportation.com) provides a shuttle by reservation only between Glacier Park International Airport and Polebridge for about $130.

Driving Tours
OUTSIDE NORTH FORK ROAD

Open year-round, the Outside North Fork Road is the easier drive of the two dirt and gravel access roads. The two-lane road runs from Columbia Falls to the Canadian border. Be prepared for washboards, potholes, ruts, dust in summer, slush or mud in fall and spring, and ice in winter. Recently, the section between Camas Road and Home Ranch Bottoms saw improvements with grading, gravel, and dust inhibitors, and a short section south of Polebridge is paved.

Locals refer to this road as simply the North Fork, dropping the "Outside," for it is the valley's main gateway. Every few years, clamor arises about paving the North Fork, which many locals oppose because pavement would change the valley's nature. The North Fork Road is intermittently plowed in winter as far as the Canadian border, but do not attempt it without good snow tires. Carry chains and emergency supplies in the car.

From Columbia Falls, the North Fork Road leaves pavement just past Blankenship Road and follows the North Fork River for 13 miles. After a junction with the paved Camas Road, an alternate access from Apgar, the road passes a few small, bucolic ranches whose pastures provide browse for cows and wild elk herds. Six miles of pavement reappears at Home Ranch Bottoms, where cattle walk the road; drive with caution. At 32 miles and a little over one hour's drive, the road meets

Polebridge Ranger Station

North Fork Wonders

TINY FAUNA

The North Fork Valley is home to the rare **northern bog lemming,** a small, brown-backed, gray-bellied rodent that seeks habitat in mats of thick, wet sphagnum moss. Weighing only one ounce (the same as one heaping tablespoon of sugar) but growing up to six inches long, the tiny cousin of the Arctic lemming is a relic of the Pleistocene ice age. Although it's rarely seen, look for the small, neat piles of clipped grass it leaves along the mossy thoroughfares en route to underground nests. One study found that bog lemmings make up 2 percent of the pine marten's diet.

Glacier's smallest predator, the **pygmy shrew,** inhabits floodplains in the North Fork Valley. This tiny carnivore is one of North America's rarest mammals. Less than 2.5 inches in length and weighing a quarter ounce, this shrew's voracious appetite for insects, slugs, snails, and carrion puts larger shrews to shame. One study watched a female eat three times her own body weight daily for 10 days. Their high metabolism echoes their respiration rate at 25 times more frequent than humans, and their hearts beat up to 1,320 times per minute when excited. To feed their high metabolic rates, pygmy shrews eat every couple of hours 24-7 year-round.

PLANTS

Carnivorous plants inhabit North Fork fens. The **sundew** attracts insects to its sparkling droplets, which look like morning dew. Sitting atop hairs lining its leaves, the sticky droplets, like wet cement, trap unsuspecting visitors. Slowly, the leaves curl around the victim as digestive juices work their magic. The **bladderwort** has also refined trapping. Buoyant bladders trap anything that swims, from mosquito larvae to fish fry. As prey passes, it brushes hairs that open a trapdoor that sucks water in along with the naive prey. Digestive enzymes make short work of the meal, with the trap reset in 15-120 minutes.

BIRDS

Birders find a feast for the eyes and ears in the North Fork. The valley teems with avian activity from 196 species and 112 nesters. Migratory birds stop on their flight highways to wintering ranges or summer nesting. To help with identification of Glacier's birds, pick up a bird list from visitors centers or on the park's website.

Raptors: Birds of prey find abundant food in the North Fork Valley. Numerous rodents, ground squirrels, songbirds, and carrion feed their appetites. The valley's forests attract sharp-shinned and Cooper's hawks. Bald eagles nest on Kintla and Bowman Lakes. Northern harriers, red-tailed hawks, goshawks, and American kestrels prowl above the prairies. At night, the hoots of large great-horned and pygmy owls haunt the air.

Waterfowl: With the Flathead River, many large lakes, swamps, and wetlands, waterfowl have no shortage of suitable habitat. Herons, ducks, grebes, geese, loons, and swans migrate through or nest in the plentiful waters.

Songbirds: The North Fork could be considered downright noisy at times. It's not from auto traffic, but from the scads of songbirds flitting among its trees and cattails. American redstarts, warbling vireos, kinglets, nuthatches, crossbills, sparrows, and warblers are just a few of the neotropical songbirds that migrate annually into the valley. In winter, you'll spot tree sparrows and redpolls.

Woodpeckers: After fires, dead standing timber attracts the three-toed woodpecker, picking away for bugs. Watch for the large red-headed pileated woodpecker seeking carpenter ants.

Polebridge Loop and the cutoff to the Merc, Inside North Fork Road, the Polebridge entrance to Glacier National Park, and **Bowman** and **Kintla Lakes.** Hand-painted signs warn drivers entering town: "Slow Down, People Breathing." Respect Polebridge's residents; speed kicks up a tremendous amount of dust in summer.

From the Polebridge junction, the road continues 22 more miles north and another hour's drive toward Canada. It accesses the upper Whitefish Range trailheads, North Fork River, and Forest Service cabins. Although drivers used to cross into Canada here, the Canadian government closed the Trail Creek port of entry.

★ INSIDE ROAD

Not for everyone, the primitive gravel **Inside North Fork Road** throws precipitous narrow drops, curves, and climbs at drivers. It's only open mid-May-October, and since 2014, flood damage has closed an 11-mile portion between Logging Creek and Camas Creek. Monster potholes and washboards are commonplace; spaces wide enough for two vehicles to pass are rare. You're definitely off the beaten path on this bumpy trek, where speeds top out at 20 mph, and two hours can be required to drive nearly 30 miles (longer with stops). Marked as Glacier Route 7 on some maps and known as simply the "Inside Road" to locals, the road requires high-clearance vehicles. Big RV rigs have trouble, and it's a rough ride for a trailer. Check with the park website, Apgar Visitor Center, or Polebridge Ranger Station for current conditions before embarking on the Inside Road. Moose, deer, coyotes, and wolves use the road as a corridor; but don't expect it to be a freeway of wildlife-watching due to thick forests.

Due to the closure between Logging and Camas Creeks, vehicles can no longer complete the 53-mile loop between Fish Creek, Inside Road, Polebridge, North Fork Road, and Camas Road. Drivers now have two accesses. From the south, one access point goes

Access the Inside Road at the bridge in Polebridge.

from Fish Creek; the other accesses the Inside Road midway at Polebridge.

From **Fish Creek,** just north of Fish Creek Campground, the road climbs through the 2003 Robert Fire. Atop the ridge, look for peekaboo views of **McGee Meadows,** a good wildlife-watching spot if you can squeeze your vehicle off the road and tolerate swarms of mosquitoes. Then compare fire regrowth as you drive through the 2001 Moose Fire to the Camas Creek closure at 6.5 miles.

From the **Polebridge entrance station,** vehicles can go north or south on the Inside Road. Travel south to reach the Logging Ranger Station, Logging Creek trailhead, and two small, remote campgrounds: Quartz Creek in 8 miles and Logging Creek in 10.5 miles. Lucky campers may hear wolf howls at night. Vehicles can also drive north on the Inside Road to **Bowman Lake** or **Kintla Lake.** A few minutes north of the Polebridge Ranger Station, the curvy Bowman Lake road turns off Inside Road for 6 miles (25 minutes) of snakelike driving up valley. Continuing northward toward Kintla, the Inside Road crosses **Big Prairie,** the largest of the North Fork's unique grasslands. **Round Prairie** follows at one-third the size. The road reenters the forest and passes through the 2003 Wedge Canyon Fire zone before dead-ending at Kintla Lake, 14 miles north of the Polebridge entrance station.

In 2016, the park service evaluated the future of the Inside Road's closed section, weighing the cost of repairs to the flood damage against preservation of the wilderness, prevention of stream degradation, and protection of threatened fisheries. If the management study opts for repairing the Inside Road, it could potentially be drivable by 2018. Check with the park for status.

Sights

★ POLEBRIDGE

Polebridge is the hub of the North Fork. The red-planked **Polebridge Mercantile** (265 Polebridge Loop, 406/888-5105, http://polebridgemerc.com, daily May-Thanksgiving, Fri.-Mon. winter, 7am-9pm summer, shorter hours in other seasons), or "Merc," listed on the National Register of Historic Places, was built in 1914. It sells local handmade jewelry and not-to-be-missed bakery goods fresh

historic Polebridge Mercantile

from the propane oven: huckleberry bear claws, cinnamon rolls, cookies, and breads. Owner Will Hammerquist has kept the Merc's historic flavor intact despite swapping out the antique cash register for computerized sales powered by solar energy.

Next door to the Merc, the tiny **Northern Lights Saloon** (255 Polebridge Loop, 406/888-9963, 4pm-midnight daily late May-mid-Sept., dinner served 4pm-9pm, $10-30) looks like a ramshackle log cabin but packs in diners, with extras spilling outside onto picnic tables. Hikers celebrate their adventures here with Montana microbrews and lounge outside, staring at Rainbow Peak, while music livens the fun.

NORTH FORK OF THE FLATHEAD RIVER

Forming the western boundary of Glacier National Park, the North Fork of the Flathead River starts in Canada and ends near West Glacier at its confluence with the Middle Fork. Descending the North Fork Valley's diverse habitats, the 59 miles of river flow through private, state, and federal lands. Designated as a Wild and Scenic River, the Class II river with six accesses is great for multiday float trips, day rafting, fishing, and scenic floating.

★ BOWMAN LAKE

Seven miles northeast of Polebridge, Bowman Lake sits in a narrow, glacier-scoured trough at the terminus of a dirt road with a bouncing ride. The lake sprawls toward nesting bald eagles and Thunderbird Peak; its 0.5-mile width squeezes in between the hulks of Numa and Rainbow Peaks, the latter rising 4,500 feet straight up from the south shore. In summer, lake waters offer solitude: Drop in a canoe, kayak, or paddleboard to tour its shoreline. In winter, the icy expanse and snow-laden crags call to cross-country skiers, who ski on the road pockmarked with wolf and elk tracks.

BIG PRAIRIE

Located 30 miles up the Inside North Fork Road, just 2 miles past the Bowman Lake turnoff and 3 miles from Polebridge, Big Prairie is the largest of four Palouse prairies in the North Fork. At 1 mile wide and 4 miles long, the prairie is a grassland with wheatgrass, fescues, oat-grass, and sagebrush. Because the Whitefish Range causes a rain shadow, the North Fork receives only 20 inches of precipitation per year, which fosters this drier flora.

★ KINTLA LAKE

Kintla Lake is a place to go only on purpose. Fifteen miles of potholed road links Polebridge with the remote lake. Its tiny campground tucked deep in the trees offers quiet, a place to decompress. Cowering between Starvation and Parke Ridges, the 0.5-mile-wide lake curves a little over 5 miles

up valley, a prelude to Upper Kintla Lake. One trail starts along the north shore and runs toward the isolated Kintla-Kinnerly peak complex and Boulder Pass. Haul a canoe or kayak to Kintla Lake for secluded, serene (motors are banned) paddling.

LOGGING CREEK RANGER STATION

The historic Logging Creek Ranger Station, built in 1907, is the oldest ranger station in Glacier National Park. With the current road closure on the Inside North Fork Road between Logging Creek and Camas Creek, the idyllic ranger station makes a good destination for a driving tour south from Polebridge.

MCGEE MEADOWS

Between Camas Road and the Inside Road, McGee Meadows is a wildlife-watching spot. During spring and early summer, the mosquito-infested fen is too wet to walk due to its soggy nature. As a fen, its low-oxygen waters build up dead plant matter, but nutrients feed it via precipitation and groundwater, making it fertile ground for diverse vegetation. The meadow is home to rare plants and over 50 species of flora: bulrushes, bladderworts, sphagnum moss, sundews, and orchids. Wildlife sightings can include bears, moose, deer, and a host of birds. Cross-country skiers tour the meadows in winter.

Recreation

DAY HIKES

Hiking in the North Fork leads to stunning vistas, but be prepared to earn your views by tromping through long, mosquito-ridden, thick-forested valleys. While day hikers trek to lakes and lookouts, backpackers gain altitude into rugged, glaciated alpine bowls above the tree line. In this undeveloped area, you're on your own to get to trailheads; no shuttle service runs up the North Fork. On opposite sides of the valley, hikes depart east into Glacier or

west into the Whitefish Range in Flathead National Forest. Those looking for hikes for the pooch should head to the national forest.

While trails in Glacier National Park are well signed and maintained, Flathead National Forest trails are less so. Signs may only show a number with no distances, destinations, or directions. For that reason, hike with a topographic map in the national forest, and know how to read it. Expect to encounter deadfall and downed trees as well as brushy routes.

North Fork Hikes

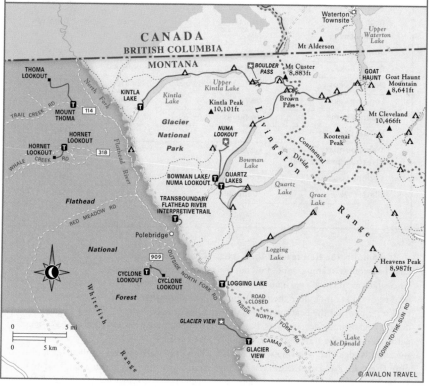

For hiking maps of Flathead National Forest, contact the **Glacier View Ranger District** (406/387-3800) in Hungry Horse. Topographic quad maps of the Whitefish Range can be purchased at outdoor sporting-goods stores in Flathead Valley. For hiking Glacier's trails, take along a topographic map, available through **Glacier National Park Conservancy** (406/892-3250, http://glacier.org).

Access to most North Fork Trails is based on snowpack. Most trailheads on the Glacier National Park side of the North Fork become accessible in May or early June; however, upper elevations will retain snow into late June. Snow lingers on high passes through July. Access to trailheads in Flathead National Forest is based on roads melting out late May-early June.

Hikers can climb Glacier View year-round, although winter requires snowshoes.

Kintla Lake

Distance: 13 miles round-trip
Duration: 6 hours
Elevation gain: 267 feet each way
Effort: easy but long
Trailhead: Kintla Lake in Glacier National Park (see map p. 72)

The gentle trail cruises along Kintla Lake's north shore with an expanding view up the lake before its midsection tours back deep in the trees. Look for woodland flowers: trilliums, twisted stalk, queen's cup, fairybells, bunchberry, and bog orchids. Toward the head of the lake, the trail returns to a shoreline tour.

North Fork Hikes

Trail	Effort	Distance	Duration
Kintla Lake	easy	13 mi rt	6 hr
Bowman Lake	easy	13 mi rt	6 hr
Quartz Lakes	moderate	13.1-mi loop	6.5 hr
Numa Lookout	moderately strenuous	10.2 mi rt	5.5 hr
Logging Lake	easy	10.4-10.8 mi rt	5.5 hr
Mount Thoma	strenuous	10 mi rt	5 hr
Hornet Lookout	easy	2 mi rt	1 hr
Transboundary Flathead River Interpretive Trail	easy	0.3-mi loop	20 min
Cyclone Lookout	moderate	5.6 mi rt	3 hr
Glacier View	strenuous	4.5 mi rt	4.5 hr

At 6.5 miles, the trail reaches the Kintla Lake backcountry campground. Pull out the binoculars, as you might see moose, bears, or bald eagles. Eat lunch near the community cooking site or on the beach rather than in or near backcountry sleeping sites. For a longer exploration, the trail continues through the 2003 Wedge Fire, growing with prolific pink fireweed, and past the dramatic Long Knife Waterfall to Upper Kintla Lake, 2.7 miles farther.

Bowman Lake

Distance: 13 miles round-trip
Duration: 6 hours
Elevation gain: minimal
Effort: easy but long
Trailhead: Bowman Lake in Glacier National Park (see map p. 73)

This easy-walking trail wanders the forested northwest shoreline of Bowman Lake to the backcountry campground at its head. For a stroll, walk it as far as you want and then turn

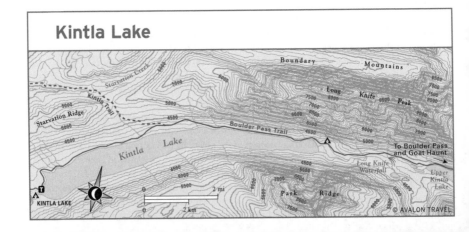

Kintla Lake

Bowman Lake Trails

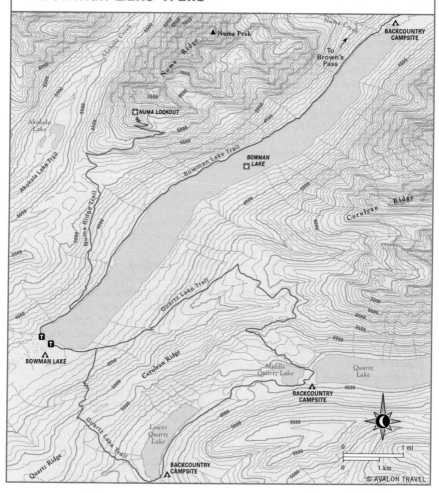

around. The brushy trail nears the shore only a few times, where rocky beaches make for good break spots after June high water recedes. Intermittent views of the Square, Rainbow, and Carter massif poke out from the trees.

At the head of the lake, a backcountry campground with a marvelous pebble beach is a great place to have lunch, but eat near the community cooking site rather than near sleeping sites. Bring binoculars, because bald eagles nest at the lake's head.

Quartz Lakes

Distance: 13.1-mile loop
Duration: 6.5 hours
Elevation gain: 1,410 feet to Upper Quartz, 910 feet on return from Lower Quartz
Effort: moderate
Trailhead: Bowman Lake in Glacier National Park (see map p. 73)

In June, early parts of the trail burst with calypso orchids while the path crossing Cerulean Ridge is still buried under snow.

Less than 0.6 mile up the trail, the path splits. You'll return to this junction at the end of the loop. Take the left fork, heading to Quartz Lake. The trail climbs through thick spruce and fir forests until it crests Cerulean Ridge. As the trail drops 1,000 feet to Quartz Lake, it enters the 1988 Red Bench burn, where lodgepole regrowth affords peekaboo views of Vulture Peak and the lakes. At Quartz Lake, lunch with a view at the patrol cabin beach located on an unmarked spur trail at the trail junction after the backcountry campsites. Hearty anglers pack in float tubes to fish for native trout.

From Quartz Lake, the trail cuts through mosquito bogs and rainforest, passing Middle Quartz Lake, and drops to a backcountry campsite at Lower Quartz Lake's outlet. From here, it climbs 1.5 miles through thick young lodgepoles to the top of Cerulean Ridge before dropping back to the junction. For families with kids, an out-and-back excursion just to Lower Quartz Lake may be easier, at 7.4 miles round-trip.

★ Numa Lookout

Distance: 10.2 miles round-trip
Duration: 5.5 hours
Elevation gain: 2,927 feet
Effort: moderately strenuous
Trailhead: Bowman Lake in Glacier National Park (see map p. 73)

Although the bulk of the trail crawls through deep forest, the view from Numa

Lookout is well worth the climb. Following the northwest shore of Bowman Lake, the trail winds 0.6 mile through damp cedars to a junction. Take the left fork. The trail climbs steadily uphill past a small, boggy pond. During mosquito season, hike fast to get past the swarms.

After the trail switchbacks up the final climb within eyesight of the lookout, the treed slope breaks into dry, open meadows. At 6,970 feet, the lookout, which is staffed during fire season, has views across Bowman Lake at the steep massif of Square, Rainbow, and Carter Peaks.

Logging Lake

Distance: 10.4-10.8 miles round-trip
Duration: 5.5 hours
Elevation gain: 469 feet
Effort: easy
Trailhead: Logging Creek on the Inside North Fork Road in Glacier National Park (see map p. 74)

The trail attracts anglers fishing for cutthroat, some with gumption enough to haul in float tubes. Above Logging Creek, the trail climbs quickly at the start but then levels out across a timbered ridgeline opened up by fire. Views span the creek canyon, aspen-flanked hillsides, and the Vulture Peak complex. At the lake, drop at the first junction to the ranger cabin beach for lunch or head to the second junction to the backcountry campsite (eat your lunch in the community cooking site rather than near the tent sites). Beaches look

Logging Lake

© AVALON TRAVEL

Numa Lookout

up-lake to Mount Geduhn and Anaconda Mountain.

Mount Thoma

Distance: 10 miles round-trip
Duration: 5 hours
Elevation gain: 2,880 feet
Effort: strenuous
Trailhead: on Trail Creek Road in Flathead National Forest
Directions: Drive north of Polebridge on the Outside North Fork Road approximately 13 miles to Trail Creek, 6 miles from the Canadian border. Turn left and drive 3 miles to the trailhead on the right.

The forested trail starts off gently but soon pitches into an uphill grunt. The brushy trail sometimes has downed trees barring the path, requiring climbing and worming through branches. But soon it breaks out into a high ridgeline meadow with bluebells. At the end of the ridge, the trail climbs a series of switchbacks to the summit.

The summit is well worth the hike for its two-nation view. Glacier's peaks sprawl to the southeast. Below, the border swath between Canada and the United States slices an unnaturally straight line across the valley. In Canada, a mosaic of clear-cuts leads up to Akamina-Kishinena Provincial Park bordering Waterton National Park. To the south, the Whitefish Range layers off peak after peak as far as the eye can see.

Hornet Lookout

Distance: 2 miles round-trip
Duration: 1 hour
Elevation gain: 747 feet
Effort: easy
Trailhead: Hornet Road's terminus in Flathead National Forest
Directions: Ten miles north of Polebridge, turn west onto Whale Creek Road (Forest Rd. 318) for 4 miles, then turn north, climbing on narrow Hornet Road (Forest Rd. 9805) for 5.2 miles.

A short climb uphill through huckleberry, fireweed, and bear grass leads to a small lookout with great views of Glacier's skyline and the North Fork Valley. Silvered trees remain from the 2003 Wedge Fire; you'll get a good look at the full scope of the burn. While the drive may take longer than the hike, the lookout makes a great kid destination with rewarding views for adults. To spend the night, rent the U.S. Forest Service lookout (for 1-2 people).

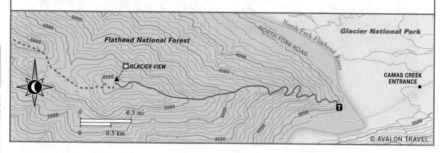

Transboundary Flathead River Interpretive Trail

Distance: 0.3-mile loop
Duration: 20 minutes
Elevation gain: flat
Effort: easy
Trailhead: on the north side of Northern Lights Saloon in Polebridge

This short trail with eight interpretive stops gives insight into the unique North Fork ecosystem that is shared with Canada. Interpretive signs cover history, fire, bears, and transboundary issues affecting the North Fork watershed.

Cyclone Lookout

Distance: 5.6 miles round-trip
Duration: 3 hours
Elevation gain: 1,034 feet
Effort: moderate
Trailhead: On the North Fork Road between Home Ranch and Polebridge, turn west into Flathead National Forest onto Forest Road 376 for 1.25 miles. Turn south onto Forest Road 909 for 4.2 miles.

The trail begins on an old road but soon narrows into a path that switchbacks up through a lodgepole forest. During huckleberry season, you may find a good crop of berries. At the summit, the lookout provides views of the Whitefish Range and straight across the North Fork Valley into the Bowman Lake region of Glacier National Park. The lookout is staffed in summer.

★ Glacier View

Distance: 4.5 miles round-trip
Duration: 4.5 hours
Elevation gain: 2,725 feet
Effort: strenuous
Trailhead: junction of Camas and North Fork Roads in Flathead National Forest; trail sign says "Demers Ridge" (see map p. 76)

A steep climb up the side of Demers Ridge leads to Glacier View. Its name says it all: Views from the top span the park's peaks. You'll even see Flathead Lake in the distance. The trail passes through the 2001 Moose Fire zone, with charred stumps and silver toothpick trees. In the valley below, you can see the fire's mosaic as it burned with different intensities and leaped tree glades. In June, wild roses scent the air amid a botanical dream of wildflower species.

Right from the start, the trail makes no bones about going uphill: There are no flats to warm up the legs. But with a decent pair of lungs, the steep ascent is not bad. Just adopt a slow, steady pace and you'll reach the top, where meadows afford a scenic top-of-the-world place to lunch with Glacier's peaks from Canada to its southern border spread across the skyline. The fire removed shade from the slopes, so the trail bakes in the August heat. In winter, snowshoers trek up.

Guides and Rentals

Glacier Guides (406-387-5555 or 800/521-7238, West Glacier, www.glacierguides.com)

has the sole guiding concession for Glacier National Park. While most day-hiking trips head elsewhere, many multiday backpacking trips begin or finish at the Bowman and Kintla trailheads. No companies run guiding services for hiking in the Whitefish Range of Flathead National Forest.

If you need to rent hiking or backpacking gear, including pepper spray, pick it up in Apgar from **Glacier Outfitters** (196 Apgar Loop Rd., 406/219-7466, www.goglacieroutfitters.com, 9am-8pm daily mid-May-late Sept., shorter hours in shoulder seasons) before coming up the North Fork.

BACKPACKING

The North Fork launches some of the most remote backpacking trips in Glacier. Two trails converge to cross the Continental Divide to reach Goat Haunt on Waterton Lake. The two most popular routes depart from Kintla and Bowman Lakes. A lack of shuttles adds a degree of difficulty to logistics.

Backpackers going overnight in Glacier need permits (adults $7 pp/night). Pick them up 24 hours in advance in person at the **Polebridge Ranger Station** (406/888-7800, daily early June-mid Sept.) or the **Apgar Backcountry Permit Office** (406/888-7859

May-Oct., 406/888-7800 Nov.-Apr.). You can apply for advance reservations online starting in mid-March (www.nps.gov/glac, $40). No permits are needed in Flathead National Forest for overnight trips.

★ Boulder Pass
33 MILES

Starting at the foot of Kintla Lake, the four- to six-day route takes in Upper Kintla Lake, Boulder Pass, Hole-in-the-Wall Cirque, and Brown Pass and finishes at Goat Haunt at the foot of Waterton Lake. A 2,800-foot climb packs in the 5.6 miles between Upper Kintla Lake and Boulder Pass, but otherwise the elevation gains are gentler. The highest camp, at Boulder Pass, boasts a wall-less pit toilet with expansive views of Agassiz Glacier and Kintla Peak, and the Hole-in-the-Wall camp is prized for meadows of rampant wildflowers. Of the nine campsites along the route, the most scenic are Upper Kintla Lake head (UPK), Boulder Pass (BOU), Hole-in-the-Wall (HOL) and Lake Frances (FRA). Due to snow clogging Boulder Pass and Hole-in-the-Wall in early summer, advance reservations are only available starting August 1. But often the route can open up by mid-July for walk-in permits 24 hours in advance. Hiking in reverse by

Glacier View yields big views of the North Fork and Livingston Range peaks.

starting at Goat Haunt spreads the elevation gain out over more miles.

Setting up shuttles is the biggest logistical challenge. Use the Waterton tour boat, east-side shuttle, and Going-to-the-Sun Road shuttles to get to or from West Glacier. Use your own car on the west side to reach Kintla Lake. During August, many backpackers rely on hitchhiking, which is legal in Montana, to get through the North Fork.

Brown Pass
28 MILES

From the trailhead at the foot of Bowman Lake, the three-day out-and-back trip goes to a lower-elevation pass, a good backpacking option earlier in summer. The brushy trail parallels the northwest shore to a large back-country campground (BOW) at the head of the Bowman Lake. Camp here for one night. With an early departure to ascend Brown Pass (BRO), you should have time to hike into the Hole-in-the-Wall cirque. Return to the trail-head in one day.

hiking from Hole-in-the-Wall to Boulder Pass

Due to the lower elevation of Brown Pass, this route is usually snow-free by mid-July. Advance reservations start for Brown Pass on July 15, but walk-in permits are available earlier if the campground melts out. Backpackers can also use this route for a point-to-point hike to Goat Haunt (24 miles total) or over Boulder Pass to Kintla Lake (38 miles total). The junction at Brown Pass links with both destinations.

BIKING

With the North Fork's rough gravel roads, mountain biking is the only way to go; road bikes won't cut it. A portion of the Outside North Fork Road is on the Great Divide Mountain Bike Route. You can rent mountain bikes in Polebridge from **North Fork Recreation** (80 Beaver Dr., 206/253-3374 or 406/888-9953, http://northforkrecmt.com, $30). Reservations are recommended.

In June, when moisture still clings to gravel and dirt, riding roads is less dusty, but you'll eat your share of mosquitoes. During dry spells, plan on drowning in clouds of dust. To dodge vehicles, ride the closed section of the **Inside Road** between Camas Creek and Logging Creek. Littered with wolf scat, the 4.5 miles from Logging Creek Ranger Station to Anaconda Creek tours along Sullivan Meadows, ponderosas, and aspens. The 6.5-mile segment from Camas Creek to Anaconda Creek climbs and drops through regrowing fire zones until reaching the steep drop down Anaconda Hill. Flooding has eroded the road-bed at Anaconda Creek; only bikers capable of carrying bikes while fording multiple creek cuts should cross the area. Due to flooding and downed trees, the route is best to ride starting midsummer after water levels drop and crews saw downed trees. Check with the park for current conditions (406/888-7800).

For mountain bikers who like challenges, including fording creeks while carrying your bike, a 53-mile loop from Apgar links together the Inside North Fork Road, Outside North Fork Road, and paved Camas Road. The Inside Road adds serious elevation gain as it climbs and drops through five creek drainages. The rugged ride requires carrying only minimal supplies as a two-day overnight. Due to the remoteness, be ready to self-rescue in case of emergency. Stay at the North Fork Hostel, dine at the Northern Lights Saloon, and breakfast on baked goodies at the Merc.

★ RIVER RAFTING, KAYAKING, AND CANOEING

Floating the Wild and Scenic **North Fork of the Flathead River** decompresses life to river pace on Class II waters. Despite the lazy ambience, the North Fork throws challenges at rafters, kayakers, and canoers. Log jams pose hazards, and braided channels can dead-end. Between Big Creek and Glacier Rim, the Class III Upper Fool Hen rapids can flip the unwary. Paddlers can avoid this stretch by taking out at Big Creek. Seven river put-ins stagger down the river's 59 miles from the Canadian border to its confluence with the Middle Fork: the border, Ford, Polebridge, Coal Creek, Big Creek, Glacier Rim, and Blankenship. Flows peak in late May, with low water in August. In July, the average float time from the border to Blankenship is 16 hours, which most floaters tend to break into three days.

Flathead National Forest's **Glacier View Ranger District** (Hungry Horse Ranger Station, 406/387-3800, www.fs.usda.gov) can answer questions on floating the river. It sells the *Three Forks of the Flathead Float Guide* ($13), which provides details on camping, rapids, and navigation. You can download its maps from the website. Solid human waste containment is required; take a toilet system, groover, or disposable biodegradable waste bags. Fire pans to prevent fire scarring are recommended.

Respect the rights of private-property owners along the river. Signage at river accesses identifies land ownership en route.

Overnights

No permits are required for floating, but all camps must be set up on the western shore rather than Glacier National Park's eastern shoreline. Camping is first-come, first-served only and is free in Flathead National Forest and on state lands. Round Prairie, on Glacier's bank, is the one exception; this backcountry campground requires a permit, which you can pick up at the **Apgar Backcountry Permit Office** (406/888-7859 May-Oct., 406/888-7800 Nov.-Apr., www.nps.gov/glac, $7 pp/night, $40 advance reservation available mid-Mar.).

Mountain bikers can tour the closed section of the Inside Road.

Tips for Wildlife-Watching

- Safety for you and safety for the wildlife is important. For spying wildlife up close, use a good pair of binoculars.

- Do not approach wildlife. Although our inclinations tell us to scoot in for a closer look, crowding wildlife puts you at risk and endangers the animal, often scaring it off. Sometimes simply the presence of people can habituate an animal to hanging around people; with bears, this can lead to more aggressive behavior.

- Let the animal's or bird's behavior guide your behavior. If the animal appears twitchy, nervous, or points eyes and ears directly at you, back off: You're too close. The goal is to watch wild animals go about their normal business, rather than to see how they react to disruption. If you behave like a predator stalking an animal, the creature will assume you are one. Use binoculars and telephoto lenses for moving in close rather than approaching an animal.

- Most animals tend to be more active in morning and evening. These are also optimum times for photographing animals in better lighting.

- Blend in with your surroundings. Rather than wearing loud colors, wear muted clothing that matches the environment.

- Relax. Animals sense excitement. Move slowly around them because abrupt, jerky movements can startle them. Look down, rather than staring animals directly in the eye.

- Don't get carried away watching big, showy megafauna like bears and moose only to miss a small carnivore like a short-tailed weasel.

- Use field guides to help with identification and understanding the animal's behavior.

- If you see wildlife along a road, use pullouts or broad shoulders to drive completely off the road. Do not block the middle of the road. Use the car as a blind to watch wildlife, but keep pets inside. If you see a bear, you're better off just driving by slowly. Bear jams tend to condition the bruin to become accustomed to vehicles, one step toward getting into more trouble.

Guides

Several river rafting companies lead overnight trips down the North Fork; however, none base their operations in the North Fork Valley. All commercial outfitters begin their trips in West Glacier. Due to the Class II nature of the river, the float trips are great for families and kids.

Rentals and Shuttles

In Polebridge, **North Fork Recreation** (80 Beaver Dr., 406/888-9985, http://north-forkrecmt.com, $60/day) rents catarafts and inflatable kayaks. Rates include paddles and life jackets. The gear is in demand, so make reservations. Rubber rafts are available to rent in West Glacier from **Glacier Outdoor Center** (406/888-5454 or 800/235-6781, www.

glacierraftco.com), which also offers vehicle shuttle services ($40-450) in your vehicle or its rigs.

BOATING

While **Kintla Lake** does not permit motorized boats, **Bowman Lake** allows motors of 10 horsepower or less. Both lakes are closed to Jet Skis and waterskiing. No boat rentals are available in the North Fork Valley; bring rentals from Flathead Valley. For sailboats and sailboarding, constrictive mountains create swirly winds that make for challenging conditions.

Boaters must pick up permits ($10 for 7-day motorized permit, $40 for annual motorized permit, free for nonmotorized boats). Boats must be cleaned, drained, and dried to avoid bringing aquatic invasive species into park lakes. The permits are available at the Polebridge entrance station. Seasonal wildlife closures at the lakes' heads, marked with orange buoys, protect nesting bald eagles.

LAKE PADDLING

The quiet waters of **Bowman** and **Kintla Lakes** appeal to kayakers and canoers. Kintla is a paddling paradise due to its ban on motorized watercraft. While both lakes make for stellar paddling on calm days, their waters can kick up with lusty winds in minutes. Wildlife closures are marked with orange buoys at the head of each lake, where bald eagles nest. Free boating permits are available at the Polebridge Ranger Station. By permit, paddlers can camp overnight in the backcountry campgrounds at the heads of Kintla and Bowman Lakes.

In Polebridge, **North Fork Recreation** (80 Beaver Dr., 206/253-3374 or 406/888-9953, http://northforkrecmt.com, $50-80) rents paddleboards, kayaks, and canoes. Rates include paddles and life jackets; reservations are recommended.

FISHING

Anglers are attracted to the North Fork for its native fish: westslope cutthroat and bull trout.

Be able to identify each, as they are catch-and-release only. Bull trout have pink or orange spots on their sides, and they lack black on their backs; cutthroats have a red slash under their jaw.

Kintla and **Bowman Lakes** are the main lakes accessible by car for fishing. Shorelines near their campgrounds rim with trails. For hikers, the three **Quartz Lakes** hop with native trout and whitefish. Along the Inside North Fork Road, most of the western creek drainages provide some fishing, with various degrees of accessibility. Fishing closures in the area include Upper Kintla Lake and Kintla Creek between the two Kintla Lakes, Bowman Creek above the lake, and Logging Creek between Logging and Grace Lakes.

The most popular North Fork Valley fishing is on the **North Fork of the Flathead River** itself, where seven river accesses (Canadian border, Ford, Polebridge, Coal Creek, Big Creek, Glacier Rim, and Blankenship) allow for fishing and raft launching. Anglers also fish around the Camas Bridge.

Several commercial outfitters guide overnight fishing trips on the North Fork River All fishing outfitters base their operations

River rafters float the North Fork of the Flathead River along Glacier's western boundary.

out of West Glacier. Find rental gear in West Glacier, too.

Licenses and Regulations

The North Fork River's high-water line on the eastern shore is Glacier National Park's western boundary. Inside the park, fishing licenses are not required, but outside the park, anglers must possess a **Montana fishing license** (Montana residents: $8-18 season, $13 adults for 2 days, free ages 1-11; nonresidents: $25 for 2 days, $44 for 10 days, $60 season, kids ages 1-14 free with adult with license for shared limit or $8 for own license). When fishing the North Fork River from the east bank, park regulations apply; when fishing from the west bank, state regulations apply. Purchase a Montana fishing license in West Glacier or Flathead Valley before you come up the North Fork; they are not sold in Polebridge. Find fishing-license information and how to order in advance online (www.fwp.mt.gov).

HUNTING

Hunting is illegal in Glacier National Park. But in the North Fork, Flathead National Forest holds popular deer, elk, and bird hunting grounds. Get regulations, seasons, and license info from **Montana Fish, Wildlife, and Parks** (406/444-2535, www.fwp.mt.gov).

CROSS-COUNTRY SKIING AND SNOWSHOEING

Roads in the North Fork Valley convert to easy, avalanche-free cross-country ski and snowshoe trails in winter. But don't expect pristine smooth snow: The North Fork thrives as a winter habitat for moose, wolves, deer, elk, snowshoe hares, coyotes, and bobcats, whose tracks pockmark the roads. Grab a track identification book to help in deciphering the prints. The nearest ski and snowshoe rentals are in Flathead Valley.

Park at the Polebridge entrance station to ski to **Bowman Lake,** touring 0.5 mile north on the Inside Road before climbing 6 miles up to Bowman Lake's frozen shores. **Big Prairie, Inside Road,** and **Hidden Meadows** all provide other routes starting from the same point. For route descriptions, pick up a free brochure on *Skiing and Snowshoeing* from Apgar Visitor Center or online (www.nps.gov/glac).

For an overnight in Flathead National Forest, skiers traverse 12 miles up Whale Creek Road to stay in Ninko Cabin on the flanks of Thompson-Seton Mountain. For information on this trip, call **Glacier View Ranger Station** (406/387-3800).

SNOWMOBILING

While snowmobiles are not permitted in Glacier, they are allowed in Flathead National Forest in the Whitefish Range, where snowfall piles up 6-12 feet deep. December-April, snowmobilers ride unplowed roads heading west off the North Fork Road. The **Flathead Snowmobile Association** (www.flathead-snowmobiler.com) grooms a few routes. **Glacier View Ranger Station** (406/387-3800) regulates snowmobile use, seasons, and closures, and it has maps; check for current conditions and restrictions. The nearest rentals are in Flathead Valley.

ENTERTAINMENT AND EVENTS

Instead of red, white, and blue marching bands, Polebridge's annual **Fourth of July Parade** has cross-dressers, beer-can draggers, bicycles, the 1956 Polebridge fire truck, and rafts. The more slightly off-kilter, the better. Hundreds of people line the dirt main street for the noon parade that's really not a parade. Parking is a nightmare, and it's a two-for-one show as the parade goes up the street and then back down the same street. Enter for free; watch for free. Who's in charge? No one knows.

Live music happens at the **Northern Lights Saloon** (255 Polebridge Loop, Polebridge, 406/888-9963, 7pm-10pm Sat. and holidays in summer). Artists include solo musicians and bands.

Accommodations

North Fork lodging is off the grid. With no electricity, power comes from generators or solar panels. Lights are propane, woodstoves provide heat, and phone lines only reach Polebridge. However, despite the rusticity, the State of Montana still charges its 7 percent bed tax.

OUTSIDE THE PARK
Polebridge

Located 0.25 mile south of the Merc and Northern Lights Saloon, the ★ **North Fork Hostel** (80 Beaver Dr., 406/888-5241, http://nfhostel.com, May-Sept., $25-80) offers a mix of hostel bunks, cabins, and unique accommodations. Reservations are strongly advised in summer. The hostel may be off the electric grid, but far from "roughing it." A huge storage battery powers phone, fax, and Wi-Fi. Propane powers the lights, cooking stove, and refrigerator, with a few kerosene lights added in. Wood heats up the cedar hot tub. The hostel has a shared living room, fully equipped kitchen, outhouses, and baths with hot showers. Lodging options include mixed dorm bunks, private guest rooms, and an assortment of tepees, cabins, and a 1950s trailer called the Green Zucchini. Bring food, towels, and sleeping bags, or rent linens ($5).

The hostel also rents two log homes at nearby **Square Peg Ranch** ($100-200). One is a 1918 homestead. Kitchens are equipped with propane lights, a fridge, and cooking range, and the buildings are heated with wood. Cold running water, solar-heated showers, and outhouses complete the rustic stay. The homes can sleep 6-8 people. Bring sleeping bags or sheets, food, towels, and containers to haul fresh drinking water from the hostel. Minimum stay is three nights.

For the newest accommodations in the North Fork, ★ **Polebridge Ranch Cabins** (8855 North Fork Rd., 406/662-1552, http://

polebridgeranch.com, May-Oct., $90-180) offers cabins sleeping up to four people. The cabins have propane heat, generator electricity, private baths with flush toilets and showers, and private fire pits. The larger cabins, named for the North Fork lakes of Bowman (3-night minimum) and Kintla (2-night minimum) have porches with outstanding views. Bowman has a fully equipped kitchen, while Kintla has a mini-fridge, coffeemaker, and gas grill. The bunk bed Numa Peak and Kootenay Cabins do not have kitchens. Rates drop for multiple nights.

Polebridge Rental Cabins (Polebridge Mercantile, 265 Polebridge Loop, 406/888-5105, http://polebridgemerc.com, $90-125) has four tiny, bare-bones cabins that have stoves, coolers, and outhouses, but no running water. You can get water at the Merc, and the stay comes with a breakfast voucher for the bakery.

Private cabins are sprinkled up and down the North Fork. Find options such as rustic one-roomers and log homes online at **VRBO** (www.vrbo.com) under "Polebridge."

North End of North Fork

For those looking to get away from it all, ★ **The Way Less Traveled Bed and Breakfast** (16485 North Fork Rd., 406/261-5880, www.thewaylesstraveled.com, year-round, $98-125) is about as remote as you can get and still have the comforts of civilization. Proprietors Paul and Nancy Winkler encourage guests to unplug in favor of soaking up nature. Located 17 miles north of Polebridge and 3 miles south of the Canadian border, the smoke-free bed-and-breakfast has three themed guest rooms. Two queen rooms share a bath, but the king room has a private bath and deck. The B&B also has a cozy cabin with a deluxe outhouse and solar shower. Breakfast is served in the dining room surrounded by wildlife-watching windows or on the deck accompanied by loons singing on a nearby lake.

Rent a 1913 homestead: Wurtz Cabin.

A generator powers lights, hot water, satellite TV, and Wi-Fi.

Flathead National Forest

The **U.S. Forest Service** maintains six rental cabins scattered across the North Fork in **Flathead National Forest** (Glacier View Ranger District, Hungry Horse, 406/387-3800, www.fs.fed.us/r1/flathead, $20-70). With a three-night maximum stay, the cabins have beds, outdoor vault toilets, kitchens equipped with propane cookstoves, outdoor fire pits, and firewood. Bring water (no running water), bedding, and food. The cabins do not permit pets, tents, or RVs. Reservations are mandatory (877/444-6777, www.recreation.gov). After confirmation, you'll get the cabin combination. You must clean up at the end of your stay and pack garbage out with you.

Three cabins are available year-round. The deck at **Schnaus** yields sweeping views of Glacier's Livingston Range, making it a local favorite for its sunrises and sunset alpenglow. The cabin, which sleeps 12, has vehicle access

right up to the front door and is less than one mile from the North Fork River. Located on the North Fork River, **Ben Rover,** which sleeps 8 and has drive-up access, is popular for skiing to Bowman Lake in winter, walking to the Merc in summer, and fishing right out the front door. The farthest north, **Wurtz Cabin,** which sleeps 12, is an old 1913 homestead with a large yard on the west side of the North Fork Road. The river is within a 15-minute walk.

Three small cabins offer seasonal lodging. In a drafty, tiny 1922 building perched atop a mountain, **Hornet Lookout** (mid-June-Oct.), which sleeps two, requires a one-mile hike from your vehicle. The lookout has a small cupola with spectacular views of Glacier. **Ford** (late May-Mar.), which was built in 1922 as part of the ranger station, sleeps eight. It has drive-up access and is adjacent to a river access site. **Ninko** (Dec.-Mar.), which sleeps seven, requires a 12-mile ski or snowmobile trek to reach its remote forested setting.

Camping

National park or national forest campgrounds are the norm. These rustic camps are first-come, first-served. Small, private campgrounds are minus hookups. If you require hookups and disposal stations, go to West Glacier or Columbia Falls.

INSIDE THE PARK

Glacier's seasonal **North Fork campgrounds** (406/888-7800, www.nps.gov/glac) are only accessible via rough dirt roads. Between rugged roads and smaller sites, these campgrounds don't accommodate huge RVs or large trailer combinations. But that's precisely their attraction: Fewer people equals solitude and quiet. They have pit toilets, fire rings, and picnic tables. While the park prohibits firewood collecting in most places, including the campgrounds, you can collect dry, downed firewood on the Bowman Lake Road and the Inside Road to Kintla Lake. Cutting live timber is not permitted. Early September-October, Bowman and Kintla Campgrounds permit primitive camping ($10). Bring water or haul it from lakes and streams to boil or purify. The four campgrounds are buggy in June, serene in August, and closed in winter when the roads are buried in snow. Midsummer, Kintla and Bowman can fill up by 11am Friday-Saturday and midafternoon Sunday-Thursday.

Kintla Lake Campground

At the foot of Kintla Lake, ★ **Kintla Lake Campground** (June-mid-Sept., $15) is 15 miles north of Polebridge. The tiny 13-site campground is tucked under large trees, with hand-pumped water and small sites. One hiking trail leads up-lake and beyond to Upper Kintla Lake and Boulder Pass. If you don't have reservations, plan to arrive early enough that if all the campsites are full, you can still drive back toward Bowman Lake.

Bowman Lake Campground

At the foot of Bowman Lake, ★ **Bowman Lake Campground** (late May-early Sept., $15) is seven miles from Polebridge. Its 48 sites, the largest of the North Fork's campgrounds, spread out under a mixed conifer forest. It has running water, and a five-minute walk leads to the lakeshore and the boat ramp. Trails connect to Quartz Lakes, Numa Lookout, Akokala Lake, and up Bowman Lake to Brown Pass.

Quartz Creek and Logging Creek Campgrounds

Two tiny campgrounds flank the Inside Road in the woods south of Polebridge. They are best for tent campers who can drive the rugged road. No running water is available, so bring your own or plan to purify stream water. Arrive by midafternoon to allow plenty of time to go elsewhere if either campground is full.

With seven campsites, **Quartz Creek Campground** (July-Nov., $10) sits six miles southeast of Polebridge adjacent to Quartz Creek. From the campground, a 6.8-mile rough trail with infrequent maintenance follows the creek up to Lower Quartz Lake. Located 8.3 miles southeast of Polebridge, **Logging Creek Campground** (July-Sept., $10), adjacent to Logging Creek Ranger Station, has only seven sites. This is a popular site for anglers heading to Logging Lake.

OUTSIDE THE PARK
Polebridge

Two small private campgrounds around Polebridge have camping in summer. Add 7 percent tax to the rates. The **North Fork Hostel** (80 Beaver Dr., 406/888-5241, http://nfhostel.com, $20) accommodates tenters, and **Home Ranch Bottoms** (8950 North

Fork Rd., 406/888-5572, www.homeranchbottoms.com, $22 RV, $10 tents) has water hookups for RVs, but no electrical hookups.

Flathead National Forest

Located 20 miles north of Columbia Falls and 13 miles from Apgar on North Fork Road, **Big Creek Campground** (Glacier View Ranger District, 406/387-3800, mid-May-late Sept., $15) is in Flathead National Forest. It can be accessed via a five-minute drive on a gravel road from the Camas Road park entrance. Several of the campground's 22 sites can accommodate 40-foot RVs and trailers among large cottonwoods and dog-hair firs. Drinking water is available, along with vault toilets. Prime campsites line the North Fork of the Flathead River, with easy fishing access. You can collect firewood here, but by August the surrounding woods are scoured. Make reservations for midsummer (877/444-6777, www.recreation.gov).

Food

OUTSIDE THE PARK
Polebridge

A rustic solar-powered restaurant in a tiny, funky old log cabin built in 1912, the ★ **Northern Lights Saloon** (255 Polebridge Loop, 406/888-9963, 4pm-midnight daily late May-mid-Sept., dinner served 4pm-9pm, $10-30) is where hikers stop to celebrate with a beer (wine and cocktails, too) and then linger over a meal. Expect to relax over your meal rather than gobble and go. New owner in 2015, Heather Matthews maintains the tradition of Friday night pizza and salads followed by Saturday night prime rib. The menu has vegan options, plus bison or elk burgers, steak, or rainbow trout. Waiting lines attest to its unique backwoods ambience. Some people even drive up the North Fork just to go to the historic restaurant. Outdoor seating makes for great people watching, and live music happens 7pm-10pm Saturday nights and holidays in summer.

For limited groceries, camping stove fuel, propane, fishing tackle, and beer, stop at the ★ **Polebridge Mercantile** (265 Polebridge Loop, 406/888-5105, http://polebridgemerc.

Locals drive up the North Fork just to go to the Northern Lights Saloon.

com, daily May-Thanksgiving, Fri.-Mon. winter, 7am-9pm summer, shorter hours in other seasons). You can pick up forgotten camping items and groceries, but don't expect a broad selection of choices. Hundreds of fresh-from-the-oven pastries, cookies, lunch breads, and cinnamon rolls based on recipes passed down through successive owners march out the door daily. Other treats include espresso and ice cream. Get deli sandwiches to-go for the road or trail.

Home Ranch Bottoms (8950 North Fork Rd., 406/888-5572, www.homeranchbottoms.

com, 10am-9pm daily Apr.-Oct.) is worth a stop to see the grizzly claw marks preserved in the floor from when a bruin tore up the building. Signed with hand-painted advertising along the road, the small store sells convenience groceries, beer, coffee, soda pop, T-shirts, firewood, and ice. Visitors can sidle up to the large log bar in **The Bottoms Tavern,** which serves burgers, barbecue, ice cream, beer in chilled glasses, wine, and cocktails. A woodstove heats the tavern on cold days, and outdoor seating accommodates warm days.

Transportation and Services

DRIVING AND PARKING

Plan on being friendly with ubiquitous dirt roads with potholes, washboards, and dust. Only a six-mile section of the Outside North Fork Road is paved around Home Ranch Bottoms. Forget public parking lots. Find parking at businesses and roadside in Polebridge.

SERVICES

You won't find strip malls or services up the North Fork. Forget the ATMs, post office, television, visitors centers, and shopping. Phone lines run only as far as Polebridge. The **Polebridge Mercantile** (265 Polebridge Loop) has a **pay phone** on its front porch, but it works intermittently. In most locations, **outhouses** and **vault toilets** take the place of flush toilets. **Showers** are available at **Home Ranch Bottoms** (8950 North Fork Rd., $7).

Gas and Repairs

Gas up before going up the North Fork. The gas sold at the **Polebridge Mercantile** (265 Polebridge Loop) is expensive. Vehicle repairs are not available; call Flathead Valley mobile vehicle services, which will charge by the mile to come to you.

Cell Phone and Internet Access

Locals head up the North Fork delighted to cut the technological umbilical cord. It's a place to get away from social media, phone calls, and surfing the 'Net. Put the phone away, and settle into a slower pace. Cell-phone reception is spotty to nonexistent. Internet access is only available on the **Polebridge Mercantile** computer or for guests at select lodging properties.

Emergencies

Call 911 for emergencies. You can also contact a ranger at 406/888-7800. The nearest hospitals are in the Flathead Valley: **Kalispell Regional Medical Center** (310 Sunny View Ln., Kalispell, 406/752-5111) and **North Valley Hospital** (1600 Hospital Way, Whitefish, 406/863-3500).

The **Polebridge Ranger Station** (406/888-7800, year-round) sits one mile from Polebridge across the North Fork River at the park entrance. During summer, **Logging Creek Ranger Station** on the Inside North Fork Road is staffed, as are stations at **Bowman and Kintla Lakes;** however, these seasonal rangers may be out patrolling miles of backcountry.

Going-to-the-Sun Road

Historic Going-to-the-Sun Road is a testament to human ingenuity and nature's wonders. In the road's 50 miles, an incomparable diversity unfolds, with surprises around each corner.

Tunnels, switchbacks, arches, and a narrow two-lane highway cutting across precipitous slopes reveal feats of engineering. Cedar rainforests give way to windblown subalpine firs, broad lake valleys lead into glacial corridors, 1,000-foot cliff walls abut wildflower gardens, and waterfalls spew from every pore. Defying gravity, ragged peaks rake the sky, crowning all.

This National Historic Landmark is a place to savor every nook and cranny. Oohs and aahs punctuate every sweep in the road as stunning scenery unfolds. Stopping at myriad pullouts along the road, many sightseers burn through their digital pixels only halfway up the alpine section. The sheer immensity of the glacier-chewed landscape leaves visitors gasping, "I can't fit it all in my camera."

To stretch your legs, well-signed short paths guide hikers through a dripping rainforest, along a glacial moraine, amid mountain goats, and beside a roaring waterfall.

Those ready to put miles on their boots should tackle at least one of the longer high alpine trails, where you'll feel you've reached the apex of the world, sending your spirit soaring.

The Sun Road, as locals call it, is one place you won't want to miss. Its rugged beauty leaves a lasting impression.

HISTORY
Early Development
By 1895, Lake McDonald boomed with tourism brought by the railroad's arrival in West Glacier. Hauling a 40-foot steamboat up from Flathead Lake, George Snyder shuttled guests from Apgar to his 12-room hotel, where Lake McDonald Lodge currently sits. With Sperry Glacier's discovery in 1896, Snyder's guests had a popular horse trip destination above his lodge. Funded by the Great Northern Railway, Dr. Lyman Sperry and 15 of his students built the Gunsight Pass and Sperry spur trail to accommodate travel between St. Mary and Lake

Previous: Avalanche Gorge; Piegan Pass Trail. **Above:** boardwalk at Logan Pass.

Look for ★ to find recommended sights, activities, dining, and lodging.

Highlights

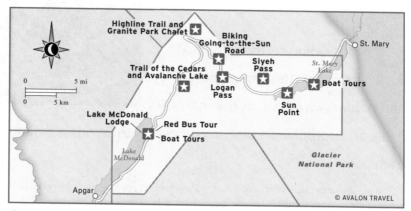

© AVALON TRAVEL

★ **Red Bus Tour:** Ride over Logan Pass in historic style. The 1937 vintage touring sedans, designed especially for national parks, roll their canvas tops back for superb views and perhaps a dousing from the Weeping Wall (page 95).

★ **Boat Tours:** See the park's two largest lakes—hop aboard *Little Chief* to see St. Mary Lake or the *DeSmet* to see Lake McDonald (page 95).

★ **Lake McDonald Lodge:** Sit on the back porch of the historic lodge gracing Lake McDonald. The lodge's rustic hunting motif harks back to a pre-national park era when the region served as a hunting preserve (page 100).

★ **Logan Pass:** Touch the Continental Divide, where waters stream toward both the Pacific and Hudson Bay. The apex of Going-to-the-Sun Road sprawls with broad alpine meadows teeming with wildflowers and mountain goats (page 103).

★ **Sun Point:** Peaks rise on both sides of this dramatic promontory in the middle of St. Mary

Lake. Views extend up to the Continental Divide. (page 105).

★ **Trail of the Cedars and Avalanche Lake:** Walk through the easternmost Pacific rainforest in the United States and then to a scenic subalpine lake (page 109).

★ **Highline Trail and Granite Park Chalet:** Hike a wildflower-packed trail clinging high on cliffs along the Garden Wall to a historic backcountry chalet where bear-watching is a worthy pastime (page 111).

★ **Siyeh Pass:** Climb over one of the most scenic and diverse trails in Glacier. The path wanders through wildflowers and descends colorful sedimentary strata, perhaps touching on every color in the rainbow (page 113).

★ **Biking Going-to-the-Sun Road:** Best in spring before the road opens to vehicles, biking Going-to-the-Sun Road is a must for cyclists. Prepare for an uphill grind to Logan Pass (page 118).

Going-to-the-Sun Road

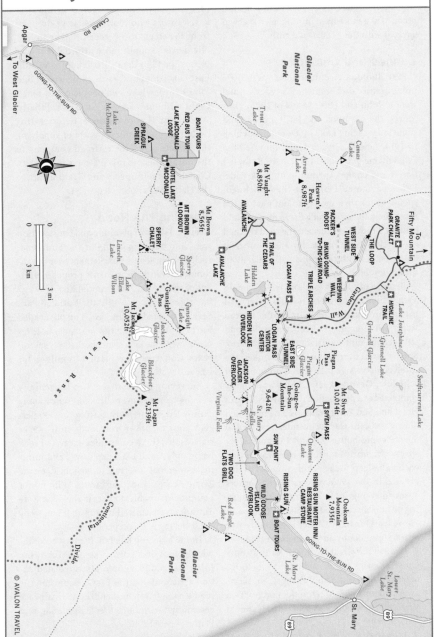

© AVALON TRAVEL

McDonald. While the west side surged with turn-of-the-20th-century tourism, on the east side, Roes Creek (Rose Creek at Rising Sun) boomed as a short-lived mining town that was vacated with the Alaska gold rush.

Lodges and Chalets

Under dubious circumstances, perhaps a poker game, ownership of Snyder's hotel went to John and Olive Lewis in 1906. They moved the old hotel and built a cedar and stone lodge facing Lake McDonald. Opening in 1914, Lewis's Glacier Hotel imitated the Swiss theme of the Great Northern Railway's hotels and chalets springing up park-wide. Lewis promoted Going-to-the-Sun Road, spending his own money to cut part of the route along the lake, grade the road, and build bridges. From West Glacier, the road reached his hotel in 1922, increasing the number of hotel visitors with the growing popularity of the automobile.

Because of Lewis's foothold in McDonald Valley, the Great Northern Railway ignored the area around the park's largest lake, instead frenetically erecting chalets between 1912 and 1914 at Sun Point, Gunsight Lake, and Sperry. Sperry's trail over Gunsight Pass linked the three chalets. A year later and quite behind schedule, Granite Park Chalet was finally completed as a destination from Many Glacier Hotel and Sun Point. With packed bunk-bed dorms and canvas tents outside, Granite and Sperry could house 144 and 152 guests, respectively, nearly four times the number that each can sleep today. Their popularity increased in the 1920s as wealthy Easterners spent an average of 21 days in the park touring on horseback with Park Saddle Company. However, Gunsight Chalet lasted only five years, wiped out by an avalanche in 1916.

In 1930 the Great Northern Railway purchased Lewis's hotel, adding it to its lodge arsenal. When ownership changed, the name swapped to Lake McDonald Lodge. Two years later, the lodge was sold to the National Park Service.

Ironically, along with the Great Depression and increased auto travel, Going-to-the-Sun Road, which was completed in 1932, hastened the demise of the chalets. Visitors who took horse trips dropped from 26 percent to 3 percent. Natty automobile drivers sought more affordable places to stay. In 1940 the railroad company built East Glacier Auto Cabins (now Rising Sun Motor Inn), where two people could rent a cabin without a shower for $1.75. Finally, World War II park closures, deteriorating buildings, and increased costs of supplying the chalets taxed the railroad company to the point where it razed Going-to-the-Sun Chalets and sold Sperry and Granite Park to the National Park Service for $1.

Building the Road

Nearly 20 years of planning and construction went into building Going-to-the-Sun Road, fueled by burgeoning excitement over the automobile. While proponents proposed various passes for the "Transmountain Highway," its original name, in 1918 the National Park Service selected Logan Pass. The plan called for 15 switchbacks up the west side, later replaced with one long switchback. Over several years, Congress appropriated $2 million for its construction.

Surveying the route required the tenacity to hang by ropes over cliffs and tiptoe along skinny ledges, perhaps causing the 300 percent crew turnover in three months. Over six seasons, three companies excavated rock using only small blast explosives and minimal power tools to create tunnels, bridges, the Triple Arches, and guard walls. With power equipment unable to reach the East Side Tunnel, crews cleared its 408-foot length by hand-boring 5.33 feet per day.

In 1932, during late fall, the first automobile chugged over Logan Pass. The following July, over 4,000 people attended dedication ceremonies at the pass, celebrating the road's completion and ending with a peace ceremony for the Blackfeet, Kootenai, and Flathead people.

Although guardrails, surfacing, and

grading were not completed until 1935, nearly 40,000 visitors flocked to the road in its first year despite its rough tread and the Great Depression. Until the late 1930s, crushed rock covered its surface. Finally, in 1938, the National Park Service embarked on a 14-year project to pave the scenic highway, which was completed at last in 1952.

Exploring Going-to-the-Sun Road

Going-to-the-Sun Road connects West Glacier and St. Mary with 50 miles of one of the most scenic highways in the United States. Crossing Logan Pass at 6,646 feet on the Continental Divide, the road links the two immense glacier-carved valleys of McDonald and St. Mary. From Lake McDonald, the road ascends 3,400 feet to the pass; from St. Mary, it rises about 2,200 feet.

VISITORS CENTER

The one place everyone wants to go is Logan Pass, but its visitors center is small, and the parking lot crowds by 8:30am. We all put up with the crowds because no one wants more pavement and a larger building impinging on the meadows. Unprepared visitors arrive expecting a resort atmosphere at **Logan Pass Visitor Center** (406/888-7800, 9am-7pm daily mid-June-Aug., hours shorten Labor

Day-mid-Sept.), but it's a seasonal outpost with an information desk, a few displays, and a tiny Glacier National Park Conservancy **bookstore** (406/888-5756, http://glacier.org).

While a fireplace crackles upstairs on cold days, one bench allows only a few to snuggle up to its heat. Flush toilets are available downstairs and vault toilets at the parking lot. The center has a water bottle refill station, but no food or beverage sales. Due to the elevation, expect harsher weather including wind, rain, and snow even in August. Don't be surprised if you left the lowlands in sunny summer only to arrive at Logan Pass in winter.

ENTRANCE STATIONS

Both ends of Going-to-the-Sun Road have entrance stations: one at **West Glacier,** the other at **St. Mary.** Staffed during daylight hours in summer and on weekends only

Logan Pass Visitor Center is only open for a few months in summer.

fall-spring, the stations hand out national park maps and the *Waterton-Glacier Guide*, the park's newspaper, updated twice annually. If you miss working hours, you can use the self-pay cash-only kiosks, on the right just beyond the booths. If you don't have an annual pass, get a seven-day pass ($30/vehicle, $25 motorcyclists, $15 hikers and bikers in summer; winter rates drop to $20, $15, and $10).

SHUTTLES AND TOURS
Shuttles
To avoid circling for a spot in the Logan Pass parking lot, **Going-to-the-Sun Road shuttles** (406/888-7800, www.nps.gov/glac, July-Labor Day) are the way to go. These shuttles also enable point-to-point hiking on some of Glacier's most popular trails. Due to their popularity, waiting lines of an hour or more often form to board. But going car-free to trailheads outweighs any waits. As of 2016, the shuttle is still free with no tickets needed, and no reservations taken. But that may change in the future due to the cost of the program.

The Going-to-the-Sun Road shuttles stop at 17 locations. Get on or off at any of the stops denoted by interpretive signs, each one featuring a different animal print. East-side and west-side shuttles begin running up the road at 7am; the last shuttles depart Logan Pass at 7pm.

On the west side, shuttles depart every 15-30 minutes, with stops at the Apgar Visitor Center, Sprague Creek Campground, Lake McDonald Lodge, Avalanche Creek, The Loop, and Logan Pass. The 32-mile ride from the Apgar Visitor Center to Logan Pass takes 90 minutes or more. Confirm the destination when boarding as some shuttles are early morning express routes, and others only go to low-elevation west-side destinations. In 2016, a pilot program extended operation of the west-side shuttle on a limited schedule through mid-September; check to see if this will continue.

On the east side, shuttles depart every 30 minutes from St. Mary Visitor Center. The 18-mile ride to Logan Pass takes one hour, with stops at Rising Sun, Sun Point, Sunrift Gorge, and trailheads for St. Mary Falls, Gunsight Pass, Piegan Pass, and Siyeh Pass before reaching Logan Pass.

By reservation only, **Xanterra** (855/733-4522, www.glaciernationalparklodges.com, one-way adults $10, kids $5) operates two pay shuttles in summer. For point-to-point hikers on the Highline and Piegan Pass Trails, a shuttle runs between Many Glacier/Swiftcurrent Motor Inn (departs 7:30am, 9am, and 4:45pm) and St. Mary Visitor Center (departs 8:15am, 10am, 5:30pm) daily July-Labor Day to aid in connections with the free park shuttle. The second shuttle conveys Amtrak travelers arriving at Belton Depot in West Glacier to Lake McDonald Lodge (daily late May-late Sept.).

Glacier Charters (406/892-3390 or 800/829-7039, www.glaciertransportation. com, $70-85 one-way) runs shuttles by reservation between Glacier Park International Airport and Lake McDonald Lodge.

free shuttle on the Sun Road

Native American Tour

A Blackfeet-led tour provides a different perspective, with emphasis on Native American cultural and natural history. **Sun Tours** (406/226-9220 or 800/786-9220, www.glaciersuntours.com, June-Sept., adults $45-100, children 6-12 $30-45) drives air-conditioned 25-passenger coaches with extra-big windows for taking in the massive mountains on Going-to-the-Sun Road. Four-hour Logan Pass tours depart daily from St. Mary (9am) with a Rising Sun pickup shortly after. The tour goes up the east side of Going-to-the-Sun Road, explores Logan Pass, and drives down the west side to Big Bend to see the Weeping Wall before returning. Make reservations at least one day in advance. West-side tours depart Apgar Visitor Center at 9am. Meals, park entrance fees, and gratuities are not included.

★ Boat Tours

Lake McDonald and St. Mary, the park's largest lakes, dominate the lowlands along the Sun Road. **Glacier Park Boat Company** (406/257-2426, www.glacierparkboats.com) runs boat tours on both. Buy tickets at the boat docks several hours in advance in midsummer or make advance reservations by phone with a credit card. Check the *Ranger-led Activity Guide* available at visitors centers for launches that have ranger naturalists aboard.

At the boat dock behind Lake McDonald Lodge, hop on the historic *DeSmet* (adults $20, kids $10) for a one-hour tour. Tours depart at 11am, 1:30pm, 3pm, 5:30pm, and 7pm daily late May-late September, although early and late cruises end on Labor Day. With a 90-passenger capacity, the 1930s-vintage 57-foot wooden boat motors to the lake's core, where surrounding snow-clad peaks pop into sight. Go for a prime seat on the top deck; bring a jacket for marginal weather.

At the Rising Sun boat dock on St. Mary Lake, catch a ride on *Joy II* or *Little Chief* (adults $28, kids $14) as it braves the lake's choppy waters. Views of Sexton Glacier and Wild Goose Island can't be beat, but be ready for some healthy wind. Daily departures

The *DeSmet* tours Lake McDonald.

★ Red Bus Tour

In historic style, red jammer buses tour visitors over Going-to-the-Sun Road in vintage 1930s White Motor Company sedans operated by **Xanterra** (855/733-4522, www.glaciernationalparklodges.com, daily mid-June-mid-Sept., Fri.-Sun. only mid-Sept.-mid-Oct., adults $35-98, children half price). On good-weather days, the jammers (tour bus drivers known for their storytelling) roll the canvas tops back for spectacular views of the Continental Divide. Without a roof, it's one of the most scenic ways to feel the expanse of the glacier-carved terrain. From Lake McDonald Lodge, Rising Sun Motor Inn, Apgar Visitor Center, and St. Mary Visitor Center, tours depart daily to explore Going-to-the-Sun Road and Logan Pass: The Crown of the Continent tour takes a full day, but half-day Logan Pass tours depart multiple times daily. Evening tours are available in July-August. Fees do not include meals, taxes, park entrance fees, and gratuities. Reservations are required.

Red Buses

Historic jammer buses tour Going-to-the-Sun Road.

Red buses are Glacier icons. Built by Ohio's White Motor Company specifically for national park touring, the red buses became a symbol of the nation's western parks. Yosemite, Yellowstone, Zion, Mount Rainier, Grand Canyon, and Bryce had their own fleets, and so did Glacier. Nearly 500 red buses toured visitors around Glacier, Yosemite, and Yellowstone alone.

Although red bus fleets disappeared from the other parks in the 1950s, Glacier steadfastly held on to its 33 scarlet prizes, upgrading parts as necessary. The canvas tops rolled back to create an open-air touring car, so guests rode in historic style over Going-to-the-Sun Road, covering up with blankets if temperatures chilled down. Nicknamed "jammers" or "gear jammers" for the tremendous noise their gears made while shifting, the vintage 25-foot-long 17-passenger vehicles first drove Glacier's curvy roads in 1936 as the park's second generation of touring sedans. Decades later, as automatic transmissions replaced the manual transmissions and power steering eased driving Going-to-the-Sun Road's curves, jammers continued to tour folks through Glacier until 1999, when safety concerns sidelined the red rigs.

The fleet was donated to the National Park Foundation, which contracted with Ford Motor Company to rehabilitate the vehicles. One was kept intact for historical purposes. For the others, Ford kept the historical appearance, but converted them to run on gasoline or propane. New wiring, interiors, and paint jobs completed the project. Check out a jammer grill up close to see both White and Ford logos.

Owned now by Glacier National Park, the red buses are back in service, each logging about 10,000 miles per summer. Fewer than 10 of the buses still run on propane due to failure of injection systems. In winter, they are housed in a new climate-controlled facility in Columbia Falls. Xanterra has begun a second rehabilitation of the buses, to the tune of $250,000 per rig, which includes restoration of vintage dashboards. Wood frames and specialized components must be crafted by hand.

launch for 90-minute cruises at 10am, noon, 2pm, 4pm, and 6:30pm daily mid-June-early September. See Baring Falls at a stop, or take a guided two-hour hike to St. Mary Falls.

Driving Tour

Of all the driving tours in Glacier National Park, **Going-to-the-Sun Road,** the 50-mile historic transmountain highway bisecting Glacier's heart, stands in a class by itself. For some, scary tight curves that hug cliff walls produce white-knuckle driving. But for most, its beauty, diversity, color, flora, fauna, and raw wildness will leave an impression like no other. For that reason, many park visitors drive it more than once during their stay. For big waterfall shows and snow left from winter, drive it in late June or early July. For alpine wildflowers, go in late July or early August. For fewer crowds, go mid-September-mid-October.

In July-August, expect crowds around Avalanche, The Loop, Oberlin Bend, Logan Pass, Lunch Creek, Siyeh Bend, St. Mary Falls, and Sun Point. To avoid the hordes, drive in early morning or early evening, when lighting is better for photography and wildlife is more active. In midsummer, the Logan Pass parking lot fills by 8:30am. Signs at the entrance sometimes include the estimated wait time for a parking space, usually 30-60 minutes or more. If the parking lot is full, forgo Logan Pass for the time being and return later in the day. While pullouts are 0.5 mile east and west of the pass, the shoulderless road does not afford safe walking to the pass, and tromping across the fragile meadows is taboo.

Although you can drive its 50 miles in less than two hours with no stops, most visitors take all day. Construction, sightseeing, and traffic slow travel. Don't be anxious with it; just sit back and enjoy the view. Pack drinking water, snacks, and lunch to avoid frustration. Most restaurants around Glacier sell box or sack lunches. The road passes through a wonderland whose development has been kept in check; no one wants to see more buildings.

SEASON AND HOURS

Going-to-the-Sun Road is open 24 hours daily mid-June-mid-October . . . usually. Weather, construction, and snow can affect its status. Due to the decade-long, federally funded Sun Road reconstruction, the seasonal opening of the Sun Road in 2017 will be mid-June at the earliest. In subsequent years, weather and plowing will dictate the spring opening. The earliest opening of the Sun Road was May 16 while its latest opening was July 13 due to snowpack. In years with heavy snow and stormy springs, Logan Pass tends to open mid-June or later. During summer the road may close temporarily for snowstorms, washouts, or accidents. The park regularly updates road status reports (406/888-7800, www.nps.gov/glac).

In fall, the road usually closes in mid-October, baring construction requiring an earlier closure. Heavy snowfall can also close the road earlier.

In spring or fall, when parts of the Sun Road are closed to vehicles for construction, plowing, or snow, bicyclists and hikers can tour the road, especially on weekends when crews may not be working. Before biking the road, check by phone or online (406/888-7800, www.nps.gov/glac) for status, as schedules and conditions change daily.

Snow buries the Sun Road in winter. The usual vehicle closure runs from Lake McDonald Lodge to St. Mary late October-spring, but cross-country skiers and snowshoers trek the lowland corridors where avalanche danger is minimal.

VEHICLE RESTRICTIONS

Large vehicles are restricted on Going-to-the-Sun Road **between Avalanche Campground and Rising Sun.** Because the road is narrow and has overhangs, **vehicles must be less than 21 feet in length, 10 feet high, and 8 feet wide.** These dimensions include side mirrors, bumpers, towed units, and bike racks. Remember to retract side extension mirrors; you'll see broken ones in the gutter claimed by cliff walls.

Driving Tips: Going-to-the-Sun Road

FOUR SIGNS OF A ROOKIE GOING-TO-THE-SUN ROAD DRIVER

- **Burning Brake Smell:** Use second gear to slow your speed on descents rather than riding the brakes down the mountain.

- **Dangling Extension Mirror:** Retract or remove those extension mirrors for fifth-wheels or trailers before driving the narrow west side below Logan Pass.

- **Center-Line Hugger:** Stay in your own lane. You're more apt to scrape another vehicle on the skinny road than drive off the cliff. Acrophobes should let someone else drive.

- **Traffic Slug:** Rather than holding up traffic by slowing to a stop in the road to take pictures, use pullouts.

narrow Going-to-the-Sun Road

OTHER TIPS

- Follow posted speed limits, and turn on your headlights.

- During high season (mid-July–mid-Aug.), the Logan Pass parking lot fills up by 8:30am, with long waits for parking spaces. Get an early start for touring Going-to-the-Sun Road.

- Take lunch, snacks, and drinks. Between Lake McDonald Lodge and Rising Sun, no food or drinks are sold.

- Watch for bicyclists. Although bicycle restrictions are in effect during July-August on Going-to-the-Sun Road's west side, the narrow roadway, lack of shoulders, and curves squeeze cyclists. Show them courtesy by slowing down to ease around them.

- Expect construction delays. Repair work usually reduces traffic to a single lane controlled by road crew personnel. When workers are not present, timed traffic lights control flow. Obey both, as the single lanes allow for no pullover room for passing.

- Check for summer closures. Heavy rain, snowstorms, fires, and accidents may close portions of the road. Entrance and ranger stations as well as lodges have current updates of the road status available.

- Be prepared for all types of weather. Sunny skies may prevail in the valleys while visitors at Logan Pass creep along slowly in a dense fog on icy pavement.

- Passengers with a fear of heights should sit on the driver's side of the car for ascending the west side and descending the east. This will put you farthest from the cliff edges.

- Cell phones get little or no service on the Sun Road. Turn them off and enjoy the views.

- For updates on Going-to-the-Sun Road status, call 406/888-7800 or check www.nps.gov/glac.

Even though smaller truck-camper units may be allowed, drivers will feel pinched on the skinny road.

ROAD CONSTRUCTION

Maintenance is interminable on Going-to-the-Sun Road. Avalanches, torrential downpours, and snows constantly wreak havoc. Summer snowstorms and heavy rains cause washouts that require annual repairs. A warming climate has turned loose snow avalanches into wet slabs that tear of rock guard walls. Because heavy snows constrict repairs to 4-6 months, summer means construction, which may reduce driving to one skinny lane in places. Road construction is a fact of life, but it's amazing to see repair action in this cliff-ridden environment far different from a normal highway. You can watch state-of-the-art road technology at work: Cranes and bobcats jockey for position along one narrow lane, somewhat akin to working on a tightrope. Anyone with a mild interest in engineering will be blown away, and you get a feel for the immensity of building the original road.

Going-to-the-Sun Road's decade-long $270 million rehabilitation project is slated to wrap up in 2017. The critical state of the road required repairs for weather damage plus wear and tear from the nearly 500,000 vehicles that travel the road annually. The work has improved road safety, pavement, parking, guardrails, drainage, cracks, and deteriorating roadbeds, all while maintaining the historic character, fabric, and width of the road. Most significant, it was done without closing the road during the peak visitor season. Road repairs frequently require traffic delays. Expect delays in summer 2017 between West Glacier and Avalanche, as this final 14-mile segment is reconstructed.

PLOWING

Every April, snowplows take to Going-to-the-Sun Road to heave more than 100,000 cubic yards of snow off the pavement. It's a big deal. Avalanche piles range 30-50 feet thick from The Loop to Logan Pass. Just east of the pass, a 50- to 80-foot-deep snowdrift, called the Big Drift, clings to a 40-degree slope. Plowing takes several months. Up to 30 equipment operators, mechanics, and snow specialists dig in with more than 20 machines: excavators, bulldozers, sweepers, loaders, and rotary blowers.

More than 60 avalanche swaths between The Loop and Siyeh Bend smash snow onto the road. Sometimes crews replow the same pavement over and over, or plow themselves

Plowing the Sun Road requires several months of work by heavy equipment operators.

out at night. Heavy rains, fog, and whiteouts also hamper progress. Debris cleanup and installation of more than 400 removable guardrails add to the challenge.

When spring snows prohibit the road opening by mid-June, everyone gets nervous, from local businesses to the governor of Montana. The opening of the road is tied to the local economy. Glacier National Park's website tracks plow progress with daily reports (www.nps.gov/glac) and photos (www.flickr.com/photos/glaciernps). The park's communications center (406/888-7800) posts road status reports, too.

Sights

Going-to-the-Sun Road is a unique driving experience. The following sights are listed as visitors see them driving from Lake McDonald to St. Mary. The road has no mileage markers to help out, so GPS coordinates are listed parenthetically. For additional details, pick up the *Going-to-the-Sun Road Driving Guide* (406/892-3250, http://glacier.org, $10) from Glacier Conservancy bookstores.

LAKE MCDONALD

The largest lake in the park, Lake McDonald (48.529423°, -113.975854° to 48.611131°, -113.881939°) fills a valley hollowed out by a monstrous, several-thousand-foot-deep glacier. Lining the trough, Howe and Snyder Ridges are lateral moraines left from that ice-age bulldozer. At 10 miles long and 1.5 miles wide, the lake is big enough to plummet to a frigid depth of 472 feet. The road hugs its southeastern shore, with frequent pullouts for access. If rare glassy waters reflect Stanton Peak, snag a photo.

★ LAKE MCDONALD LODGE

At Lake McDonald's east end, the historic Lake McDonald Lodge (48.617299°, -113.878551°) was designed to resemble a hunting lodge. The tall, stately cedar-log lobby cluttered with stuffed goats and mounted heads of bighorn sheep, deer, elk, and moose is a taxidermist's delight or an animal-rights activist's nightmare. Look for the woodland caribou still represented among the furry creatures here, even though it no longer exists in the park. Because the lodge was built prior to the road, the front door actually opens lakeside, facing the original boat approach. The lodge is a National Historic Landmark.

MCDONALD CREEK

Originating near the Continental Divide, McDonald Creek (48.641473°, -113.856666°) is the longest river in the park at 25.8 miles and definitely more than a creek, but we won't quibble about nomenclature. The Sun Road follows the river for 7 miles along tumbling

Lake McDonald Lodge

rapids and waterfalls. When stopping for a look, be extremely cautious of hazardous slippery rocks. Unseen algae, mosses, and swift cold waters have been lethal for the unwary. At **Upper McDonald Creek Falls** (48.655885°, -113.840193°), waters roil through scoured rock; wooden stairs descend to a convenient observation platform right over the falls.

TRAIL OF THE CEDARS

Trail of the Cedars (48.680204°, -113.819108°) runs through a rainforest, the easternmost in the country. A 0.9-mile wheelchair-accessible boardwalk and pavement passes water-carved Avalanche Gorge. Grandfather 500-year-old western red cedars, hemlocks, and towering black cottonwoods form a dense canopy that cools the forest floor, where mosses, lichens, Pacific yew, and devil's club grow in the rich duff. Some topple over from heavy rain, snow, and wind.

AVALANCHE PATHS

As the road sneaks through a slim corridor between the Glacier Wall and Mount Cannon (48.706329°, -113.803757°), look for avalanche paths. Snow, set in motion thousands of feet above, roars down gullies, uprooting trees and snapping them like toothpicks. In early summer, scour the slope for remnants of avalanches: ice, snow, and rock rubble piled up. Grizzly and black bears forage for carcasses along these avalanche paths in hopes of stumbling across some unfortunate mountain goat. Bring binoculars or spotting scopes to aid in bear-watching from a safe distance.

WEST SIDE TUNNEL

An engineering marvel, the West Side Tunnel (48.751062°, -113.788763°) is 192 feet long, with two stunning alcoves framing Heavens Peak. Early in the season, the alcoves drip with thin-sheeted waterfalls; hop through the spray to reach the dry, rock-hewn guardrails. Photographers especially enjoy working the alcoves into framing pictures of Heavens Peak. To walk to the alcoves, park in pullouts below the tunnel. Convertible drivers beware: early summer, a waterfall on the tunnel's uphill side splatters cars.

THE LOOP

Going-to-the-Sun Road has one massive hairpin turn known as The Loop (48.754694°, -113.800147°). With parking lots both below and above the switchback, it's a popular stop for views and a trailhead to Granite Park Chalet. Across the valley, the 8,987-foot

The West Side Tunnel cuts through a cliff.

Heavens Peak makes a stunning backdrop for a family photo. Early in the season, it will be snow-covered; by late August, only a few snowfields remain. In 2003 the **Trapper Fire** blew through The Loop; evidence of the burn lingers in skeletal trees.

BIRD WOMAN AND HAYSTACK FALLS

About two miles past The Loop, look for the sign marking **Bird Woman Falls** (48.739259°, -113.749213°). Many assume the sign denotes the cascade crossing under the road. That stair-step waterfall is **Haystack Creek,** whose ledges evolved from eroding layers of Belt Sea sedimentary rock created 800 million to 1.6 billion years ago. To see Bird Woman Falls, look across the valley for waters tumbling nearly 500 feet from a hanging valley, carved by a glacier in the last 6,000 years and lounging like a hammock in between Mount Oberlin, Mount Cannon, and Clements Peak. Early summer runoff pumps both falls full of water that dwindles to late August trickles.

GLACIATION

On one of the pullouts between Haystack Falls and the Weeping Wall, peek down McDonald Valley. Once filled with several-thousand-foot-thick ice, the valley's U shape shows the gouging, scouring, and carving of the behemoth glacier as it chugged around the Glacier Wall approximately two million years ago. Through the trough, McDonald Creek courses 26 miles and ends at Lake McDonald. Test your vertigo by gazing 2,500 feet below; you'll see Going-to-the-Sun Road, with cars looking tiny like ants as they drive the narrow corridor.

WEEPING WALL AND BIG BEND

As its name implies, the Weeping Wall (48.727042°, -113.727292°) does weep, but it's a moody thing. In early summer the wall wails profusely, enough to douse cars driving the inside lane. Roll up windows unless you want a shower. In August, drips slow to a trickle. At the Weeping Wall, the road affords no room to pull over; instead, drive ahead into the bowl named Big Bend (48.726904°, -113.724307°) to find parking on both sides of the road. Avalanches careen from Mount Gould into Big Bend, often leaving snow until mid-July.

TRIPLE ARCHES

One of the most striking engineering marvels on Going-to-the-Sun Road, Triple

Haystack Falls runs under a bridge of native stone.

The Continental Divide

At Logan Pass, you can take your photo next to a sign that says you're atop the Continental Divide. But what is it?

The Continental Divide runs the length of North America from Alaska and the Yukon to Mexico. Along the Rocky Mountains, it is the highest point in the land, dividing stream runoff in two directions: westward to the Pacific and eastward to Hudson Bay and the Gulf of Mexico. In Glacier National Park, the Continental Divide runs along the top of the Livingston Range from Canada south to Trapper Ridge and West Flattop, where it leaps to the Lewis Range.

To cross the Continental Divide, drive over Logan Pass or Marias Pass. You can hike across the divide on several passes: Brown, Swiftcurrent, Hidden Lake, Gunsight, Cut Bank, Dawson, Two Medicine, and Firebrand. Beginning in New Mexico, the 3,100-mile Continental Divide Trail ends here, with its last 110 miles in Glacier National Park.

Glacier's Continental Divide also stands in a class by itself, for it houses a tri-oceanic divide. It's the only one in the United States. (Western Canada's Mount Columbia is the continent's other significant three-way oceanic divide.) Not particularly high by Glacier's standards, Triple Divide Peak stands at only 7,397 feet above sea level. But its placement on the Continental Divide with connecting ridge spurs splits waters in three directions: Hudson Bay Creek, Atlantic Creek, and Pacific Creek. Their names cite their eventual destinations via the Saskatchewan, Missouri, and Columbia Rivers.

SIGHTS

GOING-TO-THE-SUN ROAD

Arches (48.716994°, -113.718789°) requires a slow drive to see, for no pullouts offer a view. You can see this feature only driving uphill, as it is behind downhill traffic. Approximately 1.5 miles past Big Bend, you'll come upon the arches abruptly. Start watching for them as you enter some very narrow S-turns. As you drive over the arches, don't think about the stonework repairs that suspend them.

GARDEN WALL

In the three miles from Big Bend to Logan Pass, the peaks above the road form an arête, a wall carved by glaciers on two sides. Below its top cliffs, wildflower meadows bloom with every color of the rainbow: white cow parsnip, pink spirea, yellow columbine, purple nodding onion, and blue gentian. In a short 0.5 mile, you may pass more than 30 varieties of plants. For this reason, this wild botanical wonderland has been dubbed the Garden Wall. For the best look at the Garden Wall, hike the Highline Trail from Logan Pass.

OBERLIN BEND OVERLOOK

As Going-to-the-Sun Road climbs its final mile to Logan Pass, it sweeps around a large curve below Mount Oberlin. Park on the uphill lane side for the wheelchair-accessible path to Oberlin Bend Overlook (48.699452°, -113.725173°). Mountain goats wander in the subalpine fir thickets; look for newborns with only nubbins for horns. The overlook provides the best spot for photographing the road's west-side climb plus the Continental Divide and peaks marching toward Canada. Look far north for **Mount Cleveland,** the park's highest peak.

★ LOGAN PASS

Logan Pass (48.696380°, -113.717674°) sits atop the **Continental Divide** at 6,646 feet. With its altitude and location between mountainous hulks, weather can be chilly even in midsummer. For evidence, look at the gnarled trees, growing low in krummholz or thick mats for protection against the elements. Explore the visitors center and scan surrounding slopes for goats, bighorn sheep, and bears. In June skiers and snowboarders hike the flanks of Mount Clements for turns. In late July, the pink alpine laurel, paintbrush, and monkeyflower reach their prime. Logan Pass is designated an Important Plant Area, with more than 30 rare plants and mosses. Meadows at this elevation are fragile, with short-lived flora, so stick to the paths. On the paved trails around the visitors center, special interpretive signs with hand-cranked speakers appeal to kids. Two must-do trails depart from Logan Pass: Hidden Lake and the Highline Trail to Granite Park Chalet. In 2016, the park service launched its "Bark Ranger" program, where a trained border collie herds bighorn sheep and mountain goats away from high traffic areas and confrontations with humans.

BIG DRIFT

Those driving over Logan Pass when it first opens get a treat: Big Drift (48.696927°, -113.711990°) towers on both sides of the road, making a thin corridor bounded by immense snow walls. Winds deposit heavy snows in this zone just east of Logan Pass. At a record 98 feet thick, Big Drift remains the last obstacle for spring road clearing. By August, snow piles disappear.

LUNCH CREEK

Spilling from a cirque between Piegan and Pollock Mountains, Lunch Creek (48.699799°, -113.703624°) makes for a scenic stop at the first bend east of Logan Pass. Sans picnic tables, the pullout's rock guard wall serves as a good impromptu lunch counter. Drag out your binoculars; often bighorn sheep cruise the slopes above, but they're hard to see with their camouflage tan matching the rocks. Fed by a glacier melting into an underground stream, waterfalls spew from the side of Piegan Mountain.

EAST SIDE TUNNEL

Crews excavated entirely by hand the 408 feet of the East Side Tunnel (48.697173°, -113.696044°), the larger of the road's two tunnels. For safety, flip on your headlights. To stop for photos, drive to the downhill side to find pullouts, which are also good stops for spotting bighorn sheep and shooting **Going-to-the-Sun Mountain,** from which the road acquired its name.

SIYEH BEND

Three miles below Logan Pass, the road swoops through Siyeh Bend (48.701407°, -113.667600°), with parking above and below

Logan Pass sits on the Continental Divide.

Sun Point yields a 360-degree view.

In summer 2015, the Reynolds Creek Fire burned from Jackson Overlook (48.678311°, -113.653968°) to Rising Sun (48.694461°, -113.516501°) along Going-to-the-Sun Road, opening up views of mountains and St. Mary Lake. The road cuts through patches of heavy burn and lighter flares from the 4,850-acre fire. Regeneration started the following summer: shooting stars, paintbrush, and false hellebore appeared across the burn, while woodpeckers, wind, and snow started peeling blackened bark from trees.

SUNRIFT GORGE

A narrow canyon, Sunrift Gorge (48.678545°, -113.595420°) requires a 75-foot uphill stroll to see it. Baring Creek cascades through the dark gorge like a knife slicing cake. The 2015 Reynolds Creek Fire jumped the gorge, leaving the dank rock walls as a grotto for ferns and mosses. Parking on both sides of the road is cramped, and it is a trailhead for Siyeh Pass, although most hikers opt to start at Siyeh Bend instead.

★ SUN POINT

The often windy Sun Point (48.676049°, -113.579532°) on St. Mary Lake marks the site of the park's most popular early chalet colony: Going-to-the-Sun Chalets. Accessed via boat from St. Mary, the chalets launched visitors into Glacier's interior. For the best views of the site, walk five minutes on the trail from the parking lot to the top of the rock promontory jutting into St. Mary Lake. Spectacular views from there take in Going-to-the-Sun Mountain, Fusillade Mountain, and the Continental Divide. A trail leads 0.6 mile to Baring Falls and farther to St. Mary Falls and Virginia Falls. Improvements in 2016 upgraded the restrooms, picnic loop, trail to the point, and interpretive signage.

WILD GOOSE ISLAND OVERLOOK

One of the most photographed spots in Glacier National Park, tiny Wild Goose Island

the curve. A trailhead leads to Piegan and Siyeh Passes via Preston Park, a meadowland of fuchsia paintbrush and purple fleabane. For a short stroll, walk up the creek crossing under the road to the junction of two creeks. The short walk passes gorgeous wildflower blooms in late July. From Siyeh Bend (*Siyeh* means "mad wolf"), named for the 10,014-foot barren peak towering above, you can see Blackfoot Glacier toward the south.

JACKSON GLACIER OVERLOOK

This is the best view of a glacier from Going-to-the-Sun Road, but binoculars are handy to aid vision. Although trees creep higher around Jackson Glacier Overlook (48.678311°, -113.653968°), you can still spot Jackson Glacier six miles away. Jackson Glacier joined its neighboring Blackfoot Glacier in the early 1900s, but the two glaciers melted into separate ice fields by 1939. A trail departs here for Gunsight Lake and Pass. More views are available in the next several pullouts east.

(48.691747°, -113.531285°) is dwarfed in St. Mary Lake's blue waters. Locate parking on both sides of the road from the signed viewpoint. From the overlook, the Continental Divide serves as the backdrop for the tiny island, with Fusillade Mountain as the prominent central pyramid. For the best lighting, visit this spot in early morning or at sunset. Take a photo, and then check the nearest gift shop for the same photo; you'll find it on postcards, on calendars, and in books.

RISING SUN

Rising Sun on St. Mary Lake is not really a scenic stop so much as one for necessities and services. A picnic area, campground, boat dock and ramp, camp store, restaurant, and cabins make up the area's amenities. It's also a jumping-off spot for hiking to Otokomi Lake and touring St. Mary Lake on the *Little Chief*. To walk along the beach, head to the picnic area (48.694461°, -113.516501°), but hold on to your hat, as winds often rage.

ST. MARY LAKE

The second-largest lake in the park, St. Mary Lake (48.688712°, -113.557326°) fills a much narrower valley than its larger counterpart,

Lake McDonald. At 9 miles long and 292 feet deep, it forms a blue platform out of which several stunning red argillite peaks rise. Its width shrinks in The Narrows to less than 0.5 mile, where buff-colored Altyn limestone resisted erosion. This strata contains the most ancient exposed rock in the park. While its waters attract boaters, anglers, water-skiers, and sailboarders launching from Rising Sun, frequent high winds can whip up wicked whitecaps in minutes.

TWO DOG FLATS

A series of grassland meadows interspersed by aspen groves lines the road from Rising Sun to St. Mary. Known as Two Dog Flats (48.729423°, -113.465250°), the meadows can be good areas for watching elk, coyotes, bears, and birds in early morning or late evening. From here you can see two hydrological wonders to the south: Triple Divide Peak and Divide Mountain. Triple Divide Peak sits atop the Continental Divide, and its waters head toward the Pacific Ocean, Hudson Bay, and the Gulf of Mexico. Divide Mountain, along with the sweeping moraine heading east, marks the division between the huge Saskatchewan and Missouri watersheds.

Recreation

DAY HIKES

Hikes off Going-to-the-Sun Road are top-notch. Around Lake McDonald, trails all begin in the forest, but several climb to incredible heights. At Logan Pass and eastward, most trails provide quicker access to alpine meadows and spectacular glacially carved scenery. Shorter trails are crowded in midsummer; you may feel like you're walking in a parade to St. Mary Falls or Hidden Lake Overlook. If you want to get away from the masses, head for longer hikes that will take you farther into the backcountry: Granite Park Chalet, Siyeh Pass, Piegan Pass, or Gunsight Lake. The hikes described here are

in order of their trailheads from west to east. They are all serviced by shuttle stops.

The season for Going-to-the-Sun Road hiking is limited by snow and the road's opening and closing. Even though the Sun Road may open to reach trailheads, snow buries high-elevation trails such as Mount Brown, Sperry Chalet, Sperry Glacier, Granite Park Chalet, Highline, Hidden Lake Overlook, Piegan Pass, and Siyeh Pass sometimes until mid-July. Do not attempt to cross steep snowfields without ice axes and crampons; falling can be deadly. Snow often returns to these high-elevation trails by September's end. Lower-elevation trails such as Snyder Lake,

Going-to-the-Sun Road Hikes

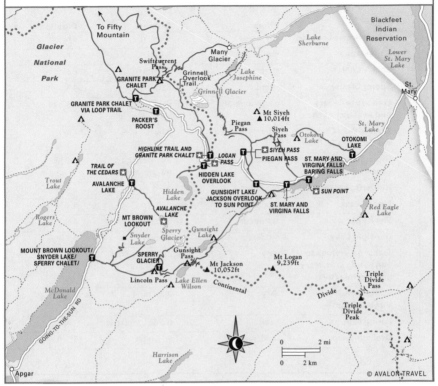

Trail of the Cedars and Avalanche Lake, St. Mary and Virginia Falls, and Gunsight Lake retain snow until early May, but can be hiked snow-free through October. Even after the Sun Road closes for winter, vehicles can still reach the Sperry trailhead at Lake McDonald Lodge; take snowshoes or skis and for upper-elevation destinations, avalanche gear (beacon, shovel, and probe).

Mount Brown Lookout

Distance: 9.9 miles round-trip
Duration: 6 hours
Elevation gain: 4,258 feet
Effort: strenuous
Trailhead: Sperry trailhead, across from Lake McDonald Lodge parking lot (see map p. 109)

One word describes this hike: *steep.* It'll feel much longer than it is. The signs may read longer until they catch up with the new GIS measurements. The trail starts out climbing through moderate switchbacks, but at 1.6 miles, turning off the Sperry Trail, the next five switchbacks are lung-busters. After these, the remaining 20 switchbacks level out into a more reasonable ascent.

Trees preclude views for most of this trail, except for snippets of Mount Edwards. Toward the top, alpine meadows bloom with bear grass and huckleberry patches as the trail works its way along the ridge to the renovated lookout. From this false summit (Mount Brown is higher to the east), you'll get dizzy peering down to Lake McDonald and the lodge. While you zoom binoculars in on Granite Park Chalet, Swiftcurrent Lookout,

Going-to-the-Sun Road Hikes

Trail	Effort	Distance	Duration
Mount Brown Lookout	strenuous	9.9 mi rt	6 hr
Snyder Lake	moderate	8.4 mi rt	4 hr
Sperry Chalet	strenuous	12.4 mi rt	6.5 hr
Sperry Glacier	strenuous	6.9 mi rt	4 hr
Trail of the Cedars and Avalanche Lake	easy-moderate	0.9-mi loop-6.1 mi rt	0.5-3 hr
Granite Park Chalet via The Loop Trail	moderate-strenuous	8 mi rt	4 hr
Highline Trail and Granite Park Chalet	moderate	7.4 mi or 11.4 mi one-way	5-6 hr
Hidden Lake Overlook	moderate	2.6-5 mi rt	2-4 hr
Piegan Pass	moderate	8.8 mi rt	4-6 hr
Siyeh Pass	strenuous	10 mi	6 hr
Gunsight Lake	moderate	13 mi rt	6.5 hr
Jackson Overlook to Sun Point via St. Mary and Virginia Falls	easy	6.7 mi one-way	3 hr
St. Mary and Virginia Falls	easy	2-3.4 mi rt	1-2 hr
Baring Falls	easy	0.6 or 1.2 mi rt	1 hr
Otokomi Lake	moderate	10.5 mi rt	5.5 hr

and the Continental Divide, protect your lunch from the overly curious mountain goats.

Snyder Lake
Distance: 8.4 miles round-trip
Duration: 4 hours
Elevation gain: 1,996 feet
Effort: moderate
Trailhead: Sperry trailhead, across from Lake McDonald Lodge parking lot (see map p. 109)
Follow the Sperry Trail up its early steep pitches until 0.1 mile beyond the Mount Brown turnoff. Turn east onto the Snyder Lake Trail, which parallels the timbered north hillside above Snyder Creek. After crossing the base of a talus slope and a brushy avalanche zone, the trail reaches the lake, a favorite for anglers.

Sperry Chalet
Distance: 12.4 miles round-trip
Duration: 6.5 hours
Elevation gain: 3,312 feet
Effort: strenuous
Trailhead: Sperry trailhead, across from Lake McDonald Lodge parking lot (see map p. 109)
The historic chalet is an attraction in itself, serving lunch and homemade desserts to hikers, but many overnight at the chalet, especially to access Sperry Glacier. The climb begins with moderate switchbacks through a hemlock forest. After crossing Snyder Creek at two miles, the trail takes a long traverse around Mount Edwards, easing up in elevation before switchbacking again up alder-strewn avalanche slopes. Because of the mule and horse trips using this same route, the trail

Mount Brown and Sperry Chalet Trails

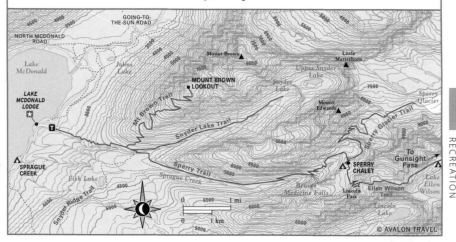

sometimes smells like a barnyard and can be miserable as you dodge equine droppings buzzing with blackflies.

With more than one mile still to climb, you'll spot the chalet clinging to a cliff top overhead. The trail crosses Sperry Creek before ascending its final switchbacks, passing the turnoff to Sperry Glacier en route. If mountain goats don't stand in your way, you'll arrive at the dining hall's door, ready for lunch and home-baked pie served inside 11:30am-5pm daily early July-early September. To spend the night, you'll need a reservation. Snowshoes or skis and avalanche gear are required in winter (chalet is closed early Sept.-early July).

Sperry Glacier

Distance: 6.9 miles round-trip
Duration: 4 hours
Elevation gain: 1,598 feet
Effort: strenuous
Trailhead: Sperry Chalet (see map p. 109)

From the chalet, drop down a few switchbacks to the Sperry Glacier trail sign. From here, the trail wraps upward around a glacial cirque below waterfalls and immense cliffs. It switchbacks up past alpine tarns, flower gardens, snowfields lingering into August, and glacially carved rock ledges before it seemingly disappears into a cliff. But voilá: A steep stairway leads through the cliff into the basin above. The trail around the lakes and through the stairway is usually snow-free late June-early October.

In the Sperry Glacier basin, a different world awaits. Snowfields, moraines, and ice mark this environment, with very sparse trees and flowers. From here, follow vertical markers across the snow-covered trail or glacial rubble to the overlook. Do not walk out on the glacier, which has hidden crevasses and waterways. Seasoned hikers can do a 19-mile round-trip Sperry Glacier hike in one day from Lake McDonald Lodge: It's a 10-hour-plus day with a 5,000-foot climb followed by a knee-pounding descent.

★ Trail of the Cedars and Avalanche Lake

Distance: 0.9-mile loop-6.1 miles round-trip
Duration: 0.5-3 hours
Elevation gain: none-477 feet
Effort: easy-moderate
Trailhead: adjacent to Avalanche Campground and Picnic Area (see map p. 110)

A boardwalk with interpretive signs guides

Trail of the Cedars and Avalanche Lake

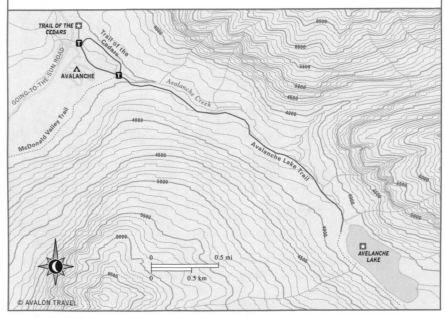

hikers through the lush rainforest on Trail of the Cedars, where fallen trees become nurse logs, fertile habitat for hemlocks and tiny foamflowers. Immense black cottonwoods furrowed with deep-cut bark and huge 500-year-old western red cedars dominate the forest. The boardwalk crosses Avalanche Creek, spitting from its narrow gorge. To finish the 0.9-mile loop, continue on the paved walkway past large burled cedars to return to the trailhead.

The trailhead to Avalanche Lake departs from the southeast end of Trail of the Cedars. Turn uphill for the short grunt to the top of the water-carved Avalanche Gorge. Be extremely careful: Too many fatal accidents have occurred from slipping. From the gorge, the trail climbs steadily through woods littered with glacial erratics. Some of these large boulders strewn when the ice receded still retain scratch marks left from the ice. At the top, 1.9 miles from the trailhead, a cirque with steep cliffs and tumbling waterfalls cradles the lake. An additional 0.7-mile path goes to the lake's less-crowded head.

500-year-old trees shade Trail of the Cedars.

High season sees streams of people, some incredibly ill prepared, with no drinking water and inappropriate footwear like flip-flops or heels. Avoid midday crowds by hiking this trail earlier or later in the day, but not at dawn or dusk. Anglers will find better fishing at the head of the lake.

Granite Park Chalet via The Loop Trail

Distance: 8 miles round-trip
Duration: 4 hours
Elevation gain: 2,402 feet
Effort: moderate-strenuous
Trailhead: The Loop (see map p. 112)

The Loop Trail is mostly used by hikers exiting the Highline Trail, but when the Highline Trail has too much snow, this trail makes a worthy hike with Granite Park Chalet as a scenic destination. Since the 2003 Trapper Fire, views have improved, but the lack of shade means there is little relief from the sun's blazing heat.

The trail crosses a tumbling creek before joining up with the Packer's Roost trail at 0.6 mile. Note this junction: You do not want to miss it when hiking back down. From here, the trail climbs two long switchbacks before it crests into the upper basin to the chalet. In June or by late September, snow can cover the last mile or so. The chalet (July-early Sept.) has no running water but does sell candy bars. Bring cash to purchase bottled water, carry your own, or filter water from the campground stream just below the chalet.

★ Highline Trail and Granite Park Chalet

Distance: 7.4 miles to Granite Park Chalet, 11.4 miles to The Loop
Duration: 5-6 hours
Elevation gain: 862 feet
Effort: moderate
Trailhead: across Going-to-the-Sun Road from Logan Pass parking lot (see map p. 112)

Many first-time hikers stop every 10 feet to take photos on this hike, which scares severe acrophobes with its exposed thousand-foot drop-offs. The trail drops from Logan Pass through a cliff walk above the Sun Road before crossing a flower land that gave the Garden Wall arête its name. At three miles, nearly all the elevation gain is packed into one climb: Haystack Saddle appears to be the top, but it is only halfway. After the high point, the trail drops and swings through several large bowls before passing Bear Valley to reach Granite Park Chalet atop a knoll at 6,680 feet.

En route, stronger hikers can add on side trails to Grinnell Glacier Overlook (1.6 steep miles round-trip) and Swiftcurrent Lookout (4.2 miles round-trip). To exit the area, some hikers opt to hike out over Swiftcurrent Pass to Many Glacier (7.6 miles) and catch shuttles; backpackers continue on to Fifty Mountain (11.9 miles farther) and Goat Haunt (22.5 miles farther). Most day hikers head down The Loop Trail (4 miles) to catch the shuttle. Due to steep, snow-filled avalanche paths, the park service keeps the trailhead at Logan Pass closed usually into early July.

The chalet (July-early Sept.) does not have running water. Plan on purchasing bottled water here, carrying your own, or filtering water from the campground stream below the chalet. Day hikers may also use the outdoor picnic tables or chalet dining room but do not have access to the kitchen. On a rainy day, a warm fire offers respite from the bluster and a chance to dry out. Sodas and candy bars are also sold.

Hidden Lake Overlook

Distance: 2.6 miles round-trip to overlook, 5 miles round-trip to lake
Duration: 2-4 hours
Elevation gain: 482 feet
Effort: moderate
Trailhead: behind Logan Pass Visitor Center (see map p. 112)

Regardless of crowds, Hidden Lake Overlook is a spectacular hike. Avoid long lines of hikers by going shortly after sunrise or in the evening. The trail is often buried under feet of snow until mid-July or later, but tall poles mark the route. Once the trail melts out, a

Granite Park Chalet Trails

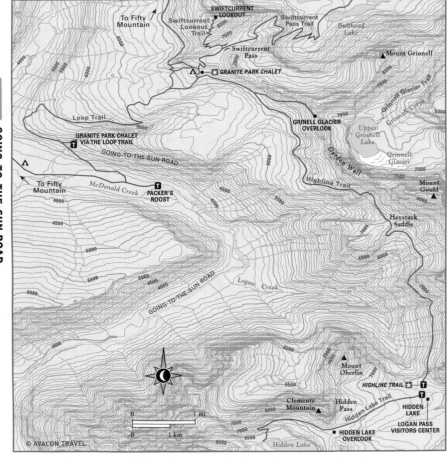

boardwalk climbs the first half through alpine meadows where fragile shooting stars and alpine laurel dot the landscape with pink. The trail ascends through argillite: Look for evidence of mud-cracked and ripple-marked rocks from the ancient Belt Sea. Above, Clements Peak reveals various sea sediments in colorful layers.

The upper trail climbs past moraines, waterfalls, mountain goats, and bighorn sheep. At Hidden Pass on the Continental Divide,

the trail reaches the platform overlooking the lake's blue waters. For ambitious hikers or anglers, the trail continues 1.2 miles down to the lake. Just remember: What drops 776 feet must come back up. After late September, bring ice cleats for walking the trail.

Piegan Pass

Distance: 8.8 miles round-trip, 11.5 miles to Many Glacier

Duration: 4-6 hours

Elevation gain: 1,739 feet

Effort: moderate

Trailhead: Siyeh Bend (see map p. 113)

Piegan Pass, named for the Pikuni or Piegan people of the Blackfeet Nation, sneaks a close look at the Continental Divide. After climbing two miles through subalpine forest and turning north at the first trail junction, the trail breaks out into Preston Park, bursting with purple fleabane, blue gentians, white valerian, and fuchsia paintbrush. During the climb, spy four glaciers: Piegan, Jackson, Blackfoot, and Sperry, the latter seen through trees. A signed trail junction splits the Piegan Pass Trail from the Siyeh Pass Trail.

Shortly after the junction, the Piegan Pass Trail heads into the seemingly barren alpine zone as it crosses the base of Siyeh Peak. But miniature flowers bloom and serve as food for pikas. The trail sweeps around a large bowl where two steep snowfields often linger into

July to Piegan [...]
Siyeh Bend, so [...]
to Many Glac[...]
to return.

★ **Siyeh**

Distance: 1

Duration:

Elevation

Effort: st

Trailhea

Siyeh Pass Trail cro[...] ecosystems that the entire trail nea[...] the park's diversity in one 10-mile segment. The trail begins with a 2-mile climb through subalpine forest broken by meadows, where it passes two well-signed junctions; go left at the first, right at the second. As the trail leads through Preston Park, one of the best flower meadows, with purple fleabane and fuchsia paintbrush, Piegan Glacier comes into view.

Piegan and Siyeh Passes

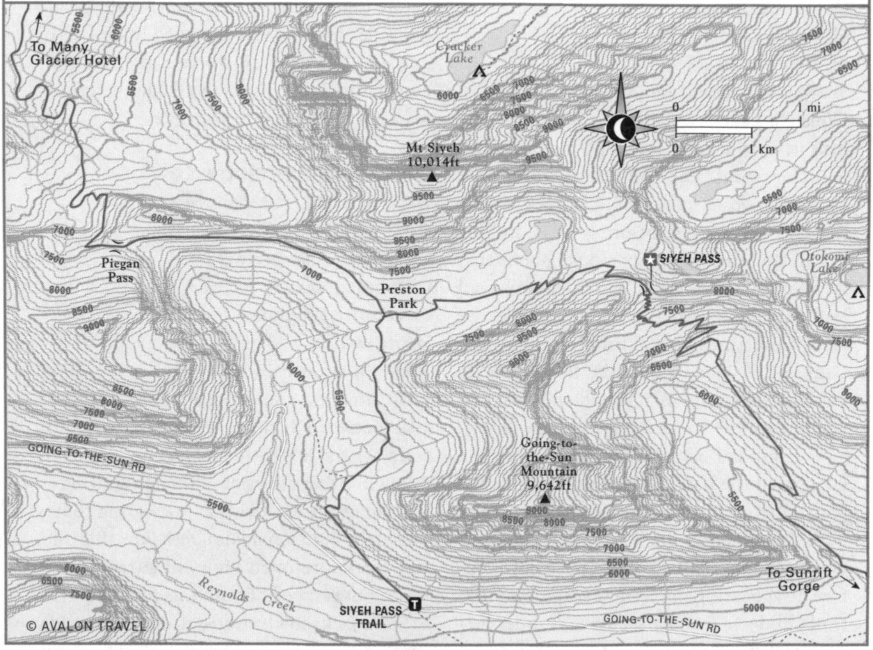

© AVALON TRAVEL

cend above the tree line, ~ides a further look at the ~n which it sits.

~backs appear to lead to a sad~ ~s Siyeh Pass. But eight more turns ~ove the pass before swinging through ~ to the divide between Boulder and ~ing Creeks. Be wary of your lunch; there ~re aggressive golden-mantled ground squirrels here. Due to the elevation, snow can bury the steep switchbacks south of the divide until mid-July. Sexton Glacier hunkers protected from the afternoon sun by Going-to-the-Sun Mountain (accessible via a 1-mile spur trail). The trail descends in 3,446 feet of elevation past goats, bighorn sheep, and a multicolored cliff band before traversing the flanks of Goat Mountain and dropping a couple hot miles through the 2015 Reynolds Creek Fire to end at the Sunrift Gorge on Going-to-the-Sun Road.

Siyeh Pass offers views of glaciers.

Gunsight Lake

Distance: 13 miles round-trip
Duration: 6.5 hours
Elevation gain: 710 feet
Effort: moderate
Trailhead: Jackson Glacier Overlook

Gunsight Lake is a tantalizer. For those who hike in for the day, more high country lures them beyond it. The trail begins with a one-mile drop down to Reynolds Creek, where the 2015 fire started, before gently climbing through a forest of boggy moose ponds that breed mosquitoes. After passing a spur trail leading to Florence Falls, the trail breaks out into flower meadows, climbing along the flanks of Fusillade Mountain. Incomparable views of the wild Blackfoot and Jackson Glaciers sprawl across the scoured basin.

Surrounded by avalanche corridors, the lake sits at the base of Jackson Peak (10,064 feet), one of the six highest peaks in the park. From here, a one-mile spur trail wanders back into the Jackson Glacier basin before disappearing in meadow seeps. Another trail climbs to Gunsight Pass (2.8 miles farther) and on to Sperry Chalet (7 miles farther)

before descending to Lake McDonald Lodge (20 miles total), a feat seasoned hikers do in one day. Be ready on the return hike from Gunsight Lake to Jackson Glacier Overlook to climb 543 feet in the last mile.

Jackson Overlook to Sun Point via St. Mary and Virginia Falls

Distance: 6.7 miles one-way
Duration: 3 hours
Elevation gain: 216 feet
Effort: easy
Trailhead: Jackson Glacier Overlook

With shuttles, you can do a point-to-point hike between Jackson Overlook and Sun Point, with side trips to St. Mary and Virginia Falls. Go either direction, although starting at Jackson Overlook yields a descending route. Due to the 2015 Reynolds Creek Fire, this trail now has more open views of surrounding peaks, but can be hot minus its forest cover.

From Jackson Overlook, drop to Reynolds Creek, where the trail forks eastward along

St. Mary Lake Trails

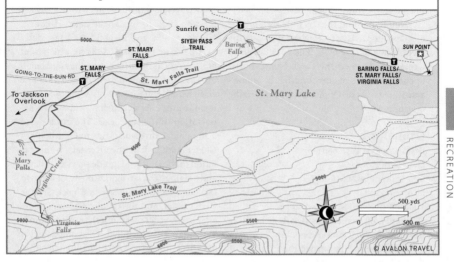

the river. At the falls junction, turn right to explore mesmerizing blue-green St. Mary Falls and climb several switchbacks to misty Virginia Falls, less than one mile farther. Return to the junction to continue east over bluffs blooming with stonecrop overlooking St. Mary Lake. (Ignore signs for Going-to-the-Sun Road parking lot spurs.) Tally up your third waterfall, Baring Falls, just before the trail climbs to Sun Point.

St. Mary and Virginia Falls

Distance: 2-3.4 miles round-trip
Duration: 1-2 hours
Elevation gain: 216 feet
Effort: easy
Trailhead: St. Mary Falls trailhead (see map p. 115)

In midsummer, the trail sees a constant stream of people, but the two falls are still gorgeous. Two trailheads depart from Going-to-the-Sun Road. The west trailhead descends from the shuttle stop. The east trailhead launches from the vehicle parking lot. Both trails connect with the St. Mary Lake Trail leading to the falls. Between the trailheads and St. Mary Falls, the 2015 Reynolds Creek Fire burned the thick forest, but it opened up views of surrounding mountains and the St. Mary River. On hot days, hike it in the morning.

The trail drops one mile through several well-signed junctions en route to St. Mary Falls, where a wooden bridge crosses blue-green pools. From here, the trail switchbacks up 0.7 mile to Virginia Falls, a broad waterfall spewing mist. A short spur climbs to the base of Virginia Falls. Be wary of slippery rocks and strong, cold currents at both falls. Look for water ouzels (American dippers) that nest near waterfalls. Recognize the dark gray birds by their dipping action, up to 40 bends per minute.

Baring Falls

Distance: 0.6 or 1.2 miles round-trip
Duration: 1 hour
Elevation gain: minimal, but 120 feet back up to Sunrift Gorge trailhead
Effort: easy
Trailhead: Sunrift Gorge or Sun Point parking lot (see map p. 115)

From Sunrift Gorge, start by dropping south of the road bridge over Baring Creek. The 0.3-mile trail follows the creek down to the trail from Sun Point. Turn right to reach Baring Falls (originally named Weasel Eyes by the Blackfeet, meaning "huckleberries").

From Sun Point, the 0.6-mile trail gradually descends to lake level where it crosses the creek below Baring Falls. The 2015 Reynolds Creek Fire burned the thick forest, but it opened up views of surrounding mountains and St. Mary Lake. On hot days, hike it in the morning.

Otokomi Lake

Distance: 10.5 miles round-trip
Duration: 5.5 hours
Elevation gain: 2,008 feet
Effort: moderate
Trailhead: behind Rising Sun Motor Inn

Otokomi Lake makes a good early or late season hike, due to its lower elevation. The 2015 Reynolds Creek Fire burned the first half of the trail on the flanks of Otokomi Mountain, reducing shade and increasing the heat factor on hot days, but opening up views. Climbing immediately uphill, the trail soon levels out into a gentle ascent above Rose Creek. Pause for breaks near the creek, where fragile shooting stars grow next to rock slabs. As the trail leads uphill, it swings southwest for the last mile of open bear-grass meadows and red argillite talus slopes. At the lake, scan the cliffs above for mountain goats, and wade the outlet to get to open lunch spots on the west shore.

Guides

Mid-June-mid-September, park naturalists (406/888-7800, www.nps.gov/glac) guide free hikes at Avalanche, Sun Point, and Logan Pass. Both the Avalanche Lake and Hidden Lake Overlook hikes are extremely popular, so expect to walk in a long train of people. They also guide longer hikes, like Siyeh Pass, and hikes with boat tours on St. Mary Lake. Pick up the *Ranger-led Activity Guide* from visitors centers or online (www.nps.gov/glac) for current destinations and schedules.

Glacier Guides (11970 U.S. 2 E., West Glacier, 406/387-5555 or 800/521-7238, www.

glacierguides.com, mid-May-Sept.) runs the trail-guiding concession in the park. Solo travelers can hook up with its weekly trips on trails to Avalanche Lake, Highline, Virginia Falls, and Piegan Pass (start dates vary pending snowpack, $98 pp), which meet at its West Glacier office. Families and small groups can arrange to meet their own guide elsewhere ($560 for up to five people). Both include guide service, deli lunch, and transportation to the trailhead. The guides also lead popular three-day trips to Granite Park Chalet ($960) including all meals, transportation to the trailhead, guide services, linens, and lodging. The six-day Ultimate Chalet trip ($2,350) splits nights at Sperry Chalet, Granite Park Chalet, and the Glacier Guides Lodge; all meals (except one dinner), transportation, and lodging are included. The company also has three- to six-day backpacking trips that depart weekly (June-mid-Sept., $190/day), some via Sun Road trailheads. Reservations are required. Plan to tip your guides at least 15 percent for day trips and 20 percent for overnights.

BACKPACKING

Going-to-the-Sun Road launches onto spectacular backpacking trails. With shuttles running in summer on the road, point-to-point trips are logistically easy. Leave your vehicle in St. Mary, Apgar, or at Lake McDonald Lodge; avoid taking up prime parking spaces at Logan Pass.

Permits (adults $7 pp/night) for these trips are in high demand. Pick them up 24 hours in advance in person at the **Apgar Backcountry Permit Office** (406/888-7859 May-Oct., 406/888-7800 Nov.-Apr.) or **St. Mary Visitor Center** (406/732-7751, late May-early Oct.), but plan to be in line at 6am. Better yet, apply online in mid-March for advance reservations (www.nps.gov/glac, $40). Pick up walk-in permits for these trips as soon as the campsites are snow-free, which can be in mid-July. But advance reservations for camps at Fifty Mountain, Lake Ellen Wilson, and Sperry are only available after August 1.

Almost Backpacking: Hiking Overnight

Between backcountry chalets and front-country cabins, hikers can sleep in a bed rather than on the ground in tents. Just load up day packs with a few essentials (water, lunch, snacks, extra clothes, and a toothbrush) to relish backpacker advantages without lugging huge, heavy packs. Restaurants and the chalets furnish meals for breakfast and dinner. Trails for these adventures usually open by mid-July. With shuttles, you can hike in one trail and out another. Plan these trips in advance: Reservations go fast in mid-January for the chalets and a year in advance for Swiftcurrent Motor Inn.

SPERRY CHALET

- **Overnighting:** The full-service chalet provides meals (dinner, breakfast, and sack lunch) and guest rooms with fresh linens and bedding.

- **Hiking:** From Lake McDonald Lodge, slog up 6.2 miles on a horse manure-laden trail that climbs 3,500 feet in elevation to Sperry Chalet. On your second day at Sperry, grab your lunch and head for the 6.9-mile round-trip trail to Sperry Glacier. To exit Sperry on the third day, hike the strenuous 14-mile route over Lincoln and Gunsight Passes to Jackson Glacier Overlook.

- **Logistics:** Leave the car at Lake McDonald Lodge. Use Going-to-the-Sun Road shuttles to connect the trailheads at Lake McDonald Lodge and Jackson Glacier Overlook.

GRANITE PARK CHALET

- **Overnighting:** Order bed linens and freeze-dried meals to avoid carrying a sleeping bag and heavy food to this hostel-type chalet. Bring a water filter.

- **Hiking:** From Logan Pass, the 7.4-mile Highline Trail goes north along the Garden Wall to the chalet on a knoll with a 360-degree view of surrounding peaks and glaciers. On the second day, leave the crowds behind by hiking 10 miles round-trip on the Northern Highline to Ahern Pass. On the third day, climb 4.2 miles round-trip to Swiftcurrent Lookout for views of the park from end to end, and after lunch, drop 4 miles downhill to The Loop.

- **Logistics:** Leave the car at Apgar Visitor Center or Lake McDonald Lodge. Use Going-to-the-Sun Road shuttles to connect with trailheads at Logan Pass and The Loop.

SWIFTCURRENT

- **Overnighting:** Stay in Swiftcurrent Motor Inn (page 159) cabins or motel rooms; dine for breakfast and dinner in its restaurant.

- **Hiking:** From Logan Pass, launch for 15.2 miles along the Highline Trail to Granite Park Chalet and then over Swiftcurrent Pass to descend past several lakes in Swiftcurrent Valley to Swiftcurrent Motor Inn. On the second day, climb the 11.5-mile trail under the Continental Divide over Piegan Pass to Siyeh Bend.

- **Logistics:** Leave the car at St. Mary Visitor Center. Use Going-to-the-Sun Road shuttles to connect with trailheads at Logan Pass and Siyeh Bend.

Gunsight Pass
28 MILES

This four-day trek is best hiked from Jackson Glacier Overlook west over Gunsight Pass to finish at Lake McDonald Lodge, but you can do it in reverse or shorten it to three days by skipping one overnight. Spend the first night at Gunsight Lake (GUN) before climbing over Gunsight Pass, often crossing a steep snowfield or two in July and encountering mountain goats. Descend to the boulder camp at Lake Ellen Wilson (ELL) for the second night. A short ascent pops over Lincoln Pass to Sperry Chalet campground (SPE). Set up camp, hang your food, and day hike up through Comeau Pass to Sperry Glacier. The chalet also invites backpackers to stop in for the social hour in the evening. On the final day, descend back into the thick forest, dodging horse manure, to Lake McDonald Lodge.

Fifty Mountain

32 MILES

Permits for this four-day trek are coveted due to the miles of high-elevation trekking along the Continental Divide. While you can do the loop either direction, most people choose to start at Logan Pass to gain the elevation by vehicle rather than on foot. Traipse along the Garden Wall to reach the backcountry campsites below Granite Park Chalet (GRN). Get an early start for the second day for 12 miles of climbs and descents through Ahern Pass, Cattle Queen basin, Mineral Creek basin, and Kootenai Pass. Snowfields can be tricky in July: A steep one bars the trail in the cliffs before Ahern, and the Cattle Queen melts into a dangerous snow bridge. Climb around to be safe. The day finishes with a long climb to the high point before dropping through gorgeous flower meadows to camp at Fifty Mountain (FIF). In the morning, take a side trip to Sue Lake Overlook (2.7 miles round-trip) before packing up to cross West Flattop to the Flattop Camp (FLA). On the last day, finish with a downhill hike to Packer's Roost. To catch the shuttle, hike 1.4 miles uphill to reach The Loop on the Sun Road.

★ BIKING GOING-TO-THE-SUN-ROAD

Going-to-the-Sun Road is an unforgettable bicycle trip. While the 3,500-foot climb up the west side seems intimidating, it's not steep . . . just a constant uphill grind amid stunning scenery. During construction in the 1920s, the road grade stayed at 6 percent because cars of the era required rigorous shifting at a steeper grade. Now, new blacktop from reconstruction smooths the riding.

Locals relish **spring riding** when the Sun Road is closed to cars. Cycling begins in early April as soon as snowplows free the pavement while the west-side road remains closed to vehicles from Lake McDonald Lodge or Avalanche, and closed on the east side from Rising Sun. Riders climb up as far as plowing

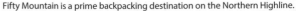

Fifty Mountain is a prime backpacking destination on the Northern Highline.

a bicycler on Going-to-the-Sun Road

Restrictions and Safety

Cyclists must be prepared to ride the narrow, shoulderless road with a constant stream of cars. Due to heavy midday traffic, **bicycles are restricted on the Sun Road during summer.** Biking is not permitted 11am-4pm daily June 15-Labor Day in two sections on the west side: along Lake McDonald between the Apgar Road junction and Sprague Creek, and climbing uphill between Avalanche Campground and Logan Pass. If starting from the west side, head out from Lake McDonald by 6:30am for adequate time to pedal to Logan Pass. In early summer, long daylight hours allow for riding after 4pm, when traffic lessens. The east side has no restrictions, but is still easier to ride early or late in the day with fewer cars on the road. Some free shuttle buses are equipped with bicycle racks in case you need a lift. Catch the shuttles only at official stops.

While laws do not mandate helmets, it'd be ill-advised not to wear one considering most drivers are gaping at the views rather than paying attention to the road. Wear bright colors for visibility, and consider tacking reflectors or flags on your bike. Be sure to carry plenty of water: exertion, wind, and altitude can lead to a fast case of dehydration. Before heading out, check your brake pads, as the screaming downhill off the Continental Divide can wear them down to nubbins. Both mountain bikes and road bikes are appropriate here, but with skinny tires, be wary of obstacles: debris, grates, rockfall, and ice. Because the Sun Road is so narrow, it is not the place for a family ride, except when the road is closed to cars. Apgar has bike rentals.

HORSEBACK RIDING

Located across Going-to-the-Sun Road from the Lake McDonald Lodge complex, **Swan Mountain Outfitters** (406/387-4405 or 877/888-5557, corral 406/888-5121, www.swanmountainoutfitters.com/glacier, early June-Sept., $45-175) departs for the best trail ride in the park. Starting mid-July, the all-day ride climbs to Sperry Chalet, where you

operations permit. By May, it is such a popular weekend activity that free bicycle-carrying shuttles run from Lake McDonald Lodge to the Avalanche road closure to expand parking options. Even tricycles and training wheels hit the flats, especially on Mother's Day. Call or consult the park website (406/888-7800, www.nps.gov/glac) to check on access, as construction or spring plowing limits cycling some days. In **fall,** as portions of the road close again to vehicles, cycling sans cars resumes.

In **summer,** when the road opens to vehicles, riders head for Logan Pass. Some riders return the way they came; others continue on to the other side. Local racers make a 142-mile loop (Going-to-the-Sun Road, U.S. 89, Highway 49, and U.S. 2) in one day; tourers take two days.

Locals also celebrate the full moon with a bone-chilling night ride. It's dangerous (injuries and at least one fatality have occurred), but an otherworldly experience. At dusk or at night, biking requires tail reflectors and a front light.

can lunch in the historic dining hall. The last two miles of the ride break out of thick trees into avalanche chutes, where you'll have better views of the steep-walled valley. Lunch is not included in the rate, so bring cash, and plan on ordering fresh homemade pie for dessert. Valley trail rides include a one-hour forest and two-hour McDonald Creek ride that depart several times daily. They tour on a trail through lichen-laden cedars and firs with peekaboo views of peaks. Wear long pants and hiking boots or tennis shoes. Kids need to be at least age 7 (age 10 for Sperry ride).

BOATING

Lake McDonald and St. Mary Lake permit motorized boats, kayaks, sailboards, and canoes, but Jet Skis are banned. Due to vehicle length restrictions (21 feet), towed boats may not cross Going-to-the-Sun Road between Avalanche and Sun Point. Pick up permits ($10 for 7-day motorized permit, $40 for annual motorized permit, free for nonmotorized boats) at St. Mary Visitor Center on the east side or on the west side at park headquarters or the Apgar Backcountry Permit Office, as directed by the orange sign near the west-side entrance station.

Lake McDonald

Lake McDonald has only one boat ramp at Apgar. For hand-carried craft, you can launch from Sprague Creek Picnic Area or several pullouts along the lake. Lake McDonald imposes a 10-horsepower limit on motorboats. At the Lake McDonald Lodge boat dock, **Glacier Park Boat Company** (dock 406/888-5727 or 406/257-2426, www.glacierparkboats.com, $18-24/hour) rents rowboats and small motorboats. Paddles, life jackets, and fishing regulations are included.

St. Mary

St. Mary Lake permits motorboats with unlimited horsepower. No boats are available to rent, but launch your own from the boat ramp at Rising Sun. Hand-carried craft can also launch easily from Rising Sun Picnic Area. Be aware: Wild winds whip up quickly on St. Mary Lake; keep alert to conditions.

PADDLING

Lake McDonald is prime for sea kayaking, canoeing, and paddleboarding. On calm days, shoreline tours are exceptionally scenic, and evening paddles yield stunning alpenglow. Launch from any of the Going-to-the-Sun Road pullouts for shoreline tours or from

a trail ride through cedar forests

the Sprague Creek Picnic Area. On St. Mary Lake, launch from the Rising Sun boat ramp to paddle to Silver Dollar Beach below Red Eagle Mountain; however, watch the weather, as high winds churn up monstrous waves quickly in the narrow valley. Although river kayakers drool at the rapids on McDonald Creek, the creek is closed to all boating due to nesting harlequin ducks.

Free permits are required to paddle on these lakes. Pick them up at St. Mary Visitor Center or park headquarters near the west entrance station.

FISHING

Glacier provides a stunning backdrop for fishing. No fishing licenses are required, but use barbless hooks for catch-and-release to protect westslope cutthroat and bull trout. Pick up current fishing regulations at visitors centers or online (www.nps.goc/glac). No fishing guide service operates inside the park.

McDonald Valley

Heavily fished, Lake McDonald is a haven for kokanee, lake trout, whitefish, and cutthroat. It has no limit on lake trout or lake whitefish. Boats tend to produce better results than shore fishing, but you'll see plenty of beach casting.

Other than Lake McDonald, fishing in McDonald Valley is sporadic at best. Although scads of anglers rim McDonald Creek, the river has a reputation for leaving hooks bare. As for Fish Lake: A 3-mile climb from Lake McDonald Lodge accesses the tiny, lily-padded shallow lake, where a few westslope cutthroat reside. Snyder Lake, a 4.2-mile climb from Lake McDonald Lodge, also has small cutthroat and is a little more open than Fish Lake's brushy shore. Ignore Avalanche Creek and head instead for Avalanche Lake, where indigenous westslope cutthroat have been kept genetically pure by the gorge's falls. This lake is heavily fished; for better action, wade to one of the chilly inlet streams on its south end.

Logan Pass

With a quick 2.5-mile access from Logan Pass,

Hidden Lake holds good-size Yellowstone cutthroat trout in spite of its elevation and its reputation as the highest lake in the park with fish. The outlet and nearby lakeshore are closed until July 31 due to bears feeding on spawning trout.

St. Mary Valley

St. Mary Lake has a reputation for beautiful scenery, but not spectacular fishing. It's best fished from boats rather than the shoreline. Upper St. Mary River isn't much better: You often see anglers below St. Mary Falls, but few catching fish. Gunsight Lake, the best fishing lake, requires a 6.5-mile hike from Jackson Glacier Overlook; expect wind, late snowpack, and brush along the shore.

Gear and Rentals

Need tackle? The camp stores at Lake McDonald Lodge and Rising Sun sell a few items, like line and flies. The nearest rental location for fishing gear is in Apgar at **Glacier Outfitters** (196 Apgar Loop Rd., 406/219-7466, www.goglacieroutfitters.com, 9am-8pm daily mid-May-late Sept., shorter hours in shoulder seasons).

WATERSKIING

While both Lake McDonald and St. Mary permit waterskiing (although Lake McDonald has a 10-horsepower limit), you won't find the lakes packed shore to shore with skiers. Frankly, these glacier-fed lakes are frigid. Those who do water-ski wear wetsuits. Precocious winds also whisk up sizable whitecaps, especially on St. Mary Lake. Serious water-skiers head to Flathead Valley's warmer, less whimsical lakes; rentals are found there, too.

WINDSURFING

Of all the park's lakes, St. Mary Lake is the one windsurfers occasionally use. Lake McDonald attracts a few, but inconsistent winds can leave sails slack. On St. Mary Lake, easterlies rage down the valley; however, high mountains and erratic valley confluences create swirly winds on its west end. The lake is not a beginner sailboarding area; experience in self-rescue is paramount. Those who sail these frigid waters usually launch from Rising Sun Picnic Area and wear a wetsuit.

SKIING AND SNOWSHOEING

Since winter buries Going-to-the-Sun Road with snow from Lake McDonald Lodge to St. Mary, the road attracts skiers and snowshoers November-early April. Touring up the gated road's lower elevations goes through relatively avalanche-free zones. The gentle grade makes for good gliding suitable for beginners. For snowshoers, etiquette requires blazing a separate snowshoe trail rather than squishing the parallel ski tracks flat. Some park ski trails are mapped online (www.nps.gov/glac).

In McDonald Valley, ski tours lead past McDonald Creek and Upper McDonald Creek Falls to Avalanche Campground (six miles). Some skiers cross the bridge at Sacred Dancing Cascade to loop back on the river's north side, but snow coverage is more variable in the trees. A gentle forest ski leads to John's Lake, but as a destination, it's not much. Some skiers head up to Snyder Lakes, but be ready for the narrow trail descending through tight trees on the way back down. Blue-sky days attract snowshoers to Mount Brown Lookout.

On the east side, a good, flat six-mile ski heads to Rising Sun along Two Dog Flats; however, high winds often strip sections of the roadway bare.

Between Rising Sun and Avalanche Creek, Going-to-the-Sun Road sees significant avalanche activity. Do not attempt to ski any of this section without experience, know-how, and safety gear (avalanche transceivers, shovels, and probes). Check current conditions at www.flatheadavalanche.org. When Logan Pass opens in June, skiers and snowboarders can hike up the Hidden Lake Overlook trail for turns on the lingering snowpack.

Guides and Rentals

Glacier Adventure Guides (406/892-2173, www.glacieradventureguides.com) leads full-day and overnight trips for cross-country touring, backcountry skiing, and snowshoeing. If you're a solo traveler, it's the best way to get accompanied into the backcountry with avalanche-certified guides to find pristine powder stashes. Lunch, snacks, and some equipment are included, although ski rentals need to be picked up in Flathead Valley. For deep backcountry, ski in to an igloo to spend the night. Call for rates; plan on tipping the guide 15-20 percent.

Entertainment and Shopping

RANGER PROGRAMS

Lake McDonald Lodge (8:30pm) and Rising Sun Amphitheater (8pm) host 45-minute nightly park naturalist programs. Check for schedules at campground information boards and hotel activity desks, or pick up the *Ranger-led Activity Guide* at visitors centers. Topics range from fires to birds. Best of all, they're free. Some of the programs feature Native American speakers, a great way to gain an understanding of the park's rich culture and history. Once per week at Lake McDonald Lodge, Jack Gladstone presents

a unique mix of music and stories of Native American legends.

Logan Pass Star Parties

With minimal light pollution, Logan Pass is one of the best places to view the night sky. The Big Sky Astronomy Club collaborates with the park service to host stargazing nights at Logan Pass with constellation tours and telescope viewing of planets, star clusters, and nebulae. Several events (9:30pm-midnight, late July-early Sept.) take place with limited admission. For admittance, each vehicle must have a ticket; they are free from Apgar or St. Mary Visitor Centers. Tickets go fast, so plan to be at the visitors center by 8am on the day before the event to get them. For dates, pick up the *Ranger-led Activity Guide* at visitors centers or check online (www.nps. gov/glac).

SHOPPING

Find gift shops in Lake McDonald Lodge, Two Dog Flats Grill at Rising Sun, and camp stores in both locations. They carry a selection of books, maps, T-shirts, postcards, and jewelry. The Logan Pass Visitor Center has a small bookstore.

Accommodations

INSIDE THE PARK

Accommodations on Going-to-the-Sun Road are scarce. The west side has Lake McDonald Lodge, 21 miles west of Logan Pass. Twelve miles east of the pass, Rising Sun offers plain cottages and motel units. For those with the feet to carry them, the incomparable Granite Park and Sperry Chalets require hiking. Most chalets and inns are National Historic Landmarks or listed on the National Register of Historic Places; none have TVs or air-conditioning. Add the 7 percent state bed tax to rates.

Lake McDonald

On the west side of Going-to-the-Sun Road, two lodging options sit near the head of Lake McDonald in a complex that has boat tours, boat rentals, red bus tours, horseback riding, trailheads, restaurants, and a camp store. Trailheads depart to Snyder Lake, Mount Brown, Sperry Chalet, Sperry Glacier, and Lincoln Pass. Limited Internet is available.

LAKE MCDONALD LODGE

Historic ★ **Lake McDonald Lodge** (288 Lake McDonald Lodge Loop, 855/733-4522, front desk 406/888-5431, www.glaciernationalparklodges.com, late May-late Sept., $105-360) graces the southeast lake shore. Centered around a massive stone fireplace and hunting lodge-themed lobby full of trophy specimens hung by John Lewis, the original owner, the complex has four types of accommodations: main lodge rooms, cabin rooms, Cobb House suites, and Snyder Hall, the latter two renovated in 2013. Lodge operator Xanterra

undertook a $3 million renovation in 2016 of some cabins, including new paint, carpets, fixtures, furniture, and upgraded bathrooms. Dial back your expectations to the mid-1900s with telephones as the only in-room amenities, and you'll be delighted with the location and historical ambience. Some lakeside rooms have views. Most rooms are small with bathrooms converted from original closets. Upstairs rooms lack elevator access. Snyder Hall has shared bathrooms. Cobb House has two-room suites with televisions. Wireless Internet is available in the lobby and reading room. Reservations are a must, opening 13 months in advance.

MOTEL LAKE MCDONALD

Glacier Park, Inc. operates the old 1950s-style two-story motel behind the camp store in the Lake McDonald Lodge complex. **Motel Lake McDonald** (3 Lake McDonald Lodge Loop, 406/892-2525 from US or 403/236-3400 from Canada, 406/888-5100 front desk, www.glacierparkinc.com, mid-June-mid-Sept., $130-170) sits in deep cedars with no lake views. Spartan rooms have no elevator access to the 2nd floor and no phones.

Rising Sun

RISING SUN MOTOR INN

It's hard to beat Rising Sun's location 12 miles from Logan Pass on the east side of Going-to-the-Sun Road. **Rising Sun Motor Inn** (2 Going-to-the-Sun Rd., 855/733-4522, front desk 406/732-5523, www.glaciernationalparklodges.com, mid-June-mid-Sept., $155-175) became the answer for motorists traveling to Glacier during World War II; it was the only facility that stayed open. Not much has changed at this funky 1940s motor inn with its board-and-batten construction, except that rooms were revamped in 2016. Expect no in-room phones, TVs, or air-conditioning, but an outdoor pay phone and portable fans are available. Cabin rooms and motel units have diminutive private baths with elbow-bumping shower stalls. The complex has a restaurant, store, limited wireless Internet, and a hiker shuttle stop. The trail to Otokomi Lake begins near the store, and access to St. Mary Lake is across the street, along with the boat tour dock. In the evening, go on a sunset cruise on St. Mary Lake or drive to look for wildlife on Two Dog Flats between Rising Sun and St. Mary. Reservations open 13 months in advance.

Backcountry

Glacier has two historic backcountry gems. The only remaining chalets built by the Great Northern Railway, **Sperry Chalet** and **Granite Park Chalet** are rustic stone and log edifices owned by the National Park Service and operated by **Belton Chalets** (406/387-5654 or 888/345-2649, www.sperrychalet.com, www.graniteparkchalet.com, early July-early Sept.). Set in scenic alpine mountain goat and grizzly bear terrain, solitude and beauty are chalet amenities. With no electricity, watching wildlife and sunsets provides quiet evening entertainment, and stargazing is spectacular. Take a flashlight to find the composting vault toilets at night (no flush toilets, no hot running water). Pack along earplugs, as snores resound through thin walls. No alcohol is sold or allowed in the dining halls, but you can pack along beverages for sipping in guest rooms and haul the containers out with you. To reach the chalets requires hiking 4-14 miles, depending on the route. Reservations are required. **Online bookings for the upcoming summer go fast, starting in early January.** Hiker shuttles stop at all the Sun Road trailheads for the chalets.

Granite Park Chalet offers 360-degree views.

SPERRY CHALET

★ **Sperry Chalet** offers hikers and horse-back riders three meals and a warm bed, which means hauling only a day pack with some extra clothing. Set in a timbered cirque, the chalet has a dining hall, dorm, and several National Park Service buildings. Seventeen dorm rooms sleep 2-6 people each ($222 first person in room, $150 per added person) in bunks or beds with bedding included. Faucets put out cold water only. Country meals with roasted turkey sate its 45 guests per night, but the menu has maintained culinary sensibilities from the 1950s, with canned fruits and vegetables. Trail lunches packed for you are plain, with a meat sandwich (no lettuce or tomato), candy bars, and fruit leather. However, outstanding bakery goods use traditional decades-old recipes for cookies, freshly baked breads, and pies. To reach Sperry, hike 6.2 miles up from Lake McDonald or 14 miles over two passes from Jackson Glacier Overlook.

GRANITE PARK CHALET

Set at the same elevation as Logan Pass, ★ Granite Park Chalet sits atop a knoll with a 360-degree view. The main chalet contains the kitchen, dining room, and guest rooms. More rooms are in another building. Twelve guest rooms sleep 2-6 people each ($106 first person in room, $80 per added person). This chalet functions somewhat like a hostel for its 35 guests per night: Bring your own sleeping bag. Meals are not supplied; haul your own food to cook in the kitchen. Pots and pans are available for cooking on the 12-burner propane stove with an oven, but you'll need to bring your own mugs, plates, bowls, eating utensils, and water filter. With no running water, guests haul water for cooking and washing from 0.2 mile away. For hikers looking to lighten their load, purchase linen service ($20 for sheets, a pillow, and blankets), preorder freeze-dried food ($2-12/item), and purchase environmentally friendly disposable plates and utensils. Most hikers reach the chalet from Logan Pass (7.4 miles), The Loop (4 miles), or Swiftcurrent (7.6 miles).

Camping

In the 50 miles of Going-to-the-Sun Road, five campgrounds stretch along the corridor, but none sit in the high alpine Logan Pass section. On the west side, Apgar, Sprague Creek, and Avalanche offer more sites than Rising Sun and St. Mary on the east side. In midsummer, the coveted Avalanche, Sprague Creek, and Rising Sun Campgrounds can fill up by early morning; all sites are first-come, first-served. Amenities include shuttle stops, flush toilets, cold running water, picnic tables, and fire rings with grills; bring your own firewood, as collecting is prohibited. Shared sites ($5 pp) accommodate hikers and bikers with bear-resistant food storage. For hookups, hit commercial campgrounds outside the park in St. Mary or West Glacier.

If campgrounds are full, oversize RVs must backtrack, because vehicles over 21 feet cannot travel the Sun Road between Avalanche Campground and Sun Point. On the west side, head to Fish Creek and commercial campgrounds in West Glacier. On the east side, aim for commercial campgrounds in St. Mary. For RVs seeking a dump station, find the closest west-side one at Apgar; Rising Sun Campground has a dump station on the east side.

INSIDE THE PARK

Sprague Creek Campground

Sprague Creek Campground (0.9 mile southwest of Lake McDonald Lodge on Going-to-the-Sun Rd., 406/888-7800, mid-May-mid-Sept., $20) is right on Lake McDonald's shore in a timbered setting with shaded sites. A few have prime waterfront. Unfortunately, several sites also abut Going-to-the-Sun Road, with a nice view of cars driving by. After dark, the road noise plummets, so it's not like tenting next to a major highway. As the smallest campground with only 25 sites accessed via a paved road, Sprague Creek does not allow towed units. Most of the parking pads are short and narrow, but a few can fit small RVs up to 21 feet. Kayakers and canoers have lakefront access, and beach sunsets rank as spectacular. At 22 miles from Logan Pass, it has quick access to the high country, and it's five minutes from Lake McDonald Lodge and the camp store. Midsummer, Sprague often fills by 8am.

Avalanche Campground

Set in a cedar-hemlock and fern rainforest, ★ Avalanche Campground (at Avalanche on Going-to-the-Sun Rd., 406/888-7800, mid-June-early Sept., $20) opens its 87 sites for a shorter season than Sprague Creek. Six miles east of Lake McDonald Lodge, Avalanche makes the closest west-side base for exploring Logan Pass, 16 miles away, and is convenient for hiking to Avalanche Lake, since the trail departs from the campground's rear. The rainforest, with its dark, overgrown forest canopy, allows little sunlight to hit picnic tables. The moist area sprouts thick patches of thimbleberries and sometimes a good collection of mosquitoes. RVs are limited to 26 feet. Midsummer, Avalanche can fill before 10am.

Rising Sun Campground

Located only 12 miles east of Logan Pass and 6 miles west of St. Mary, ★ **Rising Sun Campground** (Rising Sun on Going-to-the-Sun Rd., 406/888-7800, late May-mid-Sept., $20) tucks on the lower hillside of Otokomi Mountain by St. Mary Lake. The sun drops down early behind Goat Mountain, creating a long twilight at the campground. While the 2015 Reynolds Creek Fire bypassed the larger trees in the lower campground, it left burnt trees on the hillside above the upper campsites. Adjacent to Rising Sun Motor Inn, the 83-site campground is a few minutes' walk to a restaurant, a camp store, and hot showers. Beach access is across Going-to-the-Sun Road, with a picnic area, boat ramp, and boat tours. The Otokomi Lake trailhead is behind the adjacent inn. RVs can only be 25 feet. Midsummer, the campground can fill by 9:30am.

Food

Logan Pass has no food services, not even vending machines. The nearest restaurants on the west side are at Lake McDonald Lodge, 21 miles below the pass. On the east side, Rising Sun has the only restaurant, 12 miles from Logan Pass. **Xanterra** (855/733-4522, www.glaciernationalparklodges.com) operates these park restaurants. Local sourcing, sustainability, farm-to-table, and organic products form the backbone for their menus. Options include vegan, gluten-free, and child selections, plus flexibility with add-on toppings for salads and pastas. For hikers and sightseers on Going-to-the-Sun Road, sack lunches ($12-13) are sold at Lake McDonald Lodge and Rising Sun; order them a day in advance.

INSIDE THE PARK
Restaurants
LAKE MCDONALD LODGE

At **Lake McDonald Lodge** (288 Lake McDonald Lodge Loop, 406/892-2525, front desk 406/888-5431, daily late May-Sept.), the headliner dining room is ★ **Russell's Fireside Dining Room,** decorated with painted Native American chandeliers and full of historical ambience. The north windows have a peekaboo lake view, but during dinner the blinds usually need to be pulled down as the hot sun blazes in. Breakfast (6:30am-10am, $7-16) is a choice of continental buffet, full buffet, or menu entrées. Lunch (11:30am-2pm, $11-20) serves small plates, burgers, sandwiches, salads, and pasta. Dinner (5pm-9:30pm, $11-32) can go casual with burgers, salads, and pasta or full-on dining with charcuterie, shared appetizers, and plated entrées of fish or meats. No reservations are taken, so you may have to wait for a seat.

Also in the lodge, the cozy **Lucke's Lounge** (11:30am-10pm, $10-15), adjacent to the lodge's dining room, serves a more limited menu of appetizers, sandwiches, burgers, salads, and pasta. The bar also stocks plenty of local microbrews along with wine and craft cocktails. The best option for families is the cafeteria-style **Jammer Joe's Grill and Pizzeria** (11am-9pm, closes early

lanterns in Russell's Fireside Dining Room

When crowded with bus tours midsummer, you may have to wait for a table. If the line is really long, go six miles down the road to St. Mary for more dining options; the evening return drive offers good wildlife-watching along Two Dog Flats.

Groceries

You're best off stocking up on groceries before settling in for several days along the Sun Road. But for last-minute supplies, **camp stores** (7am-9pm daily mid-June-mid-Sept.) are located at the Lake McDonald Lodge complex and Rising Sun. Both camp stores carry limited items, but you can pick up ice, firewood, stove gas, and other camping supplies, as well as convenience-store groceries, beer, wine, gifts, and newspapers. Hikers can buy trail food for lunches.

Picnic Areas

Only four areas accommodate the picnic basket on Going-to-the-Sun Road. All except Sun Point permit fires in the fire rings with grills, but bring your own firewood, as gathering is prohibited. Picnic tables are available, but due to bears, do not leave your picnic gear unattended. Read the information on fines stapled to the tables. Adjacent to the campground, **Sprague Creek Picnic Area** tucks tightly in the trees between Going-to-the-Sun Road and Lake McDonald, with more road view than scenery; however, short paths access the shoreline. Flush toilets are available. **Avalanche Creek Picnic Area** is across the street from the campground and has larger rebuilt vault-toilet restrooms. Picnic sites are under cedar shade adjacent to McDonald Creek. Trailheads for Trail of the Cedars and Avalanche Lake are across the street. **Sun Point Picnic Area** has great views up St. Mary Valley to the Continental Divide, but watch the paper plates, as the wind can howl. Trails lead to Sun Point and Baring Falls. It has vault toilets. **Rising Sun Picnic Area** is adjacent to St. Mary Lake, with open sites slightly buffered from wind by aspen trees. If

Sept., $10-18), due to broad menu choices and foods with kid appeal. Located across from the lodge, the restaurant serves pizza, pasta, wraps, burgers, and salads. Its lunch buffet helps with quicker eating to get back on the road.

TWO DOG FLATS GRILL

Located at Rising Sun across from the motor inn, **Two Dog Flats Grill** (2 Going-to-the-Sun Rd., 855/733-4522, front desk 406/732-5523, daily mid-June-mid-Sept.) is the only restaurant inside the park on the east flank of Going-to-the-Sun Road. It serves breakfast 6:30am-10am ($6-12). Lunch and dinner are served 11:00am-10pm ($10-23), with full plated dinners starting at 5pm. The casual American fare includes sandwiches, burgers, pasta, salads, and homestyle grill dinners. Beer and wine are available, too. Ask for a south window table to see Red Eagle Peak, although pines are stretching higher into the views. No reservations are taken.

winds rage, however, hold everything down. Short paths through the trees access the shoreline. It has flush toilets.

Logan Pass has no picnic area, and the National Park Service does not allow coolers outside of vehicles except in picnic areas . . . although you can eat a sandwich anywhere. If you want to "picnic" up with the views, the best method is to pack a sack lunch to eat on a trail or at one of the many pullouts along the road. Most restaurants in and around the park sell takeout lunches ($10-13) that you can order a day in advance of your trip. Especially scenic and aptly named, **Lunch Creek pullout** (1.4 miles east of Logan Pass) has a good historic rock wall that makes a great place for a tailgate lunch. On the west side, many picnic on the rock retaining walls at The Loop or on the big boulders at Big Bend (2.3 miles below Logan Pass).

Transportation and Services

DRIVING AND PARKING

Be prepared for driving the narrow, two-lane Going-to-the-Sun Road. Between Avalanche and Rising Sun, **RVs** are not allowed: **Rigs** must be smaller than 21 feet long, 8 feet wide, and 10 feet high. Drivers who have extended side mirrors should pull them in to avoid losing them on cliffs.

Limited parking is at Logan Pass, with the lot filling up 9:30am-4:30pm. No services exist at Logan Pass. You'll enjoy your time better and in less of a rush if you pack a lunch.

SERVICES

Restrooms are few and far between on this historic highway. **Flush toilets** are available at Sprague Creek Picnic Area, Lake McDonald Lodge, Logan Pass Visitor Center, and Rising Sun. **Vault toilets** are available at Avalanche Picnic Area, Logan Creek, The Loop, Logan Pass, Jackson Glacier Overlook, and Sun Point. Only the campgrounds and lodges have **running water** for washing hands.

Showers (one token for eight minutes $3) are available at Rising Sun. For **laundry,** you'll have to go to West Glacier or St. Mary.

Lake McDonald camp store carries some supplies.

Find **ATM machines** at Lake McDonald Lodge and Rising Sun Motor Inn. The Lake McDonald Lodge complex has a small seasonal **post office** (10am-2pm Mon.-Fri. summer) across from the **camp store.**

Gas and Repairs

Gas is not available on Going-to-the-Sun Road. Gas up in West Glacier or St. Mary. Rangers can sometimes assist with minor repairs, such as jumping dead car batteries, but call mobile services from Flathead Valley for major repairs.

Cell Phone and Internet Access

While some cell phones pick up service at high elevations on the Sun Road, most do not work due to the surrounding peaks and narrow valleys. No service is available in McDonald Valley except around Apgar; St. Mary Valley gets service only in St. Mary. Granite Park Chalet has **cell service,** but be aware that many visitors go there to get away from that, so be discreet in your phone use. **Public pay phones** are at Lake McDonald Lodge, Rising Sun, and Avalanche Campground. You can purchase calling cards for them at the Rising Sun and Lake McDonald camp stores. The Sun Road is a place to break the technological umbilical cord. Public Internet access is not available.

Newspapers/Magazines

Find local newspapers in gift shops and camp stores at Lake McDonald Lodge and Rising Sun. They carry the *Great Falls Tribune* and Flathead Valley's *Daily Interlake.*

Emergencies

If you have an emergency on Going-to-the-Sun Road, call 911. If you cannot leave the scene to make a phone call, flag down a vehicle heading up or down the pass to notify the nearest ranger (usually at Logan Pass, St. Mary Visitor Center, or by phone from Lake McDonald Lodge). For other assistance, call the **National Park Service** (406/888-7800).

On the west side of the Sun Road, a seasonal **urgent-care clinic** (100 Rea Rd., West Glacier, 406/888-9224, 9am-4pm daily Memorial Day-Labor Day) operates, but the nearest hospitals are in Flathead Valley: **North Valley Hospital** (1600 Hospital Way, Whitefish, 406/863-3500) and **Kalispell Regional Medical Center** (310 Sunny View Ln., Kalispell, 406/752-5111). On the east side, the Blackfeet Reservation houses the **Blackfeet Community Hospital** (760 Government Sq., Browning, 406/338-6154).

St. Mary and Many Glacier

On Glacier's east side, mountains graze the sky and drop abruptly to wide-open grassland prairies. Below sheer cliffs, elk browse. Aspen leaves chatter in only a hint of breeze.

From valley floors, a wild panorama of Glacier's peaks runs across the western skyline, dominated by red sediments and milky sapphire lakes. Ice fields cling for dear life to cliffs as the summer sun shrinks them each year. It's a place of extravagant color, where tumbling waterfalls and pink, purple, white, and yellow wildflowers intoxicate the eyes.

Due to the Continental Divide, wind is a constant companion. It shapes trees into gnarled, bent wonders and whips up whitecaps on lakes in seconds. But every minute yields another view to fill pixels with rugged scenery. No wonder the Blackfeet called Glacier the "Backbone of the World."

While St. Mary is the eastern portal to Glacier's famed Going-to-the-Sun Road, Many Glacier is a setting of dreams: chiseled peaks, idyllic lakes, pastoral meadows. The morning sunrise gleams gold across the rampart of peaks. Loons call across glassy lakes. Grizzly bears forage on hillsides, clawing at the ground for glacier lily bulbs. By evening, when the trails vacate, the sunset paints royal hues above the Continental Divide. Dark descends, with a multitude of stars. And if you're lucky, the northern lights dance across the sky.

HISTORY
Parkhood

George Bird Grinnell first set eyes on his namesake glacier in 1887. The editor of *Forest and Stream* magazine, the precursor to *Field and Stream,* made several excursions to Glacier over two decades, during which he lobbied Congress for support for the area's preservation. Congress agreed to purchase lands from the Blackfeet to open to the public, and Grinnell helped negotiate the sale.

After the federal government purchased the land from the Blackfeet, Glacier became a forest reserve, open to prospecting and hunting. The Many Glacier Valley attracted hordes of would-be miners digging

---

Previous: Bullhead Lake on the Swiftcurrent Valley and Lookout Trail; Swiftcurrent Lake and Grinnell Point in Many Glacier. **Above:** a backpacker crosses the Belly River.

Highlights

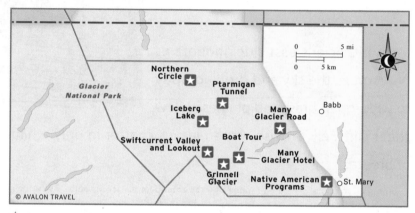

© AVALON TRAVEL

★ **Boat Tour:** The Many Glacier boat tour combines two scenic rides with unbeatable views. Launch on Swiftcurrent Lake and stroll to Lake Josephine for the second boat (page 138).

★ **Many Glacier Road:** On a scenic evening drive into Many Glacier, sunsets turn the peaks rosy with alpenglow, and wildlife is frequently afoot (page 139).

★ **Many Glacier Hotel:** The park's grandest lodge takes advantage of its idyllic setting with an enormous four-story log lobby and two-story floor-to-ceiling dining room windows (page 142).

★ **Grinnell Glacier:** See Grinnell Glacier before it melts completely. Hikers on the trail to the glacier often spot grizzly bears (page 147).

★ **Swiftcurrent Valley and Lookout:** Climb atop the Continental Divide where you'll survey glaciers and peaks for as far as you can see (page 148).

★ **Iceberg Lake:** Swim with icebergs! Tucked below goat-studded cliffs, the lake gleams with ice floating in blue waters (page 149).

★ **Ptarmigan Tunnel:** Climb to a hiker's tunnel built in the 1930s. A walk through its dark corridor ends with a burst of reds and blues (page 149).

★ **Northern Circle:** Backpack this historic 52-mile route through Ptarmigan Tunnel, the Belly River, fishing lakes, two passes, and countless wildflower meadows (page 151).

★ **Native American Programs:** Gain a better understanding of Blackfeet culture through storytelling, song, and dance (page 157).

St. Mary and Many Glacier

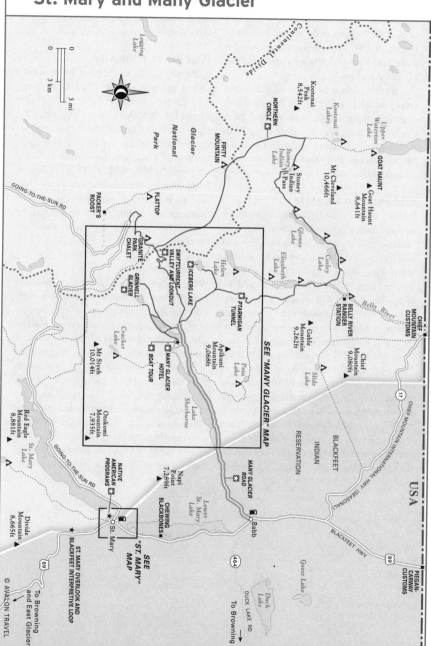

© AVALON TRAVEL

for copper, silver, and gold. In 1898 the mining boom gave rise to Altyn, a town site located where Sherburne Reservoir is today. At its peak, the burg housed 800 residents, but by December 1902 it was a ghost town. Meager yields could not compete with the lure of the Klondike gold rush.

Grinnell pressed on in his efforts to preserve Glacier. Finally, in 1910, President Taft signed the act creating Glacier National Park, the United States' 12th national park. In recognition of Grinnell's efforts, the Many Glacier area bears his name on a glacier, peak, point, and two lakes.

Lodges and Chalets

On old wagon roads, the Great Northern Railway built a dirt road in 1911-1912 from Midvale (now East Glacier) to St. Mary and Swiftcurrent Valley, which was soon to be the home of the "showplace of the Rockies," Many Glacier Hotel. When dry, the road was drivable; when rains fell, it mutated into treacherous muck. In the hustle to create guest lodging for train passengers, the train company threw up Many Glacier and St. Mary Chalets in 1912-1913. Guests rode the 36 miles from Midvale to St. Mary by car in 2.5 hours or by stagecoach in 4 hours. Others arrived via the Inside Trail on an overnight horseback trip, stopping at Cut Bank Chalets. After avalanches demolished two of the Many Glacier chalets and the dining hall, poor site selection prompted choosing another location for the grand Many Glacier Hotel. The hotel on

Swiftcurrent Lake opened its doors in 1915 with luxuries of hot and cold running water, steam heat, telephones, and electric lights in every room.

Blackfeet Highway

In the late 1920s, the State of Montana rerouted and paved the Midvale to St. Mary road, known as the Blackfeet Highway (Hwy. 49 and U.S. 89). The new route bypassed St. Mary Chalets, which fell into disuse as growing automobile traffic diverted to Going-to-the-Sun Road, and the town of St. Mary sprouted. Saddled with the Depression and fewer people who could afford pricey hotels, the park service pressured the railroad company into building Swiftcurrent Cabins in 1933. They soared into popularity at $2.25 per night.

1936 Fire

When high winds forced the 1936 Heavens Peak fire over the Continental Divide, it made a beeline down Swiftcurrent Valley, eating up 33 of the Swiftcurrent cabins en route to Many Glacier Hotel. Employees doused the hotel roof with water to protect the lodge. They telegrammed the railroad's vice president, apprising him of their success at saving the hotel. His reply: "Why?" The hotels and chalets had become a financial noose around the railroad's neck. The St. Mary chalets were torn down in 1948; the Many Glacier chalets succumbed to fire and avalanches. Only the historic showplace Many Glacier Hotel remains.

Exploring St. Mary and Many Glacier

Glacier's eastern ecosystem sprawls across national park lands and the Blackfeet Reservation, divided by an artificially straight border. Bears and elk know no boundaries, and sometimes neither do cattle, ranging astray inside Glacier.

Blackfeet Reservation

Bordering the park's eastern boundary are 1.5 million acres of Blackfeet Nation lands. The boundary slices across the summits of Chief Mountain, Napi Point, and Divide Mountain, crossing the lower end of Sherburne Reservoir and sliding between the two St. Mary Lakes.

St. Mary

BLACKFEET INDIAN RESERVATION

Lower St. Mary Lake

WEST SHORE RD

ST. MARY KOA

River

To Babb

89

ST. MARY

St. Mary River

NATIVE AMERICAN PROGRAMS

JOHNSON'S OF ST. MARY/ JOHNSON'S WORLD FAMOUS HISTORIC RESTAURANT

ST. MARY VISITOR CENTER

PARK CAFÉ

RED EAGLE MOTEL

ST. MARY ENTRANCE

GOING-TO-THE-SUN RD

PARK GROCERY

St. Mary Lake

ST. MARY LODGE AND RESORT

COTTAGES AT GLACIER

ST. MARY SUPERMART

1913 RANGER STATION

89

Glacier National Park

ST. MARY SCENIC OVERLOOK AND BLACKFEET INTERPRETIVE LOOP

Red Eagle Trail

0   500 yds
0   500 m

© AVALON TRAVEL

Permits are required for camping, fishing, hiking, and boating on the reservation.

St. Mary

St. Mary is the eastern portal to Going-to-the-Sun Road. At the junction of the Sun Road and the Blackfeet Highway (U.S. 89), the town clusters at the park boundary along the highway. Only the visitors center and St. Mary Campground are within the park; the town, restaurants, grocery stores, lodging, and commercial campgrounds are on the Blackfeet Reservation.

Many Glacier

Get used to the lingo here: Although the popular Many Glacier Hotel is in the Swiftcurrent Valley, locals refer to the area simply as Many Glacier, even though that is technically not its name; only the hotel and the campground actually use that name. Many Glacier derived its name from the string of small glaciers that populate its peaks: Grinnell, Salamander, Gem, North Swiftcurrent, and South Swiftcurrent.

Babb

Between St. Mary and Many Glacier is Babb, a blink-and-you'll-miss-it village about one block long. A few houses are tucked behind a small year-round grocery store, along with two bars, two restaurants, and a tiny motel. In the middle of nowhere, it seemingly has no purpose, but its year-round post office and elementary school serve families ranching between St. Mary and the Canadian border.

Belly River

North of Many Glacier in two valleys lined with good fishing lakes, the Belly River is home to tales of Joe Cosley, one of the park's most notorious rangers. Guides and rangers tell stories of his poaching and womanizing exploits. The Belly, as locals call it, is

Many Glacier

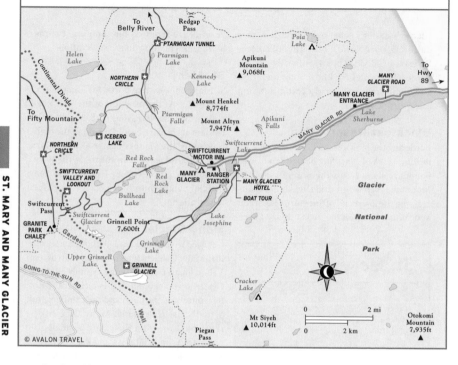

To Belly River
Redgap Pass
Poia Lake
⚑ PTARMIGAN TUNNEL
Helen Lake
Ptarmigan Lake
Apikuni Mountain 9,068ft
To Hwy 89
Continental Divide
NORTHERN CRICLE
Kennedy Lake
MANY GLACIER ROAD
MANY GLACIER ENTRANCE
To Fifty Mountain
Ptarmigan Falls
▲ Mount Henkel 8,774ft
Lake Sherburne
Mount Altyn 7,947ft ▲
Apikuni Falls
MANY GLACIER RD
★ ICEBERG LAKE
NORTHERN CRICLE
Red Rock Falls
Swiftcurrent Lake
SWIFTCURRENT MOTOR INN
★ SWIFTCURRENT VALLEY AND LOOKOUT
Red Rock Lake
MANY GLACIER
RANGER STATION
MANY GLACIER HOTEL
Glacier
Bullhead Lake
BOAT TOUR
Swiftcurrent Pass
Swiftcurrent Glacier
Grinnell Point 7,600ft
Lake Josephine
National
GRANITE PARK CHALET
Garden
Grinnell Lake
Park
GOING-TO-THE-SUN RD
Upper Grinnell Lake
★ GRINNELL GLACIER
Cracker Lake
Wall
Mt Siyeh 10,014ft
0   2 mi
0   2 km
Otokomi Mountain 7,935ft ▲
Piegan Pass

© AVALON TRAVEL

undeveloped backcountry with no hotels or restaurants. While day hikers can reach a couple of the Belly's lakes in one long day, the area is best explored by backpacking.

VISITORS CENTERS

Located at the St. Mary entrance to Glacier National Park, the **St. Mary Visitor Center** (406/732-7751, www.nps.gov/glac, 8am-5pm daily late May-early Oct., open until 7pm midsummer, backcountry permit desk 7am-4:30pm) is the largest visitors center in the park. Indoors houses a small Glacier National Park Conservancy **bookstore** (406/892-3250, http://glacier.org), theater, and displays on Native American cultural history. Astronomy programs take place outdoors. Walk to the visitors center via a wooden bridge and trail from the campground or on the paved pathway from St.

Mary; drive through the park entrance to reach the parking lot.

Inside the center, find backcountry permits, fishing regulations, Going-to-the-Sun Road updates, *Junior Ranger Activity Guides,* and information on free guided hikes and presentations with park naturalists in the *Ranger-led Activity Guide.* The theater hosts slide presentations, evening naturalist programs, and the popular Two Medicine Lake Singers and Dancers.

The visitors center is also a shuttle stop: To avoid parking hassles at Logan Pass, park your car here all day for free and catch the free shuttle up Going-to-the-Sun Road.

In Many Glacier, between the picnic area and Swiftcurrent parking lot adjacent to the campground, the small **Many Glacier Ranger Station** (milepost 12.4, Many Glacier Rd., 406/732-7740, 8am-5pm daily late May-mid-Sept.) has hiking info, maps, trail conditions, bear-sighting information, guidebooks, and backcountry permits.

ENTRANCE STATIONS

The park staffs entrance stations at **St. Mary** at the eastern gateway of Going-to-the-Sun Road and in **Many Glacier.** Both have self-pay cash-only kiosks for when the stations are unstaffed. If you don't have an annual pass, get a seven-day pass ($30 per vehicle, $25 motorcyclists, $15 hikers and bikers summer; $20, $15, and $10 winter). The St. Mary entrance is open year-round, but with the road open only to St. Mary Campground in winter. Many Glacier usually opens May-Oct.

SHUTTLES AND TOURS
Shuttles

St. Mary Visitor Center serves as the eastside transit hub where you can catch the **free Going-to-the-Sun Road shuttles** to Logan Pass. No tickets are needed, and no reservations are taken. Starting at 7:30am daily, the shuttle leaves every 40-60 minutes for Logan Pass, with six stops en route at trailheads. Riding to Logan Pass takes about one hour, even though it's only 18 miles. At Logan Pass, you can catch the west-side shuttles into Lake McDonald Valley. The last buses leave Logan Pass at 7pm daily to return to St. Mary.

Two shuttle systems operate between St. Mary and Many Glacier, especially helpful for hikers and backpackers. Find their respective schedules online, and make reservations to ensure seats. For point-to-point hikers on the Highline or Piegan Pass Trails, **Xanterra** (855/733-4522, www.glaciernationalparklodges.com, July-Labor Day, adults $10, kids $5) runs a shuttle between Many Glacier and St. Mary Visitor Center to link with the free Going-to-the-Sun Road shuttle to the trailheads. Two departures are scheduled each way in the morning and one in late afternoon. **Glacier Park, Inc.** (406/892-2525, www.glacierparkinc.com, early June-late Sept., $15-75 one-way) runs shuttles on the east side of the park. Shuttles go northbound and southbound between St. Mary and Many Glacier, plus connect with Glacier Park Lodge in East Glacier, Two Medicine, Cut Bank Creek, Chief Mountain Customs, and Prince of Wales Hotel in Waterton.

Glacier Charters (406/892-3390 or 800/829-7039, www.glaciertransportation.com) runs shuttles by reservation only between Glacier Park International Airport and St. Mary, Many Glacier, or Chief Mountain

St. Mary Visitor Center serves as a shuttle hub.

Customs for the Belly River trailhead ($275-375 one-way).

Bus Tours

While tours can travel to the east side of Glacier in early summer, they may not access Logan Pass and the entire Going-to-the-Sun Road until it is open. Rates for tours do not include meals, taxes, park entrance fees, and gratuities. Reservations are required.

Daily tours leave Many Glacier Hotel and St. Mary on **historic red buses** (Xanterra, 855/733-4522, www.glaciernationalparklodges.com, early June-mid-Sept., adults $38-90, kids half price). Departure times vary based on pickup location: Many Glacier Hotel, Swiftcurrent Motor Inn, St. Mary Lodge, or Rising Sun Motor Inn. These scenic buses are charmers; on good-weather days, the jammers (tour bus drivers) roll back the canvas tops for unlimited skyward views. No air-conditioning needed! Full-day and several-hour tours head to Logan Pass, hitting almost every scenic stop on Going-to-the-Sun Road. The Old North Trail tour heads to Two Medicine and Glacier Park Lodge in East Glacier.

From St. Mary, **Sun Tours** (406/226-9220 or 800/786-9220, www.glaciersuntours.com, daily mid-May-mid-Sept., $45) drives air-conditioned 25-passenger buses with extra-large windows for big scenery, an asset on the historic Going-to-the-Sun Road. Led by local Native American guides who grew up on the reservation, the tours highlight Glacier's rich connection with the Blackfeet, Native American history in the park, traditional medicines, stories behind peak names, and life in buffalo days. A four-hour tour departs at 9am from several locations in St. Mary.

★ Boat Tour

In Many Glacier, jump on a pair of historic wooden boats for a tour of two lakes with **Glacier Park Boat Company** (406/257-2426, www.glacierparkboats.com, daily mid-June-mid-Sept., round-trip adults $28, children $14). Catch the 1961-vintage *Chief Two Guns* at Swiftcurrent Lake's boat dock behind Many Glacier Hotel. In 75 minutes, you'll cruise across the lake, hike five minutes over a hill, hop aboard the 1945 *Morning Eagle* for a cruise on Lake Josephine, and return. Don't forget your camera, although you may have difficulty cramming the view into the lens. Tours depart at 9am, 11am, 2pm, and 4:30pm from mid-June-mid-Sept., with additional launches at 1pm and 3pm from July 1, and 8:30am from mid-July. Two of the launches offer guided two-mile round-trip walks to Grinnell Lake, and the earliest boat has a ranger-led hike to Grinnell Glacier. Tours sell out, but you can make reservations by phone with a credit card or in person at the dock one day in advance.

On St. Mary Lake, boat tours depart from Rising Sun on Going-to-the-Sun Road.

Hikers also use the boats as **shuttles** to cut down trail mileage. Hikers can catch one-way return boats (half price) at the Lake Josephine upper dock; pay cash as you board. You may have to wait for a few launches to get on, but

a boat tour on Lake Josephine

park entrance station in Many Glacier

the captain runs the boat until all hikers are shuttled.

Driving Tours

Visitors to St. Mary have options for touring in all directions. Since St. Mary is the eastern portal for **Going-to-the-Sun Road,** most people head to Logan Pass when the road is open. Winding along St. Mary Lake and Two Dog Flats, the Sun Road reaches Logan Pass in 18 miles before dropping 32 miles to West Glacier.

In this region, all roads are two-laners. On the Blackfeet Reservation, roads cross open range where **cattle or horses wander onto the roads.** Slow down and give them room. Ol' Bessie may just stand there staring at you and refuse to budge. If so, a toot on the horn can sometimes help, but avoid being obnoxious. If necessary, carefully pass in the other lane. Even though the speed limit sign says 70 mph, slow down at night due to livestock. Brakes frequently screech as drivers nearly hit animals.

BLACKFEET HIGHWAY

The Blackfeet Highway (U.S. 89, open year-round) runs entirely on the Blackfeet Reservation along the east side of Glacier National Park from the Canadian border to Browning. Most of it traverses aspen ranchland.

Driving north from St. Mary, the highway undulates past **Lower St. Mary Lake** and Thunderbird Island. This section is one of the few roads with shoulders, making driving easier. Rounding the lake's outlet, watch for waterfowl and views to the north of Chief Mountain and Old Sun Glacier on Mount Merritt. The road passes Duck Lake Road (7.3 miles north of St. Mary), Many Glacier Road and Babb (9 miles), and Chief Mountain Highway (14 miles) before reaching the Canadian border (24 miles). The highway becomes Alberta Highway 2 in Canada.

Driving south from St. Mary, the Blackfeet Highway heads to **Two Medicine, Browning,** and **East Glacier.** Two miles up the hill, stop at **St. Mary Scenic Overlook and Blackfeet Interpretive Loop** for panoramic views of the St. Mary Valley. As the road climbs to St. Mary Ridge through the 2006 Red Eagle Fire, it crosses Hudson Bay Divide, which sends water to the Missouri and Saskatchewan Rivers. Several lanes allow for passing, but within a few miles the road pinches into a curvy, rolling, narrow, shoulderless trek through willow bogs and beaver ponds divided by aspen groves. Turns are blind; take them slowly to avoid cyclists or cows on the road. At 20 miles from St. Mary, turn right onto Highway 49 (closed in winter), a road with more curves than a snake, heading toward Two Medicine (38 miles) and East Glacier (33 miles), or stay left to reach Browning (32 miles).

★ MANY GLACIER ROAD

The 12-mile-long Many Glacier Road (Glacier Route 3, open May-Oct.) is a stunning drive into **Swiftcurrent Valley.** Drive slowly to deal with wildlife, copious potholes, and torn-up pavement. From Babb, the road follows

Swiftcurrent Creek upstream across Blackfeet Nation lands. Watch for bears, particularly around dusk. If you spot a bear, drive by slowly to watch rather than stop and create a bear jam, which conditions bears to be comfortable around cars. Above all, stay in the car for safety.

After the road rises to reach Sherburne Dam (mile 4.8), it follows the reservoir's north shore, crossing into the park over the cattle grate, but you won't reach the park entrance station for another three miles. Check the shoreline for deer, bears, and errant cows straying into the park. Wildflower meadows with early July's pink sticky geraniums and lupine line the road. Scenic stops have views of Sherburne Reservoir and up the valley to **Grinnell Glacier.**

At the end of the road, you'll reach **Many Glacier Hotel** (turn south at 11.5 miles), the picnic area (mile 12.1), and ranger station and campground (mile 12.3). It terminates at Swiftcurrent Motor Inn and trailheads.

DUCK LAKE ROAD

Highway 464, known locally as the Duck Lake Road (open year-round), leaves U.S. 89 at the east end of Lower St. Mary Lake (7.3 miles north of St. Mary, 1.7 miles south of Babb). Locals use this road via Browning for faster access between the park's northeast sections and East Glacier. Although the mileage is longer (53 miles from St. Mary to East Glacier rather than 33 miles via U.S. 89), the straighter

road affords easier driving, especially for RVs. It's also faster: Speed limits reach 70 mph on stretches. The road climbs over St. Mary Ridge, passing Duck Lake at 3 miles. From the top of the ridge above Duck Lake, which is the divide between the Missouri and Saskatchewan drainages, the road heads southward across the Blackfeet Reservation to Browning (34 miles from U.S. 89) through bison and cattle ranches, with Glacier's peaks dominating the western skyline.

CHIEF MOUNTAIN INTERNATIONAL HIGHWAY

A seasonal road, Chief Mountain International Highway links Glacier and Waterton Parks. Its season and hours are those of the Canadian and U.S. immigration and customs stations at the border (9am-6pm daily mid-May-June and Sept., 7am-10pm daily June-Labor Day). With its start 4 miles north of Babb, the 30-mile road undulates over rolling aspen hills and beaver ponds on the Blackfeet Reservation as it curves around blocky Chief Mountain to the border. A few unmarked pullouts offer good photo ops.

As the road rounds Chief Mountain, it enters Glacier National Park. There is no entrance station here, and no payment is required. The road reaches the international border and Chief Mountain border crossing at 15 miles. Passports are required for crossing into Canada.

Sights

ST. MARY RIVER

Between St. Mary Visitor Center and St. Mary Campground, Going-to-the-Sun Road crosses the St. Mary River, a waterway connecting the two St. Mary Lakes. You can park near the stone bridge to take a look. Find larger parking at the visitors center and walk 0.3 mile through prairie smoke flowers to a scenic wooden bridge that connects to the campground. Watch for killdeers, among other

birds. For anglers, this river offers some of the best local fishing. You can drop a line in from the wooden footbridge, but not from the Going-to-the-Sun Road bridge.

ST. MARY LAKES

In pockets left from 1,200-foot-deep Pleistocene ice age glaciers, **St. Mary Lake** and **Lower St. Mary Lake** stand as testament to glacial forces. The lakes collect water from snowmelt and some of the largest glaciers left in the park: Blackfoot and Jackson Glaciers. Their waters meander toward the Canadian border and into the Saskatchewan River to Hudson Bay. With the valley sucking air down from the Continental Divide, frequent winds swirl up large whitecapped waves. See the lakes from Going-to-the-Sun Road and U.S. 89.

ST. MARY SCENIC OVERLOOK AND BLACKFEET INTERPRETIVE LOOP

Two miles south of St. Mary on U.S. 89, the **St. Mary Scenic Overlook** offers a panoramic view of the upper St. Mary Valley, St. Mary Lake, and Continental Divide. Under construction in 2016, the paved, wheelchair-accessible **Blackfeet Interpretive Loop** begins from the overlook's parking area and tours metal tepee sculptures, while signage tells stories of the Blackfeet culture and lands. The loop is shorter than 0.2 mile, and boasts two more viewpoints. It's slated for completion by 2017.

DIVIDE MOUNTAIN

Divide Mountain rises 8,665 feet in elevation, the last in a string of peaks guarding St.

Mary Valley's south. Charred remnants of the 2006 Red Eagle Fire flank its slopes. From the summit, the mountain drops east to St. Mary Ridge, running for miles onto the prairie. The ridge is a lateral moraine, deposited by a Pleistocene glacier that formed the valley. This ridge, along with Divide Mountain, separates the waters flowing into the Saskatchewan and Missouri Rivers.

1913 RANGER STATION

Follow the signs on a five-minute drive from Going-to-the-Sun Road (0.2 mile from the junction with U.S. 89, just south of St. Mary Visitor Center) to the 1913 Ranger Station. A small parking area leads uphill on a three-minute walk to the historic building. Adjacent to it is the Lubec Ranger Station Barn, which was moved here in 1977. With its restored weather-split logs and chinking, the barn is more photoworthy than the original ranger station.

GRINNELL GLACIER

Like all glaciers in northwest Montana, Grinnell Glacier is melting. Located in Many Glacier, the ice field reached its peak size around 1850, when it filled the entire hanging valley under Mount Gould and connected

St. Mary Overlook and Blackfeet Interpretive Loop

with Salamander Glacier. Lateral moraines mark its original size. By 1930, the glacier receded, separating from Salamander and forming a lake at its snout. Today, the ice has thinned and shrunk considerably. See a bit of the glacier with binoculars from the Many Glacier Road, or for a closer inspection, hike to the most-visited glacier in the park.

SWIFTCURRENT LAKE

Originally called McDermott Lake, Swiftcurrent Lake took its name from the Blackfeet term for swift-flowing water, a name that George Bird Grinnell promoted for the area. The lake, however, does not have fast-flowing waters. Located in Many Glacier, its bays attract loons and mergansers. Moose eat the shoreline willows. A beaver lodge sits at the inlet of Swiftcurrent Creek. Enjoy the lake by paddling, riding the tour boat, circling it by trail, or sitting on Many Glacier Hotel's deck.

★ MANY GLACIER HOTEL

Built in 1915, the National Historic Landmark **Many Glacier Hotel** (milepost 11.5, Many Glacier Rd., 406/892-2525, www.glacier-parkinc.com, mid-June-mid-Sept.) graces Swiftcurrent Lake's shore. Listed as one of the 11 most endangered places in the country, the five-story 211-room hotel is owned by the National Park Service and is operated by Xanterra. A $30 million restoration continuing through 2017 straightened the leaning structure, restored the dining room to its historic look, revamped the lobby, rebuilt the historic helical stairway to the lower level, and replaced windows, doors, the roof, siding, and decks. Warm up on a cold day around the huge fireplace in the massive lobby, or lounge on its large deck overlooking Swiftcurrent Lake and a mountainous panorama. Join park naturalists for a tour of the historic hotel: Check the *Ranger-led Activity Guide* for the current schedule.

ALTYN-HENKEL WILDLIFE

Bears congregate heavily in the Swiftcurrent Valley due to abundant food sources. One of the best places to see them is feeding on the slopes of Mount Altyn and Mount Henkel on the north side of the Many Glacier Road. With binoculars, you can see bears, along with mountain goats and bighorn sheep, from the Many Glacier Hotel deck. Rangers set up a spotting scope in the Swiftcurrent parking lot for wildlife-watching.

Grinnell Glacier

Recreation

DAY HIKES

Around **St. Mary,** hiking options are limited to mosquito-ridden beaver ponds, a lake, or a peak scramble. For hiking, most visitors go up Going-to-the-Sun Road or drive 21 miles to Many Glacier where options are plentiful.

In **Many Glacier,** because routes lead quickly to stunning high country, trails are crowded. Most trailheads are accessed from Many Glacier Hotel, Swiftcurrent parking lot, or the picnic area. Although trail junctions are extremely well signed, maps are helpful to navigate the maze, especially trails

crisscrossing Grinnell Valley. St. Mary Visitor Center and Many Glacier Ranger Station have free non-topographic maps of hiking trails in both areas. They are also online (www.nps.gov/glac). Using the Many Glacier-St. Mary shuttle and the Going-to-the-Sun Road shuttles, visitors can do point-to-point hikes on Piegan Pass Trail or the Highline Trail over Swiftcurrent Pass to or from Many Glacier.

Because of dense bear populations and heavy hiker traffic in Many Glacier, trails are closed from time to time to let an aggressive or feeding bear cool off. Check for current trail

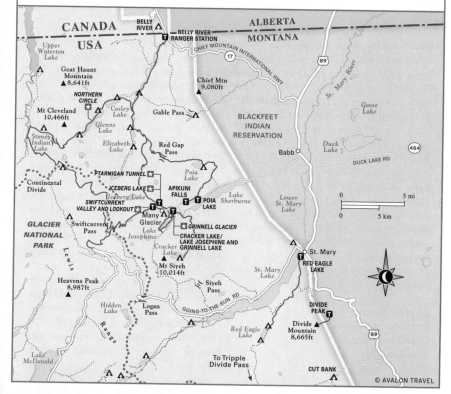

St. Mary and Many Glacier Hikes

© AVALON TRAVEL

St. Mary and Many Glacier Hikes

Trail	Effort	Distance	Duration
Divide Peak	strenuous	5 mi rt	3.5 hr
Red Eagle Lake	easy	16 mi rt	7.5 hr
Apikuni Falls	moderate	1.6 mi rt	1 hr
Poia Lake	moderate	13.2 mi rt	6.5 hr
Cracker Lake	moderate	12.5 mi rt	6 hr
Lake Josephine and Grinnell Lake	easy	2.2-7.8 mi rt	1-4 hr
Grinnell Glacier	moderate-strenuous	11 mi rt	6 hr
Swiftcurrent Valley and Lookout	easy-strenuous	3.6-16.2 mi rt	2-8 hr
Iceberg Lake	moderate	10.4 mi rt	5 hr
Ptarmigan Tunnel	moderate-strenuous	11.4 mi rt	5 hr
Belly River Ranger Station	moderate	12 mi rt	6 hr

status with the ranger station, Many Glacier Hotel's activity desk, or online.

Trails are accessible depending on road openings (Many Glacier and Chief Mountain Highway) and snow. Snow usually blankets trails late October-late May. Most lower-elevation trails on the east side of Glacier melt out in May, and the park service starts installing seasonal bridges over rivers; most are removed in late September. Higher-elevation trails in Many Glacier, such as Cracker Lake, Grinnell Glacier, Swiftcurrent Pass, Ptarmigan Tunnel, and Iceberg Lake retain snow as late as mid-July and usually get snow-covered again by October. Check trail status reports at ranger stations and online (www. nps.gov/glac) for updates.

Hikes are listed in order from the south at St. Mary north to the Canadian border.

Divide Peak

Distance: 5 miles round-trip
Duration: 3.5 hours
Elevation gain: 1,832 feet
Effort: strenuous

Trailhead: unmarked end of a dirt road on the Blackfeet Reservation

Directions: Take U.S. 89 south of St. Mary; turn off the highway at milepost 25.5 at the top of St. Mary Ridge onto the unmarked dirt road.

On Blackfeet land, this hike requires a Tribal Conservation Permit ($10 pp), available at the St. Mary Visitor Center. You'll have to poke around a bit to find the trail (there are several) that wanders through the 2006 Red Eagle Fire. Not only is the trail unmarked, but it's very steep. Only those confident in their backcountry scrambling skills should attempt this. Several routes lead up to an old hexagonal fire lookout on Divide Mountain's northeast ridge. Pick one, scouting constantly ahead for where it goes. If you don't like the steepness of what's ahead, head back down and try another trail.

At the lookout, incredible views take in the St. Mary Valley up to the Continental Divide and prairies to the east. From the lookout, a 45-minute scramble leads to the top of the peak, where you can stand atop the divide between the Saskatchewan and Missouri drainages.

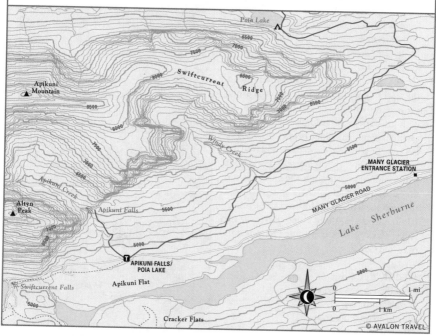

© AVALON TRAVEL

Red Eagle Lake

Distance: 16 miles round-trip
Duration: 7.5 hours
Elevation gain: 480 feet
Effort: easy but long
Trailhead: at the 1913 Ranger Station parking lot in St. Mary

After following an old road for one mile, the trail climbs gently through the 2006 Red Eagle Fire, where wildflowers are madly growing back. The burn continues to the lake, where it started. Watch for bear diggings, where grizzlies rototill for glacier lily bulbs or go after ground squirrels. Red Eagle Mountain looms ahead, and grand views northwest to Going-to-the-Sun Mountain unfold. About halfway, the trail crosses Red Eagle Creek twice on swinging bridges. Between the two bridges, the St. Mary Lake Trail splits off.

In the 1920s, Red Eagle Lake was home to a large tent camp, famous for its fishing.

Today, die-hard anglers hike in with float tubes hitched to their packs.

Apikuni Falls

Distance: 1.6 miles round-trip
Duration: 1 hour
Elevation gain: 570 feet
Effort: moderate
Trailhead: Grinnell Glacier interpretive site, 10.4 miles west on Many Glacier Road (see map p. 145)

Apikuni Falls springs from a hanging valley, which you can see from the trailhead. The short walk starts out across a flat meadow but soon climbs steeper uphill. In July, wildflowers bloom thickly here: geraniums, arrowleaf balsamroot, paintbrush, lupine, and stonecrop. The trail climbs to the cliffs between Mount Altyn and Apikuni Mountain, where the falls drop out of the basin above. Those with scrambling skills can climb a rough trail into the upper hanging valley.

Poia Lake

Distance: 13.2 miles round-trip
Duration: 6.5 hours
Elevation gain: 1,511 feet
Effort: moderate
Trailhead: Grinnell Glacier interpretive site, 10.4 miles west on Many Glacier Road (see map p. 145)

One of Many Glacier's less crowded routes, the trail to Poia Lake climbs through aspen groves and wildflower meadows blooming with pink sticky geraniums to crest the forested Swiftcurrent Ridge before dropping to the lake. Be prepared for manure and trail destruction from the daily horseback trail-ride concession. Pass through the campground and drop to the lake, where spur paths cut through the willows to the beach. The return trip requires a 600-foot climb back over the ridge. Backpackers continue on from Poia over Red Gap Pass.

Cracker Lake

Distance: 12.5 miles round-trip
Duration: 6 hours
Elevation gain: 1,182 feet
Effort: moderate
Trailhead: south end of Many Glacier Hotel parking lot (see map p.146)

If you can stand the muddy, horse-rutted, manure-filled first 1.5 miles, where trail rides travel multiple times a day, the rest of the hike is extremely scenic and not nearly as crowded as other Many Glacier hikes. If you meet horses, step below, not above, the trail to let them pass. At the Cracker Flats junction, leave the messy trail behind and stomp the mud and manure from your boots. Climb up switchbacks into the Cracker Valley, where avalanche paths break up the forested trail and give way to bluebell and lupine meadows in the final stretch.

Once you reach Cracker Lake, bypass the backcountry campground and drop to the inlet for the best lunch spot on the shore. Glacial flour clouds the lake water, turning it a rich milky turquoise. The gutsy take a quick dive in the frigid water. Siyeh Peak, at 10,014 feet, rises abruptly up a gigantic cliff face, a skyscraping 4,000 feet above the lake.

Cracker Lake

Lake Josephine and Grinnell Lake

Distance: 2.2-7.8 miles round-trip
Duration: 1-4 hours
Elevation gain: minimal
Effort: easy
Trailheads: on the south side of Many Glacier Hotel, at Swiftcurrent Picnic Area, or via the tour boat (see map p. 147)

For a two-mile round-trip walk, catch the tour boat across Swiftcurrent Lake and Lake Josephine to hike to Grinnell Lake. For a longer hike, begin from Many Glacier Hotel, following the trail winding around Swiftcurrent Lake to the boat dock opposite the hotel. A

Grinnell Glacier Trails

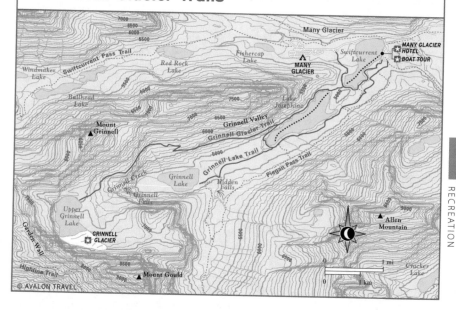

third starting point begins at the picnic area, where it follows Swiftcurrent Lake to that same boat dock.

From the boat dock, pop over the hill to Josephine Lake, where the trail hugs the north shore until it splits off to Grinnell Glacier. Stay on the lower trail to wrap around Josephine's west end to the Grinnell Lake junction. Turn right and follow the trail over a swinging bridge. At the lakeshore, enjoy Grinnell's milky turquoise waters and the falls tumbling into the lake from the hanging valley above. Although you can return to the trailheads via the south lakeshore trail, it is not as scenic, buried in deep forest. Shorten the hike by catching the tour boat back.

★ Grinnell Glacier

Distance: 11 miles round-trip
Duration: 6 hours
Elevation gain: 1,619 feet
Effort: moderate-strenuous
Trailheads: on the south side of Many Glacier Hotel, at Swiftcurrent Picnic Area, or via the tour boat (see map p. 147)

In early summer, a large steep snowdrift frequently bars the path into the upper basin until early July; check with the ranger station for status before hiking. The most accessible glacier in the park, Grinnell Glacier still requires stamina to access, for most of its elevation gain is within 2 miles. For that reason, many hikers take the boat shuttle, cutting the length to 7.8 miles round-trip, or just trimming 2.5 miles off the return. To hike the entire route from the picnic area, follow Swiftcurrent Lake's west shore to the boat dock. From Many Glacier Hotel, round the southern shore to meet up with the same dock. Bop over the short hill and hike around Lake Josephine's north shore.

Toward Josephine's west end, the Grinnell Glacier Trail diverges uphill. As the trail climbs through multicolored rock strata, Grinnell Lake's milky turquoise waters come into view below. In the glacial basin above, you'll spot Gem Glacier and Salamander

Swiftcurrent Valley, Iceberg Lake, and Ptarmigan Tunnel

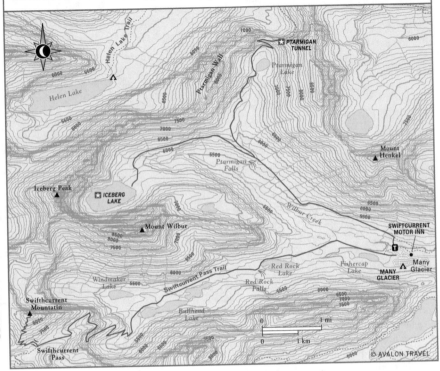

© AVALON TRAVEL

Glacier, both shrunken to static snow-fields, long before Grinnell Glacier appears. The trail ascends on a cliff stairway where a waterfall douses hikers before passing a rest stop with outhouses. A steep grunt up the moraine leads to a stunning view. Trot through the maze of paths crossing the bedrock to Upper Grinnell Lake's shore, but do not walk out on the glacier's ice, as it harbors deadly hidden crevasses.

★ Swiftcurrent Valley and Lookout

Distance: 3.6-16.2 miles round-trip
Duration: 2-8 hours
Elevation gain: 100-3,496 feet
Effort: easy-strenuous
Trailhead: Swiftcurrent parking lot in Many Glacier
(see map p. 148)

This popular trail leads to various destinations along a scenic path dotted with lakes, waterfalls, moose, glaciers, and wildflowers. The trail winds through pine trees and aspen groves as it rolls gently up to Red Rock Lake and Falls at 1.8 miles. At the top of the falls, a knoll provides a viewpoint to scan hillsides with binoculars for bears. The trail continues level through meadows rampant with Sitka valerian in July to Bullhead Lake at 3.9 miles, a shorter destination. Scan scree slopes for bighorn sheep.

From the lake, the trail switchbacks up-hill. It cuts around a cliff face before reaching the pass at 6.6 miles. From here, Granite Park Chalet is 0.9 mile downhill. To reach the lookout, take the spur trail up 1.4 more miles of switchbacks; you'll lose count of them. The lookout surveys almost the entire

glacial lakes of Swiftcurrent Valley

park: glaciers, peaks, wild panoramas, and the plains. Many Glacier Hotel looks minuscule. Enjoy the one-of-a-kind view from the outhouse. For a different descent, drop to The Loop to catch a shuttle.

★ Iceberg Lake
Distance: 10.4 miles round-trip
Duration: 5 hours
Elevation gain: 1,193 feet
Effort: moderate
Trailhead: behind Swiftcurrent Motor Inn cabins in Many Glacier (see map p. 148)

One of the top hikes in Glacier, the trail to Iceberg Lake begins with a short, steep jaunt straight uphill, with no time to warm up your muscles gradually. Within 0.4 mile you reach a junction. Take note of the directional sign here, and watch for it when you come down. On the return, some hikers in zombie-walk mode blaze right on past it.

From the junction, the trail maintains an easy railroad grade to the lake. Make noise on this trail, known for frequent bear sightings.

Wildflowers line the trail in July: bear grass, bog orchids, penstemon, and thimbleberry. One mile past the junction, the trail rounds a red argillite outcropping with views of the valley. As the trail swings north, it enters a pine and fir forest and crosses Ptarmigan Falls at 2.6 miles, a good break spot where aggressive ground squirrels will steal your snacks. Do not feed them; feeding only trains them to be more forceful. Just beyond the falls, the Ptarmigan Tunnel Trail veers right. Stay straight to swing west through multiple avalanche paths. After crossing a creek, the trail climbs the final bluff, where a view of stark icebergs against blue water unfolds. Brave hikers dive into the lake, but be prepared to have the frigid water suck the air from your lungs.

★ Ptarmigan Tunnel
Distance: 11.4 miles round-trip
Duration: 5 hours
Elevation gain: 2,304 feet
Effort: moderate-strenuous
Trailhead: behind Swiftcurrent Motor Inn cabins in Many Glacier (see map p. 148)

Depending on snowpack, the tunnel doors usually open mid-July-late September; check with the ranger station to confirm the status. Traversing the same trail as Iceberg Lake, the route begins with a steep uphill climb before leveling out into a gentle ascent around Mount Henkel. Just past Ptarmigan Falls, at 2.8 miles the Ptarmigan Tunnel route veers right off the Iceberg Trail. The climb goes aggressively uphill for a mile before assuming an easier uphill grade through meadows to Ptarmigan Lake.

From the lake, the route to the tunnel leads up another 800 feet via two switchbacks on a scree slope. Tiny, fragile alpine plants struggle to survive on this barren slope: Protect them by staying on the trail rather than cutting the switchbacks. The 183-foot tunnel, 6 feet wide and 9 feet tall, cuts through Ptarmigan Wall. Walk through for the burst of red rock color on the other side. Admire the trail engineering along the north side's cliff wall and drop down 0.25 mile to see Old Sun Glacier on Mount Merritt.

Belly River Ranger Station

Distance: 12 miles round-trip
Duration: 6 hours
Elevation gain: 745 feet on return
Effort: moderate
Trailhead: Chief Mountain border crossing parking lot on Chief Mountain Highway

A trail used by backpackers to access Elizabeth, Helen, Cosley, Glenns, and Mokowanis Lakes, the Ptarmigan Tunnel, and Stoney Indian Pass, the Belly River Trail attracts day hikers for the views of Chief Mountain and Pyramid Peak in the distance. Anglers also drop lines into the Belly River. The trail begins with a descent down to the valley floor. Look for scratches in the aspen bark where elk have rubbed to remove the velvet from their antlers.

As the trail undulates gently across the valley floor, it traverses aspen groves and open meadows blooming with lupine and paintbrush. At the pastoral Belly River Ranger Station, listed on the National Register of Historic Places, you can envy the backcountry rangers who spend their summers staring at Gable Mountain's colorful strata, the spires of the Stoney Indian Peaks, and Mount Cleveland, the highest peak in the park.

Guides

In Many Glacier and St. Mary, options abound for guided hikes. The National Park Service leads hikes to various scenic destinations mid-June–mid-September, including full-day hikes to Grinnell Glacier and Iceberg Lake in Many Glacier. Some trips combine with boat tours to cross Swiftcurrent Lake and Lake Josephine. Although the hikes are free, you'll need to pay for the boat ride. The park's guided hikes are great for solo hikers to be in the company of others in bear country and to glean tidbits of natural history, but be prepared for hiking in very large groups; some have more than 30 people in midsummer. For schedules, pick up the *Ranger-led Activity Guide* from visitors centers, online (www.nps.gov/glac), at ranger

Iceberg Lake

stations, or at hotel activity desks. For full-day hikes, pack along water, snacks, lunch, and extra clothes.

Glacier Guides (406/387-5555 or 800/521-7238, www.glacierguides.com) leads day hikes and backpacking trips in the park's northeast region. While solo travelers can join the weekly Iceberg Lake hike (Fridays July-Aug., $98 pp), families and small groups can hire a guide (June-Sept., $560 for up to five people) for any trail. The guide will meet you at your lodge or campground in St. Mary or Many Glacier to do hikes in Many Glacier or on Going-to-the-Sun Road. All hikes require reservations and include guide service, deli lunch, and transportation to the trailhead. The company also has three-, four-, and six-day backpacking trips that depart weekly (June-mid-Sept., $190/day), some via St. Mary and Many Glacier trailheads and frequently in the Belly River. Plan on 15 percent gratuity for day trips and 20 percent for overnights.

BACKPACKING

Popular backpacking trails follow historic horse-packing routes from the 1920s in this region, and shuttles aid in reaching trailheads. In June, the Belly is outstanding for backpacking when snow still buries high passes.

Permits (adults $7 pp/night) for these trips are in high demand. Pick them up 24 hours in advance in person at the **Apgar Backcountry Permit Office** (406/888-7859 May-Oct., 406/888-7800 Nov.-Apr.), **St. Mary Visitor Center** (406/732-7751, late May-mid-Sept.), or **Many Glacier Ranger Station** (406/732-7740, late May-mid Sept.). Lines begin forming an hour before the 7am opening. Permits are available until 4pm. Better yet, apply for advance reservations online starting in mid-March (www.nps.gov/glac, $40).

★ Northern Circle
52 MILES

Hike the five- to seven-day Northern Circle in either direction to take in prime fishing lakes and high passes. The loop makes logistics easy. Start and finish at one of five trailheads: Swiftcurrent, Iceberg-Ptarmigan Tunnel, Poia Lake, Chief Mountain Customs, or Goat Haunt.

The classic route is from Many Glacier. Launch up to Ptarmigan Tunnel to drop into the Belly River drainage. Then connect Elizabeth, Cosley, and Glenns Lakes (fording the outlet river at Cosley) to ascend the Mokowanis River drainage. The route pitches up to Stoney Indian Pass and quickly plunges to Stoney Indian Lake, where the wall-less pit toilet takes in surrounding peaks. After descending into Waterton Valley, the trail climbs to the immense meadows at Fifty Mountain. A long day traipses up and down through multiple high-elevation basins along the Continental Divide to the Granite Park Chalet before crossing over Swiftcurrent Pass to return to Many Glacier, exiting at the Swiftcurrent trailhead.

Of the 12 backcountry campsites on or near the route, the best are at the foot of Elizabeth Lake (ELF), Cosley Lake (COS), Stoney Indian Lake (STO), Fifty Mountain (FIF), and Granite Park (GRN). Ptarmigan Tunnel usually opens mid-July, and the park service usually blasts steep snowfields between Fifty Mountain and Granite Park by late July. Get walk-in permits for July, but advance reservations for Fifty Mountain and Stoney Indian Lake are only available starting August 1. Prepare for high-elevation snow in September.

The Northern Circle links the Belly River with the Northern Highline.

Belly River Country

North of Many Glacier, the Belly River is wild backcountry. With no roads accessing the valley, entry is on foot or horseback. From Many Glacier, two routes cross into the Belly: Ptarmigan Tunnel and Red Gap Pass via Poia Lake. Three other trails reach the Belly via other routes: The shortest is from the Chief Mountain border crossing; longer routes go from Goat Haunt over Stoney Indian Pass or from Lee Ridge. To locals, the area is simply known as the Belly.

The Belly is home to the headwaters of the Saskatchewan River, which flows to Hudson Bay. The **Belly River** may have been named for the Gros Ventre (French for "Big Belly") people, and the **Mokowanis River** for a Blackfeet term that refers to a buffalo's stomach. Thirty-three backcountry campsites are strung up and down the two valleys, as well as lakes: Elizabeth, Helen, Cosley, Glenns, and Mokowanis. At the confluence of the two valleys, the historic Belly River Ranger Station, which is staffed in summer, sits idyllic amid aspen groves and fields of wild sticky geraniums staring up at Stoney Indian Peaks and Mount Cleveland, the park's highest peak.

For **backpackers,** the Belly is the place to go in June. Backcountry campsites at the low-elevation lakes open weeks before higher-elevation trails. For **anglers,** the rivers and lakes hop with fish.

Red Eagle Lake and Triple Divide Pass
30 MILES

Plan three days for an out-and-back trip to Red Eagle Lake and Triple Divide Pass, south of St. Mary Lake. Camp at the head (REH) or foot (REF) of the lake for two nights. Anglers should take rods, as the lake has yielded record trout. From the trailhead near St. Mary, the rolling route crosses through aspen groves and wildflower meadows and over two swinging bridges to reach Red Eagle Lake. On the middle day, ford Red Eagle Creek and climb 15 miles round-trip to Triple Divide Pass, a summering range for bighorn sheep.

To extend the trip to Two Medicine (32 miles total, 4-5 days), continue south from the pass on the Inside Trail to Morning Star Lake (MOR). From there, go over Pitamakin Pass to Old Man Lake (OLD) or up Pitamakin and Dawson Passes to No Name Lake (NON). Both routes end at Two Medicine Lake.

The passes are usually snow-free by mid-July, although a few steep snowfields can linger on north slopes. Advance reservations start at Red Eagle Lake in mid-June, but not until July 15 for Morning Star, Old Man Lake, and No Name Lake.

BIKING

Bicycling the east side of Glacier National Park is all about big scenery road biking, as trails do not permit mountain bikes. No bike rentals are available, so bring your own. The National Park Service campgrounds at St. Mary and Many Glacier provide shared biker-hiker campsites ($5-8 pp) on a first-come, first-served basis. The sites have bear-resistant food storage containers.

East-side roads are generally narrow with no shoulders, a challenge for novice riders. Some vehicles nearly push riders off the road. Due to heavy traffic during July-August, riding earlier or later in the day is easier. Outside the park, roads cut through open range; cow herds and horses may be on the road, plus plentiful cow pies. Moose and bears are also common, especially early and late in the day. With bears capable of running up to 40 mph, you won't be able to outride them. Carry bear spray; some cyclists whoop or holler to make noise to alert bears to their presence.

East-side roads are notorious for high winds. Expect strong easterlies. Heading in the right direction produces a nice tailwind; pushing against the bluster is tough.

Scenic Roads

Cyclists riding on **Going-to-the-Sun Road** the 18 miles from St. Mary to Logan Pass have no restrictions. Bicycling the 12-mile **Many Glacier Road** is extremely picturesque, but keep at least one eye on the road for potholes, cattle grates, and a few short gravel sections. Bicycling **Chief Mountain International Highway** 15 miles to the customs station provides sustained climbs and sailing descents while rounding the imposing Chief Mountain. Watch for a few rough gravel patches and catttle.

Blackfeet Highway

Cycling the Blackfeet Highway (U.S. 89) from the Canadian border to St. Mary is easier than pedaling other roads in the area. The undulating road is wider, straighter, and has small shoulders. Riding south on U.S. 89 from St. Mary to East Glacier starts on a wide thoroughfare with big shoulders for a climb atop St. Mary Ridge. But then the spacious road suddenly squeezes into a skinny, curvy ribbon with blind corners and little place to go when large vehicles hog the road. From a cycling perspective, it's a fun ride with the rolling terrain, but blind corners have a tendency to make riders brake for safety and then curse the loss of momentum.

HORSEBACK RIDING

Adjacent to the Many Glacier Hotel parking lot, **Swan Mountain Outfitters** (406/387-4405 or 877/888-5557, corral 406/732-4203, www.swanmountainoutfitters.com/glacier, June-mid-Sept., $45-175) guides one- and two-hour rides departing several times daily for Lake Josephine and Cracker Flats. Half-day rides leave twice daily for Swiftcurrent Ridge. All-day rides (lunch not included) head through aspen parklands and wildflower meadows to Poia Lake or Cracker Lake. This is trail riding; the nose of one horse will be in the tail of another, sometimes in a long string of 15 horses. However, the scenery is well worth the ride. Wear long pants and hiking boots or tennis shoes for these rides. Kids must be at least eight years old. Reservations are strongly advised.

BOATING AND WATERSKIING

No motorized boats are permitted in Many Glacier. Sans motors, only sailboats, kayaks, rowboats, and canoes quietly ply the waters. The public boat ramp on **Swiftcurrent**

a trail ride in Many Glacier

Lake sits adjacent to the picnic area. **St. Mary Lake** permits motorized craft with no horsepower limit plus nonmotorized boats such as canoes, kayaks, rowboats, and rafts. The boat launch is at Rising Sun. Boating regulations in Glacier require boats to pick up permits ($10 for 7-day motorized permit, $40 for annual motorized permit, free for nonmotorized boats). Boaters must show that their boats have been cleaned, drained, and dried to avoid bringing aquatic invasive species into park lakes. Permits are available at the St. Mary Visitor Center or Many Glacier Ranger Station.

On the Blackfeet Reservation, boats can launch onto **Lower St. Mary Lake** via the public boat ramp at Chewing Blackbones Campground (milepost 37.3, U.S. 89, $20 launch fee plus $10 conservation permit). Motorboats are also allowed on **Duck Lake** (milepost 29 on Duck Lake Rd., Hwy. 464) but not waterskiing.

PADDLING

High east-side winds deter many paddlers from the larger lakes. Instead, most head to more protected waters, such as Many Glacier's **Swiftcurrent Lake,** which is less prone to big whitecaps and often affords sightings of moose, bears, and birds. A popular kayak trip crosses the lake and paddles the connecting slow-moving Cataract Creek upstream to Lake Josephine, where a shoreline loop makes a wonderfully scenic tour. Launch this tour from the public boat dock adjacent to Swiftcurrent Picnic Area. Pick up free boating permits at St. Mary Visitor Center or Many Glacier Ranger Station.

Rent canoes, kayaks, and rowboats at the boat dock behind the Many Glacier Hotel. **Glacier Park Boat Company** (406/732-4480 summer, 406/257-2426, www.glacierparkboats.com, daily mid-June-mid-Sept., $15-20/hour) rents boats for use only on Swiftcurrent Lake. Paddles and life jackets are included.

FISHING

Glacier's east side is noted more for lake fishing than stream or river fishing. Inside Glacier National Park, no license is required for fishing, although you must be aware of fishing regulations. Outside park boundaries, visitors on the Blackfeet Reservation need a Blackfeet fishing permit available online (http://blackfeetfishandwildlife.net, $20 one day, $45 three days, $75 season).

St. Mary

St. Mary Lake doesn't support much in the way of good fishing with its raging winds. But it does have lake whitefish, brook trout, and rainbows. For better fishing, head instead to St. Mary River's deep channels below the lake for rainbow trout. The best local fishing requires a 7.5-mile hike to **Red Eagle Lake;** here a state-record 16-pound native westslope cutthroat was caught. Those with serious commitment and willpower pack in float tubes.

Duck Lake

While 8-pound trophy rainbow trout used to be the norm, anglers now pull 16-inch brown or cutthroat trout from Duck Lake's waters. Although you can keep the fish from this stocked fishery, you may find your fishing over within an hour if you don't throw some back. The fishing is better from a boat or a float tube. In winter, ice fishing is permitted on the lake.

Many Glacier

With its numerous lakes, the Many Glacier Valley offers lots of fishing holes. Grinnell, Josephine, Swiftcurrent, Red Rock, Bullhead, Windmaker, and Ptarmigan Lakes all support varying trout populations, but don't be deceived into carrying your rod to Iceberg, Upper Grinnell, or Poia Lakes, which have no fish. Cracker and Slide Lakes are closed to fishing. Lake Sherburne, a dam-controlled reservoir partly on Blackfeet land and

Wildlife in Many Glacier

Many Glacier is regaled as a wildlife-watching area. So where are the best places to spot wildlife? The park service often sets up a spotting scope in the Swiftcurrent parking lot for watching wildlife 5:30pm-7pm.

Bighorn Sheep: Open slopes, pruned of tall vegetation by winter avalanches, make good bighorn sheep habitat. They prefer broken cliffs for protection and meadows for feeding. Use binoculars to see them above tree line on the slopes of Mount Altyn and Mount Henkel. Look for them in the final mile around the moraine on the Grinnell Glacier Trail and in grassy meadows in the upper portion of the Iceberg Lake Trail.

Grizzly Bears: Due to plentiful food sources, Many Glacier has one of the thickest concentrations of grizzly bears in Glacier. They frequent the trails, so make noise to let them know you are there. From the Swiftcurrent Trail around Red Rock Lake, use binoculars to scan the lower slopes of Grinnell Point for bears. From Many Glacier Road near Swiftcurrent Lake, look on the lower slopes of Mount Altyn.

Moose: With abundant lakes, Many Glacier provides excellent moose habitat. Not only can you spot them while driving the road, but also when hiking trails or sitting on the Many Glacier Hotel deck in the early morning. The Swiftcurrent Trail passes three lakes where moose hang out: Fishercap, Red Rock, and Bullhead. They swim across Grinnell Lake and eat water plants in Swiftcurrent and Josephine Lakes.

Mountain Goats: These white denizens of Glacier's alpine find safety in cliffs and adjacent high meadows. In fact, the kids can navigate cliffs within 24 hours of birth. Binoculars are useful for watching them. Spot mountain goats in the upper red cliffs on Mount Altyn and Mount Henkel. They also scamper around the steep cliffs surrounding Iceberg Lake and Grinnell Point.

Pika: These non-hibernating members of the rabbit family collect flowers and greens all summer to dry for winter food. High-elevation talus slopes and large rockfalls with adjacent meadows yield the best habitat. You can find them around Apikuni Falls, and most likely will hear their telltale "eep" before you spot them.

Wolverines: These elusive weasels prefer high elevations near snowfields and glaciers. Hiking to lingering snowfields and ice around Swiftcurrent Pass, Grinnell Glacier, and the north side of Piegan Pass provide the best possibility of spotting them. You might even see pairs hunting together.

partly in the park, supports northern pike. Cataract Creek between Lake Josephine and Swiftcurrent Lake contains brookies, but other creeks in the area don't offer much.

Belly River

Those willing to heft a backpack should hike through Ptarmigan Tunnel or from the Chief Mountain border crossing into **the Belly.** Pools and riffles along the Belly and Mokowanis Rivers, plus multiple lakes provide endless angling. **Elizabeth Lake,** in particular, holds arctic grayling and rainbow trout.

WINDSURFING

Sturdy winds attract a few windsurfers to the bigger St. Mary Lakes, but only the skilled. Wear wetsuits or dry suits, as the water is extremely cold. Launch onto **St. Mary Lake** at Rising Sun after passing a boat inspection at St. Mary Visitor Center. On **Lower St. Mary Lake,** the public boat launch is at Chewing Blackbones Campground (milepost 37.3, U.S. 89). For **Duck Lake,** launch at Duck Lake Campground. Tribal conservation/recreation permits ($10) are required, available at St. Mary Visitor Center.

The Legend of Joe Cosley

The Belly River backcountry is rife with legends of the park's favorite renegade ranger, **Joe Cosley.** A fur trapper long before Glacier became a national park, Cosley trapped animals for hides in Glacier and Waterton and carved his name on thousands of trees.

When Glacier achieved parkhood in 1910, Cosley was hired as the Belly's first ranger. But for Cosley, ranger duties became a vehicle for poaching, even near West Glacier right under the superintendent's nose. He sold hides in Canada and furnished paying clients with big game.

Cosley's mountain man reputation grew due to self-generated legends. He told more than one woman he named Elizabeth Lake for her, said he buried a diamond ring in a Belly poplar, and claimed to have hiked 35 miles between Polebridge and Waterton in 3.5 hours for a dance.

Finally, in 1914, after sending rangers to nab him poaching, the superintendent threw Joe off the payroll. After serving with Canadian forces in World War I, Joe weaseled his way back into the Belly to trap and hunt. Meanwhile, the new 24-year-old Belly ranger, **Joe Heimes,** discovered footprints leading to one of Cosley's caches. Heimes arrested Cosley, who was twice his age. After repeated attempts at escape, Cosley succumbed only when Heimes tied his feet. Heimes made Cosley carry a pack with the evidence of traps and beaver pieces for the long snowy hike over a pass, a drive, and a train ride to jail in Belton (now West Glacier).

In 1929, Glacier saw its most notorious trial. Cosley pleaded guilty but claimed Heimes framed him with the evidence. The commissioner pronounced him guilty with a $125 fine and 90 days in jail. Claiming a fatal disease, Cosley asked for clemency. To avoid a death in his jail, the commissioner suspended the sentence due to Joe's visibly fast-failing health. Friends paid his fine; Cosley walked free.

Two hours later, supplied with snowshoes and trail grub, the cured Cosley hiked over the Continental Divide to his cache in the Belly. Within two days after his trial, he sold 55 beaver, 21 marten, and 22 mink hides for $4,129 in Canada.

For more of Cosley's adventures, read *Belly River's Famous Joe Cosley* by Brian McClung.

Entertainment and Shopping

RANGER PROGRAMS

The park service runs many free programs during summer about natural history, wildlife, and astronomy. Check the current *Ranger-led Activity Guide* or online (www.nps.gov/glac) for schedules.

Park naturalists present 45-minute **evening programs** in Many Glacier Hotel, Many Glacier Campground Amphitheater, St. Mary Campground Amphitheater, and St. Mary Visitor Center nightly at 7:30pm or 8pm, depending on location. Indoor programs include slide shows; outdoor programs feature speakers.

Other naturalist programs take place in various locations. During the day, the park service leads **tours of the historic Many Glacier Hotel.** In the Swiftcurrent parking lot, rangers usually set up a **spotting scope** 5:30pm-7:30pm to watch bighorn sheep, mountain goats, and bears on the hillsides.

Astronomy programs take place at the St. Mary Visitor Center parking lot. **Late night stargazing** (10pm-midnight) happens when weather and dark skies permit. On sunny days, rangers set up a **solar telescope** for viewing solar activity (11am-2pm, July-Aug.).

★ NATIVE AMERICAN PROGRAMS

During summer months, Native Americans feature their talents around Glacier. Look for shows in park lodges, St. Mary Visitor Center, and at campground amphitheaters. Check the *Ranger-led Activity Guide* for the current schedule and location of presentations.

For more than two decades, Glacier's naturalist programs have included the acclaimed **Native America Speaks** program. Once a week, the free 45-minute evening campground amphitheater shows feature members of the Blackfeet, Salish, and Kootenai people. Speakers use storytelling, humor, and music to share their culture and heritage. Catch the programs at the Apgar, Many Glacier, Rising Sun, and Two Medicine campground amphitheaters and Lake McDonald Lodge.

At the St. Mary Visitor Center's auditorium, the **Two Medicine Lake Singers and Dancers** draw standing-room-only crowds for demonstrating Blackfeet dances in full traditional regalia once a week during summer. Traditional, jingle, fancy, and grass dances display different footwork and body movements. For the finale, visitors can join in the Round Dance. Tickets (adults $5, kids 12 and under free) go on sale in the morning for the 90-minute show, and they sell out quickly.

Jack Gladstone, a Blackfeet, presents his **Triple Divide: Heritage and Legacy** (www. jackgladstone.com), which blends storytelling and music into a one-hour multimedia walk through Glacier's history from the Blackfeet perspective. Gladstone has won awards and been nominated for a Grammy. Look for his evening performances once a week at St. Mary Visitor Center.

SHOPPING

St. Mary has a handful of gift shops. Expect to see merchandise heavily branded with popular moose and bear themes. Many Glacier Hotel (milepost 11.5) has a gift shop below the lobby; access it via the helical stairway.

Catch Native American programs at St. Mary Visitor Center.

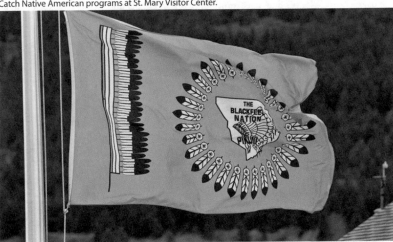

Accommodations

St. Mary has access to Going-to-the-Sun Road and a modern hotel; Many Glacier has a destination location. While St. Mary is convenient for exploring Logan Pass and taking day trips to Many Glacier, Waterton, and Two Medicine, Many Glacier is the best place to be smack in the heart of hiking country. You can park the car for a few days without using it. In both locations, that 7 percent Montana bed tax will still find its way onto your bill.

INSIDE THE PARK

In Many Glacier, **Xanterra** (855/733-4522, front desk 406/732-4411, www.glaciernationalparklodges.com) runs two lodges. These are historic locales with no TVs or air-conditioning. Make reservations starting 13 months in advance. You can sometimes pick up last-minute rooms due to cancellations.

Many Glacier Hotel

★ **Many Glacier Hotel** (milepost 11.5, Many Glacier Rd., mid-June-mid-Sept., $186-528) is the most popular and largest of the park's historic lodges due to its stunning location. Set on Swiftcurrent Lake with access to boating, trail riding, red bus and boat tours, the lodge centers around its massive four-story lobby with a huge fireplace. The guest rooms and suites (some with decks) facing the lake have outstanding peak views. East-side guest rooms get the sunrise, with a unique morning wake-up call as the horses jangle to the corral. A Swiss theme pervades the hotel, with bellhops dressed in lederhosen and gingerbread cutout deck railings.

From being the "showplace of the Rockies," the hotel slipped into disrepair, prompting Congress to allocate $30 million to renovate the National Historic Landmark. An extensive rehabilitation slated to continue through 2017 straightened the structure, repaired decks, replaced windows, and renovated guest rooms by re-enameling old-fashioned claw-foot tubs and adding insulation to the walls, making the guest rooms quieter. But the baths are small; many were created from the original closets. Some guest rooms have tiny sinks and skinny shower stalls instead of tubs. No elevators access the upper floors. Upscaling to 60

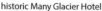

historic Many Glacier Hotel

rooms should be completed for summer 2017. Rooms have phones, and the lobby has limited wireless Internet. A restaurant, lounge, convenience store, and gift shop are on-site. When the hotel opened in 1915, it was considered the epitome of luxury; today that is hardly the case, but what the hotel lacks in amenities it makes up for in historical ambience, dramatic scenery, bear-watching, and convenience to trailheads. Trails to Cracker Lake, Grinnell Lake, Piegan Pass, and Grinnell Glacier depart from the hotel. Other trails depart from Swiftcurrent, one mile away.

Swiftcurrent Motor Inn

At Many Glacier Road's terminus, **Swiftcurrent Motor Inn** (2 Many Glacier Rd., front desk 406/732-5531, mid-June-mid-Sept., $95-175) has cabins and simple motel rooms. Cabins come with or without bathrooms. For austere units without baths, a central comfort station and shower house with lukewarm water awaits. It's similar to camping, but with a bed, heat, walls, and a roof for inclement weather. New Loop "I" cabins, including an ADA cabin, were added in 2014. Guest rooms have no in-room phones. Pay phones are outside the camp store, and wireless Internet is in the lobby; the complex also

has laundry and a restaurant. Historic charm isn't the lure but rather the price and utter convenience to trailheads such as Red Rock and Bullhead Lakes, Granite Park Chalet, Swiftcurrent Pass and Lookout, Iceberg Lake, and Ptarmigan Tunnel.

OUTSIDE THE PARK
St. Mary

St. Mary is located outside the park on the Blackfeet Reservation at the eastern portal of Going-to-the-Sun Road. Lodging in the seasonal town consists of a large resort complex, one older motel, and cabins. Amenities are limited, especially Internet access. In most locations, Wi-Fi is slow and usually only available in lobbies.

RESORTS

A large complex of hotel rooms, cabins, and motel rooms at the entrance to Going-to-the-Sun Road, ★ **St. Mary Lodge and Resort** (junction of U.S. 89 and Going-to-the-Sun Rd., 406/892-2525 from US or 403/236-3400 from Canada, front desk 406/732-4431, www.glacierparkinc.com, early June-late Sept., $90-630) spans both sides of the highway. The resort surrounds itself mostly with parking lots rather than natural landscape, and the 82-acre

St. Mary Lodge and Resort has small family cabins.

complex has shopping, restaurants, a bar, a coffee shop, and a grocery. You can walk five minutes to the park entrance and St. Mary Visitor Center.

St. Mary Lodge and Resort has several different options ranging from value rooms to upscale accommodations. At the high end, the three-story 48-room **Great Bear Lodge** contains modern hotel comforts in chic lodge style with satellite TV (limited channels), air-conditioning, wet bars, mini-fridges, and the only elevator in the immediate Glacier environs. Superior guest rooms include fireplaces and jetted tubs, and all rooms enjoy the sound of the creek and stunning views of Singleshot Mountain from private decks. Third-floor guest rooms have larger panoramic mountain views.

Less-pricey guest rooms cluster in older lodges and small cabins. Great for small families, the **Glacier Cabins** line up along Divide Creek. The cozy, modern one-bedroom cabins include kitchenettes and porch picnic tables for enjoying the creek ambience. The older **main lodge** has tiny cedar-walled guest rooms with small baths. Upgraded guest rooms in the **West Lodge** include satellite TV and air-conditioning. Older **East Motel** guest rooms do not have either, but they allow pets. Due to the proximity to the highway, some of the rooms have road noise.

CABINS

St. Mary has an abundance of cabins. In addition to the cabins at St. Mary Resort, cabins range from rustic to upscale.

Located high on the bluff above St. Mary with spectacular views of Glacier, the five upscale ★ **Cottages at Glacier** (3 Going-to-the-Sun Road E., 406/309-4231, www.thecottagesatglacier.com, mid-May-mid-Oct., $250-490) offer big picture windows with the most dramatic scenery in St. Mary. The spacious two-bedroom cabins can sleep seven and have large decks facing the mountains, gas barbecues, fully equipped kitchens, rock fireplaces, air-conditioning, satellite TV, DSL Internet, and a sleeper sofa in the

living room. The lower rates apply early or late in the season. A two-night minimum is required.

The ★ **St. Mary KOA** (106 West Shore Dr., 406/732-4122 or 800/562-1504, www.go-glacier.com, mid-May-Sept., $95-800) has a variety of cabins, including several large new cabins. The cheapest have no baths or kitchens and require you to bring sleeping bags and use the communal building showers and toilets. The higher-end cabins are homes that come with baths, kitchens, and bedding. Amenities at the KOA include barbecues, outdoor pool, hot tub, splash park, and wireless Internet. **Johnson's of St. Mary** (0.5 mile north of junction of Going-to-the-Sun Rd. and U.S. 89, 406/732-5565, www.johnsonsofstmary.squarespace.com, May-late Sept.) and the **Red Eagle Motel** (16 Red Eagle Tr., 406/732-4453, www.redeaglemotelrvpark.com, May-Oct.) rent a few odds and ends of cabins and modular homes.

Located 2.5 miles north of St. Mary, the **Glacier Trailhead Cabins** (milepost 34.4, U.S. 89, 406/732-4143, http://glaciertrailheadcabins.com, late May-Sept., $160-390) are quiet, removed from the bustle of town and set back from the highway among aspens. The 12 spartan, smoke-free, knotty-pine log cabins maintain quiet without TVs, Internet access, and phones (a phone is available in the office). Each cabin sleeps 2-4 people with a private bath, electric heat, microwaves, fridges, and a porch with a mountain view; one cabin is wheelchair accessible, and one includes a kitchen. Otherwise, cook your own meals in the communal kitchen pavilion, which has an outdoor grill, sinks, a stove, picnic tables, running water, dishes, utensils, and pots.

MOTEL

For inexpensive motels, St. Mary has only one choice, and it's old. Sitting on a bluff overlooking St. Mary, **Red Eagle Motel** (16 Red Eagle Tr., 406/732-4453, www.redeaglemotelrvpark.com, mid-Apr.-Oct., $95-115) has 23 plain nonsmoking guest rooms that have small baths with showers but no tubs. It's a place to sleep rather than lounge, but with great views of Napi Point.

Babb

Babb has two no-frills lodging options. Located three miles south of Babb, **Montana's Duck Lake Lodge** (3215 Duck Lake Rd., 406/338-5770, http://ducklakelodge.com, year-round, $130-200) is a rustic, family-owned lodge for anglers, hunters, and snowmobilers, with Duck Lake one mile away and access to local Native American hunting and fishing guides. Renovated in 2014, nine upstairs guest rooms have shared bath facilities. In Babb, the older **Thronson's Motel** (4013 U.S. 89, 406/732-5530, May-Sept., $100-150) has 14 rooms above the general store with a restaurant across the street. It is run by a fifth-generation Babb family.

Camping

While Many Glacier has only one campground with no hookups, St. Mary has commercial campgrounds with hookups for RVs. If the inside park campgrounds fill up, head to a commercial one in St. Mary rather than up Going-to-the-Sun Road to Rising Sun, which usually fills up first.

St. Mary is convenient for exploring Going-to-the-Sun Road, and it works as a home base for day trips to Waterton, Many Glacier, and Two Medicine. However, if you envision parking the car, setting up a tent for a couple of days, and hiking straight from the campground, then Many Glacier is where you need to be. Cell service is available at St. Mary campgrounds, but not in Many Glacier.

INSIDE THE PARK

The inside-park campgrounds run by the National Park Service (406/888-7800, www.nps.gov/glac) have flush toilets, dump stations, picnic tables, fire rings with grills, and running water. Bring your own firewood; collecting it is illegal. Check online for historic fill times and status to know when to arrive for first-come, first-served campsites. For the summer, make reservations (877/444-6777, www.recreation.gov, $9 reservation fee) starting six months in advance.

St. Mary Campground

St. Mary Campground (milepost 0.9, Going-to-the-Sun Rd., mid-May-mid-Sept., $20-23) has 183 sites sitting in open meadows or tucked among aspens. Sites fill midsummer by 8am. For the best views, the C loop sites stare at Divide and Red Eagle Mountains, but in August heat, they can be hot. Four token-operated showers with lukewarm water are available. A few campsites can fit RVs up to 35 feet, but most are shorter. A trail crosses the St. Mary River on a wooden bridge to connect with the visitors center, St. Mary's restaurants, shuttles, and shops, but it has no access to St. Mary Lake. This campground has shoulder-season primitive camping (late Apr.-mid-May and late Sept.-Nov., $10) and winter camping (free) with pit toilets and no water.

Many Glacier Campground

Located at the end of Many Glacier Road, ★ **Many Glacier Campground** (406/888-7800, late May-mid-Sept., $20-23) packs 110 shaded sites into a treed setting at the base of Grinnell Point. As the most coveted campground in the park, plan to arrive by 7am to claim one of the first-come, first-served campsites in the front loops; back loop campsites are by reservation. A few sites can fit RVs up to 35 feet, but most fit RVs only up to 21 feet. Nearby trails depart for Red Rock, Bullhead, and Iceberg Lakes as well as Ptarmigan Tunnel and Swiftcurrent Pass. From the picnic area, a five-minute walk down the road, trails depart to Lake Josephine and Grinnell Lake, Grinnell Glacier, and Piegan Pass. Across the parking

The Extinction of Glaciers

"Where's the best place to go to watch the glaciers go by?" Locals chuckle when someone who slept through 7th-grade earth science asks this question. Glaciers don't move like a herd of elk, but they are moving ice. Due to climate change, scientists from the U.S. Geological Survey (USGS) estimate the park's glaciers will melt by 2030.

WHAT ARE GLACIERS?

Glaciers are moving ice. A glacier's upper end, called the accumulation zone, piles with snow, compressing into the ice's mass. With a mass of at least 100 feet deep and 25 acres of surface area, glaciers move inches per day here. That movement separates glaciers from static snowfields.

Glaciers may look similar to snowfields, but they aren't. They have crevasses, debris bands, and moraines. When ice inches over rocky humps, the rigid surface cracks into crevasses; some shoot hundreds of feet deep. Bands of rock debris pile atop the ice, carried along in lines that reveal the glacier's movement. When the ice melts, rock rubble is left in lateral or terminal piles, known as moraines. Snowfields lack these features.

HOW MANY GLACIERS REMAIN?

Once glamorous diamonds, the park's current glaciers are relics from a mini ice age that peaked around 1850 with more than 150 glaciers. Since then, the glaciers have thinned, shrunk, broken into pieces, or melted entirely. While early melt rates tended to be slow, the last century saw warmer summers and less snow trigger rapid melting that sped up each decade. A glacier shrinks when the math doesn't add up: when more ice melts annually than it makes. In 2016, fewer than 25 glaciers remained; some may no longer be glaciers due to halting movement.

WHY ARE THE GLACIERS MELTING?

Glacier National Park is a laboratory for studying climate change because the park's higher elevations have warmed at three times the rate of the overall planet. Average temperatures in Glacier now run 2°F hotter than they did in the mid-1900s, and the park now sees 30 fewer days with below-freezing temperatures. Warmer summers with more days above 90°F and shorter snowpack seasons are the norm. The USGS monitors the park's glaciers as climate barometers, using surface measurements, aerial photography, and repeat photography for comparisons between years.

HOW ARE THE GLACIERS MELTING?

As glaciers retreat, they fracture into patches, form lakes at their snouts, or split in two—all actions that speed up melting. In the Mount Jackson area, 27 glaciers once clustered over 5,300 acres; now

lot, Swiftcurrent Motor Inn has a restaurant, laundry, hot showers, and a camp store. If bears frequent the campground, tent camping may be restricted, with only hard-sided vehicles allowed. Primitive camping (mid-Sept.-Oct., $10) has pit toilets and no water.

OUTSIDE THE PARK
St. Mary

In St. Mary, commercial campgrounds have flush toilets, hot showers, picnic tables, laundries, camp stores, Wi-Fi, and hookups for electricity, water, and sewer (and will add a 7 percent state bed tax to your bill). One mile away from the hubbub of St. Mary and on Lower St. Mary Lake, **St. Mary KOA** (106 West Shore Dr., 406/732-4122 or 800/562-1504, www.goglacier.com, mid-May-Sept., tents $45-55, RV hookups $65-90, $5-10 pp beyond two) is on the St. Mary River and Lower St. Mary Lake in a huge meadow where elk appear in spring and fall. Prime campsites flank the river. You can rent kayaks to paddle the lake. The outdoor pool and huge hot tub claim

Grinnell Glacier is fast melting into a lake.

15 of those glaciers have disappeared, and those remaining have broken into multiple pieces. The warming climate caused Grinnell and Salamander Glaciers, once joined, to split into two separate glaciers, and since the 1930s, Grinnell Glacier shrinks every year, while Upper Grinnell Lake, at its snout, grows larger.

WHAT WILL HAPPEN WHEN THE GLACIERS MELT?

Glacier National Park's ecosystem will change; the most obvious will be an increase in forest elevations. More trees aren't necessarily disastrous, but with more forests eventually come more fires. Animals and birds, especially those living on the fringes of their habitat, may seek a food base elsewhere. Heat-intolerant pikas, for instance, may not survive warmer temperatures. Water, now seemingly so abundant, may not shed from the mountains in the sustained runoff from glaciers or at temperatures kept cool by the ice, threatening the survival of cold-loving bull trout and affecting irrigation and salmon runs.

Follow the ongoing study of Glacier National Park's glaciers and see comparative photography at www.usgs.gov. Pick up the *Climate Change* flier at visitors centers and ranger stations for more information.

mountain views, and kids go for the splash park. Amenities include espresso, pet sitting, bike rentals, and an outdoor restaurant (late June-Aug.), which serves breakfasts and barbecue dinners.

Sitting atop a bluff with panoramic view of Glacier from premium RV sites, the older **Johnson's Campground** (21 Red Eagle Rd., 406/732-4207, http://johnsonsofstmary. squarespace.com, mid-May-late Sept.) overlooks St. Mary. It sprawls in a grassy setting broken up by chattering aspens. With 75 tent sites ($30-35) plus 82 RV sites with hookups ($45-60), the campground can usually accommodate latecomers when inside-park campgrounds are full. The bathrooms are old. Amenities include a camp store, laundry, a dump station, a restaurant, and wireless Internet in the lobby. Restaurants and shops in St. Mary are a five-minute walk down the hill.

Red Eagle Motel (16 Red Eagle Tr., 406/732-4453, www.redeaglemotelrvpark. com, May-Oct., $35) has a 22-site RV park

Stay in a tipi at Chewing Blackbones Campground.

with full hookups, but no shower or bathroom facilities.

Babb

Reopened in 2016, **Chewing Blackbones Campground** (3719 Hwy. 89, 406/732-4045, blackfeetcountry.com, June-Sept., tents $20, RV hookups $40-50) sits on Lower St. Mary Lake. Run by the Blackfeet Tribe, the campground has tepee rentals ($125), RV hookups, tent sites, showers, flush toilets, laundry, a camp store, and a boat launch ($20 plus $10 conservation fee). Grass surrounds most campsites. Named for a renowned Blackfeet warrior, the campground hosts handgame demonstrations on Tuesdays and dancing exhibitions with storytellers on Wednesdays (6pm-8pm).

Food

Because Many Glacier has minimal choices, locals staying here for several days will drive to Babb (12 miles away) or St. Mary (21 miles away) to hit other eateries. Nothing beats driving back into Many Glacier at sunset, with ample opportunities for wildlife-watching. Be aware that restaurants and grocery stores in Babb and St. Mary do not serve alcohol during North American Indian Days, a reservation-wide four-day celebration beginning the second Thursday in July. Alcohol sales are also prohibited on other selected days, such as graduation in June. Because of their location in the park rather than on the reservation, restaurants in Many Glacier can still serve alcohol on those days.

For hikers and travelers, sack lunches ($9-13) are sold at St. Mary Lodge, Many Glacier Hotel, and Swiftcurrent; order these a day in advance.

INSIDE THE PARK

Many Glacier has three restaurants, all operated by **Xanterra** (855/733-4522, www.glaciernationalparklodges.com, daily mid-June-mid-Sept.) No reservations are accepted for any of them, so you may have to wait for a table in midsummer. Menus rely on local, fresh, and organic sourcing served with healthy, gluten-free, vegan, and child options plus choices for toppings and portions. Except for Heidi's, all restaurants serve craft cocktails, beer, and wine.

Restaurants
MANY GLACIER HOTEL
In Many Glacier Hotel (milepost 11.5, Many Glacier Rd.), the ★ **Ptarmigan Dining Room** underwent a renovation in 2012 that removed the drop ceiling to unmask the original railroad beams and take the restaurant back to its historic look. Massive windows look out on Swiftcurrent Lake, Grinnell Point, and Mount Wilbur. For the best views to watch the bears, ask to sit near the north windows facing Mount Altyn. For breakfast (6:30am-10am, $7-17), choose between a continental buffet, full buffet, or menu entrées. Lunch (11:30am-3pm, $10-25) serves pasta, salads, sandwiches, and burgers. Dinner (5pm-9:30pm, $10-57) has prime rib, Wagyu steak, duck, fish, or more casual burgers, pasta, and salads. Grab small plates, sandwiches, salads, and pasta in the adjacent **Swiss Room** bar (11:30am-10pm, $10-20).

SWIFTCURRENT MOTOR INN
At the Swiftcurrent Motor Inn complex, **'Nell's** (2 Many Glacier Rd., front desk 406/732-5531, 6:30am-10pm, breakfast and lunch $4-20, dinner $9-23) got a new menu, interior, and decor in 2016, including tables with maps for discussing trails. Named in honor of George Bird Grinnell, the café crowds at mealtimes due to its location adjacent to the campground, cabins, and motel. Breakfast is served all day. Appetizers, sandwiches, pasta, pizza, and salads frame the diner-style lunch and dinner menu, with full dinners of roast turkey, pot roast, pork chops, and trout starting at 5pm.

Groceries
In Many Glacier, you'll find only two small options for groceries. In the basement of Many Glacier Hotel, **Heidi's Snack Shop** (milepost 11.5, Many Glacier Rd.,

855/733-4522, 6am-9:30pm daily mid-June-mid-Sept.) sells coffee, espresso, soda pop, snacks, sandwiches, newspapers, beer, wine, and other convenience-store items. Located across the parking lot from Many Glacier Campground in the Swiftcurrent Motor Inn, the **Swiftcurrent Campstore** (milepost 12.5, Many Glacier Rd., 855/733-4522, 7am-10pm daily mid-June-mid-Sept.) carries groceries, camping and hiking supplies, T-shirts, gift items, newspapers, beer, wine, firewood, and ice. Hikers can cobble together trail snacks and lunches from either store.

Picnic Areas
Many Glacier's small picnic area (milepost 12.2, Many Glacier Rd.) crams with picnickers toting binoculars to scan for bears on Mount Altyn. It's a popular picnic site and can be crowded in midsummer. If you want to roast marshmallows in one of the fire pits, bring your own firewood, because gathering wood is prohibited. The picnic area is also one of the trailheads for hiking to Lake Josephine, Grinnell Lake, Piegan Pass, and Grinnell Glacier.

OUTSIDE THE PARK
St. Mary
RESTAURANTS
Located in **St. Mary Lodge and Resort** (junction of Going-to-the-Sun Road and U.S. 89, 406/892-2525, front desk 406/732-4431, www.glacierparkinc.com, daily early June-late Sept.), the **Snowgoose Grille** looks up at striking Singleshot Mountain. The dining room serves up breakfast (6:30am-10am, $9-15) with omelets and pancakes. Lunch (11:30am-2:30pm, $12-16) includes salads, sandwiches, and burgers, while dinner (5pm-9:30pm, $14-31) concentrates on steak, fish, and vegetarian options. No reservations are taken, which can sometimes mean waiting in line. For hikers and those who need an early start, the restaurant sells bag lunches ($9). For an alternative, you can order sandwiches and appetizers in the adjacent **Mountain Bar** (11:30am-10pm daily), or on warm days sit on

the deck overlooking Divide Creek to watch the sunset with a Montana microbrew. **Curly Bear Café** (10am-8:30pm, $6-10), located in the mini shopping strip near the gas pumps, is the closest thing in St. Mary to fast food, with subs and ice cream. Find espresso at **Glacier Perk** (inside St. Mary Lodge, 406/892-2525, 6am-7pm daily).

St. Mary is home to two family-run cafés, where reservations are not taken and no alcohol is served. The Hilton family runs the **Park Café** (3147 U.S. 89, 406/732-4482, http://parkcafe.us, 7:30am-9pm daily early June-mid-Sept., hours shorten early and late season, $9-20). Homemade fruit pies are baked every morning. Breakfast has pancakes and Benedicts, while lunch and dinner serve burgers, wraps, greens, Tex-Mex, grilled meats, and a few vegetarian options. For a throwback experience, ★ **Johnson's World Famous Historic Restaurant** (21 Red Eagle Rd., 406/732-5565, http://johnsonsofstmary.squarespace.com, 7am-9pm daily mid-May-late Sept., $8-26) serves up most of its daily large-portion specials family style with homebaked bread. Located at Johnson's Resort of St. Mary, the small, old-fashioned restaurant with red-checked tablecloths serves its eggs, bacon, and hash browns all on one big platter for the entire table. Lunch soup shows up in a large tureen; ladle it yourself. Dinner features country foods, served individually or family style.

GROCERIES

In St. Mary, you can stock up on supplies at two grocery stores on U.S. 89. The largest grocery store, the **St. Mary Supermarket** (St. Mary Lodge and Resort, 406/892-2525, www.glacierparkinc.com, 8am-8pm daily June-Sept.), is more like a glorified convenience store with beer and wine rather than a full market. It carries minimal fresh produce, meats, and camping, fishing, and automotive supplies. Shoulder seasons see skimpy fresh fare. The **Park Grocery and Gift Shop** (3147 U.S. 89, 406/732-4482, http://parkcafe.us, 7:30am-10pm daily July-Aug., shorter hours daily late May-June and Sept.) carries Montana microbrews, along with convenience-store items, groceries, fishing tackle, and backpacking supplies. St. Mary stores do not sell alcohol during Blackfeet celebration days, including North American Indian Days (2nd Thurs.-Sun. in July). For big grocery stores, head to Browning.

The Snowgoose Grille is the headliner restaurant at St. Mary Lodge and Resort.

Babb

RESTAURANTS

In Babb, the Thronson family runs
★ **Glacier's Edge Café** (4013 U.S. 89,
406/732-5530, 7:30am-8pm daily June-Sept., $8-16), serving up diner fare for breakfast, lunch, and dinner, including burritos, burgers, and barbecue pork. Plates have big portions, and the huckleberry milkshakes are huge. South of Babb, in a bright purple building with the walls inside covered with license plates and bumper stickers, **Two Sisters Café** (3600 U.S. 89 N., 406/732-5535, www.twosistersofmontana.com, 11am-10pm daily June-Sept., $10-25) serves up homemade fare, with hand-cut fries and big portions for lunch and dinner. Cajun grilled chicken and the Red burger topped with bacon, cheese, grilled mushrooms, onions, and Creole sauce are the house specialties along with monstrous ice cream sandwiches or huckleberry cheesecake for dessert. Montana microbrews, wine, cocktails, and margaritas are served.

Not for vegetarians, the **Cattle Baron Supper Club** (junction of U.S. 89 and Many Glacier Rd., 406/732-4033, 5pm-10pm daily, mid-June-Sept., $25-66) is a meat palace. Up the log spiral staircase above the Babb Bar, once known as the roughest bar in Montana, the restaurant serves dinners where the baked potato isn't the biggest thing on the plate. Be ready to gorge, for steak cuts are humongous and rib eyes even larger. Sides include bread from a 4-generation recipe and hot from the oven. The log lodge pays tribute to Blackfeet history with painted wall stories and a sculpture of a buffalo jump. During midsummer, make reservations.

GROCERIES

Located in Babb, **Thronson's General Store** (4013 U.S. 89, 7am-9pm daily summer, shorter hours Mon.-Fri. fall and spring, closed winter) stocks convenience items, fishing and camping supplies, but no beer or wine.

Transportation and Services

DRIVING AND PARKING

Two-lane roads connect St. Mary with Many Glacier. Find public parking at the St. Mary Visitor Center, Swiftcurrent, Many Glacier, and trailheads.

SERVICES

In Many Glacier, **public showers** ($3), which are often cold to lukewarm, and **laundry facilities** are available behind Swiftcurrent Campstore; purchase tokens for both in the store.

Find **showers** ($5-10) at St. Mary KOA and Johnson's Campground in St. Mary, and at Chewing Blackbones Campground in Babb. St. Mary KOA and Chewing Blackbones have **coin-op laundries.** Find **ATMs** and **pay phones** at Many Glacier Hotel, Swiftcurrent Motor Inn, the supermarket in St. Mary, and St. Mary Lodge.

At the junction of Many Glacier Road and U.S. 89, Babb has a **year-round post office.** St. Mary has a **seasonal post office** at Johnson's Campground.

Gas and Repairs

Two gas stations are in St. Mary on U.S. 89, one on either side of the junction with Going-to-the-Sun Road. Babb has a gas station across from Thronson's General Store. Many Glacier has no gas services. Repairs need to be made by mobile services.

Cell Phone and Internet Access

Planning to use your cell phone in Many Glacier? Keep dreaming. There's **no coverage.** If you require **cell service,** stay in St. Mary. **Limited wireless Internet** is available for guests in the lobbies of select motels and St. Mary's commercial campgrounds.

Newspapers/Magazines

The local newspaper is the *Great Falls Tribune*.

Emergencies

In an emergency, call 911. To contact a ranger, call 406/888-7800. The nearest hospital is on the **Blackfeet Reservation** (Blackfeet Community Hospital, 760 Government Sq., Browning, 406/338-6154).

Rangers like to keep apprised of all bear sightings and encounters, especially bears close to the trail. Report your sightings to the **St. Mary Visitor Center** (at the St. Mary entrance to Glacier National Park, 406/732-7751, 8am-5pm daily late May-early Oct., open until 7pm midsummer, backcountry permit desk 7am-4:30pm) or **Many Glacier Ranger Station** (milepost 12.4, Many Glacier Rd., 406/732-7740, 8am-5pm daily late May-mid-Sept.). Backpackers who need assistance in the Belly can find the **Belly River Ranger Station** in the backcountry at the junction of the Cosley Lake, Elizabeth Lake, Gable Pass, and Chief Mountain Trails.

Two Medicine and East Glacier

Look for ★ to find recommended sights, activities, dining, and lodging.

Highlights

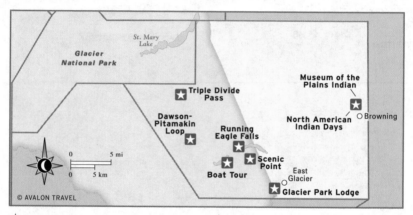

★ **Boat Tour:** Hop on the historic *Sinopah* for the best way to see Two Medicine Lake. The wooden tour boat has plied these waters since 1927 (page 175).

★ **Running Eagle Falls:** Water changes seasonally, plunging from the top and from an underground chute in this falls named for Pitamakin, a Blackfeet woman warrior (page 178).

★ **Glacier Park Lodge:** Gardens lead up to the front door of this headliner hotel, and three-story Douglas firs hold up its massive lobby (page 178).

★ **Museum of the Plains Indian:** Sample Blackfeet history and culture in Browning at this tiny museum (page 179).

★ **Scenic Point:** Hike high above Two Medicine Lake to a top-of-the-world view. Stare across the plains, and if it's clear enough, you may see Minneapolis (page 181).

★ **Dawson-Pitamakin Loop:** Skitter on a narrow trail along the Continental Divide thousands of feet above blue lakes and forested valleys for broad views of peaks and glaciers (page 183).

★ **Triple Divide Pass:** Climb to this scenery-laden, less-traveled pass in bighorn sheep summering terrain (page 185).

★ **North American Indian Days:** This colorful festival in Browning features Blackfeet regalia, horse racing, and rodeos (page 190).

Quiet and removed, Glacier's south-east corner harbors a less-traveled wonderland. It's a favorite part of the park for many locals.

It's away from the harried corridor of Going-to-the-Sun Road with its endless line of cars. With no hotel in Two Medicine, you'll find trails far less clogged on day hikes than at Many Glacier. Just because it sees fewer people, however, does not make it less dramatic.

A string of three lakes curves through the Two Medicine Valley below Rising Wolf Mountain, a red hulking monolith. Its sheer mass is larger than any other peak in the park. Even though glaciers vacated this area within the past 150 years, their footprints are left in swooping valleys, cirques with blue lakes, and toothy spires. Two Medicine Lake, the park's highest road-accessible lake at a mile high in elevation, shimmers in a valley strewn with hiking trails.

Around the corner, the tiny East Glacier burg on the Blackfeet Reservation buzzes in summer. The Great Northern Railway's historic headliner hotel, Glacier Park Lodge, dominates the town with its immense Douglas fir lobby. Train travelers taste the history as

they step from the depot across a garden walkway to the hotel, framed by the mountains of Dancing Lady and Henry. Hiking, golf, Native American and red bus tours, horseback riding, and swimming delight guests. At night, quiet stretches across the sky, broken only by the rumble of trains rolling by.

HISTORY

Two Medicine acquired its name from Blackfeet legends. According to one story, two Piegan tribes planned to meet for a medicine ceremony in the valley. Failing to find each other, they both celebrated independently. In another version, two lodges for the sun dance sat on either side of Two Medicine Creek. Either way, the name stuck.

The 1896 land sale between the Blackfeet and the federal government included the Two Medicine area. Starving and nearly decimated as a nation, the Blackfeet swapped part of their reservation land from the Continental Divide to the current reservation boundary for $1.5

Previous: tour and rental boats at Two Medicine Lake; bison. **Above:** North American Indian Days celebration.

Two Medicine and East Glacier

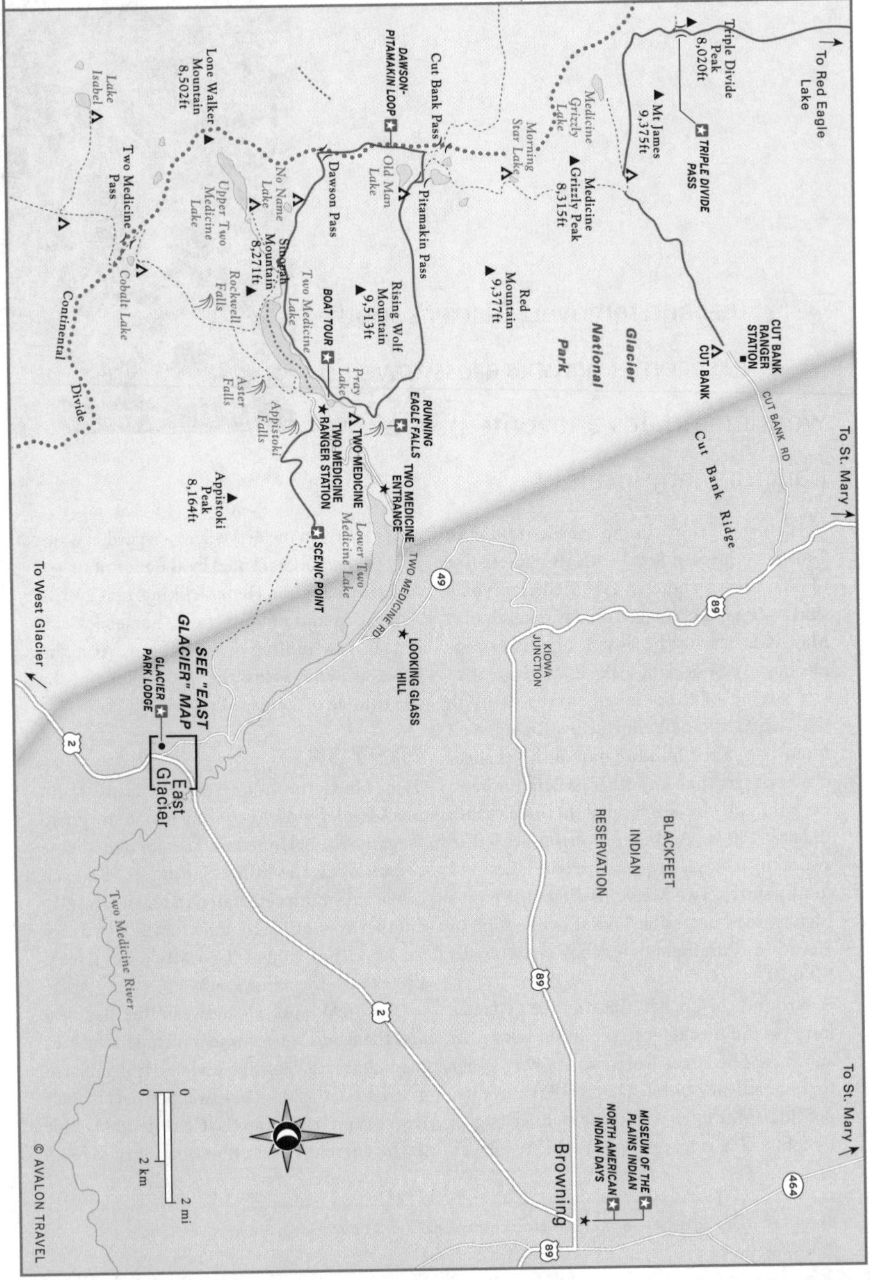

To Red Eagle Lake

Triple Divide Peak 8,020ft

To Red Eagle Lake

Lake Isabel

DAWSON-PITAMAKIN LOOP

Lone Walker Mountain 8,502ft

Cut Bank Pass

Medicine Grizzly Lake

Mt James 9,375ft

TRIPLE DIVIDE PASS

Cut Bank Creek

Medicine Star Lake

Two Medicine Pass

Dawson Pass

Old Man Lake

Pitamakin Pass

Medicine Grizzly Peak 8,315ft

Glacier

CUT BANK RANGER STATION

Upper Two Medicine Lake

No Name Lake

Sinopah Mountain 8,271ft

Rockwell Falls

Two Medicine Lake

Rising Wolf Mountain 9,513ft

Red Mountain 9,377ft

National

CUT BANK

CUT BANK RD

Cobalt Lake

Continental Divide

Aster Falls

Appistoki Falls

BOAT TOUR

Pray Lake

RUNNING EAGLE FALLS

TWO MEDICINE ENTRANCE

Park

Cut Bank Ridge

To St. Mary

Appistoki Peak 8,164ft

TWO MEDICINE RANGER STATION

Lower Two Medicine Lake

TWO MEDICINE RD

49

89

SCENIC POINT

LOOKING GLASS HILL

KIOWA JUNCTION

To West Glacier

SEE "EAST GLACIER" MAP

GLACIER PARK LODGE

East Glacier

2

BLACKFEET INDIAN RESERVATION

To St. Mary

Two Medicine River

89

2

Browning

MUSEUM OF THE PLAINS INDIAN NORTH AMERICAN INDIAN DAYS

464

89

0 2 km
0 2 mi

© AVALON TRAVEL

million, a mere pittance considering the worth of the park lands.

Great Northern Railway began laying tracks in 1891 from Cut Bank to Midvale (East Glacier) and west over Marias Pass. As railroad developer James J. Hill sought means to increase ridership on his new line, he spawned a grand plan: a lodge to greet Eastern guests first arriving at Glacier and several chalets sprinkled in the park's most scenic spots for places to tour. For early visitors getting off the train in Midvale in 1911, a bumpy wagon ride led to a tent enclave with canvas walls and wooden floors at Two Medicine Lake. The successful camp prompted the railroad to add a dormitory and a dining hall. By 1915, guests arrived on horseback via trail, the first leg on the Inside Trail connecting to Cut Bank and St. Mary Chalets, on three-day Park Saddle Horse Company tours costing $13.25. In 1913, the railroad's headliner hotel, Glacier Park Lodge, finally welcomed arriving train guests. Built on land purchased from the Blackfeet, the posh lodge touted high-class amenities: a plunge pool, electric lights, and steam heat. The nine-hole golf course followed 14 years later, but employees were not allowed to play it for fear of upsetting class-conscious tourists.

Great Northern introduced in 1929 the *Empire Builder,* named after J. J. Hill, as a modern train for the Chicago-Seattle trip that packaged in Glacier Park. This is still the name for the Amtrak line. It's the only U.S. train in the Lower 48 that stops at a major national park.

In the wake of the Depression, World War II closures, and increasing auto traffic, the Two Medicine Chalets met their demise. They were torn down; only the dining hall remained, now the Two Medicine store.

Today, East Glacier is home to less than 400 year-round residents. Brutal winters keep it small. High winds accompanied by frigid temperatures pound the town. Winds have blown strong enough to push trains off the tracks.

Blackfeet dancing at the annual North American Indian Days

Exploring Two Medicine and East Glacier

RANGER STATIONS

The **Two Medicine Ranger Station** (406/888-7800, 7am-5pm daily summer), on Two Medicine Road at the campground junction, has current trail information and issues backcountry campsite permits. You can also pick up copies of the *Ranger-led Activity Guide* for park naturalist programs, fishing information, and free non-topographic maps of trails in the area. The ranger station plots bear sightings on a large wall map, which is worth a look just for bear trivia, and sells annual Blackfeet conservation permits ($10 pp) for those hiking over Scenic Point to East Glacier. The **East Glacier Ranger Station** (824 Hwy. 49, 406/888-7800) has a small staff year-round, but it doesn't maintain public hours.

ENTRANCE STATION

East Glacier sits outside park boundaries, but Two Medicine is within the park, with an entrance station location approximately four miles up **Two Medicine Road.** It is staffed during daylight hours daily in the summer.

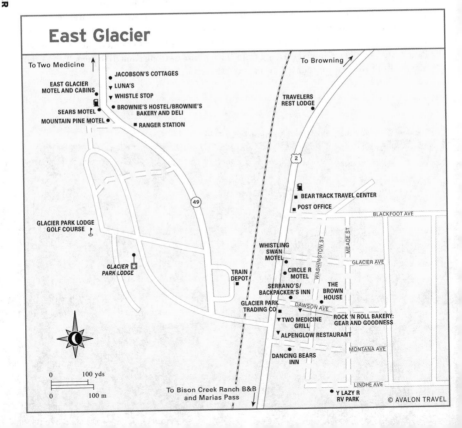

East Glacier

To Two Medicine

JACOBSON'S COTTAGES
LUNA'S
EAST GLACIER MOTEL AND CABINS
WHISTLE STOP
SEARS MOTEL
BROWNIE'S HOSTEL/BROWNIE'S BAKERY AND DELI
MOUNTAIN PINE MOTEL
RANGER STATION

To Browning

TRAVELERS REST LODGE

2

BEAR TRACK TRAVEL CENTER
POST OFFICE

BLACKFOOT AVE

49

GLACIER PARK LODGE GOLF COURSE

WHISTLING SWAN MOTEL
WASHINGTON ST
MEADE ST
GLACIER AVE

GLACIER PARK LODGE

TRAIN DEPOT
CIRCLE R MOTEL
THE BROWN HOUSE
SERRANO'S/ BACKPACKER'S INN
GLACIER PARK TRADING CO
DAWSON AVE
ROCK 'N ROLL BAKERY: GEAR AND GOODNESS
TWO MEDICINE GRILL
ALPENGLOW RESTAURANT
MONTANA AVE

DANCING BEARS INN

0   100 yds
0   100 m

LINDHE AVE

To Bison Creek Ranch B&B and Marias Pass

Y LAZY R RV PARK
© AVALON TRAVEL

The *Sinopah* provides boat tours and shuttles.

Medicine, Cut Bank Creek, St. Mary Lodge, and Many Glacier Hotel and once daily to Chief Mountain Customs and Prince of Wales Hotel in Waterton Lakes National Park, Canada. Reservations are required; a schedule is online.

Bus Tours

For those who have limited time to explore, bus tours go from East Glacier to Going-to-the-Sun Road and Logan Pass. Reservations are required. Rates do not include meals, park entrance fees, taxes, and gratuities. Plan to tip guides about 15 percent.

Historic **red buses** (855/733-4522, www.glaciernationalparklodges.com, daily mid-June-mid-Sept., adults $92, kids $46) depart at 9am from Glacier Park Lodge in East Glacier. Driven by storytelling jammer drivers who roll the canvas tops back when the weather permits, the vintage tour buses are a treat for their historical ambience and the whole-sky views. The full-day **Big Sky Circle Tour** loops around and through the park.

Departing East Glacier or Browning, **Sun Tours** (29 Glacier Ave., 406/226-9220 or 800/786-9220, www.glaciersuntours.com, 8am daily mid-June-mid-Sept., adults $85, kids $45) runs 25-passenger air-conditioned buses with extra-large windows to catch the big views. Tours go through St. Mary to Logan Pass and back. Led by local guides who live on the reservation, the full-day tour highlights Glacier's connection with the Blackfeet. You'll learn the background of peak names as well as the cultural history of the park. The storytelling guides explain plants, wildlife, and geology.

★ Boat Tour

The *Sinopah* (Glacier Park Boat Company, 406/257-2426, www.glacierparkboats.com, early June-mid-Sept., adults $14 round-trip, kids half price) started service on Two Medicine Lake in 1927 and has never left its waters. The 45-foot, 49-passenger wooden boat cruises up-lake five times daily for 45-minute tours (9am, 10:30am, 1pm, 3pm,

During shoulder seasons, staffing is reduced to weekends only or not at all, but you can use the self-pay cash-only kiosk. If you don't have an annual pass, get a seven-day pass ($30 per vehicle, $25 motorcyclists, $15 hikers and bikers summer; $20, $15, $10 winter). Maps and the biannual *Waterton-Glacier Guide* are available.

Even though the Cut Bank Road enters the park, it lacks both an entrance station and a self-pay kiosk.

SHUTTLES AND TOURS
Shuttles

Glacier Charters (406/892-3390 or 800/829-7039, www.glaciertransportation.com, $140-160) runs shuttles by reservation only between Glacier Park International Airport and East Glacier.

An east-side shuttle operated by **Glacier Park, Inc.** (406/892-2525, www.glacierparkinc.com, early June-late Sept., $15-75 one-way) runs several times daily between Glacier Park Lodge in East Glacier, Two

Blackfeet Nation

Bordering Glacier National Park on the east side, Blackfeet land extends from the Canadian border to south of East Glacier, covering 1.5 million acres. Nearly two-thirds of the nation's 16,000 members live on the reservation.

Originally from north of the Great Lakes, the Blackfeet are related by language to the Algonquin peoples. As Europeans landed in North America in the 1600s, the Blackfeet were one of the first nations to move westward, adopting a nomadic lifestyle hunting buffalo in what is now Saskatchewan, Alberta, and Montana. Small bands, each led by a chief, met for summer medicine-lodge or sun-dance rituals before separating for winter.

The loose Blackfeet Confederacy contained three nations: The **North Blackfeet** and **Bloods** gravitated into Alberta, and the **Piegan** to Montana. All three hunted using buffalo jumps, lighting fires to stampede bison over a cliff. (*Siksika*, or "black feet," may have referred to moccasins ash-darkened from these prairie fires.) When the Blackfeet acquired horses in the 1700s from the Kootenai, Flathead, and Nez Perce and guns from French fur traders, their hunting methods altered.

The 1800s brought devastating misery to the Blackfeet. A smallpox epidemic in 1837 killed 6,000 people, two-thirds of the population. Buffalo herds declined, leading to Starvation Winter in 1884, claiming the lives of 600 Blackfeet. By the middle of the 19th century, the first treaty with the U.S. government defined Blackfeet territory as two-thirds of eastern Montana, starting at the Continental Divide. White settlers arrived, rankling the Blackfeet, who raided settlements. To squelch hostilities, in 1870 the U.S. Army sent Colonel E. M. Baker to kill the raid leader, Mountain Chief. But Baker mistakenly attacked Heavy Runner's peaceful band, slaughtering 200 and capturing 140 women and children.

Blackfeet leaders, desperate to help their destitute people, negotiated with the U.S. government for their survival. They sold off portions of the reservation in trade for tools, equipment, and cattle. Glacier, from the Continental Divide to the eastern boundary, was one of these trades, purchased by the U.S. government for a mere $1.5 million in 1896.

Today, the Blackfeet economy is based on some cattle ranching, but 90 percent of tribal income depends on oil and gas extraction. While making strides to preserve the language and culture, the tribe struggles with high unemployment and its accompanying social ills. Browning, the center of Blackfeet culture, houses the small but educational **Museum of the Plains Indian,** which chronicles their history and displays amazing beadwork. In July, the nation celebrates **North American Indian Days** (406/338-7521, www.blackfeetnation.com), hosting regional indigenous people for a four-day powwow that includes rodeos, games, dancing, traditional regalia, singing, and drumming.

BEST WAYS TO EXPLORE NATIVE AMERICAN ROOTS

The Blackfeet once used Glacier for hunting and sacred ceremonies. You can learn about Blackfeet history and culture by visiting Browning to tour the **Museum of the Plains Indian,** to sleep in a tepee at the **Lodgepole Gallery and Tipi Village,** or to attend **North American Indian Days.** Narrated by Native American guides, **Sun Tours** guides bus tours from East Glacier and Browning up Going-to-the-Sun Road to Logan Pass. Take in a **Native America Speaks** program once a week on summer evenings at the Two Medicine Campground Amphitheater; check *Ranger-led Activity Guide* for schedules.

and 5pm) while the captain narrates history, trivia, and natural phenomena. Two trips daily also incorporate a guided hike to Twin Falls (0.9 mile one-way). Purchase tickets at the boat dock, or make reservations by phone with a credit card at least one day in advance.

Hikers use the tour boat as a **shuttle.** It shortens the 10-mile round-trip Upper Two Medicine Lake hike to 4.4 miles round-trip. For a nearly 3-mile jaunt, hike one-way along the northern lakeshore through avalanche gullies under Rising Wolf's flanks and hop the boat back. You can pay half price in cash for one-way return rides on boarding. If too many people are waiting, the boat runs extra trips to retrieve all hikers waiting at the upper dock.

Blackfeet Reservation Tours

Darrell Norman, a Blackfeet member who runs the Lodgepole Gallery and Tipi Village in Browning, leads private **Blackfeet Cultural Historical Tours** (406/338-2787, www.black-feetculturecamp.com, May-Sept., $120-180 for 1-4 people) to buffalo jumps and tepee ring sites on the Blackfeet Reservation. He accompanies up to four people in your car for half-day or full-day tours.

Driving Tours
TWO MEDICINE ROAD

Four miles north of East Glacier, Two Medicine Road diverges off Highway 49 for a 7.5-mile scenic venture up Two Medicine Valley. Beginning on the Blackfeet Reservation, it winds through quaking aspen above Lower Two Medicine Lake. In September, the aspens turn bright yellow, almost emitting a light of their own. **Scenic Point** rises across the lake, and the red flanks of **Rising Wolf** fill the upper valley. Three miles up, you'll enter the park, crossing over a cattle guard, but you won't reach the entrance station until 4 miles. At 5.2 miles, you'll reach the **Running Eagle Falls** interpretive site

before the road climbs into the Two Medicine basin. Look for blue camas in early July. Once in the basin, the peaks of Two Medicine pop out: Sinopah, Lone Walker, and Rising Wolf. After passing the campground and picnic area entrance (7.1 miles), the road terminates in the parking lot at **Two Medicine Lake.** The road is usually open late May-October.

LOOKING GLASS HILL-BROWNING LOOP

From East Glacier, a 49-mile scenic drive twists up Highway 49 and loops through Browning. Because the section from Two Medicine Road to Kiowa Junction is closed November-April, this tour is a summer drive only. State law restricts the size of trailer combinations and RVs to 21 feet on Highway 49, and motorcycles should use caution. Expect chewed-up pavement, potholes, gravel portions, and slumps. As the road climbs to a high vantage point on Looking Glass Hill above **Lower Two Medicine Lake,** 3 miles past the Two Medicine junction, find unmarked pull-outs overlooking the valley for great photo ops before descending to Kiowa Junction.

Drive slowly: "Open range" means no fences. Cattle wander willy-nilly where they please. You may have to wait for cows standing in the middle of the road. They are not speedy creatures, but they can dent your car with a good kick, so give them room. Because the road is narrow and curvy, take it slow. You'll have less chance of putting a cow imprint across your grille.

At Kiowa, turn east onto U.S. 89 toward **Browning** to make the loop through the Blackfeet Reservation. At the Museum of the Plains Indian, turn back to East Glacier on U.S. 2 past the Blackfeet Nation Bison Reserve. From Kiowa, an alternate tour continues north on U.S. 89 to St. Mary along the Rocky Mountain Front on a scenic but narrow, curvy drive.

Sights

TWO MEDICINE LAKE

The largest of three lakes, Two Medicine Lake is the highest road-accessible lake in Glacier, sitting almost one mile high and flanked by peaks rich in Blackfeet history. Its waters collect snowmelt from peaks over 8,000 feet high but devoid of glaciers. The lakes are all that remain of the 1,000-foot-thick ice field that covered nearly 500,000 acres, flowing out onto the prairie past Browning. To explore Two Medicine Lake, jump on the historic *Sinopah* tour boat, or if the waters are calm, paddle its shoreline, swim in its chilly clear waters, or fish for brook trout.

TWO MEDICINE CAMPSTORE

Little remains of Two Medicine Chalets, but the dining hall, now operating as the Two Medicine Campstore, is designated a National Historic Landmark. Built in 1912-1913, the chalets replaced the original tepee camp. The log two-story chalet was once the hub of the small colony, the first stop on the Inside Trail horse trip with the Park Saddle Horse Company in the 1920s. The dining hall hosted Franklin Delano Roosevelt when he addressed the nation from here in an unofficial fireside chat in 1934.

★ RUNNING EAGLE FALLS

A short nature trail (0.6 mile round-trip) leads to Running Eagle Falls, also known as Trick Falls. In high runoff, water gushes over the top of the falls, spraying those standing nearby. But in lower flows, you can see the trick. Part of the falls runs underground and spits out through a cavern halfway down the cliff face. Running Eagle, the Blackfeet name for the falls, honors a female warrior named Pitamakin who had her vision quest here. She gained renown for stealing horses from the Kootenai but was eventually killed during a raid.

★ GLACIER PARK LODGE

In East Glacier, **Glacier Park Lodge** (1 Midvale Rd., 406/892-2525 from US or 403/236-3400 from Canada, front desk 406/226-5600, www.glacierparkinc.com) stands as the headliner hotel for the historic chain of Great Northern hostelries built throughout Glacier. Set within the Blackfeet Reservation, the 155-room hotel, built in 1915, started its life providing train visitors with a first taste of Glacier. Since the advent of Going-to-the-Sun Road, additional avenues into the park stole some of the lodge's thunder. Today, the hotel is listed on the National Register of Historic Places. Even if you are not staying here, walk the gardens leading up to the front door and lounge in its massive lobby

Running Eagle Falls

Rising Wolf

The most prominent feature in Two Medicine Valley is the hulking 9,513-foot **Rising Wolf Mountain.** It is named for the first person of European descent to meet the Blackfeet. Born Hugh Monroe in Quebec, Canada, in 1798, the 16-year-old traveled west as an apprentice for the Hudson's Bay Company.

With an intense interest in the Indians, he was sent to live with the Small Robes band of Piegans, a tribe of the Blackfeet nation, to learn their language and to find beaver-trapping territory. The band's chief, **Lone Walker,** took a liking to the congenial Monroe. After several seasons with the Piegans, Monroe married **Sinopah,** Lone Walker's daughter, and lived permanently with them.

When officially admitted to the band, Monroe was given the name Rising Wolf. Despite the lack of written records, it is presumed that Monroe was the first person of European descent to set eyes on St. Mary Lake and much of Glacier's eastern lands. He served as a guide and interpreter for territorial survey teams and early reconnaissance of Glacier National Park. He later left the Hudson's Bay Company for the American Fur Company, which established trading posts on the Marias River in Blackfeet country.

While there is some discrepancy as to Monroe's birth date, it is apparent he lived to a ripe old age, even after losing sight in one eye in a fight with a Sioux. He died in 1892, just as Great Northern Railway laid tracks over Marias Pass. Many of Monroe's descendants still live on the Blackfeet Reservation. Lone Walker Peak sits at the head of Upper Two Medicine Lake; Sinopah rises straight out of Two Medicine Lake opposite Rising Wolf.

held up by 500- to 800-year-old Douglas firs. Peruse the historical photo display chronicling the hotel's glory days.

BLACKFEET SENTRIES

Blackfeet artist Jay Laber gives new life to garbage in what he calls "reborn Rez Wrecks." Using farm tools, jewelry, hubcaps, and barbwire, he sculpted a not-to-be-missed sculpture series. The *Blackfeet Reservation Sentries* are posted on the reservation's four boundaries. Each pair of life-size sentries rides atop horses. Posted in East Glacier, one pair guards the reservation's western entrance (U.S. 2, 0.2 mile west of town).

BLACKFEET NATION BISON RESERVE

While driving between East Glacier and Browning, you may catch sight of the buffalo herd managed by the Blackfeet. Bison provided food, shelter, and clothing for the nomadic Blackfeet until the buffalo were exterminated in the 1800s.

★ MUSEUM OF THE PLAINS INDIAN

Located adjacent to the roundabout at U.S. 2 and 89 in Browning, the **Museum of the Plains Indian** (406/338-2230, www.blackfeetcountry.com, 9am-5pm Tues.-Sat. June-Sept., adults $5, seniors $4, kids $1, under age 6 free, cash only; 10am-4:30pm Mon.-Fri. Oct.-May, all ages free winter) is a tiny but informative center for Blackfeet culture and history. Displays cluster phenomenal beadwork, leather, tools, and clothing to tell the story of the Northern Plains Indians. Seeing the life-size beaded ceremonial regalia is worth the price of admission. The museum also exhibits contemporary artists and craftspeople.

Recreation

DAY HIKES

Hiking at Two Medicine is in a class by itself. Except for a few short hikes from the lake's upper boat dock, hikers here find solitude even on the busiest summer days. For hikes on reservation land (those leaving directly from East Glacier or the latter half of the Scenic Point-East Glacier trail), a Blackfeet recreation permit ($10) is required, available at the Two Medicine Ranger Station or Bear Track Travel Center (Exxon gas station) in East Glacier.

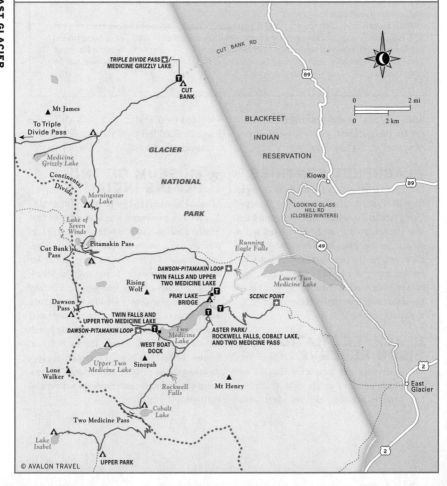

Two Medicine and East Glacier Hikes

© AVALON TRAVEL

Trail	Effort	Di	
Scenic Point	moderate-strenuous	7.4 mi	
Aster Park	easy	3.8 mi rt	
Rockwell Falls, Cobalt Lake, and Two Medicine Pass	easy-strenuous	6.8-15.8 mi rt	
Two Medicine Lake Loop, Twin Falls, and Upper Two Medicine Lake	easy-moderate	2-10.7 mi rt	1-5
Dawson-Pitamakin Loop	strenuous	15.3 or 17.6 mi	7-9 hr
Medicine Grizzly Lake	moderate	12 mi rt	6 hr
Triple Divide Pass	strenuous	14.8 mi rt	7.5 hr

With a maze of trail junctions breaking off the north-shore and south-shore Two Medicine Lake trails, the park's non-topographic trail map can be helpful. Find these at the ranger station and the Glacier Park Lodge activity desk. For longer hikes, such as the Dawson-Pitamakin Loop, take a good topographic map; you can buy one in the Two Medicine Campstore.

In Two Medicine, hikers use the tour boat as a shuttle to prune miles off hikes and get farther into the backcountry faster. Glacier Park, Inc. also runs a shuttle from Glacier Park Lodge to Two Medicine for hiking; the shuttles arrive in time to catch the boat across Two Medicine Lake.

Two Medicine trailheads usually can be accessed mid-May-October, or as long as the road is open. Lower-elevation trails melt out by late May, but higher elevations retain snow through June. Use caution on steep snowfields in early summer; use ice axes for crossing high-angled snow slopes. Seasonal bridges are usually installed in May and removed in late September. Consult the ranger station or online (www.nps.gov/glac) for trail status updates.

★ Scenic Point

Distance: 7.4 miles round-trip
Duration: 4 hours
Elevation gain: 2,124 feet
Effort: moderate-strenuous
Trailhead: milepost 6.9 up Two Medicine Road (see map p. 182)

Scenic Point is one short climb with big scenery. The trail launches up through a thick subalpine fir forest. A short side jaunt en route allows a peek at Appistoki Falls. As switchbacks line up like dominoes, stunted firs give way to silvery dead and twisted limber pines. Broaching the ridge, the trail enters seemingly barren alpine tundra. Only alpine bluebells and pink mats of several-hundred-year-old moss campion cower in crags.

The trail traverses a talus slope (avoid the early summer steep snowfield by climbing a worn path that goes above it) before descending to Scenic Point. To reach the actual Scenic Point above the trail, cut off at the sign, stepping on rocks to avoid crushing fragile alpine plants. At the top, views plunge several thousand feet straight down to Lower Two Medicine Lake and across the plains. Return the way you came, or drop seven miles to East Glacier, passing outside the park boundary,

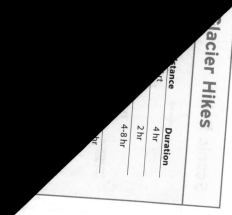

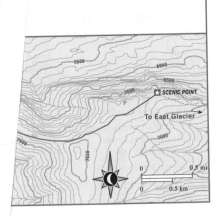

...available at the ranger station.

Aster Park

Distance: 3.8 miles round-trip
Duration: 2 hours
Elevation gain: 610 feet
Effort: easy
Trailhead: adjacent to Two Medicine boat dock (see map p. 184)

Beginning on the South Shore Trail, Aster Park is reached via a spur trail just past Aster Creek. About 1.2 miles southwest of the boat dock, turn left at the signed junction and follow the trail past Aster Falls as it switchbacks up to a flower-covered knoll. This overlook provides grand views of Two Medicine Lake and Rising Wolf.

Rockwell Falls, Cobalt Lake, and Two Medicine Pass

Distance: 6.8-15.8 miles round-trip
Duration: 4-8 hours
Elevation gain: minimal-2,518 feet
Effort: easy-strenuous
Trailhead: adjacent to Two Medicine boat dock

Follow the gentle South Shore Trail along Two Medicine Lake past beaver ponds and bear-scratched trees to Paradise Creek, crossing on a swinging bridge. At 2.3 miles, turn left at the signed junction. The trail wanders through avalanche paths with uprooted trees shredded like toothpicks. At 3.4 miles, you reach Rockwell Falls. Spur trails explore the falls.

Continuing on to Cobalt Lake, the trail climbs up several switchbacks into an upper basin, crossing the creek. It ascends at a moderate pitch for the last 2 miles. Tucked in the uppermost corner of the basin, Cobalt Lake sits below mountain-goat cliffs.

Another 2.2 miles climbs above the tree line through alpine tundra along the windblown Two Medicine Pass. From the high point atop Chief Lodgepole Mountain, you'll stare straight down a dizzying drop to Cobalt Lake with Two Medicine Lake in the distance.

Two Medicine Lake Loop, Twin Falls, and Upper Two Medicine Lake

Distance: 2-10.7 miles round-trip
Duration: 1-5 hours
Elevation gain: 0-424 feet
Effort: easy-moderate
Trailhead: North Shore Two Medicine Lake Trailhead at Pray Lake Bridge in Two Medicine Campground, South Shore Two Medicine Lake Trailhead near boat launch, Two Medicine Lake west boat dock (see map p. 184)

Two Medicine and Upper Two Medicine Lake are a set of subalpine lakes formed by the immense Two Medicine Glacier. As an added

hiker on Scenic Point Trail

Trailhead, connecting the two trailheads with 0.8 mile of road walking. Other routes vary depending on starting trailheads, ending points, and whether or not you opt to use the Two Medicine Lake boat as a shuttle. Taking the boat round-trip across the lake makes for the shortest hikes (2 miles round-trip for Twin Falls and 4.2 miles round-trip for Upper Two-Medicine Lake at 4.2 miles). Hiking the North Shore Trail, Twin Falls, and Upper Two Medicine Lake to end at the west boat dock for a one-way shuttle (pay cash when boarding, $7 adults, half-price for children) across the lake makes for mid-sized hikes (4.6 miles for Twin Falls and 7.2 miles for Upper Two Medicine Lake). All trail junctions have signage, but maps help with clarifying routes.

★ Dawson-Pitamakin Loop

Distance: 15.3 or 17.6 miles
Duration: 7-9 hours
Elevation gain: 2,909 feet
Effort: strenuous
Trailhead: Two Medicine Lake west boat dock, or Pray Lake Bridge in Two Medicine Campground (see map p. 184)

Although this loop can be done from either direction, both with the same elevation gain up to 8,000 feet, the approach to Dawson Pass is much steeper than to Pitamakin Pass. It crams all the elevation gain within a shorter distance, while Pitamakin Pass spreads it out over more than double the miles. So pick your route based on your preference or aversion to uphill grunts and knee-pounding descents. Taking the Two Medicine boat one direction or the other shortens the route to 15.3 miles.

In its loop around Rising Wolf, the route actually crosses three passes: Pitamakin, Cut Bank, and Dawson. The latter two passes have frequent winds that are sometimes strong enough to knock you off-balance. Much of the route crosses through bighorn sheep summering terrain, offering opportunities to see new lambs. Going counterclockwise from the Pray Lake Bridge in Two Medicine Campground, the trail climbs the southeast

treat for hikers, the trail also takes in Twin Falls, a double flume of cascades. The North Shore and South Shore Trails connect at the west end of Two Medicine Lake to form the loop, a route that cuts through forest, avalanche chutes, huckleberry bushes, and meadows. The South Shore Trail takes in beaver ponds, a swinging bridge over Paradise Creek, and the precipitous slopes of Mount Sinopah, while the North Shore Trail trots along the base of Rising Wolf, the biggest peak in the area, and captures views of Pumpelly Pillar. A spur trail at the west end of the lake leads to Twin Falls and Upper Two Medicine Lake below Lone Walker Mountain. In early summer, water floods the upper lake's beach, leaving only a brushy shoreline. For lunch, help maintain the safety of those sleeping in the backcountry campground by sitting in the cooking area to eat.

To hike the Two Medicine Lake Loop, Twin Falls, and Upper Two Medicine Lake (10.7 miles), go either direction starting at the North Shore Trailhead or South Shore

Two Medicine Lake Trails

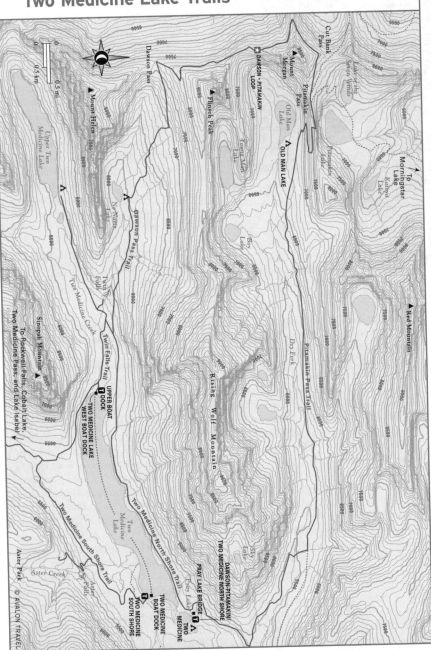

0   0.5 km
0   0.5 mi

Mount Helen

Upper Two
Medicine Lake

Dawson Pass

DAWSON-PITAMAKIN
LOOP

Mount
Morgan

Cut Bank
Pass

Pitamakin
Pass

Old Man
Lake

Lake of the
Seven Winds

Flinsch Peak

Young Man
Lake

OLD MAN LAKE

To
Morningstar
Lake

Pitamakin
Lake

Katoya
Lake

Dawson Pass Trail

No Name
Lake

Boy
Lake

Pitamakin Pass Trail

Dry Fork

Red Mountain

Twin Falls
Twin Falls Trail

Two Medicine Creek

Sinopah Mountain

Rising Wolf Mountain

To Rockwell Falls, Cobalt Lake,
Two Medicine Pass, and Lake Isabel

UPPER BOAT
DOCK

TWO MEDICINE LAKE
WEST BOAT DOCK

Two Medicine North Shore Trail

Sky
Lake

DAWSON-PITAMAKIN/
TWO MEDICINE NORTH SHORE

PRAY LAKE BRIDGE

Two
Medicine Lake

Two Medicine South Shore Trail

Aster Park

Aster Creek

Aster
Falls

TWO MEDICINE
BOAT DOCK

TWO MEDICINE
SOUTH SHORE

Two Lake

TWO
MEDICINE

© AVALON TRAVEL

Flinsch Peak on the Dawson-Pitamakin Loop Trail

flank of Rising Wolf and drops to cross Dry Fork Creek before ascending the valley through forests and meadows to Old Man Lake junction at mile 6.1. The lake contains cutthroat trout that will steal flies off an angler's lines. From the lake, climb switchbacks to Pitamakin Pass at mile 7.6 to cross the narrow arête perched 700 feet above Pitamakin Lake. The climb continues through alpine tundra overlooking Lake of the Seven Winds to reach the high point at the south end of Cut Bank Pass. A top-of-the-world traverse heads south to Dawson Pass at 10.9 miles. Those with a fear of heights will be uncomfortable, but it's the best part of the trail, walking a tightrope between vertigo and soaring. Midway, between Mount Morgan and Flinsch Peak, the trail overlooks Old Man Lake and Dry Fork Valley. From Dawson Pass, the trail plunges to the North Shore Trail, at mile 14.3, along Two Medicine Lake. Go left for 3.3 miles to complete the loop or go right, and then left at all junctions, to reach the boat dock in 1 mile.

Medicine Grizzly Lake

Distance: 12 miles round-trip
Duration: 6 hours
Elevation gain: 540 feet
Effort: moderate
Trailhead: terminus of Cut Bank Road
Directions: Locate the signed Cut Bank Road six miles north of Kiowa Junction on U.S. 89. Follow the narrow dirt road over cattle grates into the park and past the ranger station. The trailhead is about four miles up, just before the campground.

Fewer people populate this trail due to its off-the-beaten-path location. For anglers, Medicine Grizzly Lake harbors 12-inch rainbows, but expect to battle a brushy shoreline for casting. Check with the ranger station before leaving, as bear activity frequently closes the lake and its spur trail.

The trail follows Atlantic Creek up a forested drainage to a signed junction at 4 miles. Turn right, climbing past the Atlantic Creek Campground for 0.6 mile to the junction for the lake or Triple Divide Pass. Continue straight for 1.4 miles to reach Medicine Grizzly Lake, set below high cliffs of the Continental Divide.

★ Triple Divide Pass

Distance: 14.8 miles round-trip
Duration: 7.5 hours
Elevation gain: 2,223 feet
Effort: strenuous
Trailhead: terminus of Cut Bank Road
Directions: Locate the signed Cut Bank Road six miles north of Kiowa Junction on U.S. 89. Follow the narrow dirt road over cattle grates into the park and past the ranger station. The trailhead is about four miles up, just before the campground.

The less-visited Cut Bank location puts fewer people on this trail than Two Medicine trails. The trail is part of the historic Inside Trail that connects Two Medicine and St. Mary. From the trailhead in a meadow, the easygoing route follows Atlantic Creek up a forested drainage to a signed junction (4 miles). Turn right, ascending past the Atlantic Creek Campground for 0.6 mile to a second junction. Turn right to begin the climb to the pass.

Soon the trail bursts out of the trees, traversing a rocky face below Mount James as it looks down on Medicine Grizzly Lake. After winding into a large bowl, look for bighorn sheep that summer here. The pass tucks at the base of Triple Divide Peak, a three-way continental watershed to the Pacific Ocean, Atlantic Ocean, and Hudson Bay. The pass actually stands on the split between the Saskatchewan and Missouri River drainages, beginning here as Hudson Bay Creek and Atlantic Creek.

Guides

The National Park Service guides free hikes (mid-June-mid-Sept.) to a variety of destinations in Two Medicine: Upper Two Medicine Lake, Scenic Point, Dawson Pass, Rockwell Falls, and Cobalt Lake, as well as a daily boat ride and hike to Twin Falls. (The hike is free, but you still need to pay for the boat ride.) Grab the *Ranger-led Activity Guide* from the ranger station for the current schedule.

Glacier Guides (406/387-5555 or 800/521-7238, www.glacierguides.com) leads a weekly group hike up Scenic Point. The group meets at its office in West Glacier; transportation, lunch, snacks, and guiding are included in the rate (Sat., mid-June-late Sept., $98 pp). Bring your pack, sunscreen, insect repellent, water, and extra clothes. You can also hire a guide ($560 for 1-5 people) to meet you in East Glacier or Two Medicine for a guided hike. The guide service also has 3-6-day backpacking trips (June-mid-Sept., $190/day) that depart weekly, some on routes out of Two Medicine. Reservations are mandatory.

BACKPACKING

Two Medicine trails offer short trips to lakes perfect for children and longer, high-elevation treks for those looking for higher challenges. Pick up permits (adults $7 pp/night) 24 hours in advance in person at the **Two Medicine Ranger Station** (7am-5pm daily summer), **Apgar Backcountry Permit Office** (406/888-7859 daily May-Oct., 406/888-7800 Nov.-Apr.), or **St. Mary Visitor Center** (406/732-7751, daily late May-early Oct.). For

advance reservations, apply online starting in mid-March (www.nps.gov/glac, $40).

Dawson-Pitamakin Loop
18.4-32 MILES

Although this route can be done as a day hike, you can also stretch it out to make a backpacking trip of it. The Dawson-Pitamakin Loop takes a top-of-the-world Continental Divide traverse between high passes through bighorn sheep summering habitat and alpine tundra. Hike this loop in either direction, starting from the trailhead at Two Medicine Campground. For an 18.4-mile, three-day trip, camp a night at Old Man Lake (OLD) and a night at No Name Lake (NON). For four days and 25 miles, add a night at Morning Star Lake (MOR) in the middle, but be prepared for the plunge to the lake and a 2,000-foot climb back up the next day. The route is snow-free some summers by early July, but advance reservations are not available until July 15.

To extend this hike up the historic Inside Route (32 miles total, 4-5 days), head north from Pitamakin Pass to Morning Star Lake (MOR), Triple Divide Pass, and Red Eagle Lake (REH or REF) to reach St. Mary. The east-side shuttle aids in returning to your vehicle.

Cobalt Lake and Lake Isabel
28-31 MILES

Cobalt Lake and Lake Isabel anchor both sides of the lofty Two Medicine Pass. A 28-mile, four-day backpacking trip leads to prime fishing at Lake Isabel with utter solitude. The long trek across Two Medicine Pass goes through alpine tundra surrounded by jagged peaks; it's worth doing both directions. Camp on the first and third nights at Cobalt Lake (COB) and the second night at Lake Isabel (ISA). Snow can melt from the route by mid-July, allowing for walk-in permits, but advance reservations are not available for Cobalt until August 1.

A one-night trip to Cobalt is a good destination for kids. An alternative point-to-point route from Isabel descends down Park Creek 17 miles to Essex with or without an additional night at Lower Park camp (PAR); the

31-mile route avoids the return climb over Two Medicine Pass, but requires a shuttle.

BIKING

Bicycling around the park's southeast corner is usually restricted to narrow, curvy, shoulderless roadways. Be prepared to have large RVs nearly shove you off the road, simply due to their size in comparison to the skimpy pavement. It's an area where you may encounter bears on the roadway, especially on Two Medicine Road; on Highway 49, with open range, you can round a corner into a small herd of cows. For some reason, no matter which direction you're riding, a strong headwind always blasts. Since mountain biking is not permitted on trails within Glacier, riding is restricted to roadways and, for kids, the campground loops. Bicyclists do day tours from East Glacier to Two Medicine Lake and back. Bike rentals are not available.

For bicyclists, Two Medicine Campground has shared hiker-biker campsites ($5-8 pp). These have bear-resistant food storage containers on-site.

HORSEBACK RIDING

Across the street from Glacier Park Lodge on Highway 49, **Glacier Gateway Trailrides**

(406/226-4408 or off-season 406/338-5560, June-early Sept., $35-190) leads trail rides and cowboy-style horseback rides; the latter tour cross-country rather than riding single file. Led by Native American guides, the tours roam outside Glacier National Park on adjacent Blackfeet Reservation land. Rides wander along Two Medicine River Gorge through aspens and blooms of early season shooting stars and late summer lupine at the foot of the park's front range. Rides lasting 1-3 hours depart twice daily. Those dreaming of riding the open range rather than riding head-to-tail can take a full-day ride (minimum six people) to two buffalo jumps. Wear long pants and sturdy shoes, such as hiking boots or tennis shoes. Kids must be at least seven years old and have some experience riding. Reservations are recommended, especially in midsummer.

BOATING AND PADDLING

Two Medicine is one of the windiest lakes in the park. Boaters need to keep an eye on waves; if whitecaps pop up, paddlers should consider getting off the lake. Two Medicine Road terminates at the public boat ramp, so it's easy to find. Hand-powered craft and up to

Bike on Two Medicine Road.

Leave No Trace

To keep Glacier pristine, visitors to this unique park need to take an active role in maintaining its well-being.

- **Plan ahead and prepare.** Hiking in Glacier's backcountry is inherently risky. Three miles here may be much harder than three miles through your neighborhood park back home. Choose appropriate routes for mileage and elevation gain with this in mind, and carry hiking essentials.

- **Travel and camp on durable surfaces.** In both front-country and backcountry campgrounds, camp in designated sites. Protect fragile plants by staying on the trail, refusing to cut switchbacks, and walking single file on trails even in the mud. If you must walk off the trail, step on rocks, snow, or dry grasses rather than wet soil and delicate plants.

- **Leave what you find.** Flowers, rocks, and goat-fur tufts on shrubs are protected park resources, as are historical cultural items. For lunch stops and camping, sit on rocks or logs where you find them rather than moving them to accommodate your camp.

- **Properly dispose of waste.** Whatever you bring in, you must pack out. Pack out all garbage. If toilets are not available, pack out toilet paper. Urinate on rocks, logs, gravel, or snow to protect soils and plants from salt-starved wildlife, and bury feces 6-8 inches deep at least 200 feet from water.

- **Minimize campfire impacts.** Make fires in designated fire pits only, not on beaches. Use small, wrist-size dead and downed wood, not live branches. Be aware that fires and collecting firewood are not permitted in many places in the park.

- **Respect wildlife.** Bring along binoculars, spotting scopes, and telephoto lenses to aid in watching wildlife. Keep your distance. Do not feed any wildlife, even ground squirrels. Once fed, they become more aggressive.

- **Be considerate of other visitors.** Where cell service is available, be considerate to others around you who are trying to enjoy the quiet.

For more information, visit Leave No Trace online at www.LNT.org.

10-horsepower motorized boats are allowed, but Jet Skis are not. The lake generally maintains a pleasant quiet. On calm days, kayaks, canoes, and paddleboards tour the shoreline.

Boating regulations in Glacier require permits for boats ($10 for 7-day motorized permit, $40 for annual motorized permit, free for nonmotorized boats). Boats must be cleaned, drained, and dried to avoid bringing aquatic invasive species into park lakes. Permits are available at the **Two Medicine Ranger Station** (7am-5pm daily summer).

Located at the Two Medicine boat dock, **Glacier Park Boat Company** (406/226-4467 summer, 406/257-2426, www.glacierparkboats.com, $15-20/ hour) rents canoes, kayaks, and rowboats.

FISHING

The Two Medicine River links together three lakes by the same name, with brook trout populating much of the water. For fishing **Upper Two Medicine Lake,** hike about two miles after taking the boat shuttle across Two Medicine Lake. It's an attractive lake to fish, but with a brushy shore and outlet clogged with downed timbers. Anglers in **Two Medicine Lake** may have more success tossing in a line from a boat rather than fishing from the heavily timbered and brushy shore. On the valley's south side, Paradise Creek harbors some trout, but Aster and Appistoki Creeks are empty. On the dam-controlled **Lower Two Medicine Lake,** half of which is in the park with the other half on the Blackfeet

406/226-5342, www.glacierparkinc.com, early June-mid-Sept., greens fees $40, cart rental $35, club rentals $21) is the oldest grass greens in Montana. The nine-hole course winds through aspen groves with views of the Dancing Lady, Henry, Calf Robe, and Summit peaks. Don't be surprised if bears (or more commonly stray dogs) roam across the course. Because the course is on Blackfeet land, each hole is named after a former Blackfeet Nation chief: Rising Wolf, Bad Marriage, Long Time Sleeps, and Stabs-by-Mistake. If weather permits, the course can open earlier in spring.

A public nine-hole pitch-and-putt miniature golf course covers half of the front lawn of Glacier Park Lodge. Pick up clubs and a souvenir ball ($10 pp) at the front desk. Ground squirrel holes add challenge to the course.

CROSS-COUNTRY SKIING

Cross-country skiers can tour roads late December-April. But because winds can scour the road free of snow in places, you may need to take your skis off and walk portions. Headwinds also frequently blow in both directions. **Two Medicine Road** (15 miles round-trip) makes a delightfully moderate but long ski, with frozen Two Medicine Lake as the destination. Snow piles up enough to bury the restrooms. The gentle terrain undulates, except for one long climb into the lake basin. It's a stunning trip, with relatively little avalanche danger.

When snow permits, skiing **Looking Glass Hill** on Highway 49 is also popular. An eight-mile round-trip tour leads from the junction with Two Medicine Road to spectacular overlooks of Two Medicine Valley and Lake Creek.

No equipment rentals are available in East Glacier; the nearest rentals are at the Izaak Walton Inn (milepost 179.7, U.S. 2, Essex). Be prepared for winter travel: Do not venture out without a complete pack full of emergency gear, ready for self-rescue.

Glacier Park Lodge Golf Course

Reservation, only a few anglers go after the 10-12-inch rainbows and brookies due to difficult access with no public trails. Other area lakes, such as **No Name** and **Old Man,** support trout, but Cobalt is barren. In the Cut Bank Valley, **Medicine Grizzly Lake** lures anglers, but reality doesn't live up to legend, and the lake is frequently closed due to bear activity.

Licenses and Regulations

No fishing license is required inside Glacier, but pick up park fishing regulations at Two Medicine Ranger Station. On Lower Two Medicine Lake or the Two Medicine River, you will need a Blackfeet fishing permit ($20 one day, $45 three days, $75 season). Purchase Blackfeet fishing permits at **Bear Track Travel Center** (Exxon station, 20958 U.S. 2, East Glacier, 406/226-5504).

GOLF

Built in 1927, the **Glacier Park Lodge Golf Course** (406/892-2525, tee times

Entertainment and Shopping

RANGER PROGRAMS

On summer evenings, National Park Service naturalists present free 45-minute talks (8pm daily) on natural history and wildlife in the Two Medicine Amphitheater. Once a week, the presentations feature **Native America Speaks,** storytellers who bring to life the history of local indigenous people and their involvement in Glacier. For a current schedule, pick up the *Ranger-led Activity Guide* at Two Medicine Ranger Station.

From time to time, Glacier Park Lodge sponsors entertainers and musicians. Check the sign in the lobby near the front desk for the current schedule.

★ NORTH AMERICAN INDIAN DAYS

Over four days beginning the second Thursday in July, **North American Indian Days** (406/338-7521, www.blackfeetcountry.com) celebrates native culture in vibrant, stunning color. In Browning, behind the Museum of the Plains Indian, the powwow grounds (4th Ave. NW and Boundary St.) become home to tepees, dancing, drumming, singing, games, rodeos, horse racing, sporting events, food, and crafts. Hosted by the Blackfeet, this family event draws regional indigenous people from the United States and Canada. Traditional regalia show off exceptional craftsmanship with feathered headdresses and beadwork. Nonnative people are welcome to attend, and it's free to watch the performances and events. No alcohol is sold on the reservation during North American Indian Days.

SHOPPING

East Glacier has a few gift shops to browse, and it is home to the unique **Spiral Spoon** (1012 Hwy. 49, 406/226-4558, www.thespiralspoon.com), which creates artfully hand-carved spoons from different woods. The old post office converted into the **Rock 'n Roll Bakery: Gear and Goodness** (34 Dawson Ave., 406/226-5553, www.seeglacier.com) and stocks a small selection of quality-brand backpacking and hiking essentials such as hiking poles, rain gear, socks, maps, and hydration packs.

For the largest collection of Native American art, stop in Browning at the **Blackfeet Heritage Center and Art Gallery** (333 Central Ave., 406/338-5661, 9am-6pm daily June-Sept.). It houses the beadwork, jewelry, paintings, and sculptures of more than 500 artists and craftspeople. Some art comes on rawhide, buffalo hides, and bison skulls. The center also has on display a baby Tyrannosaur skeleton that was found on the reservation.

CASINO

Gaming and slot machines on the Blackfeet Reservation are at **Glacier Peaks Casino** (46 Museum Loop, Browning, 406/338-2274 or 877/238-9946, www.glacierpeakscasino.com, 10am-2am daily), located at the roundabout junction of U.S. 2 and 89. The 33,000-square-foot casino contains 300 slot machines, live poker, a lounge, and a restaurant.

Accommodations

Two Medicine has no lodging, but offers a spectacular campground. Browning, tribal center of the Blackfeet Reservation, has minimal tourist amenities: Lodging includes the **Holiday Inn Express and Suites** (50 Museum Loop, 406/338-2400 or 866/264-5744), built in 2013 adjacent to Glacier Peaks Casino, and the smaller, family-owned **Going-to-the-Sun Inn and Suites** (121 Central Ave. E., 406/338-7572), remodeled in 2013.

OUTSIDE THE PARK
East Glacier

Most visitors prefer to stay in **East Glacier.** Outside the park boundary and located on the Blackfeet Reservation, it caters to tourists with multiple restaurants and motels, cabins, lodges, and hostels. Bring earplugs for the clatter of passing trains and highway trucks.

a garden walkway leads to Glacier Park Lodge

On the west side of the railroad tracks, historic Glacier Park Lodge is on Highway 49 along with a compact strip of motels—think very rustic, not a highway megastrip. On the east side of the tracks along U.S. 2, East Glacier has several motels within a few blocks of restaurants. All of these fill completely in midsummer, so reservations are strongly advised. Add on a 7 percent tax to all rooms. **VRBO** (www.vrbo.com) lists vacation rentals that range from small cabins to large homes in the East Glacier vicinity and on the Blackfeet Reservation.

LODGE

Historic ★ **Glacier Park Lodge** (1 Midvale Rd., 406/892-2525 from US or 403/236-3400 from Canada, front desk 406/226-5600, www.glacierparkinc.com, early June-mid-Sept., $140-500) is right across from the train depot. It's the only historic park lodge with an outdoor swimming pool (heated, but still chilly), golf course, and pitch-and-putt. In the gigantic lobby, huge Douglas firs hold aloft a multistory ceiling. The main lodge connects to guest rooms in the west wing via a scenic enclosed walkway. Get a room facing the mountains to enjoy the sunrises and sunsets casting orange glows. Lodge rooms, suites, and family rooms are available, along with a chalet and home. West-wing guest rooms tend to be larger. Expect rustic: tiny baths converted from original closets, thin walls, slanted floors, cantankerous hot water, and no TV, air-conditioning, or elevators. The lobby has limited Wi-Fi. Revel in the historical ambience instead. Make reservations for summer a year in advance.

A restaurant, lounge, snack shop, and gift shop are near the lobby, and Remedies Day Spa offers massages for trail-weary muscles. Red bus tours depart from the hotel, and trail riding is across the street. Trails to Scenic Point and Firebrand Pass depart nearby.

CABINS

On the east edge of town amid aspen trees, ★ **Travelers Rest Lodge** (20987 U.S. 2 E., 406/226-9143 summer, 406/378-2414 winter, http://travelersrestlodge.net, May-mid-Oct., $130-155) has roomy log cabins with gas fireplaces and fully equipped kitchenettes. Each is positioned so that its covered deck has privacy and views of the Bob Marshall Wilderness. The nicely decorated cabins sleep 2-4 in log-hewn beds; there are TVs and CD players but no phones (a phone is available in the office). In one of the cabins, owners Diane and Bob Scalese have their engraving workshop.

Located 1.5 miles from East Glacier, **Bison Creek Ranch B&B** (milepost 207.4, 20722 U.S. 2, 406/226-4482 or 888/226-4482, www.bisoncreekranch.com, mid-May-Sept., $90-140 for two people, $15 additional person) combines rustic cabin stays with a breakfast. Remodeled one-bedroom Gandy Dancer cabins (built as bunkhouses for railroad repair workers) and two-bedroom A-frame chalets are spread among the firs and meadows. It appeals to those who want real quiet without phones, Internet, or TVs but with electricity and private baths. Be ready for slow-arriving hot water. An on-site restaurant serves Western dinners.

MOTELS

East Glacier has seven basic, older family-run motels, some with cabins and all within walking distance to restaurants, stores, and the train station. Advance reservations in midsummer are wise. Some motels offer pickups at the train depot.

Four summer-only motels line Highway 49's strip north of Glacier Park Lodge adjacent to restaurants. The area hops in midsummer, but highway traffic virtually disappears at night. Train noise still filters through the trees to some of the motels. Most drop their rates in spring and fall. The **Mountain Pine Motel** (909 Hwy. 49, 406/226-4403, www.mtnpine.com, May-late Sept., $86-195) offers 25 tidy guest rooms lined up surrounding a lawn tucked under tall, shady trees. The non-smoking guest rooms have queen beds, wireless Internet access, and TVs. Some adjoin for families. **East Glacier Motel and Cabins** (1107 Hwy. 49, 406/226-5593, May-mid-Oct., $80-160) has six motel rooms and 11 small cabins with private baths, some with kitchenettes. **Sears Motel** (1023 Hwy. 49, 406/226-4432, www.searsmotel.com, June-Sept., $72-90) maintains 16 motel rooms with double beds. **Jacobson's Cottages** (1204 Hwy. 49, 406/226-4422, www.jacobsonscottages.

Travelers Rest Lodge

com, May-Sept., $70-135) offers queen-bed cottages with or without kitchens.

Three year-round motels are in "downtown" East Glacier, south of the tracks. Rates are highest in summer and lowest in winter. The ★ **Whistling Swan Motel** (512 U.S. 2, 406/226-4412 or 406/226-9227, www.seeglacier.com, $65-160) is run by the same family that owns the Two Medicine Grill, Glacier Park Trading Company, and Rock 'n Roll Bakery. Its 10 pine-walled guest rooms offer various bed configurations, and you can get loads of advice from the owners, who are avid hikers. The **Dancing Bears Inn** (40 Montana Ave., 406/226-4402, www.dancingbearsinn.com, $90-190) has 16 guest rooms with continental breakfast and wireless Internet access. Some guest rooms have kitchenettes. The **Circle R Motel** (406 U.S. 2, 406/226-9331, www.circlermotel.net, $65-205) has newer rooms added in 2015, older rooms, and nearby cabins.

GUESTHOUSE

Art aficionados can rent a room from a professional potter and sculptor at ★ **The Brown House** (402 Washington St., 406/226-9385, June-Sept., $90-95), which has three non-smoking guest rooms, each furnished with antiques. Each room has a private entrance and bath. The upstairs guest room has a view of the park's peaks. Originally a 1920s store, the building still has some of the fixtures from that era. The gift shop also sells the works of local artisans.

HOSTELS

For budget travelers, East Glacier has two hostels open May-September. Located one block from the train depot, **Backpacker's Inn** (29 Dawson Ave., 406/226-9392, www.serranosmexican.com) has three dorms ($20 pp, bring sleeping bags), plus two cabins ($50, queen bed) located in the backyard of Serrano's Mexican Restaurant. It's a little outdoor oasis in the middle of town that serves as a common area. Buildings are renovated original 1920 prefab cedar Sears and Roebuck homes. **Brownie's Hostel** (1020 Hwy. 49, 406/226-4426, www.brownieshostel.com) is in a renovated old two-story 1908 building that used to house railroad workers. A six-block walk from the train station and adjacent to restaurants, the hostel has a fully equipped communal kitchen, three dorms ($22-24 pp), private bedrooms ($35-70), and a deli, convenience store, and Internet. Cinnamon rolls scent the morning air from the downstairs bakery.

Camping

RVers requiring hookups will need to stay in East Glacier or Browning, as Glacier National Park campgrounds have no hookups. If the campgrounds are full, check the Marias Pass and Essex districts.

INSIDE THE PARK

Two National Park Service campgrounds are in Glacier's southeast corner. Campsites have picnic tables and fire rings with grills. Bring your own firewood; gathering wood in the park is prohibited. All campsites are first-come, first-served.

Two Medicine Campground

★ **Two Medicine Campground** (406/888-7800, late May-late Sept., $20) yields views of bears foraging on Rising Wolf Mountain, especially from the A and C loops. Riverfront sites are 95, 99, and 100. In early summer, ruby-crowned kinglets call out "teacher, teacher" from the trees. The campground surrounds the calmer waters of small Pray Lake, a good place for paddling, fishing, or chilly swimming. With 99 sites, the campground may have sites available later than those nearer Going-to-the-Sun Road, but it can fill up midsummer before 11am. Tenters should choose sheltered sites due to abrupt high winds that can flatten poles. Flush toilets, water, and a dump station are provided. The Loop C restrooms were rebuilt in 2015. The north-shore trail departs right from the campground, leading in both directions around Rising Wolf Mountain. A seven-minute walk or a few-minute drive connects with the boat tour and rental dock. Only 13 sites can handle RVs up to 32 feet. Primitive camping (late Sept.-Oct., $10) has pit toilets and no water.

Cut Bank Campground

Located 19 miles north of East Glacier off U.S. 89, **Cut Bank Campground** (406/888-7800, early June-early Sept., $10) is at the end of a five-mile potholed dirt road. The ultra-quiet campsites can only fit very small RVs, and trailers are not recommended. The campground has pit toilets and no running water. Atlantic Creek runs nearby, but you'll need to filter the water or boil it for five minutes. With only 14 sites set in deep shade under large firs, it's a great place to escape the crowds. Atlantic Creek has fishing, and a nearby trailhead departs to Medicine Grizzly Lake and Triple Divide Pass. To locate the road, look for the campground sign six miles north of the junction of Highway 49 and U.S. 89.

OUTSIDE THE PARK
East Glacier

A small three-acre campground on the Blackfeet Reservation, **Y Lazy R RV Park** (junction of Lindhe Ave. and Meade St., 406/226-5505, mid-May-Sept., tents $23, hookups $25-28) is two blocks off U.S. 2. With only a few aspen trees, its open, rough grass-and-dirt setting overlooks Midvale Creek and affords big views of surrounding mountains. Amenities include flush toilets, picnic tables, coin-op showers, a dump station, a large laundry, and hookups for electricity, water, and sewer. The campground is an easy few blocks' walk from restaurants. Bring earplugs for the hoards of nearby trains.

Two Medicine Campground surrounds Pray Lake.

Browning

On a prairie wildflower knoll west of Browning in view of Glacier's peaks, the ★ **Lodgepole Gallery and Tipi Village** (U.S. 89, 2.5 miles west of Browning, 406/338-2787, www.blackfeetculturecamp. com, May-Sept., $68 first person, $16 each added adult, $10 kids) provides an authentic experience in 10 traditional double-walled canvas tepees with inside fire pits and the ground for the floor. Supplied wood heats the tepees on cooler nights. Bring your sleeping bag, air mattress, and flashlight, or rent them ($12). A central bathhouse has flush toilets and showers. You can watch a small herd of nearly extinct Spanish mustangs, the original Indian horse, run free on the property. Breakfast or a traditional southern Blackfeet dinner are available by reservation. A Blackfeet art gallery and art classes are on-site, and the owners can arrange Blackfeet-guided tours, fishing trips, and horseback riding.

West of Browning, with views of Glacier's

eastern front range, **Aspenwood Resort** (980 U.S. 89 W., 9.5 miles west of Browning or 2.3 miles east of Kiowa Junction, 406/338-3009, www.aspenwoodresort.com, mid-May-mid-Oct., $25-40) is on the Blackfeet Reservation with two beaver ponds that offer fishing, paddleboating, wildlife-watching, and walking. The cam[...] toilets, hookups for elec[...] and RV campsites, showe[...] tion, and a restaurant. The[...] ranges for Native American-g[...] trips, tours, and horseback ridi[...] horses are welcome.

Food

Two Medicine has only a tiny café, and eateries in Browning are fast food. Most visitors hit East Glacier to dine out. During special days on the Blackfeet Reservation, such as graduation and North American Indian Days, none of the restaurants, groceries, or bars serves alcohol, including East Glacier. The four-day celebration is usually scheduled beginning the second Thursday in July.

INSIDE THE PARK

On the shore of Two Medicine Lake, **Two Medicine Campstore** (end of Two Medicine Rd., 8:30am-6pm daily summer) operates in what used to be the historic dining hall for Two Medicine Chalets. A tiny café in the back of the store sells espresso, soft-serve ice cream, cold drinks, muffins, cinnamon rolls, breakfast burritos, soup, bison chili, and several types of pasties.

Two Medicine has the only **picnic area,** adjacent to the campground. With running water and flush toilets, it is in a scenic spot right on the shore of Two Medicine Lake amid cottonwoods. Most of the sites have some trees, which provide a good windbreak on days when the wind howls, but scant shade on hot days. Sites include a picnic table and a fire ring with a grill, but bring your own firewood; it's illegal to gather wood here.

OUTSIDE THE PARK
East Glacier

Given the small size of the town, you can walk to most of the restaurants from your accommodations.

CASUAL DINING

In the historic Glacier Park Lodge, the **Great Northern Dining Room** (1 Midvale Rd., 406/892-2525, front desk 406/226-5600, daily late May-late Sept.) has the best views of any restaurant in town. Ask to be seated near the west windows facing Dancing Lady Mountain and Mount Henry: The sunrise smears them orange, and the sunset backlights them with a pink glow. The view and the historical ambience draw diners to the restaurant, which doesn't take reservations. Breakfast (6:30am-10am, $10-15) is frequently a huge buffet ready for those with big appetites, or off-the-menu traditional breakfast dishes. Lunch (11:30am-5pm, $13-17), served in the adjacent bar rather than the dining room, features burgers, sandwiches, and a few entrées. Dinner (5pm-9:30pm, $18-33) has steak, fish, and vegetarian dishes. Order bag lunches ($9) one day in advance. Adjacent to the restaurant, the **Empire Bar** (11:30am-midnight) serves Montana microbrews, wine, cocktails, lunch, and dinner.

Located 1.5 miles west of East Glacier, **Bison Creek Ranch** (20722 U.S. 2, 406/226-4482 or 888/226-4482, www.bisoncreekranch.com, 5pm-9pm daily May-Sept., $11-36) has served up the Schauf family's Western home cooking since the 1950s. The house favorite is fried chicken, but the large menu has rib eyes, steaks, fish, burgers, sandwiches, and salads. Dinners are large, and must be topped with dessert. The restaurant does not sell alcohol, but allows you to bring your own.

porch of **[...]urant** (29 **[...]** w.serran- **[...]** ay-Sept., **[...]** made- **[...]** hilada **[...]** alties. **[...]** oads **[...]** ling **[...]** an **[...]** with wooden **[...]** deck out back while **[...]** sunset. Either way, the margar- **[...]** go down easy.

CAFÉS

Two cafés flank U.S. 2 opposite the train station. ★ **Two Medicine Grill** (314 U.S. 2, 406/226-9227, www.seeglacier.com, 6:30am-9pm daily spring-fall, closes earlier in winter, $6-16) is a local hangout for diner-type meals, espresso drinks, gooey homemade cinnamon rolls, wild huckleberry shakes, bison burgers, and pie. You can sit on one of the eight stools at the bar, or eat in the tiny dining room. Built in Choteau in 1935, the funky diner building moved to East Glacier where it serves as the only year-round place to eat and a place where

locals connect. Formerly the Glacier Village Café, the **Alpenglow Restaurant** (304 U.S. 2 E., 406/226-4464, 8am-9pm daily) launched under new owners in July 2016 serving breakfast ($10-12), lunch ($12-20), and dinner ($12-30). It serves burgers in multiple sizes, plus fish, steaks, and limited pizza, and has a salad bar. As of 2016, it does not have a beer and wine license. Opening hours and days decrease in winter.

Two other cafés sit on the Highway 49 strip across from motels. In a log cabin, ★ **Luna's Restaurant** (1112 Hwy. 49, 406/226-4433, www.lunasrestaurant.com, 7am-9pm daily mid-May-Sept., $7-18) serves up café fare: omelets, breakfast burritos, zucchini or green bean fries, bison brats, Indian tacos, and a variety of burgers and sandwiches that you can customize with a selection of ingredients. Luna's huckleberry pie is made with a graham cracker crust and a cream cheese layer. Food is not pre-cooked, so have a beer or glass of wine while waiting. Reservations and a few outdoor seats are available. At the **Whistle Stop Restaurant** (1024 Hwy. 49, 406/226-9292, www.brownieshostel.com, 7am-9pm daily June-Sept., $6-28), plan to settle in to indoor or outdoor seating and relax for your meal in this ramshackle building. The

Serrano's Mexican Restaurant

Glacier Park Trading Company

Kathryn Hiestand. Her double butter crust triple berry and huckleberry pies can be purchased whole at the bakery or by the slice à la mode at Two Medicine Grill.

Brownie's Bakery and Deli (1020 Hwy. 49, 406/226-4426, www.brownieshostel.com, 7am-9pm daily May-Sept.) churns out muffins, bagels, cookies, breads, and brownies, plus espresso and ice cream. Pick up deli sandwiches or wraps for hiking.

GROCERIES

Two East Glacier stores sell groceries daily year-round. **Glacier Park Trading Company** (316 U.S. 2 E., 406/226-9227, www.seeglacier.com, 8am-9pm daily summer, 9am-8pm daily winter) sells fresh veggies, dairy products, wine, meat, and staples. It also carries a broad selection of Montana microbrews. The deli makes sandwiches for hiker lunches, plus pizzas to go. The **Bear Track Travel Center** (Exxon station, 20958 U.S. 2, 406/226-5504, 7am-10pm daily summer, 7am-8pm daily winter) sells convenience-store foods, ice, firewood, camping and fishing supplies, beer and wine, propane, and fishing licenses. In summer, **Brownie's Bakery and Deli** (1020 Hwy. 49, 406/226-4426, www.brownieshostel.com, 7am-9pm daily May-Sept.) is a convenience store in addition to a bakery and deli.

Browning

For a full-size grocery store, you'll need to head 12 miles east to Browning to **Glacier Family Foods** (601 SE Boundary St., 406/338-7283). On the Blackfeet Reservation, alcohol sales are banned during graduation, North American Indian Days, and other holidays.

breakfast specialty is deep-fried huckleberry-stuffed French toast, but they also serve a variety of omelets. Barbecue ribs or chicken in different styles and portions are the dinner specialties. Beer and wine are available, as is a single-crust huckleberry pie topped with whipped cream.

BAKERIES

The **Rock 'n Roll Bakery: Gear and Goodness** (34 Dawson Ave., 406/226-5553, www.seeglacier.com, 7:30am-2pm daily May-Sept.) serves up baked goods, including pesto popovers, braids, and muffins. The bakery also scored with hiring premier pie baker

Transportation and Services

DRIVING AND PARKING

Two-lane roads are ubiquitous. Some are very narrow and curvy. In East Glacier, find parking streetside or in a potholed dirt parking lot south of the train depot. In Browning, find parking at businesses. In Two Medicine, find parking at the road terminus at Two Medicine Lake, in the picnic area, and at trailheads.

SERVICES

Car rentals are available in East Glacier May-September through **Dollar** at **Sears Motel** (1023 Hwy. 49, 406/226-4432 or 800/457-5335, www.searsmotel.com) or **Avis** and **Budget** car rentals at **Glacier Park Trading Company** (316 U.S. 2, 406/226-9227 or 800/230-4898, www.seeglacier.com).

ATMs are at Glacier Park Trading Company and Glacier Park Lodge. There is a **post office** (15 Blackfoot Ave., East Glacier, 8:30am-noon and 1:30pm-5pm Mon.-Fri.). The area's daily newspaper is the *Great Falls Tribune*.

In East Glacier, a **launderette** is at **Y Lazy R RV Park** (Lindhe Ave. and Meade St.), and it offers **coin-op showers** available to drop-ins.

Gas and Repairs

Two Medicine has no gas station, but East Glacier has two: an **Exxon** at the **Bear Track Travel Center** at the east end of town on U.S. 2 and **Grizzly Gas** on Highway 49 at the Sears Motel. Browning has several gas stations. For repairs, go to Browning.

Cell Phone and Internet Access

Some cell phones have reception in East Glacier, Browning, and Cut Bank Campground. No reception is available at Two Medicine. In East Glacier, Internet access is available at Brownie's, Bear Track Travel Center, and some accommodations.

Emergencies

Call 911 in emergencies. To contact a park ranger, call 406/888-7800. You can also walk into the **Two Medicine Ranger Station** (7am-5pm daily summer), on Two Medicine Road at the campground junction. The nearest hospital is on the **Blackfeet Reservation** (Blackfeet Community Hospital, 760 Government Sq., Browning, 406/338-6154).

Marias Pass and Essex

Look for ★ to find recommended sights, activities, dining, and lodging.

Highlights

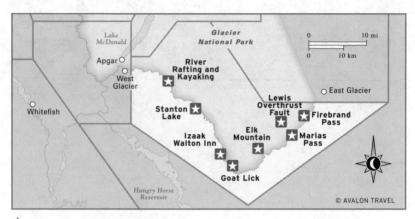

★ **Marias Pass:** Drive over the Continental Divide on one of the lowest passes through the Rockies. From the pass, peaks sweep up above 8,000 feet, revealing remarkable geology (page 205).

★ **Lewis Overthrust Fault:** Sixty-five million years ago, the Lewis Overthrust pushed older rock on top of younger sediments. See this stone story in the cliff face along Summit and Little Dog Mountains (page 206).

★ **Goat Lick:** Mountain goats congregate May-early July at the Goat Lick. Bring your binoculars to see the shaggy white beasts strutting across death-defying cliffs (page 206).

★ **Izaak Walton Inn:** Don cross-country skis and glide across the groomed trails at this historic inn. Warm up with a hot lunch in the dining

room before tackling more trails in the afternoon (page 207).

★ **Firebrand Pass:** Climb uphill through wildflowers and circle around Calf Robe Mountain to reach this pass. Keep your eyes peeled for bighorn sheep (page 210).

★ **Elk Mountain:** Climb this steep, little-traveled trail to the summit where a lookout used to be. A sea of peaks stretch north into Glacier and south into the Bob Marshall Wilderness (page 211).

★ **Stanton Lake:** Take this popular, family-friendly hike to a subalpine lake (page 213).

★ **River Rafting and Kayaking:** Float the Middle Fork of the Flathead River below the Goat Lick. You'll stare up at the nimble creatures cavorting along the cliffs (page 216).

The Theodore Roosevelt Highway (U.S. 2) runs 2,119 miles from Minnesota to Washington, with 57 of its miles bordering Glacier National Park. The Rocky Mountain corridor's history, as much as its scenery, adds to its appeal.

Tiny, rustic mountain enclaves dot the route. Both Marias Pass and Essex gained their notoriety through the railroad: Marias Pass as the route chosen for the railroad to cross the Continental Divide, Essex as a train community to work the tracks.

Running through John F. Stevens Canyon, the year-round highway accesses wild country. With 1.5 million acres of the Bob Marshall Wilderness Complex to the south and Glacier's one million acres to the north, the road bisects the largest grizzly bear habitat in the Lower 48. The Middle Fork of the Flathead River, designated a Wild and Scenic River, races through the canyon, creating a playground for rafters, kayakers, and anglers. The canyon also draws mountain goats in search of minerals and bighorn sheep and elk for wintering. From this passageway, most of Glacier is only accessible on foot. Hikers soak up solitude on remote trails, while horseback riders, anglers, and hunters dive into the Bob Marshall Wilderness.

Backwoodsy and removed from the accoutrements of civilization, the southern route around Glacier is devoid of stores and fast-food restaurants. Services are few and far between. Most visitors just drive through, but for hikers, anglers, and river floaters, it's an area rich with recreation.

HISTORY
Marias Pass

When Lewis and Clark passed through Montana in 1805, they failed to find Marias Pass. They came within 25 miles but swung south on the Missouri River to cross the Continental Divide on a much higher and more difficult pass. Lewis named the Marias River, calling it "Maria's River" after his cousin. The apostrophe got lost through history, much like the pass with the same name.

Previous: fishing the Middle Fork of the Flathead River; snowshoeing in view of Mount St. Nicholas.
Above: the trail to Firebrand Pass in September.

Marias Pass and Essex

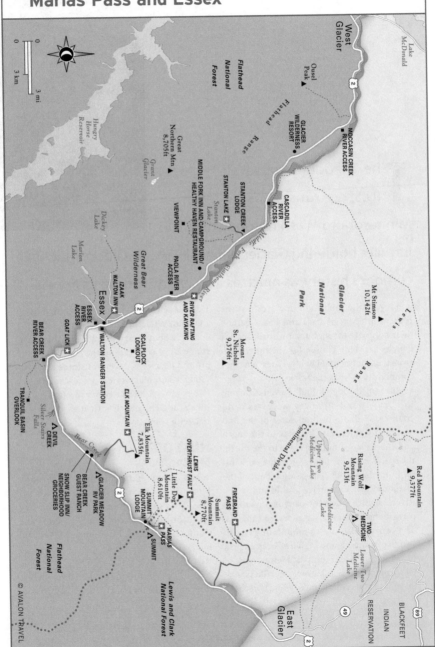

© AVALON TRAVEL

Reports of a "lost" pass filtered through the ranks of fur traders and mountain men. Government-funded expeditions went looking, but to no avail, while mountain men and Native Americans wandered through the real Marias Pass, yet "undiscovered." Rumors of the pass reached Great Northern Railroad developer J. J. Hill, prompting him to dispatch railroad engineer John F. Stevens and his Flathead guide Coonsa to see if the fable was true. While temperatures plummeted to -40°F in December 1889, the pair traveled on rawhide snowshoes through deep snow. Unable to slog on, Coonsa stayed behind with a fire as Stevens ventured on solo. He found the lost pass, deeming it appropriate for the railroad crossing. Within two years, Hill had a rail line built across the Continental Divide at Marias Pass in his push to complete his transcontinental railroad.

Building a Highway

As auto travel enchanted Americans, the demand for a road through John F. Stevens Canyon rose to a clamor. To transport an auto over the Continental Divide, you had to cough up $12.50 to put your car on a Great Northern Railway flatbed. While building Going-to-the-Sun Road dragged on for 20 years, the road over Marias Pass went through in a jiffy. Finished in 1930, the road over Marias Pass was much easier to build than chipping a route through the cliffs over Logan Pass.

Lodges

In 1906, the Great Northern Railway built Summit Station at Marias Pass as one of its early depots. When Glacier Park Lodge and its depot in East Glacier attracted more visitors, Summit's use died.

In 1939, the Great Northern Railway constructed Izaak Walton Inn to house railroad workers who cleared the tracks of snow in winter. The railroad planned to convert it to guest lodging when the park service built a southern road entrance into Glacier. When the Depression and World War II sent park visitation plummeting, the park scrapped the south entrance. Today, Glacier's southern valleys remain remote bastions of wilderness, accessible only by trail, some only after fording the Middle Fork. The building eventually became an inn, but not under the Great Northern Railway's umbrella.

Amtrak and freight trains run today on tracks built by the Great Northern Railway.

Public Lands

Many people find it confusing to differentiate the various types of public land. In the greater Glacier ecosystem, national park lands border national forests and wilderness areas. National parks, national forests, and wilderness areas are each managed with different purposes:

- **National parks** fall under the U.S. Department of the Interior. Parks are set aside for their historical, geological, cultural, or biological significance and are geared toward public recreation. Hunting is not permitted, nor is picking mushrooms or berries for commercial use. Mining and logging are also taboo. Leases for developing recreation like ski resorts are not available. Generally, dogs are not allowed on trails; neither are mountain bikes. Permits are needed for backcountry camping.

- **National forests** come under the U.S. Department of Agriculture. Hunting, timber harvesting, and commercial berry picking are generally allowed by permit. National forest land is leased for recreational development, such as ski areas. Your pooch can go with you on hikes; you can mountain bike as long as no special designation says otherwise. Permits are not needed for backcountry camping.

- **Wilderness areas** are administered usually by the national forest that contains the wilderness boundaries. Two concepts set wilderness apart: no mechanical transportation and no permanent human inhabitants. Wilderness areas do not have roads inside them. While hunting is permitted and Fido can go along on the trail, mountain biking is not allowed. Permits are not needed for backcountry camping.

Exploring Marias Pass and Essex

The public lands of Glacier National Park, Lewis and Clark National Forest, Flathead National Forest, and the Bob Marshall Wilderness Complex surround U.S. 2. They add up to 2.5 million acres. Only small strips of private land line the valley floor. The result is a necklace of tiny mountain blink-and-miss communities, none barely large enough to warrant the title of "village." Midway, the highway enters Glacier National Park for 3.5 miles with no entrance fee required.

SHUTTLES AND TOURS

No hiker shuttles regularly run along U.S. 2. You either have to drive yourself to trailheads or use your thumb, which is legal in Montana. By reservation, you can arrange for a shuttle with **Glacier Charters** (406/892-3390 or 800/829-7039, www.glaciertransportation.com, $100-120 one-way) to go from Glacier Park International Airport to Izaak Walton Inn. For **backpackers** hiking point-to-point trails, call

for rates to drop you off at one trailhead and pick you up at another several days later.

Bus Tour

For tours on Going-to-the-Sun Road to Logan Pass, **Sun Tours** (406/226-9220 or 800/786-9220, www.glaciersuntours.com, mid-May-Sept., $100) picks up riders in summer at Izaak Walton Inn. Air-conditioned 25-passenger coaches with extra-big windows for taking in the massive mountains tour the east side of Glacier National Park. The full-day tours depart at 7:30am.

Driving Tour
U.S. 2

After driving the dramatic Going-to-the-Sun Road, most visitors are less impressed with this southern highway. But this two-lane road still has gorgeous scenery. The drive from East Glacier to West Glacier takes 70 minutes or so. Locals use the road as a faster route

Marias Pass crosses the Continental Divide.

midsummer. Large RVs and trailers must use it, as they are banned from driving Going-to-the-Sun Road. You can start from East Glacier or West Glacier.

You'll see several white crosses along this highway. One cross equals one traffic fatality. Begun in 1953, the American Legion-sponsored program works with the Montana Department of Transportation to use the crosses as safety reminders. An estimated 2,000 sobering crosses line the state's highways.

U.S. 2 is considerably easier to maintain than Going-to-the-Sun Road. It is wider, more gradual, and, for the most part, follows a fairly long, gentle 2,000-foot ascent from West Glacier to Marias Pass. However, even though Marias Pass is 1,500 feet lower than Logan Pass, winter still poses difficulties. While plows clear and sand the road frequently to keep it passable for winter travel, cornices thousands of feet above break loose, sending avalanches careening down across its path. In some winters the highway is closed for several days while road crews clear a path through ice, rock, and tree debris.

across the Continental Divide when too many cars clog Going-to-the-Sun Road in

Sights

U.S. 2 sights are listed here from East Glacier to West Glacier.

LEWIS AND CLARK NATIONAL FOREST

From south of East Glacier to Marias Pass, U.S. 2 passes through the Lewis and Clark National Forest. Its 1.7 million acres serve as the headwaters for the mighty Missouri River. High prairies at 4,500 feet in elevation climb up to Rocky Mountain Peak, at 9,362 feet, along the Rocky Mountain Front in an extremely diverse ecosystem that is home to species like lynx and grizzly bears. Around milepost 198, you'll get good views south of 46,000 burned acres from the 2007 Skyland Fire.

★ MARIAS PASS

At 5,220 feet, Marias Pass (milepost 197.9) is the lowest **Continental Divide** saddle north of New Mexico. Two monuments mark the pass: A statue of John F. Stevens commemorates his discovery of the route for the railroad, and a tall obelisk stands in memory of Theodore Roosevelt, for whom the highway is named. Legend has it that he visited Many Glacier in 1910, but no official records indicate that. At the pass, the 3,100-mile Continental Divide Trail crosses into Glacier National Park, where hikers and skiers launch onto Autumn Creek Trail. With the area's broad flat forest, you'd be hard-pressed to realize you were crossing the Continental Divide. Bypass the ill-kept restrooms here in favor of the ones at the Goat Lick or Walton Picnic Area.

★ LEWIS OVERTHRUST FAULT

Opposite Marias Pass, the Lewis Overthrust Fault shoved older 1.6-billion-year-old rocks on top of 80-million-year-old stones. This fault exposed some of the oldest sediments in North America; these ancient Precambrian rocks formed as Belt Sea sediments solidified. On the face of Summit and Little Dog Mountains, look for an obvious upward line where the younger Cretaceous rock from the dinosaur age shows up as black or brown. This is the site where in the 1890s geologists discovered the Lewis Overthrust Fault, which extends into Canada and sets Glacier apart as a World Heritage Site.

SILVER STAIRS FALLS

Tumbling thousands of feet, an unmarked and unsigned pullout on the highway's south side stares up Silver Stairs Falls (milepost 188.2). The waterfall cascades down stair steps created from eroding sedimentary layers. In June-July, water rages down in torrents, but by late August it slows to a trickle. You can catch a glimpse with a drive-by, but with trees surrounding the falls, you'll get a better view by stopping.

★ GOAT LICK

Much of Glacier National Park's wildlife tends to be mineral deficient. Because their bodies crave minerals from their winter-deprived condition, during spring and early summer, mountain goats congregate at the Goat Lick (milepost 182.6). The lick is actually a huge mass of gray rock cliffs, an exposed fault containing salts like calcium, magnesium, and potassium. Goats hop sure-footedly along the steep cliff faces as if they were on flat land to slurp the minerals. The well-marked overlook has a couple of viewing areas: one at the interpretive sign and the other at the end of a short, wheelchair-accessible walkway widened in 2016. Bring your binoculars for better viewing. You can also catch sight of the goats on the slopes above the Goat Lick bridge on the highway.

BOB MARSHALL WILDERNESS COMPLEX

While Glacier rises to the north of the highway, to the south the Bob Marshall Wilderness Complex spans nearly 1.5 million acres. It actually comprises three wilderness areas: the

The Lewis Overthrust Fault is visible on Summit Mountain.

Mountain goats congregate at the Goat Lick.

winter, it becomes a cross-country skiing destination. Loaded with historical photos and memorabilia, the inn makes you feel almost like you've been transported back to a different era. In the downstairs bar, check out photos of avalanches burying the railroad tracks. Cozy up to the warm lobby fire.

MOUNT ST. NICHOLAS

The toothy 9,376-foot spire of St. Nicholas is easy to pick out on the skyline, especially when rimmed with winter snow. Look for a notched spire with precipitous cliffs on its southern face. Get good views of this forbidding-looking peak driving eastward on U.S. 2. For more in-your-face views, hike Grant Ridge Loop counterclockwise or climb to Scalplock Lookout.

JOHN F. STEVENS CANYON

Named for the Great Northern Railway engineer who verified the feasibility of Marias Pass as a railroad route, John F. Stevens Canyon begins just west of the pass and follows Bear Creek and the Middle Fork of the Flathead until its terminus near West Glacier. U.S. 2 and the railroad traverse the canyon's entire 40-mile distance. In places the canyon broadens into wide valleys; in others it tightens up into narrow channels, frothing with wild waters. Although its more dramatic sections are best seen from a raft or kayak on the river, several highway pullouts offer good photo ops.

FLATHEAD NATIONAL FOREST

From the Continental Divide west past Flathead Valley and extending 120 miles south of the Canadian border, Flathead National Forest is broken up by state and private land but still tallies up a healthy 2.3 million acres. Within its glaciated mountains, it has 2,600 miles of trails. Over 46 percent of the forest is designated wilderness area. Spruce, Douglas fir, lodgepole, larch, and pine cover its slopes, which house wolverines, grizzly bears, and wolves.

Bob (as locals call it), the Great Bear, and the Scapegoat. The Great Bear is the section bordering U.S. 2. The Bob Marshall was one of the country's first wilderness areas, dedicated in 1964 concurrent with the Wilderness Act. Scapegoat was added in 1972, and Great Bear six years later. While roads do not enter the wilderness areas and mechanized vehicles are prohibited (no mountain bikes or snowmobiles), a plethora of trails lead off U.S. 2. Short day hikes access the Great Bear, while longer overnight treks reach the Bob, a world-class area for horse packing, fishing, and big-game hunting.

★ IZAAK WALTON INN

Listed on the National Register of Historic Places, **Izaak Walton Inn** (milepost 179.7, 290 Izaak Walton Inn Rd., 406/888-5700, www.izaakwaltoninn.com) is opposite the southernmost point of Glacier National Park at Essex. The hotel stands adjacent to the train tracks, luring train aficionados and those looking for something a bit different, like sleeping in a renovated caboose. In the

Bob Marshall Wilderness Complex

The largest wilderness area in Montana, the Bob Marshall Wilderness Complex straddles 1.5 million acres along 110 miles of the Continental Divide. It is home to a huge ungulate population of deer, elk, moose, mountain goats, and bighorn sheep. They feed predators like lynx, grizzlies, black bears, mountain lions, and wolves. Over 1,000 miles of trails crisscross its ranges, with peaks reaching 9,000 feet high. The 1,000-foot-high Chinese Wall escarpment runs for 22 miles along the Continental Divide.

The complex is named for Bob Marshall, a young forester who became a local legend in 1925 with marathon 30-mile mountain treks around the Missoula area. Later, he penned *The Problem of Wilderness*, a treatise defining principles that would shape the movement to preserve the country's wildlands. In a one-man crusade as the U.S. Forest Service's Lands Division chief, he placed 5.4 million acres of vulnerable land under wilderness protection. Along with Aldo Leopold and others, he launched the Wilderness Society in 1935, but he died four years later at age 38.

In 1941, the South Fork, Pentagon, and Sun River areas south of Glacier were set aside as primitive zones, and finally, after 66 drafts, the 1964 Wilderness Act protected them from development. As part of the act, the three primitive-zone areas were combined to create the one-million-acre **Bob Marshall Wilderness.**

Unprecedented lobbying by a citizens group from the town of Lincoln led by a hardware store owner resulted in the adjacent **Scapegoat Wilderness,** adding 239,936 acres to the south end of the area in 1972. Scapegoat is home to 50 miles of the 3,100-mile-long Continental Divide Trail. Six years later, the **Great Bear Wilderness** added 286,700 acres of land to the northwest side of the complex. Tucked between Hungry Horse Reservoir and Glacier National Park, the Great Bear has 300 miles of trail; the elevation tops out at 8,700 feet on Great Northern, the sweeping peak seen from Flathead Valley.

Together these three wilderness areas, along with Glacier National Park, provide 2.5 million acres of habitat for species such as grizzly bears, lynx, and wolves. The wilderness complex is managed jointly by Flathead, Lewis and Clark, Lolo, and Helena National Forests.

MIDDLE FORK OF THE FLATHEAD RIVER

Draining Glacier National Park and the Bob Marshall Wilderness Complex, the Middle Fork of the Flathead River is no small tributary. Designated a Wild and Scenic River, its 95-mile length is known for some of the best white-water rafting and kayaking in Montana. Dropping at 35 feet per mile, the Great Bear section teems with Class III-IV rapids; the lower waters break up long, scenic floats with Class II-III rapids with such names as Jaws and Bonecrusher. Hook up with one of the four West Glacier rafting companies to splash in its waves, or float it yourself.

WINTERING RANGE

Belton Mountain, to the road's north (mileposts 155-157), is quite a different ecosystem from the heavily forested south slopes. Fires, winds, and a dry exposure have minimized forest growth. Winds create a lower snowpack, and south-facing slopes melt off early. Those are factors that make the area a prime wintering range for ungulates such as deer, elk, and bighorn sheep. Grizzly and black bears also forage on its slopes. Even in summer, it's worth a stop at one of the several pullouts to scan the slopes with binoculars.

Recreation

DAY HIKES

U.S. 2 is one road where hiker shuttles are not available; you must get to the trailheads on your own. Most of Glacier's trails on the south end are long valley hikes accessing little-used areas. Additional short hikes, mostly in the Great Bear Wilderness, round out the options, especially for hikers with Fido. While trails within Glacier do not allow dogs, canine friends can tag along on a leash in the wilderness area. However, hiking in bear country with a dog will not guarantee protection from bears.

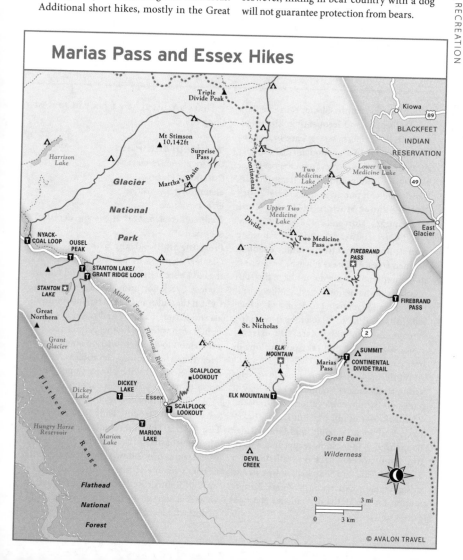

Marias Pass and Essex Hikes

Marias Pass and Essex Hikes

Trail	Effort	Distance	Duration
Firebrand Pass	moderate	9.6 mi rt	4.5 hr
Elk Mountain	strenuous	7 mi rt	6 hr
Scalplock Lookout	strenuous	9.4 mi rt	5 hr
Marion Lake	strenuous	3.4 mi rt	2 hr
Dickey Lake	moderate	4.8 mi rt	2.5 hr
Stanton Lake	easy	2 mi rt	1 hr
Grant Ridge Loop	strenuous	10.2-mi loop	5 hr
Ousel Peak	very strenuous	5.2 mi rt	3.5 hr

While trails within Glacier National Park are well signed and frequently maintained, trails in the wilderness areas are not; signs, if any, may be just a wooden trail number or name nailed to a tree. Don't expect to see mileages. Take a good topographic map, which you can purchase from the **Hungry Horse Ranger Station** (10 Hungry Horse Dr., Hungry Horse, 406/387-3800, www. fs.fed.us/r1/flathead), and know how to read it. Be prepared to encounter deadfall, downed trees, and heavy brush. Trail crews in the national forests do not have the staff numbers of the national park trail crews; it takes them longer to get to damaged or buried trails. Unlike in Glacier, bear-warning signage does not exist, except in extreme cases. Make noise and take precautions in bear country.

While snow melts from most lower-elevation trails such as Stanton Lake in May, it hangs on the upper elevations of Firebrand Pass, Elk Mountain, Marion Lake, Dickey Lake, Scalplock Lookout, and Grant Ridge Loop through June. Snow reappears on those trails in October. Check on trail status for Firebrand, Elk, and Scalplock online (www. nps.gov/glac); call Hungry Horse Ranger Station for the status of Flathead National Forest trails.

Hikes are listed here from east to west along U.S. 2.

★ Firebrand Pass

Distance: 9.6 miles round-trip
Duration: 4.5 hours
Elevation gain: 2,210 feet
Effort: moderate
Trailhead: at milepost 203 on the north side of U.S. 2 (see map p. 211)

From the trailhead, the path crosses into Glacier, wanders by beaver ponds, passes the old Lubec ranger station site, and follows Coonsa Creek northward. At 1.4 miles, turn right at the Autumn Creek Trail junction and ascend through aspens and meadows thick in July with valerian, lupine, paintbrush, and penstemon to another junction about a mile later. Take a left, gaining elevation as the trail circumvents Calf Robe's lower slopes. Make noise, for this is prime bear country.

As the trail breaks out of the trees, you'll have views of Dancing Lady Mountain and East Glacier. The trail rounds Calf Robe into a hanging basin and then ascends to the pass, where you can look down Ole Creek and into Glacier's remote southern peaks. Scrambles up Calf Robe or Red Crow lend even better views, but don't go off-trail unless you're ready to deal with steep scree hillsides.

Firebrand Pass

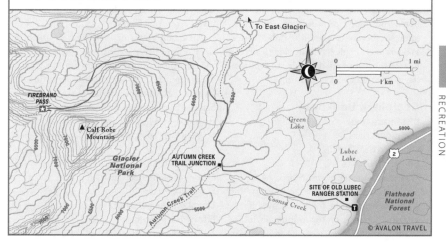

FIREBRAND PASS

Calf Robe Mountain

Glacier National Park

AUTUMN CREEK TRAIL JUNCTION

To East Glacier

Green Lake

Lubec Lake

SITE OF OLD LUBEC RANGER STATION

Coonsa Creek

Flathead National Forest

Autumn Creek Trail

© AVALON TRAVEL

★ Elk Mountain

Distance: 7 miles round-trip
Duration: 6 hours
Elevation gain: 3,332 feet
Effort: strenuous
Trailhead: Turn north off U.S. 2 at Fielding (milepost 192) and follow the dirt Forest Road 1066 about 0.5 mile to the trailhead.

Hike up through private logged land to the railroad tracks and cross into Glacier. The trail starts off deceptively easy enough, but shortly after turning right at the junction near a ranger cabin, the trail climbs and climbs. *Steep* does not come close to describing the pitch as it ascends to an open saddle. No wonder you have so much solitude here. Ahead, you can see the remainder of the trail, climbing sharply again across a talus slope to the summit.

descending from Elk Mountain in early summer

From the top, among debris from what was once the lookout, the views make the grunt worthwhile. Panoramas both north and south line up peak tops for miles into Glacier's remote southern sector and the Bob Marshall Wilderness Complex. A knife ridge leads east toward the Continental Divide, and the view down Autumn Creek is dizzying.

Scalplock Lookout

Distance: 9.4 miles round-trip
Duration: 5 hours
Elevation gain: 3,079 feet
Effort: strenuous
Trailhead: Walton Picnic Area (milepost 180.5)

This can be a gorgeous hike in early July, with bluebells in the high meadows, but be prepared for snow on top in June. Beginning in the Walton Picnic Area, the trail wanders along the Middle Fork of the Flathead in the first mile, crossing Ole Creek on a swinging bridge over a small gorge and ascending to the Ole Creek Trail. Turn west onto this trail for 0.4 mile to a second junction where the climb

begins. In the remaining 3 miles, the trail grunts up switchbacks at nearly 1,000 feet per mile as the sounds of the highway and train reverberate from below.

Peekaboo views of the Middle Fork of the Flathead River are the only respite from the relentless ascent. Near the top, the trail breaks out of the trees to climb up a ridge flanked with wildflower meadows. At the top, Scalplock Lookout has a commanding view of the entire Middle Fork drainage, with Mount St. Nicholas's spire in your face.

Marion Lake

Distance: 3.4 miles round-trip
Duration: 2 hours
Elevation gain: 1,739 feet
Effort: short but strenuous
Trailhead: Turn south onto Dickey Lake Road (milepost 178.7 on Forest Rd. 1640) at Essex and follow the left fork 2.3 miles to the Flathead National Forest-signed trailhead.

The trail is popular and sees quite a bit of summer traffic, making it well-worn and quite obvious to follow until you encounter heavy foliage. From the start, it taxes your lungs on its steep climb up Marion Creek Valley. You will encounter thick, heavy brush in the trail's midsection. Cow parsnip, nettle, elderberry, and false huckleberry nearly suffocate the trail. Make noise here to avoid surprising a bear.

You know you're nearing the lake when the trail assumes a more moderate pitch. Marion Lake sits in a photo-worthy glacial cirque surrounded by cliffs with its outlet congested with logs. Anglers should bring rods, as the lake harbors westslope cutthroat trout up to 12 inches long.

Dickey Lake

Distance: 4.8 miles round-trip
Duration: 2.5 hours
Elevation gain: 1,446 feet
Effort: moderate
Trailhead: Turn south onto Dickey Lake Road (milepost 178.7 on Forest Rd. 1640) at Essex and follow

Scalplock Lookout

Stanton Lake makes a great destination for kids.

★ Stanton Lake

Distance: 2 miles round-trip
Duration: 1 hour
Elevation gain: 600 feet
Effort: easy
Trailhead: Stanton Lake trailhead on U.S. 2 at milepost 169.9 in the Flathead National Forest (see map p. 214)

A favorite of families with little kids, this trail takes hikers and anglers to the shores of Stanton Lake in the Great Bear Wilderness. From the trailhead, a steep grunt heads straight uphill. But it soon levels out into a nice forested walk that leads into the basin cradling Stanton Lake. From the foot of the lake, you see Great Northern Mountain. Anglers should bring rods to fish for westslope cutthroat, rainbows, and mountain whitefish in the outlet creek.

Grant Ridge Loop

Distance: 10.2-mile loop
Duration: 5 hours
Elevation gain: 3,605 feet
Effort: strenuous
Trailhead: Stanton Lake trailhead on U.S. 2 at milepost 169.9 in the Flathead National Forest (see map p. 214)

This loop explores the scenic Grant Ridge in the Great Bear Wilderness. You can hike this loop in either direction, starting with the ascent to Stanton Lake but turning left at the first junction to ford Stanton Creek, or hiking 0.5 mile east along the highway to where the trail dives into the forest for a switchback ascent of the ridge. Soon, rest stops yield peekaboo views into Glacier. When the trail breaks out of the forest, it climbs through steep wildflower meadows with frontal views of Grant Peak and Grant Glacier. Turn around for spectacular views of Glacier's southern monoliths and the Middle Fork of the Flathead River far below. On the descent, the trail cuts toward Great Northern, the highest peak in the Great Bear Wilderness, before a long, forested descent to ford Stanton Creek and join the Stanton Creek Trail back to the trailhead.

the right fork three miles to an unmarked spur where the Flathead National Forest trail begins.

This short trail in the Great Bear Wilderness gives rather decent rewards for its efforts, and anglers will want to tote a fishing rod. After wading Dickey Creek, the forested trail climbs up a large bowl riddled with avalanche paths, which means deadfall, limbs, and uprooted and downed trees. In places, thick brush chokes the path, but you can still follow it to the headwall near the basin's end. From here, a rock cairn, which may be buried in snow that hangs late in the season, marks the trail, ascending steeply through false huckleberry bushes dangling with pale apricot blossoms and into a hanging valley.

Upon reaching the upper basin, the trail pops out on the edge of Dickey Lake. The shallow tarn, flanked by meadows and steep talus slopes, is a scenic lunch spot. You'll most likely find solitude here. Anglers will enjoy fishing for cutthroats in the small lake.

Stanton Lake and Grant Ridge Loop

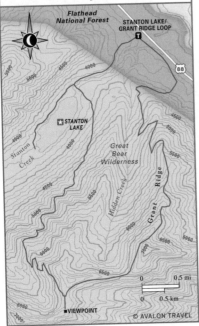

Ousel Peak

Distance: 5.2 miles round-trip
Duration: 3.5 hours
Elevation gain: 3,818 feet
Effort: very strenuous
Trailhead: milepost 159.6 on U.S. 2 in the Flathead National Forest

Do the math: This trail gains well over 1,000 feet per mile, and from the first minute it makes no bones about heading straight uphill. If the uphill doesn't tax your lungs, the downhill will pound your knees. Nevertheless, the view from the top is outstanding and well worth the effort or pain. Sitting on the northern edge of the Great Bear Wilderness, the trail climbs through a forest canopy littered with various microclimates, from wet seeps to dry, arid slopes. The path finally breaks out of the forest with glimpses of Glacier's peaks. At the top, remnants of the old lookout scatter across the hillside amid tiny yellow stonecrop.

Look into Glacier to see Mounts Jackson and Stimson along with Harrison Glacier.

Guides

Glacier Guides (11970 U.S. 2 E., West Glacier, 406/387-5555 or 800/521-7238, www.glacierguides.com, mid-May-Sept.) leads a few day hiking and backpacking trips that depart from U.S. 2. Solo travelers can hook up with weekly hikes to Firebrand Pass (start dates vary pending snowpack, $98 pp) that meet at the company's West Glacier office. Families and small groups can arrange to meet their own guide elsewhere ($560 for up to five people). Reservations are required. Plan to tip your guides at least 15 percent for day trips.

BACKPACKING

Backpacking from U.S. 2 offers two different experiences, depending on whether you hike north or south. Trails north go into Glacier National Park, which require backcountry camping **permits** ($7 pp/night). Get them 24 hours in advance in person at the **Apgar Backcountry Permit Office** (406/888-7859 May-Oct., 406/888-7800 Nov.-Apr.) or **St. Mary Visitor Center** (406/732-7751, late May-early Oct.). You can also get them at **Two Medicine Ranger Station** (406/226-4484, daily late May-mid Sept.). For advance reservations, apply online starting in mid-March (www.nps.gov/glac, $40). Trails heading south of the highway go into the Bob Marshall Wilderness, where no permit is required. Consult **Hungry Horse Ranger Station** (406-387-3800, http://www.fs.usda.gov/flathead) or *Hiking Montana's Bob Marshall Wilderness* by Erik Molvar.

Nyack-Coal Loop
46 MILES

Prepare for wild on this lengthy, forested, old Kootenai trail in southern Glacier National Park. It starts and ends with fording the Middle Fork of the Flathead River at Nyack Creek or Coal Creek, or adding more miles to start at Walton Ranger Station. The route, which can be done in either direction, circles

Stimson Peak, a monolith over 10,000 feet. Route-finding skills are required; the trail can be overgrown, washed out, and buried in downfall, and part of it burned in summer 2015. Many creeks also require fording; there are no bridges. Due to its difficulty, it guarantees solitude. Plan to camp at Coal Creek (COA), Beaver Woman Lake in Martha's Basin (BEA), Upper Nyack (UNY; burned in 2015), and Lower Nyack (LNY). High water in June precludes access and makes for treacherous stream crossings. Only those with experienced backcountry savvy should tackle its primitive isolation, but wilderness solitude is the reward. Advance reservations are not available until July 15.

Continental Divide Trail
117 MILES

Of the 3,100 miles of the Continental Divide National Scenic Trail (CDT), the northernmost miles are in Glacier National Park. Strong backpackers can cover Glacier's CDT in a week, but most prefer at least 10 days. Weaving together backcountry campsites (by permit) and shared hiker campsites in front-country campgrounds, you can launch a CDT trek from Marias Pass and finish by hiking across the border at Waterton Lake into Canada. En route, the trail crosses high vistas usually snow-free after mid-July: Scenic Point, Pitamakin Pass, Triple Divide Pass, Piegan Pass, Swiftcurrent Pass, and Northern Highline. Because the route uses popular backcountry campsites, apply for an advance reservation permit mid-March.

On the north side of Marias Pass, embark on the CDT via the Autumn Creek Trail, with which it joins, heading 14 miles to East Glacier or 24 miles to Two Medicine. Many hikers opt to stay their first night in East Glacier hostels before climbing over Scenic Point to Two Medicine. Portions of this trail require a Blackfeet Tribal Conservation Permit ($10). At Two Medicine Campground, stay in a shared hiker campsite and augment food supplies at the camp store. Going north, camp at Old Man Lake (Old), Morningstar Lake (MOR) or Atlantic Creek (ATL), Red Eagle Lake Head (REH) or Foot (REF), and Reynolds Creek (REY). After climbing over Piegan Pass to Many Glacier, camp in a shared hiker campsite at Many Glacier Campground, take a break from trail food by dining at 'Nell's in the Swiftcurrent Motor Inn, and resupply at the camp store. After departing Many Glacier, overnight at Granite Park (GRN), Fifty Mountain (FIF), and Kootenai Lakes (KOO). Finish the route by hiking the Waterton Lakeshore Trail across the boundary to the Waterton Townsite in Canada. Passports are required.

For those without passports or when snow clogs the Northern Highline in early summer or late fall, an official alternate route diverges from Many Glacier over Red Gap Pass for a total of 107 miles. Camp at Poia Lake (POI), Elizabeth Lake Foot (ELF), and optionally at Gable Creek (GAB) to reach the border and trailhead at Chief Mountain Customs.

BIKING

Cross-country cyclists use U.S. 2 to cross the Continental Divide when Going-to-the-Sun Road is not open. Many use it also to make a big loop through and around Glacier (Going-to-the-Sun Rd., U.S. 89, Hwy. 49, and U.S. 2). Compared to the rest of Glacier's roads, U.S. 2 is definitely an easier ride, because it has shoulders in some sections and is a bit wider and less curvy. However, due to heavy traffic in summer, it can be downright dangerous, with large rigs that nearly blow cyclists off the road. Tackle it only if you can handle riding with semis and RVs whipping by your elbows at 60 mph.

Be prepared for winds, especially at Marias Pass. They are usually blowing eastward, so those riding toward West Glacier encounter substantial headwinds. Also, be extra cautious in the five curvy miles east of West Glacier, as severe turns reduce the visibility of drivers on the road. Even though no law requires wearing a helmet, think twice about leaving your brain bucket off. Most drivers here are gawking at scenery or trying to spot wildlife rather than keeping their attention totally on the road.

While you can mountain bike on some trails in the national forests, biking is not permitted on trails in the wilderness areas or in Glacier National Park.

★ RIVER RAFTING AND KAYAKING

Designated as a Wild and Scenic River, the **Middle Fork of the Flathead River** is the local hot spot for rafting and kayaking. The river has two sections: the wilderness above Bear Creek and the lower section below Bear Creek.

With headwaters starting in the Great Bear Wilderness, you'll need to fly in to Schaeffer Meadows or pack in on a horse to float the upper 26 miles. Contact the **Flathead National Forest ranger station** (406/387-3800, www.fs.fed.us/r1/flathead) in Hungry Horse for details on rafting and floating this upper wild section. The normal float season (Class III-IV) runs mid-May-mid-July. During peak runoff in May, the trip can often be more challenging, with several rapids becoming Class V and spring snows chilling the air.

From Bear Creek to the confluence with the North Fork of the Flathead, the river runs 46 miles, with easy river access from locations on U.S. 2: Bear Creek (milepost 185), Essex (milepost 180), Paola (milepost 175.2), Cascadilla (milepost 166), Moccasin Creek (milepost 160.5), and West Glacier (follow signs to the golf course). With the float season running mid-May-early September, the river accesses make for easy half-day or full-day float trips. Between Bear Creek and Cascadilla, rapids rate Class III-IV. Waters flatten to a float trip from Cascadilla to Moccasin Creek, but be wary of deadly log jams. From Moccasin to West Glacier, rapids range Class II-III, with some Class IV stretches during late May high water. The average float time in July from Bear Creek to Cascadilla is usually 6.5 hours, and from Moccasin Creek to West Glacier 2.5 hours.

Flathead National Forest manages the river, even though it borders Glacier National Park. Consult the **Hungry Horse Ranger Station** (10 Hungry Horse Dr., Hungry Horse, 406/387-3800, www.fs.fed.us/r1/flathead), located nine miles west of West Glacier, for assistance in planning a self-guided overnight trip. Toilet systems are required for overnights, and fire pans are required in the wilderness. Rafters and kayakers should purchase the *Three Forks of the Flathead Floater's*

Calm float sections alternate with white water on the Middle Fork of the Flathead River.

21

Guide ($13), available through the ranger station or downloadable free online (www.fs.usda.gov/flathead), for locations of rapids and public land for camping. No permits are needed for overnights, but no camping is allowed on the Glacier National Park side. In the Great Bear Wilderness, sites are not restricted, but in the section below Bear Creek, private land abuts national forest land, much of it unmarked.

Guides

Four local river companies operate out of West Glacier, guiding half-day, full-day, and overnight trips on the Middle Fork of the Flathead. **Glacier Raft Company** (406-888-5454 or 800/235-6781, www.glacierraftco.com) is the only one that guides trips in the wilderness section above Bear Creek. Glacier Raft Company, **Montana Raft Company** (406/387-5555 or 800/521-7238, www.glacierguides.com), **Great Northern Whitewater** (406/387-5340 or 800/735-7897, www.gnwhitewater.com), and **Wild River Adventures** (406/387-9453 or 800/700-7056, www.riverwild.com) guide trips between Bear Creek and West Glacier.

Rentals and Shuttles

One company in West Glacier rents rafts, kayaks, camping gear, toilet systems, and fire pans: **Glacier Raft Company** (406/888-5454 or 800/235-6781, www.glacierraftco.com). It also provides shuttle services on the Middle Fork in your vehicle or its rigs ($20-315).

FISHING
Rivers and Streams

In Glacier National Park, Ole, Park, Muir, Coal, and Nyack Creeks are closed to fishing. However, anglers can drop lines in Summit, Railroad, and Badger Creeks, which flow from Marias Pass east through Lewis and Clark National Forest and onto the Blackfeet Reservation. **Badger Creek,** in particular, has a good reputation for rainbow trout. **Bear Creek,** good for westslope cutthroat, mountain whitefish, and some rainbow trout,

drops west from Marias to its confluence with the Middle Fork of the Flathead River. The **Middle Fork** has plenty of river accesses for fishing: Bear Creek, Essex, Paola, Cascadilla, and Moccasin.

Lakes

Inside the park, good cutthroat trout fishing lakes such as Ole, Harrison, and Isabel usually require backpacking or fording the Middle Fork of the Flathead. It's actually easier to get to lakes in the Great Bear Wilderness on the south side of the highway. **Stanton Lake** is a quick destination with westslope cutthroat trout, mountain whitefish, and rainbow trout, but it's somewhat overfished because of its ease of access. Dickey and Marion Lakes also harbor cutthroat.

Guides

For guided fishing on Blackfeet Nation lands, contact **Blackfeet Fish and Wildlife** (406/338-7207, www.blackfeetfishandwildlife.com) for a list of licensed outfitters. From West Glacier, four fishing companies guide fly-fishing trips on the Middle Fork of the Flathead River: **Glacier Guides** (11970 U.S. 2 E., 406/387-5555 or 800/521-7238, www.glacierguides.com), **Montana Fly-Fishing Guides** (Great Northern Resort, 12127 U.S. 2 E., 406/387-5340 or 800/735-7897, www.greatnorthernresort.com), **Wild River Fishing Guides** (11900 U.S. 2 E., 406/387-9453 or 800/700-7056, www.riverwild.com), and **Glacier Anglers** (Glacier Outdoor Center, 11957 U.S. 2 E., 406/888-5454 or 800/235-6781, www.glacierraftco.com).

Licenses and Regulations

Fishing regulations along U.S. 2 vary depending on land ownership. Check carefully where you are before dropping a line into the water; the road passes through Blackfeet land, Glacier National Park, and national forests. No licenses are required inside Glacier, although you must be aware of fishing regulations. Elsewhere you'll need to plan ahead to get the appropriate fishing licenses, as none are available along the highway. Purchase Blackfeet fishing permits ($20 one day, $45 three days, $75 season) at **Bear Track Travel Center** in East Glacier (Exxon station, 20958 U.S. 2, 406/226-5504). For **Montana fishing licenses** (Montana residents: $8-18 season, $13 adults for 2 days, free ages 1-11; nonresidents: $25 for 2 days, $44 for 10 days, $60 season, kids ages 1-14 free with adult with license for shared limit or $8 for own license), go to **Glacier Outdoor Center** (11957 U.S. 2 E., 406/888-5454 or 800/235-6781, www.glacier-raftco.com) in West Glacier.

HUNTING

Hunting is illegal in Glacier National Park, but south of U.S. 2, the famed Bob Marshall Wilderness boasts world-renowned big-game hunting for bighorn sheep, elk, and black bears. East-side grasslands are also famous for bird hunting. For hunting in the Bob Marshall Wilderness or in national forests, get regulations and license info from **Montana Fish, Wildlife, and Parks** (406/444-2535, www.fwp.mt.gov). The **Blackfeet Reservation** (406/338-7207, www.blackfeetfishandwildlife.com) has separate regulations and licenses for its land. Check also with each entity for the names of licensed outfitters.

CROSS-COUNTRY SKIING AND SNOWSHOEING

In winter, ski and snowshoe routes off U.S. 2 are popular for their ease of access. Trails, groomed snowmobile routes, and roads turn into popular trails.

Izaak Walton Inn

With 20 miles of track groomed daily for skate and classic skiing late November-mid-April, **Izaak Walton Inn** (290 Izaak Walton Inn Rd., Essex, 406/888-5700, www.izaakwaltoninn.com) becomes a great cross-country skiing destination in winter. At the inn, trails range from easy meanders to steep grunts. One short section of trail is lit for night skiing. Trail passes for day skiers and inn guests cost $12 per day. Although the area never feels crowded, the most popular time is late December-late February. Lessons are available from the lodge as well as ski and snowshoe rentals, and the rentals can be taken elsewhere to use.

Autumn Creek Trail

One of the most popular ski trails in Glacier is Autumn Creek Trail at Marias Pass, which can be skied point-to-point if you set up a

Izaak Walton Inn offers groomed ski trails in winter.

car shuttle or hitchhike, which is legal in Montana. Park for the west trailhead at milepost 193.8 on U.S. 2, and ski up the railroad access road and across the tracks. Park for the other trailhead at Marias Pass and locate the trailhead north of U.S. 2 and the railroad tracks. Orange markers on trees denote the six-mile trail. Beginners will find the Marias Pass section easier than the steep Autumn Creek section. To avoid the narrow, steep 660-foot downhill plummet, begin on the west end and finish at the pass.

Guides

Guided cross-country skiing, backcountry skiing, and snowshoeing tours are available by reservation through **Glacier Adventure Guides** (406/892-2173 or 877/735-9514, www. glacieradventureguides.com, Dec.-Mar.). The avalanche-certified guides lead single- or multi-day trips. Lunch, snacks, park entrance fees, and equipment are included.

Check online for rates; plan on tipping the guide 15-20 percent.

SNOWMOBILING

Snowmobilers gravitate to groomed and ung-roomed roads in **Lewis and Clark National Forest** (406/791-7700) and **Flathead National Forest** (406/758-5204). The most popular snowmobiling is in the Marias Pass and Skyland-Challenge complex, both straddling the Continental Divide south of U.S. 2. The Cut Bank Snowgoers and Flathead Snowmobile Association groom about 40 miles of trail, which are open for snowmobiling December-mid-May. Contact them via the **Montana Snowmobile Association** (406/788-2399, www.m-s-a.org). Snow depths in both of these snowmobiling areas vary 150-250 inches. Some restrictions apply to the designated connecting trails, so get a good snowmobile map from the Forest Service. The nearest rentals are in Flathead Valley.

Accommodations

OUTSIDE THE PARK
Along U.S. 2

Along U.S. 2, lodging includes historic inns, rustic cabins, and tiny motels. Regardless of the type, that 7 percent Montana state bed tax will find your bill. Many lodging properties boast of being near Glacier, but from U.S. 2, the only access is on foot, horseback, or by raft, with the exception of Walton Picnic Area and the Goat Lick.

RESORT

With some of the most unique lodging around Glacier, ★ **Izaak Walton Inn** (290 Izaak Walton Inn Rd., Essex, 406/888-5700, www.izaakwaltoninn.com, $110-490), located down a road just off U.S.2, celebrates its railroad heritage with accommodations in historic lodge rooms, cabooses, a luxury locomotive, and log cabins. Pet-friendly rooms are available in its plain roadside Half Way

House motel located 1.5 miles west on U.S. 2. From the lobby fireplace to the Dining Car Restaurant or the swinging seat on the porch, the nonsmoking National Historic Landmark is a place to relax. The inn maintains its historical ambience with no TVs, in-room phones, air-conditioning, or elevators; a pay phone is off the lobby. Lodge guest rooms vary in size, although most baths are fairly small. A short walk over a footbridge above the railroad tracks leads to four heated cabooses set in the trees that sleep four each, with kitchenettes and full baths. In the same glen, six log cabins with kitchens sleep up to six in bedrooms and lofts. One locomotive and three additional cabooses offer luxury accommodations. Two nights minimum are required for the cabooses, locomotive, and cabins. The inn also operates a house rental.

Amenities include a sauna, hot tub, coin-op laundry, wireless Internet in the main lodge, restaurant, cross-country ski trails in winter, walking trails, rental cars, and railroad ambience. You can arrive and depart by train, as it's an Amtrak stop. Bring earplugs, as trains rumble by each night. You can rent skis or snowshoes in winter. In summer, Sun Tours picks up riders here for an all-day tour on Going-to-the-Sun Road. Check the inn's packages, which include skiing, rafting, park sightseeing, and special weekends for railroad fans.

MOTELS

Several small, no-frills, family-run motels with restaurants dot U.S. 2, all within close earshot of the highway and train noise. Bring earplugs to survive the night. The **Snow Slip Inn** (milepost 180, 15644 U.S. 2 E., Essex, 406/226-4400, www.snowslipinn.com, $65-100) has six motel rooms and wireless Internet access. At milepost 173.8, **Glacier Haven Inn** (14305 U.S. 2, Essex, 406/888-5720, www.glacierhaveninn.com, $160 d, $15/added person, discounted in off-season) has eight small guest rooms with two double beds, wireless Internet, and satellite TV. Two family-sized cabins ($300-350, late May-early Sept.) are also available. Call for reservations, as the property is for sale.

CABINS

New owners resurrected the 1906 Summit Station that used to serve train riders at Marias Pass before it was moved to its present location. After remodeling the nine cabins, all named for park peaks, they opened ★ **Summit Mountain Lodge** (16900 U.S. 2, 406/226-9319, www.summitmtnlodge. com, mid-May-Sept., $175-320). The nonsmoking cabins, which come in different configurations for couples or families up to 12 people, include private bathrooms and log beds. Smaller cabins come with mini-fridges and microwaves, but the large family cabins have full kitchens. Sinopah and Running Rabbit cabins garner superb mountain views of Summit and Little Dog. Early season discounts are available, a prime time for wildlife-watching. The main lodge houses the restaurant, saloon, and wireless Internet. A short nature trail tours to local beaver ponds.

Flathead National Forest (406/387-3809, www.fs.fed.us/r1/flathead) rents two quiet, rustic cabins (reservations 877/444-6777, www.recreation.gov, $9 reservation fee) with three-night maximum stays. Both are accessible from U.S. 2 and must be reserved. Decked out with propane, mattresses, and kitchen utensils, the cabins are warmed with

You can stay in a caboose or engine at Izaak Walton Inn.

Summit Mountain Lodge

off U.S. 2; turn at milepost 191.9 and drive two miles, following the signs. In winter, it requires a ski or snowshoe trip to reach the front door. Bring your own food and sleeping bags. Both cabins are nonsmoking, and neither allows pets.

The closest lodging to West Glacier, **Glacier Wilderness Resort** (milepost 163 on U.S. 2, 406/888-5664, www.glacierwildernessresort.com, $225-300) is in a woodsy setting abutting the Great Bear Wilderness. With an indoor heated pool, its 11 time-share 1-2-bedroom log cabins sleep 4-6 people and come with fireplaces, satellite TV, DVD players or VCRs, fully equipped kitchens, and private hot tubs. In summer, you can use an outdoor picnic pavilion and walking trails. In winter, cross-country skiing and snowshoeing trails tour the property. A minimum stay of three nights is required.

BED-AND-BREAKFAST

If you prefer horseback riding, **Bear Creek Guest Ranch** (milepost 192, U.S. 2, 406/226-4489, www.bearcreekguestranch.com, June-mid-Sept.) specializes in riding clinics, cattle drives, and Western weeks. But the ranch, which has been operating since 1933, also serves as a B&B ($190 for two people, $20/extra person) with lodging in rustic log cabins with private baths.

either propane heat or woodstoves (wood is supplied). A seven-mile ski or snowmobile ride up Skyland Road (milepost 195.8 on U.S. 2), tiny one-room **Challenge Cabin** (Dec.-Mar., $30) sleeps six people stacked like sardines. A much larger two-bedroom cabin that sleeps eight, **Zip's Place** (June-Mar., $55) is

Camping

OUTSIDE THE PARK
Along U.S. 2

U.S. 2 has no drive-in national park campgrounds; to camp in Glacier requires backpacking. U.S. Forest Service and private campgrounds line the highway, where noise from trains and trucks permeates the night.

U.S. FOREST SERVICE CAMPGROUNDS

Two smaller, summer-only Forest Service campgrounds are adjacent to U.S. 2, tucked in dog-hair timbers and monitored by campground hosts. Expect to find picnic tables (some wheelchair accessible), fire rings with grills, vault toilets, drinking water, bear-proof food storage boxes, but no hookups. Pack out your trash. No firewood is provided, but you can collect it in the woods.

At Marias Pass, the **Summit Campground** (Lewis and Clark National Forest, 406/791-7700, June-Sept., $10) has 16 sites that are first-come, first-served, so get there by early afternoon in high season, especially if you want to nab one of the campsites farthest from the highway. Across the highway and railroad tracks, the Autumn Creek Trail tours below Glacier's peaks.

At milepost 190, **Devil Creek Campground** (Flathead National Forest, 406/387-3800, late May-Sept., $14) has 14 sites, a few of which can handle up to 40-foot RVs. From the campground, a trail leads 5.9 miles up to Elk Lake or 8.2 miles to Moose Lake. Make reservations for midsummer (877/444-6777, www.recreation.gov).

PRIVATE CAMPGROUNDS

Two private campgrounds are available along U.S. 2. If these fill up, a couple of restaurant-bar-cabin businesses also offer a few campsites. The 7 percent Montana bed tax is added to the rates, which usually cover two people; each additional person is $5. Bring earplugs, because both are near the highway and train tracks.

Located 16 miles west of East Glacier between mileposts 191 and 192, ★ **Glacier Meadow RV Park** (406/226-4479, www.glaciermeadowrvpark.com, mid-May-Sept., tents $26-28, hookups $40-45, $6/added person after two) has 41 sites on a 58-acre meadow and forest setting with a dump station, laundry, a playground, full hookups, flush toilets, showers, and wireless Internet access. All the sites are open, providing good satellite dish reception, but not much privacy from the highway and neighboring campers. The trail to Elk Mountain is nearby.

Between mileposts 173 and 174 west of Essex, **Glacier Haven Campground** (14297 U.S. 2 E., 406/888-5720, www.glacierhavenrv-campground.com, Apr.-Oct., tents $33, hookups $50, $5/extra person after two) is part of the Glacier Haven Inn. The treed campground snuggles between the highway and the railroad tracks, with 19 RV hookup campsites, including three that can accommodate large RVs, and room for four tents in a large camping zone. Facilities include flush toilets, showers, full hookups, launderette, and a four-person camping cabin with linens ($95, $15/extra person after two). Kids nine and under are free. The property is for sale, so call first.

Food

OUTSIDE THE PARK
Along U.S. 2

Restaurants along U.S. 2 vary from old dives to family cafés and a couple of casual-dining restaurants. Off-season, don't be surprised if one is closed when its hours say otherwise; if the fish are biting, the owners may lock up.

CASUAL DINING

Located three miles west of East Glacier, **Ramsey's Firebrand Food and Ale** (20629 U.S. 2, 406/226-9374, 4pm-10pm daily $10-30) has a mixed menu of burgers, sandwiches, pasta, fish, and steaks along with more than 50 types of beer. The food rates much better than the building would imply, and it fills with local characters. It's convenient for

dining after hiking to Firebrand Pass or cross-country skiing the Autumn Creek Trail.

Travelers can once again enjoy the 1906 Summit Station that used to be the train stop at Marias Pass. New owners reopened the station in 2014 as ★ **Summit Mountain Lodge** (16900 U.S. 2, 406/226-9319, www.summitmtnlodge.com, mid-June-mid-Sept., 4pm-9pm, $12-38). The intimate dining room and enlarged deck yield outstanding views of Summit and Little Dog Mountains. The steak house offers a lineup of grilled meats, burgers, and pastas, and the attic saloon serves up beer, wine, and cocktails.

At Izaak Walton Inn, the ★ **Dining Car Restaurant** (290 Izaak Walton Inn Rd., Essex, 406/888-5700, www.izaakwaltoninn.

com, 7am-8pm daily, $10-30) serves up scrumptious meals as trains rumble past the window. The cozy restaurant serves breakfast, lunch, and dinner with a menu that changes with the seasons and includes vegetarian and kid options. Dinners feature elk tenderloin, buffalo rib eye, and trout. Leave room for the huckleberry cobbler dessert. Be sure to head downstairs to the Flagstop Bar for a nightcap or at least to look at the historical photos of local railroad disasters.

CAFÉS

Inexpensive family-run cafés, favorites for locals and good for after-hike burgers, are the mainstay of U.S. 2. Lighter meals at these establishments run $7-10; full dinners run up to about $20. Located six miles west of Marias Pass, the **Snow Slip Inn** (15644 U.S. 2 E., Essex, 406/226-4400, www.snowslipinn.com, 8am-10pm daily) bases its homestyle cooking on local, fresh products as much as possible. It still has its 1945 historic bar. Located west of Essex, the three-generation family-run ★ **Healthy Haven Café** (14305 U.S. 2 E., 406/888-5720, www.glacierhaveninn.com, 6pm-8pm Tues.-Sat. mid-June-Labor Day) serves homestyle dinners with fresh ingredients: salmon, steaks, and buffalo burgers. Leave room to finish dinner with real huckleberry pie. The café is for sale, so check on its status first. Closest to West Glacier, the small **Stanton Creek Lodge** (13951 U.S. 2 E., 406/888-5040, www.stantoncreeklodge.com, 11am-7pm daily mid-May-Oct., bar open later Fri.-Sat.)

serves lunch and dinner. Its location is convenient for refueling after hiking the Grant Ridge Loop. This is one of Montana's funky old bars, where patrons used to ride horses through the building and shoot at the floor. If you see the buck sing, you've stayed too long.

GROCERIES

You can pick up a few groceries at the small Neighborhood Grocery store that opened in summer 2016 at the **Snow Slip Inn** (15644 U.S. 2 E., Essex, 406/226-4400, www.snowslipinn.com). To stock up for camping or traveling, find seasonal grocery stores in East Glacier and West Glacier. Larger food markets are in Browning on the east side or Hungry Horse and Columbia Falls on the west side.

PICNIC AREAS

There is only one designated picnic area on U.S. 2, and that is **Walton** (milepost 180.5). Behind the Walton Ranger Station, the small picnic area is under thick trees adjacent to the Middle Fork River. Picnic tables, pit toilets, and fire rings with grills are available, but you'll need to bring your own firewood; gathering wood is prohibited. Trails to Ole Creek, the Middle Fork, and Scalplock Lookout depart from the picnic area.

With several **river accesses** along the Middle Fork of the Flathead, there are plenty of additional places sans tables for picnicking at a scenic spot and soaking your feet in cold water. **Cascadilla** and **Paola** offer the best beaches.

Transportation and Services

DRIVING AND PARKING

U.S. 2 is a narrow, curvy, two-lane mountain highway. Because it's a trucking route, large semis will whiz by and press behind you. This is the route for **RVs**, as they are not permitted across Going-to-the-Sun Road.

Find parking at signed river accesses and trailheads.

SERVICES

While you can find some newspapers sold in the inns and restaurants along the highway, you'll need to head to East Glacier or West Glacier for **ATMs, laundry services,** and **groceries**. The closest **post offices** are in East Glacier and West Glacier. For **hot showers** ($5-10), you can pop in to Glacier Meadow RV Park or Glacier Haven Campground.

Even though U.S. 2 lacks many services, **public restrooms** are plentiful. Most are vault toilets with no running water and are open spring-fall. Find these at all river access points, Walton Picnic Area, the Goat Lick, and Marias Pass.

Gas and Repairs

This 60-mile corridor through wild, untamed wilderness is a road where the usually expected conveniences of civilization are not available. You won't find gas stations between East Glacier and West Glacier; fill up in either of those towns before you leave. For car repairs, call mobile repair services in Flathead Valley.

Cell Phone and Internet Access

Because of surrounding steep mountains, you'll find cell reception nonexistent on U.S. 2, but you can stop to use old-fashioned **public pay telephones** at Stanton Creek Lodge, Izaak Walton Inn, and Snow Slip Inn. Internet services are only available for guests at a few private campgrounds and inns.

Newspapers/Magazines

A few of the inns and restaurants sell the *Great Falls Tribune, Hungry Horse News,* or Flathead Valley's *Daily Interlake.*

Emergencies

For highway, river, or wilderness emergencies, call 911. A seasonal **urgent-care clinic** (100 Rea Rd., West Glacier, 406/888-9224, 9am-4pm daily Memorial Day-Labor Day) operates in West Glacier. Regional hospitals in Flathead Valley include **Kalispell Regional Medical Center** (310 Sunny View Ln., Kalispell, 406/752-5111) and **North Valley Hospital** (1600 Hospital Way, Whitefish, 406/863-3500). The east side is served by the **Blackfeet Community Hospital** (760 Government Sq., Browning, 406/338-6154).

The **Walton Ranger Station** (milepost 180.5, U.S. 2, 406/888-7800), at Walton Picnic Area on the southernmost tip of Glacier National Park, is staffed only in summer, and not full time, as the rangers patrol miles of backcountry trails. If you need assistance, use the pay phone at **Izaak Walton Inn** (0.8 mile west of the Walton Ranger Station) to call Glacier National Park **headquarters** (406/888-7800). For maps, guidebooks, and information on outdoor activities in the Great Bear Wilderness and the Bob Marshall, contact the **Hungry Horse Ranger Station** (10 Hungry Horse Dr., Hungry Horse, 406/387-3800, www.fs.fed.us/r1/flathead). For Lewis and Clark National Forest information, call the **Rocky Mountain Ranger Station** (1102 Main Ave. NW, Choteau, 406/466-5341, www. fs.fed.us/r1/lewisclark).

Waterton

Look for ★ to find recommended
sights, activities, dining, and lodging.

Highlights

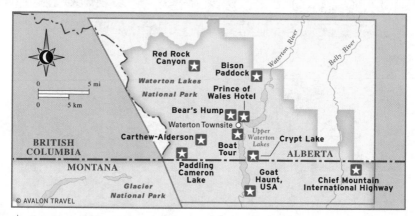

★ **Boat Tour:** Hop aboard the historic MV *International* for a ride on the deepest lake in the Canadian Rockies. You'll float across the international boundary to Goat Haunt, USA (page 233).

★ **Chief Mountain International Highway:** Cross into Canada to reach Waterton on this two-nation scenic road which circles around a mountain sacred to the Blackfeet (page 233).

★ **Prince of Wales Hotel:** This 1927 hotel maintains British ambience with kilt-wearing bellhops and afternoon high tea (page 236).

★ **Goat Haunt, USA:** Accessible only by boat or on foot, Goat Haunt is a launchpad to Glacier's remote northern trails (page 236).

★ **Bison Paddock:** In a tribute to the great wild herds that once roamed the prairies, Parks Canada maintains a small herd of these large mammals (page 238).

★ **Crypt Lake:** A boat ride leads to the trailhead, where switchbacks ascend to what looks like impassable cliffs. But a hidden tunnel curls into a hanging valley holding an idyllic lake (page 241).

★ **Bear's Hump:** Climb up the short grunt for a grand panoramic view of Waterton Townsite and Waterton Lake (page 242).

★ **Carthew-Alderson:** Cross over a high, windswept alpine pass and you'll be wowed by peaks and icy blue jewels (page 243).

★ **Red Rock Canyon:** Its colorful mosaic of sediments is evidence of the canyon's origins as an ancient inland sea (page 245).

★ **Paddling Cameron Lake:** Paddle this idyllic lake and look for grizzlies above the southern shore (page 251).

22

For such a small park, Waterton Lakes National Park packs a punch. Located at a nexus of major bird migration routes and weather systems, it houses a plethora of wildlife and rare plants found nowhere else.

On the Continental Divide's east side, mountains meet the prairie; with no transitional foothills, eastern peaks plummet directly to grasslands, a phenomenon caused by geological overthrusts that exposed the oldest sedimentary rock in the Canadian Rockies. Although active glaciers vacated Waterton's borders years ago, the results of ice gnawing on its landscape left lake pockets strewn through the park. A long, glacier-gouged trough forms Upper Waterton Lake, the deepest lake in the Canadian Rockies and one that straddles the U.S.-Canadian border. The lake frequently kicks up with winds, proving the park's ranking as the second-windiest place in Alberta.

Dominated by the Prince of Wales Hotel and Waterton Lake, the park serves as a destination itself as well as an entrance to Glacier's remote north country. On any summer day, the Waterton Townsite bustles with shoppers, bicyclists, backpackers, boaters, and campers. It's a quintessential Canadian mountain town that embodies what Banff used to be before booming commercialism. The MV *International* shuttles hikers and sightseers across Waterton Lake and the international boundary to Goat Haunt, USA. Only two roads pierce the park's remarkable interior, both gateways to lakes, waterfalls, canyons, peaks, and wildlife.

HISTORY

In 1858, Lieutenant Thomas Blakiston, a European explorer, scoured southern Alberta for a railroad route through the Canadian Rockies. Arriving at Waterton Lakes, he named them for the British naturalist Charles Waterton, who never visited the area.

The area became Kootenay Lakes Forest Park in 1895, Canada's fourth national park and the brainchild of Pincher Creek rancher F. W. Godsal. The legendary Kootenai Brown took the reins as the first game guardian

---

Previous: paddleboarding in Upper Waterton Lake; Prince of Wales Hotel. **Above:** swimming in Upper Waterton Lake.

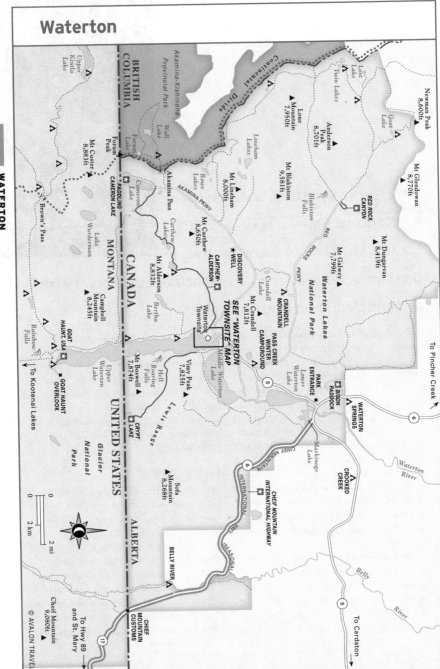

© AVALON TRAVEL

Kootenai Brown

John George "Kootenai" Brown was influential in the formation of Waterton Lakes National Park, but he also became the stuff of legend. Born in Ireland in 1839, he served with the British Army in India before coming to North America in 1861. With no money, he followed the Cariboo Gold Rush to Barkerville, British Columbia. He spent the money he made from gold, departing several years later broke.

At age 26, he crossed the Continental Divide at South Kootenay Pass in what would become Waterton Lakes National Park. He fell in love with the area, called Kootenay Lakes at the time, and inherited his name through his close ties to the Kootenai people.

Local legend is full of Brown's escapades. When Blackfeet shot him in the back with an arrow, he reputedly pulled the arrow out himself and cleaned the wound with turpentine. He spent 12 years in Montana as a trader, a pony express rider, a scout for Custer, and a buffalo hunter. When buffalo became scarce, he hunted wolves. While he rode for the U.S. Army pony express, Chief Sitting Bull and the Sioux captured him, stripping him and tying him to a stake while they debated his fate. He escaped in the middle of the night.

In 1869, he married and started a family with a Métis woman, Olivia Lyonnais. After being hauled into a Fort Benton court on murder charges and acquitted, he and his family packed up and went to Alberta. He built a cabin by Upper Waterton Lake, working as a guide, commercial fisherman, hunter, rancher, trader, and scout for the Rocky Mountain Rangers during the 1885 North-West Rebellion, the same year Olivia died. He later married Isabella, a Cree.

When Canada established the Kootenay Lake Forest Reserve in 1885, Brown became its first game warden and fisheries officer. In 1910, he was promoted to Forest Ranger in Charge. A year later, when Kootenay Lakes officially became Waterton Lakes, he stepped in as its first superintendent.

Kootenai Brown died in 1916 and is buried with his two wives along the entrance road to Waterton.

---

and fisheries inspector. In 1911 he became Waterton's first superintendent, and the park's name officially changed to Waterton Lakes National Park.

Waterton produced western Canada's first oil well in 1902, but within four years the site closed down as the yield trickled to nothing. Meanwhile, an oil well near Cameron Falls produced one barrel a day and prompted building the Waterton Townsite. When oil riches dissipated in 1910, tourism arrived, fueled in part by Great Northern Railway's Glacier development. The Townsite sprouted cottages, a hotel, a golf course, packhorse outfitters, and boating.

In 1913 the Great Northern Railway scouted Waterton for an appropriate hotel site, but World War I and a proposed dam in Waterton delayed its construction. Ironically, Prohibition in the United States prompted it to be built. Alcohol, after all, was still legal in Canada, attracting scads of Montanans for thirst quenching. In 1927 the Prince of Wales Hotel finally opened on the wind-battered knoll above the town, and the 72-foot MV *International* took its first sightseers up Waterton Lake. Within five years the park gained status in conjunction with Glacier as the world's first International Peace Park.

Parks Canada started a historic $107 million in infrastructure improvements in Waterton in 2016. Projects are slated from 2016-2020 to revamp trails, trailheads, parking areas, roads, campgrounds, picnic areas, water, sewer, park service buildings, and construct a new visitors center.

ECOLOGICAL SIGNIFICANCE

Despite its tiny size, Waterton is a nexus. The park is on a narrow north-south wildlife corridor and is at the axis of two major migratory bird flyways. Over 250 bird species nest or use the park's rich habitat for migration stopovers. It is one of the last places in North America where grizzly bears roam into the fringes of their original grassland habitat. Over 45 different habitats shelter 10 species of amphibians and reptiles, 24 species of fish, and 60 species of mammals. Rare trumpeter swans nest here, as do Vaux's swifts.

Because arctic and Pacific weather systems collide at Waterton, a breadth of vegetation abounds. With more than 1,370 plants, mosses, and lichens, Waterton is home to more than half of Alberta's plant species, 179 of which are considered rare and 22 of which are found nowhere else in the province. Moonwort, a small fern, grows in eight varieties; one is found only in Waterton. The park's diminutive acreage has more plant diversity than the much larger Banff, Jasper, Kootenay, and Yoho parks combined. Because of its extremes and such rarities, the United Nations Educational, Scientific, and Cultural Organization (UNESCO) has named Waterton a Biosphere Reserve and a World Heritage Site.

Waterton is also bordered by two provincial parks: Akamina-Kishinena and Castle Wildlands, the latter created in 2015. Together, they enhance the Crown of the Continent ecosystem.

Exploring Waterton

Waterton's 52 square miles are tiny compared to Glacier. The Townsite is at 4,200 feet in elevation, but surrounding peaks climb to 9,000 feet. While the Townsite is home to about 100 people in winter, in summer it balloons to nearly 2,000 residents. The park sees about 475,000 annual visitors; that's about 16 percent of Glacier's crowds.

Waterton and Glacier meet at the 49th parallel, which is the international border, yet the parks are connected because they form one ecosystem, recognized by UNESCO as a **World Heritage Site** and a **Biosphere Reserve.** Humans can cross between the two via Waterton Lake, and grizzly bears roam back and forth. The two parks, which include part of the longest undefended border in the world at 5,525 miles, form **Waterton-Glacier International Peace Park.**

VISITORS CENTER

The small **Waterton Lakes Visitor Information Centre** (7.2 km/4.5 miles south of the park entrance station on the park entrance road, 403/859-5133, www. pc.gc.ca, 8am-7pm daily July-Aug., 9am-5pm daily early May-June and Sept.-early Oct.) is across from the entrance road to Prince of Wales Hotel. It provides information, wilderness-use permits, road conditions, fishing licenses, maps, and the Bear's Hump trailhead. In winter, you can get the same information, licenses, and permits from the **Parks Canada office** (215 Mount View Rd., 403/859-2224, www.pc.gc.ca, 8am-4pm Mon.-Fri. year-round). With construction slated for 2018, a new $7.6 million Waterton Lakes National Park Visitor Reception Centre on Windflower Avenue adjacent to the playground is expected to open in 2019.

ENTRANCE STATION

The **entrance gate** is **open 24-7 year-round,** but only staffed early May-early October. U.S. park passes are not valid in this Canadian park, although many Americans expect them to be. Even though Waterton-Glacier is an International Peace Park, no combined park pass is sold. To enter Waterton, you must purchase a separate **Parks Canada day pass** valid until 4pm the following day (C$4-8 pp, single-vehicle C$20, May-Oct.; C$3-6 pp, single-vehicle C$15, Nov.-Apr.). For multiday visits, the annual Waterton pass

Waterton Townsite

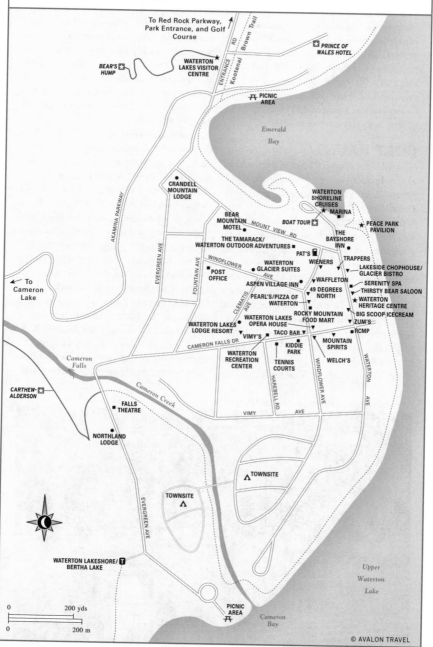

To Red Rock Parkway, Park Entrance, and Golf Course

PRINCE OF WALES HOTEL

BEAR'S HUMP

WATERTON LAKES VISITOR CENTRE

ENTRANCE RD

Kootenai Brown Trail

PICNIC AREA

Emerald Bay

CRANDELL MOUNTAIN LODGE

WATERTON SHORELINE CRUISES

MARINA

BOAT TOUR

PEACE PARK PAVILION

BEAR MOUNTAIN MOTEL

MOUNT VIEW RD

THE BAYSHORE INN

THE TAMARACK/ WATERTON OUTDOOR ADVENTURES

PAT'S

WIENERS

TRAPPERS

AKAMINA PARKWAY

EVERGREEN AVE

FOUNTAIN AVE

WINDFLOWER AVE

WATERTON GLACIER SUITES

LAKESIDE CHOPHOUSE/ GLACIER BISTRO

POST OFFICE

WAFFLETON

SERENITY SPA

THIRSTY BEAR SALOON

ASPEN VILLAGE INN

49 DEGREES NORTH

To Cameron Lake

CLEMATIS AVE

PEARL'S/PIZZA OF WATERTON

WATERTON HERITAGE CENTRE

ROCKY MOUNTAIN FOOD MART

BIG SCOOP ICECREAM

WATERTON LAKES OPERA HOUSE

ZUM'S

WATERTON LAKES LODGE RESORT

VIMY'S

TACO BAR

RCMP

CAMERON FALLS DR

Cameron Falls

MOUNTAIN SPIRITS

CARTHEW-ALDERSON

WATERTON RECREATION CENTER

KIDDIE PARK

TENNIS COURTS

WELCH'S

FALLS THEATRE

Cameron Creek

HAREBELL RD

WINDFLOWER AVE

WATERTON AVE

NORTHLAND LODGE

VIMY AVE

TOWNSITE

TOWNSITE

EVERGREEN AVE

WATERTON LAKESHORE/ BERTHA LAKE

PICNIC AREA

Upper Waterton Lake

Cameron Bay

0   200 yds
0   200 m

© AVALON TRAVEL

might be more economical (C$20-40 pp, single-vehicle C$99). A one-year Parks Canada pass is valid for entry to 27 Canadian national parks (C$34-68, single-vehicle C$137). Children under six are admitted free, and seniors can get discounts. Admission to the park is free on Canada Day (July 1) and Parks Day (July 17). During 2017, entry is free all year to celebrate the 150th anniversary of the Confederation. A proposal has kids under 18 getting free entry starting in 2018.

GOAT HAUNT

Located at the southern tip of Waterton Lake and only accessible by foot or boat, **Goat Haunt** is in Glacier National Park in the United States. Visitors may debark the boat to tour the **Peace Park Pavilion** and walk to the **Goat Haunt Pavilion** and back without going through immigration control; however, hikers must go through immigration at the ranger station (11am-5:30pm daily June-Sept.) to access Glacier's trails and backcountry campsites. All hikers must have appropriate **passports** or **passport cards.** Those entering Waterton from Glacier via Goat Haunt-area trails are required to call the **Canada Border Services Agency** (403/653-3535 or 403/653-3009) from the Waterton Townsite.

SHUTTLES AND TOURS
Shuttles
INTERNATIONAL SHUTTLES

The international border complicates shuttling between Glacier and Waterton. Pay shuttles run daily early June-late September, but different companies cover various segments and directions. Check online with the companies for schedules, which can alter due to construction. **Reservations are required** for these shuttles.

From Glacier's east side, get to Waterton on the northbound shuttle operated by **Glacier Park, Inc.** (GPI, 406/892-2525, www.glacierparkinc.com, schedule online, adults $15-75, kids half price). The shuttle picks up riders at Glacier Park Lodge, Two Medicine, Cut Bank Creek, St. Mary Lodge, Many Glacier Hotel, Chief Mountain Customs, and terminates service at Prince of Wales Hotel in Waterton.

For the return connection between Waterton and Glacier, riders may not originate in Canada with GPI. Instead, use the *Chief Mountain Connector* operated by **Waterton Outdoor Adventures** (The Tamarack, 214 Mount View Rd., 403/859-2378, www.hikewaterton.com, $20 pp). The shuttle departs The Tamarack in the afternoon for the Chief Mountain border crossing,

Goat Haunt is only accessible by tour boat or hiking.

where you walk through the border control station to catch the southbound GPI shuttle at the Chief Mountain Customs Trailhead to go down Glacier's east side. This shuttle also provides a return service from the Waterton side of the customs station for backpackers exiting Glacier at the Chief Mountain Customs Trailhead and returning to the Waterton Townsite to retrieve a car.

For connections between Glacier Park International Airport and Waterton, **Glacier Charters** (406/892-3390 or 800/829-7039, www.glaciertransportation.com, $380-390 one-way) runs shuttles by reservation.

WATER SHUTTLES

Waterton Shoreline Cruises (403/859-2362, www.watertoncruise.com) operates two boat services that serve as hiker shuttles to trailheads. The **Crypt Lake Water Shuttle** (daily late May-early Oct., adults C$25 round-trip, children C$12) departs from the marina for a 15-minute ride across Upper Waterton Lake to Crypt Landing, where the Crypt Lake trail begins. Shuttles depart the marina at 10am; earlier departures are added to the schedule June-early September at 8:30am and 9am. Return boats leave Crypt Landing at 5:30pm, with a 4pm boat added in summer. Purchase tickets a day in advance, or arrive at least 20 minutes before departure to buy tickets.

A tour boat to **Goat Haunt** (daily June-late Sept., one-way adults C$32 and kids C$12-16, round-trip adults C$49 and kids C$16-24) functions also as a hiker shuttle. It accesses trailheads in northern Glacier and provides transportation back to Waterton after hiking the Lakeshore Trail to Goat Haunt. Buy your return ticket in the morning before hiking down the lake. You can also pay in cash (exact change in U.S. or Canadian dollars) when you board in Goat Haunt. Day hikers should catch the 10am boat from Waterton Townsite to Goat Haunt, notify the ticket agent of which boat you plan to catch to return, and be prepared for immigration requirements at Goat Haunt.

LAND SHUTTLES

Departing from The Tamarack, **Waterton Outdoor Adventures** (214 Mount View Rd., 403/859-2378, www.hikewaterton.com) runs shuttles to trailheads on Red Rock and Akamina Parkways. The **Cameron Express** (8am daily June-Aug., 8:30am Sept., C$14) takes hikers to the popular Carthew-Alderson trailhead for a point-to-point hike back to the Townsite. Mountain bikers can take the shuttle to ride the Akamina trails and then ride back to town. Reservations are a good idea midsummer and required for cyclists; make them with a credit card by phone. By reservation, the company also shuttles backpackers to trailheads for point-to-point hikes.

★ Boat Tour

Waterton Shoreline Cruises (at the marina at junction of Mount View Rd. and Waterton Ave., 403/859-2362, www.watertoncruise.com, 10am, 1pm, 4pm, and 7pm daily July-Aug., 10am and 1pm daily May-June and Sept.-early Oct., adults C$49 round-trip, kids C$16-24, under age 4 free) operates the historic *International* on Upper Waterton Lake. During the two-hour tour on the wooden 200-passenger boat, which has been cruising here since 1927, knowledgeable guides punctuate their patter with humor. For the best views, go for a sunny seat on the boat's top deck. If the weather is brisk, just bundle up. June-mid-September, the boat docks for 30 minutes at Goat Haunt, allowing enough time to walk to the ranger station pavilion to see the full length of the lake. Shoulder season launches, which are often on the *Miss Waterton* instead, do not stop at Goat Haunt. Buy tickets at least one hour in advance; to guarantee space, buy them a day in advance.

Driving Tours
★ CHIEF MOUNTAIN INTERNATIONAL HIGHWAY
The Chief Mountain International Highway provides a connection between Glacier and Waterton National Parks. Its season and hours are linked to the Canadian and U.S.

Akamina-Kishinena Provincial Park

Where Waterton Lakes National Park meets the Continental Divide, Akamina-Kishinena Provincial Park begins. It flanks the international boundary of Montana's Glacier National Park and runs westward to the North Fork of the Flathead River. This remote 27,000-acre park is accessible only on foot from Akamina Parkway in Waterton Lakes or on trails from the end of a 109-kilometer (68-mile) dirt road that starts 16 kilometers (10 miles) south of Fernie, British Columbia.

The small park is part of the same slice of the Rockies that provides corridors for grizzly bears and wolves. Geologic wonders display themselves in Forum Peak's 1.3-billion-year-old sedimentary rocks, and rare plants like the pygmy poppy grow here.

From Waterton, hikers and mountain bikers can access the park via a circa-1920 trail that connects the Cameron Valley to the North Fork of the Flathead Valley. At Akamina Pass, the boundary between Waterton National Park and the provincial park, you can mountain-bike to Wall Lake or hike to Forum Lake.

On both sides of the international border, a growing movement is lobbying to make Akamina-Kishinena a national park. The addition would complete the protection of the "Crown of the Continent" ecosystem, matching the entire distance of Glacier's international boundary with lands protected under the Canadian national park system.

Contact **British Columbia Parks** (205/489-8540, www.gov.bc.ca/bcparks) for information on visiting the park. For information on lobbying efforts, see www.flathead.ca.

immigration and customs stations at the border (daily mid-May-Sept., 7am-10pm June-Labor Day, 9am-6pm May and Sept.). You may want to top off on gas in the United States since gas is generally more expensive in Canada. The nearest gas is in Babb, Montana, or in Waterton Townsite. The 30-mile road undulates over rolling aspen hills and past beaver ponds as it curves around Chief Mountain, imposing and alone on Glacier's northeast corner. A few unmarked pullouts offer good photo ops. Drive this open range carefully, for cows wander the road. Your car also may need a good cleaning if wet cow pies litter the road, but the 2016 repaving of the Waterton section smoothed out the tread.

From the United States, as the road rounds Chief Mountain, it enters Glacier National Park. There is no entrance station here, and no payment is required. The road reaches the international border and Chief Mountain border crossing at 18.6 miles. After crossing the border, the road enters Alberta and Waterton Lakes National Park, but you won't reach a park entrance station until nearly at the Townsite. After the road crosses the Belly River, it briefly exits the park, crossing the

Blood Indian Reserve (the Blood are part of the Blackfoot family) before reentering the park. Regrowth from the 1998 Sofa Mountain Fire lines both sides of the road. As you crest a big rise, stop at the overlook (45 kilometers, 28 miles) to gaze at the Waterton Valley. For the descent, shift into second gear to avoid burning your brakes.

PARK ENTRANCE ROAD

From Highway 6, the eight-kilometer (5-mile) year-round road connecting the park entrance station with Waterton Townsite is worth a drive with a pair of binoculars. Linnet, Maskinonge, and Lower Waterton Lakes attract scads of birds as well as moose, bears, elk, and smaller wildlife. Stop at a picnic area along the route for wildlife-watching: Knight's Lake (1 km/0.6 mile), Hay Barn (4 km/2.5 miles), or Marquis (6.5 km/4 miles). The Waterton Lakes Visitor Information Centre is 7.2 kilometers (4.5 miles) from the entrance station.

AKAMINA PARKWAY

Resurfaced in 2016, the 16-kilometer (10-mile) Akamina Parkway climbs along the base of

Chief Mountain International Highway connects Glacier and Waterton.

Crandell Mountain to Cameron Lake. The paved road is open year-round, although in winter plowing only goes as far as Little Prairie. West of the Waterton Lakes Visitor Information Centre, the signed Akamina Parkway turns off and climbs steeply from Waterton Townsite as it curves above Cameron Creek Gorge. It passes the **Oil City Historic Site** as well as trailheads to Crandell Lake, Lineham Falls, Rowe Lakes, Akamina Pass, and Forum Lake. Picnic tables, pit toilets, and shelters are at McNeally's (6.4 km/4 miles) and Little Prairie (13 km/8 miles). You'll see signs of washouts, now repaired, from 2013's torrential rains. The road ends at **Cameron Lake.** For the return descent to the Townsite, shift into second gear; you can always smell the hot brakes of those who don't.

RED ROCK PARKWAY

Repaving in 2016 removed the copious potholes from Red Rock Parkway (open May-Oct.); the pleasant drive terminates at Red Rock Canyon. Locate the signed turnoff on the park entrance road (3.5 km/2.2 miles from the Townsite; 4 km/2.5 miles from the park entrance station). The 15-kilometer (9.3-mile), narrow road climbs through grasslands, squeezes through a canyon, and opens up into meadows along Blakiston Creek. Early July often brings on a wildflower show. Bring binoculars for watching bears and bighorn sheep. The road is quite narrow but passable for trailers and RVs, and it reaches Crandell Mountain Campground (6.8 km/4.2 miles) about midway. The parkway ends at two parking areas, which have restrooms. A self-guided trail leads around **Red Rock Canyon.** To picnic along Red Rock Parkway, you'll find tables, pit toilets, and shelters at three spots: Coppermine Creek (8 km/5 miles), Dungarvan (13 km/8 miles), and Red Rock (15 km/9.3 miles).

Sights

CHIEF MOUNTAIN

Located along Chief Mountain Highway, Chief Mountain abruptly rises 9,080 feet from aspen parklands and prairie. It is the northeasternmost peak in Glacier National Park. Legend tells of a young Flathead brave who carried a bison skull to its summit and remained there for four nights wrestling the Spirit of the Mountain. When he finally prevailed, the spirit gave him a protection totem to keep him safe in battle and hunting.

★ PRINCE OF WALES HOTEL

Designated a Canadian National Historic Site, the 122-foot-tall, four-story, 90-room **Prince of Wales Hotel** (406/892-2525 or 403/236-3400, www.glacierparkinc.com, daily early June-mid-Sept.) took more than a year to build. Constructed by the Great Northern Railway as a link in its Glacier chain, the hotel opened its doors in 1927. Even if you are not staying here, drop in to see its massive lobby with floor-to-ceiling windows looking down Waterton Lake. Kilt-wearing bellhops haul luggage, and the lobby serves high tea in the afternoon. Walk out on the bluff for the best photographic views of Waterton Lake. Beware the howling winds that can rip off hats.

WATERTON LAKE

Set in a north-south trough gouged by Pleistocene ice age glaciers, Waterton Lake is the deepest lake in the Canadian Rockies. (It's actually Upper Waterton Lake, which feeds Middle and Lower Waterton Lakes, but no one calls it that.) Its 487-foot depths hold 50-pound lake trout and opossum shrimp, which are tiny relics of the ice age. Spanning the international boundary, the 0.5-mile-wide and nearly seven-mile-long lake conveys visitors over its waters in the 1927 wooden *International* tour boat.

THE U.S.-CANADIAN BORDER

For Waterton visitors, the border inside the park is an attraction. The long, straight swath is cleared every 20 years by the International Boundary Commission. The boat tour down Waterton Lake crosses this unnatural forest line en route to Goat Haunt, where visitors can debark for 30 minutes without going through immigration control. Hikers can also walk over the border swath on the Waterton Lakeshore Trail.

★ GOAT HAUNT, USA

A tiny seasonal enclave housing rangers, Goat Haunt, USA, is at Waterton Lake's southern end in Glacier National Park. Accessed only by boat or on foot, Goat Haunt sees hundreds of visitors per day in midsummer. Most arrive via the *International* tour boat. Goat Haunt's International Peace Park Pavilion displays tell the story of the peace park. Trailheads depart to Goat Haunt Overlook, Kootenai Lakes, Rainbow Falls, and beyond.

PEACE PARK PAVILIONS

Two small interpretive pavilions commemorate Waterton and Glacier as the first International Peace Park in the world. After razing the old Peace Park Pavilion in 2016 between the Bayshore Inn and the marina, Waterton is slated to install its new pavilion in 2018. The U.S. pavilion sits at Goat Haunt.

CAMERON LAKE

Tucked in a glacial cirque at the terminus of Akamina Parkway, Cameron Lake reflects the steep slopes of Mount Custer. Facilities were reconstructed in 2016. Across the glacially fed lake sits Herbst Glacier in Montana, where avalanches preen the slopes into good bear habitat. Rent a rowboat or canoe to paddle around the lake's shoreline, or saunter the Lakeshore Trail along the west shore, watching for moose, shorebirds, and bears. From here, hikers also climb the Carthew-Alderson trail to trek to the Townsite.

WATERTON HERITAGE CENTRE

Operated by the Waterton Natural History Association, **Waterton Heritage Centre** (117 Waterton Ave., 403/859-2267, 10am-6pm daily May-late Sept., free) is a very tiny museum housed in the old fire hall with displays on Waterton's natural and cultural history, including local favorite renegade Joe Cosley. Books ranging from hiking guides to coffee-table picture books are also sold here.

CAMERON FALLS

Picturesque Cameron Falls is on the edge of Waterton Townsite on Evergreen Avenue. In June, water roars through its slots, but the flow drops substantially by August. Cameron Creek has eroded a massive fold of the Waterton Formation, a 600-million-year-old rock layer. Sit on a bench at the base, or climb the short, steep trails on both sides of the creek to reach overlooks. Opt for the north-side switchback trail for better views.

WATERTON TOWNSITE

A quaint little tourism town frequented by bighorn sheep and deer, Waterton Townsite is in a dramatic location at the foot of Waterton Lake. Paved walking trails lead through the town, connecting the few-blocks-long shopping district with the campground and picnic areas. Find two International Peace Park commemorative markers adjacent to the marina, where a new pavilion is to be built in 2018. Waterton Townsite hums in summer with visitors riding surrey bikes but is quiet in winter under the snow. New streetlights provide darker skies for better stargazing.

MASKINONGE LAKE

Birders and wildlife-watchers migrate to Maskinonge Lake for its rich diversity. Located east of the park entrance, the aspen-rimmed lake attracts waterfowl, ospreys, trumpeter swans, yellow-headed blackbirds, and kingfishers. Because Waterton is on the axis of two migratory flyways, it sees over 250 species of birds. The lake also attracts huge Shiras moose, weighing 1,500 pounds, plus muskrats, mink, and tiny vagrant shrews. When rare trumpeter swans nest here in midsummer, some of the area closes to protect their offspring. Bring binoculars and

Hikers reach immigration at Goat Haunt.

spotting scopes for wildlife-watching. Rent binoculars at **Pat's Gas Station** (224 Mount View Rd., 403/859-2266, www.patswaterton. com, $15/day).

★ BISON PADDOCK

Roaming the plains in vast numbers 150 years ago, wild bison, also called buffalo, have all but vanished from North America. Two kilometers (1.2 miles) west of the park entrance road on Highway 6, the Bison Paddock contains a small herd. Bison weigh close to 2,000 pounds and look like shaggy cows. But don't be lured into thinking they are docile: They may look big, lunky, and dumb, but they are extremely unpredictable and aggressive. You can see the bison from a viewing area or via a four-kilometer (2.5-mile), narrow, potholed road with broken pavement looping through the grassland paddock. No trailers are allowed.

DISCOVERY WELL AND OIL CITY

Located on the Akamina Parkway, two stops mark the site of western Canada's first oil well and its accompanying town site. Find the 1902 Discovery Well site eight kilometers (5 miles) up the road. Continue on a bit to the original

bison grazing in Waterton's Bison Paddock

town site for Oil City, where a five-minute walk leads to the foundation of the hotel. It's all that remains of the 20-block city that became a ghost town within four years.

Recreation

DAY HIKES

Waterton has more than 200 kilometers (124 miles) of trails. Among them, three kilometers (1.8 miles) of paved and dirt walking trails connect sights, restaurants, lodging facilities, the campground, and picnic areas in Waterton Townsite. From the marina to Cameron Bay, the trail follows the shoreline. Trails also connect to the Falls Theater, Cameron Falls, Bertha Lake and Waterton Lakeshore trailheads, Emerald Bay, and the Prince of Wales Hotel. Contrary to Glacier's backcountry rules, Waterton's trails permit dogs on a leash, but keep your pet under control and away from wildlife.

For updated trail conditions, look at current reports on the Parks Canada website (www.pc.gc.ca) under "Public Safety." The visitors center also has trail conditions information, but if you want to talk to the experts about trails, head to **The Tamarack**, home of **Waterton Outdoor Adventures** (214 Mount View Rd., 403/859-2378, www.hikewaterton.com), to check the hike board and get advice.

For hiking, you'll find the best Waterton topographic map at the visitors center and The Tamarack. The **Gem Trek map** (877/921-6277, www.gemtrek.com, C$14), also available online, includes roads, trails, bike routes,

Waterton Hikes

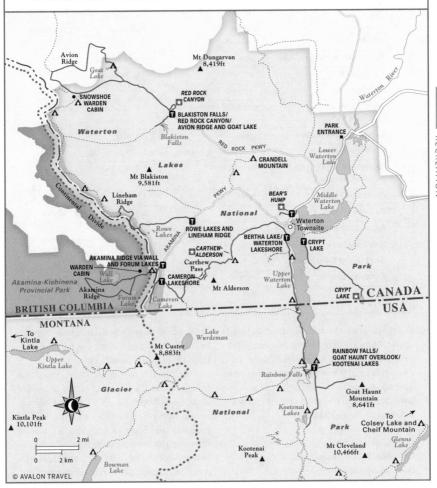

and trail descriptions for easy, moderate, and strenuous hikes, plus trails in Akamina-Kishinena Provincial Park and at Goat Haunt.

Shuttles by water and land make for easy trailhead access. **Waterton Shoreline Cruises** (403/859-2362, www.watertoncruise.com) operates the Crypt Lake and Goat Haunt boats. **Waterton Outdoor Adventures** (The Tamarack, 214 Mount View Rd., 403/859-2378, www.hikewaterton.com) operates the land shuttles. **Pat's Gas Station**

(224 Mount View Rd., 403/859-2266, www.patswaterton.com, C$20/day) rents bear spray.

Lower-elevation trails (Bear's Hump, Waterton Lakeshore) usually become snow-free in May. Snow melts off other trails in June, but can linger on high-elevation trails (Avion Ridge, Carthew Pass, Bertha Lake, Lineham Ridge) into early July. Use ice axes for crossing steep snowfields. Consult the visitors center or online (www.pc.gc.ca) for current trail status. Goat Haunt trails are subject

Waterton Hikes

Trail	Effort	Distance	Duration
Bertha Lake	strenuous	7 mi rt	3-4 hr
Waterton Lakeshore Trail	easy	8 mi one-way	4 hr
Crypt Lake	moderate-strenuous	10.6 mi rt	5.5-8 hr
Bear's Hump	strenuous	1.7 mi rt	1.25 hr
Rowe Lakes and Lineham Ridge	moderate-strenuous	5.2-10.6 mi rt	2.5-6 hr
Cameron Lakeshore	easy	1.9 mi rt	1 hr
Carthew-Alderson	moderate-strenuous	11.2 mi one-way	6 hr
Akamina Ridge via Wall and Forum Lakes	strenuous	5.4-11.4 mi rt	6-7 hr
Blakiston Falls	easy	1.2 mi rt	45 min
Red Rock Canyon	easy	0.6-mi loop	30 min
Avion Ridge and Goat Lake	moderate-strenuous	7.8-14 mi rt	4-7 hr
Rainbow Falls	easy	1.4 mi rt	1 hr
Goat Haunt Overlook	very strenuous	1.9 mi rt	2 hr
Kootenai Lakes	easy	5.6 mi rt	3-3.5 hr

to access when the immigration station is open (11am-5:30pm daily June-Sept.). Take your **passport,** as hikers must show valid passports or approved passport cards to go beyond the station. Look online (www.nps.gov/glac) for updated status reports for trails in Glacier National Park.

Bertha Lake

Distance: 11.4 km (7 miles) round-trip
Duration: 3-4 hours
Elevation gain: 1,480 feet
Effort: strenuous
Trailhead: southwest corner of Waterton Townsite off Evergreen Avenue (see map p. 241)

From the parking lot reconstructed in 2016, the trail starts as a signed interpretive path to Lower Bertha Falls. The path climbs gradually along the western shore of Waterton Lake to an overlook with views of Mount Cleveland, the highest peak in Glacier National Park. At the junction, take the right fork and head across the dry, open hillside to Lower Bertha

Falls, where pounding waters crash through bedrock. For a destination, the falls is 6.4 kilometers (4 miles) round-trip.

To continue to Bertha Lake, cross the bridge below the falls and climb incessant switchbacks up through a forested hillside beside Upper Bertha Falls, a larger sister of the lower falls. Soon the trail crests a timbered knoll high above narrow Bertha Lake for the best view of the lake. To reach the shore, descend 160 meters (525 feet) to the campground near its outlet.

Waterton Lakeshore Trail

Distance: 13 km (8 miles) one-way
Duration: 4 hours
Elevation gain: minimal
Effort: easy by elevation gain, moderate by length
Trailhead: southwest corner of Waterton Townsite off Evergreen Avenue (see map p. 241)

Bordering the west lakeshore of Waterton Lake, the trail begins at the Bertha Lake trailhead. After 1.5 kilometers (1 mile), the trails

Waterton Lakeshore Trail

© AVALON TRAVEL

diverge, with the Waterton Lakeshore Trail dropping in a quick, steep descent to Bertha Bay Campground on the lakeshore. The trail climbs up and down with some lake views until the international boundary at 6.1 kilometers (3.8 miles).

After the trail crosses the border, it becomes more level until entering the well-signed maze of trails at the end of Waterton Lake. Follow signs to Goat Haunt and catch the boat back to the Townsite. Before you leave in the morning, buy your return ticket with Waterton Shoreline Cruises. Bring your passport for immigration control in Goat Haunt.

★ Crypt Lake

Distance: 17 km (10.6 miles) round-trip
Duration: 5.5-8 hours
Elevation gain: 2,300 feet
Effort: moderate-strenuous
Trailhead: Crypt Landing, accessible by boat from Waterton (see map p. 242)

From the marina in the Waterton Townsite, catch the water taxi operated daily by **Waterton Shoreline Cruises** (403/859-2362, www.watertoncruise.com, May-early Oct., adults C$25, kids half price) to cross Upper Waterton Lake to Crypt Landing. July-early September, it departs the marina at 8:30am, 9am, and 10am and Crypt Landing at 4pm and 5:30pm. Spring and fall boats go only at 10am and 5:30pm. The startup date in May depends on snowmelt on the trail. Buy tickets the day before or at least one hour in advance.

From Crypt Landing, the climb bolts up 19 switchbacks through a wooded hillside along Hellroaring Creek. At the sixth switchback, an alternate, steeper route drops and climbs the edge of Hellroaring Creek to see its waterfalls; you can take one route up and one down. Soon the trail passes Twin Falls, and lodgepole pines give way to open meadows and boulder fields at Burnt Rock Falls, where the trail shoots up another 18 switchbacks. This exposed climb can be a scorcher, but yields a full view of 600-foot-high Crypt Falls.

The trail appears to dead-end in the headwall, but a hidden route leads to a narrow,

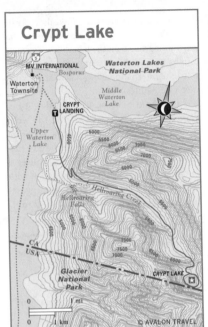

Crypt Lake

MV INTERNATIONAL
Bosporus
Waterton Lakes National Park

Waterton Townsite

CRYPT LANDING

Middle Waterton Lake

Upper Waterton Lake

Hellroaring Creek

Hellroaring Falls

CA
USA

Glacier National Park

CRYPT LAKE

0   1 mi
0   1 km

© AVALON TRAVEL

an underwater channel. The international boundary crosses the lake's southern end. To catch the return boat, hikers jump up to speed down the trail en masse. Take the earliest and latest boats (8:30am, 5:30pm) to have the maximum time for hiking, especially if you want to add on the 1.8-kilometer (1.1-mile) loop around the lake. For wildflowers, the trail is best in early July.

★ Bear's Hump

Distance: 2.8 km (1.7 miles) round-trip
Duration: 1.25 hours
Elevation gain: 550 feet
Effort: strenuous but short
Trailhead: Waterton Lakes Visitor Information Centre parking lot

The trail heads promptly uphill, piling on switchback after switchback in a vertical ThighMaster. At least it offers benches along the way to rest. Partially forested and thick with thimbleberry and virgin's bower, the hike is cool in early morning or late afternoon after the hump shades the east slope from the sun. For a trail guide, pick up a free interpretive brochure at the visitors center or download the phone app (www.pc.gc.ca).

Topping out on the Bear's Hump, a rocky outcropping on Mount Crandell's ridge,

10-foot steel ladder that climbs up to a tunnel. Its four-foot height demands an awkward walk or crawl. The 60-foot-long tunnel emerges on a cliff with a steel cable for assistance in crossing. The trail breaks into a tight cirque housing Crypt Lake, which drains from

Crypt Lake requires a cliff walk aided by a cable.

the trail offers one of the best views of the Waterton Townsite, the Prince of Wales Hotel, Waterton Lake, Glacier National Park, and the prairie. On top, three benches offer good spots to gaze at the scenery before you tackle the knee-pounding descent.

Rowe Lakes and Lineham Ridge

Distance: 8.4 km (5.2 miles) round-trip to Lower Rowe Lake; 12.8 km (7.9 miles) round-trip to Upper Rowe Lakes; 17.2 km (10.6 miles) round-trip to Lineham Ridge
Duration: 2.5-6 hours
Elevation gain: 3,116 feet
Effort: moderate-strenuous
Trailhead: Rowe Tamarack trailhead, 10.9 km (6.7 miles) up Akamina Parkway

In July this trail bursts with wildflowers: yellow arnica, paintbrush, and purple lupine. The climb starts through thin forest broken by avalanche paths, following Rowe Creek. At 3.9 kilometers (2.4 miles), a 10-minute spur trail splits off to Lower Rowe Lake, a destination for those wanting the shortest trek. Continuing on from the junction, the trail ascends into a broad meadow at the base of a giant cirque. After you cross the creek at 5.2 kilometers (3.2 miles), the left fork climbs steep switchbacks to Upper Rowe Lakes, a pair of scenic shallow lakes fringed with alpine larch.

For Lineham Ridge, the right fork after the creek crossing swings around the cirque to climb from subalpine wildflower meadows into alpine tundra. Red argillite colors the mountainside. From the ridge, Lineham Lakes appear below. At the saddle below Mount Lineham, you can opt to climb off-trail east to the peak or continue on the rugged trail west up Lineham Ridge to look down Blakiston Creek.

Cameron Lakeshore

Distance: 3.2 km (1.9 miles) round-trip
Duration: 1 hour
Elevation gain: none
Effort: easy
Trailhead: end of Akamina Parkway (see map p. 244)

This short trail follows the lake's western shoreline to a wooden platform and small interpretive display called Grizzly Gardens, where trees are starting to cut the view. Although the trail is flat, watch your footing on tree roots. Several points reach the shoreline for photos of Mount Custer and Herbst Glacier. At the trail's terminus, scan the avalanche slopes for grizzly bears feeding on glacier lilies. Do not continue farther; bears depend on quiet here for denning, feeding, and rearing cubs.

★ Carthew-Alderson

Distance: 18 km (11.2 miles) one-way
Duration: 6 hours
Elevation gain: 1,440 feet
Effort: moderate-strenuous
Trailhead: end of Akamina Parkway (see map p. 244)

Catch the **Cameron Express hiker shuttle** (www.hikewaterton.com, mid-June-Sept. C$15, reservations required) to Cameron Lake or set up your own shuttle. One of the most popular hikes in Waterton, the trail climbs 7.2 kilometers (4.5 miles) to Carthew Summit, where alpine tundra stretches along a windswept ridge. Be prepared for strong winds, even on a sunny summer day. Some winds may even force you to crawl over the pass. From the summit, views span deep into Glacier National Park's interior.

The descent is a knee pounder, dropping over 3,000 feet in elevation to reach the Waterton Townsite. From the summit, the trail passes several high tarns, sometimes flanked with snowfields in June or rimmed with wildflowers in late July. The path plunges along a cliff wall before reaching Alderson Lake. Once you depart the lake, only peekaboo views of avalanche chutes break out from the thick timber en route to Cameron Falls at Waterton Townsite.

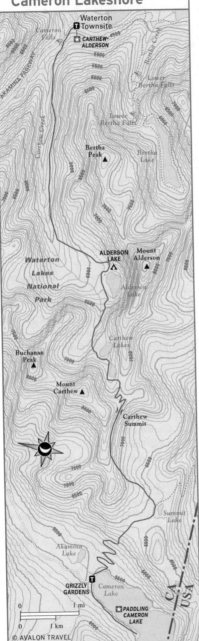

Carthew-Alderson and Cameron Lakeshore

Akamina Ridge via Wall and Forum Lakes

Distance: Akamina Ridge Loop, 18.3 km (11.4 miles); 8.8 km (5.4 miles) round-trip to Forum Lake; 10.4 km (6.4 miles) round-trip to Wall Lake

Duration: 6-7 hours

Elevation gain: 3,199 feet

Effort: strenuous

Trailhead: Akamina Pass trailhead, 14.8 km (9.2 miles) up Akamina Parkway

This hike begins in Waterton Park, but within one mile reaches low, forested Akamina Pass, where it crosses over the Continental Divide and into Akamina-Kishinena Provincial Park. Hikers looking for shorter adventures can choose either lake as a destination, but the longer loop hike gets the views. Continue 700 meters (0.4 mile) to the Forum Lake junction, turning left; Wall Lake is to the right, and it's the way you will return. The trail climbs to the snowmelt-fed Forum Lake, surrounded by steep talus and larch slopes. From the lake, follow the rough unmaintained trail that ascends the western ridge up through a 16-foot rock band where you'll need to use your hands for climbing. Once above the band, the ridge walk begins.

The five-kilometer (3.1-mile) Akamina Ridge walk is truly spectacular. Rolling over peaks and knolls, the alpine tundra is devoid of trees but rampant with miniature plants like pink moss campion struggling to survive. To the south, Glacier's remote Kintla Peak stands with Agassiz Glacier while a sea of peaks stretches in all directions. At the end of the ridge, the trail drops steeply back into forest to Wall Lake, a dramatic cirque tucked against abrupt limestone walls. From Wall Lake, hike three kilometers (1.8 miles) back to the Forum Lake junction and return to the trailhead over Akamina Pass.

Blakiston Falls

Distance: 2 km (1.2 miles) round-trip

Duration: 45 minutes

Elevation gain: 100 feet

Effort: easy

on the Carthew-Alderson Trail

Trailhead: end of Red Rock Parkway

Turn left just after you cross Red Rock Creek. After crossing Bauerman Creek, turn right and ascend through a coniferous forest. At Blakiston Falls, two wooden decks reconstructed in 2016 stair-step down to platforms to overlook the roaring falls of Blakiston Creek with Mount Blakiston looming above.

★ Red Rock Canyon

Distance: 1 km (0.6 mile) loop
Duration: 30 minutes
Elevation gain: 130 feet
Effort: easy
Trailhead: end of Red Rock Parkway

From the bridge over Red Rock Canyon, walk down and up either side of the loop. Water chiseled the canyon, exposing the lustrous red mudstone. Iron-rich argillite sediments are layered on top of each other, some turning red from oxidization, others remaining green. Evidence of the ancient Belt Sea appears in mud cracks and ripple marks. These are some of the region's oldest exposed sedimentary rock, created 1.5 billion years ago. At the top of the loop, you'll stare down a dizzying drop more than 23 meters (75 feet) to the creek, a distance that took up to 10,000 years to carve.

Avion Ridge and Goat Lake

Distance: Avion Ridge Loop, 22.5 km (14 miles); 12.6 km (7.8 miles) round-trip to Goat Lake
Duration: 4-7 hours
Elevation gain: 1,750 feet
Effort: moderate-strenuous
Trailhead: end of Red Rock Parkway

The Avion Ridge Loop begins and ends on the Snowshoe Trail, an old overgrown roadway that permits bicycles. It's easiest done clockwise, but some hikers prefer the vertical ascent via Goat Lake in favor of a less-steep descent. At four kilometers (2.5 miles) up the Snowshoe Trail, you'll reach the Goat Lake junction. Those heading to Goat Lake abruptly climb a relentless uphill into the hanging valley above to Goat Lake, known for its rainbow trout.

For Avion Ridge Loop, continue up the Snowshoe Trail from the Goat Lake junction. At 8.2 kilometers (5.1 miles), you'll reach the Snowshoe Warden Cabin and campsites. Take the trail heading north toward Lost Lake and climb to Avion Ridge. An eight-kilometer (5-mile) unmaintained trail ascends the ridgeline through larch before popping out of the trees on a barren, windswept ridge. The trail circles above a cirque right on the boundary of Waterton National

Park (you'll see signs). Endless peaks parade in all directions. As the trail swings north, it descends to a saddle, traverses a steep side-hill, and reaches a pass above Goat Lake. A knee-pounding descent through wildflower meadows plummets to the lake and then to the Snowshoe Trail junction. Turn left to return to the trailhead.

Rainbow Falls

Distance: 2.3 km (1.4 miles) round-trip
Duration: 1 hour
Elevation gain: minimal
Effort: easy
Trailhead: behind the ranger station at Goat Haunt in Glacier National Park (see map p. 247)

Rainbow Falls is one option for a short hike from the boat tour on Waterton Lake. Check with Waterton Shoreline Cruises for the boat schedule that will allow enough time to complete your hike. Take your passport to pass through immigration control in Goat Haunt.

Follow the paved trail to the first junction, taking the right fork onto dirt. The trail wanders through thick forests, filled with mosquitoes in early summer. Just before reaching the Waterton River, take a left turn at the signed junction, heading up the east bank toward Rainbow Falls. The falls is actually a series of cascades cutting troughs in the bedrock, but it's a great place to sit.

Red Rock Canyon exposes a slice of red mudstone.

A hike along Akamina Ridge yields views into Glacier National Park's remote Agassiz Glacier.

Goat Haunt Overlook

Distance: 3.2 km (1.9 miles) round-trip
Duration: 2 hours
Elevation gain: 844 feet
Effort: very strenuous
Trailhead: behind the ranger station at Goat Haunt in Glacier National Park (see map p. 247)

Goat Haunt Overlook is another option for a short but steep hike from the boat tour on Waterton Lake. Check with Waterton Shoreline Cruises for the boat schedule that will allow enough time to complete your hike.

Take your passport to pass through immigration control in Goat Haunt.

Follow the paved trail past the first right-hand turn to a dirt trail and hike 160 meters (525 feet) on the Continental Divide Trail, heading south toward Fifty Mountain. At the signed junction, turn left. The trail climbs gently for a few hundred feet before it turns straight up a steep uphill. It's a grunt, but the view is well worth the climb. At the overlook, you can gander down-lake to the Waterton Townsite and the Prince of Wales Hotel.

Goat Haunt Trails

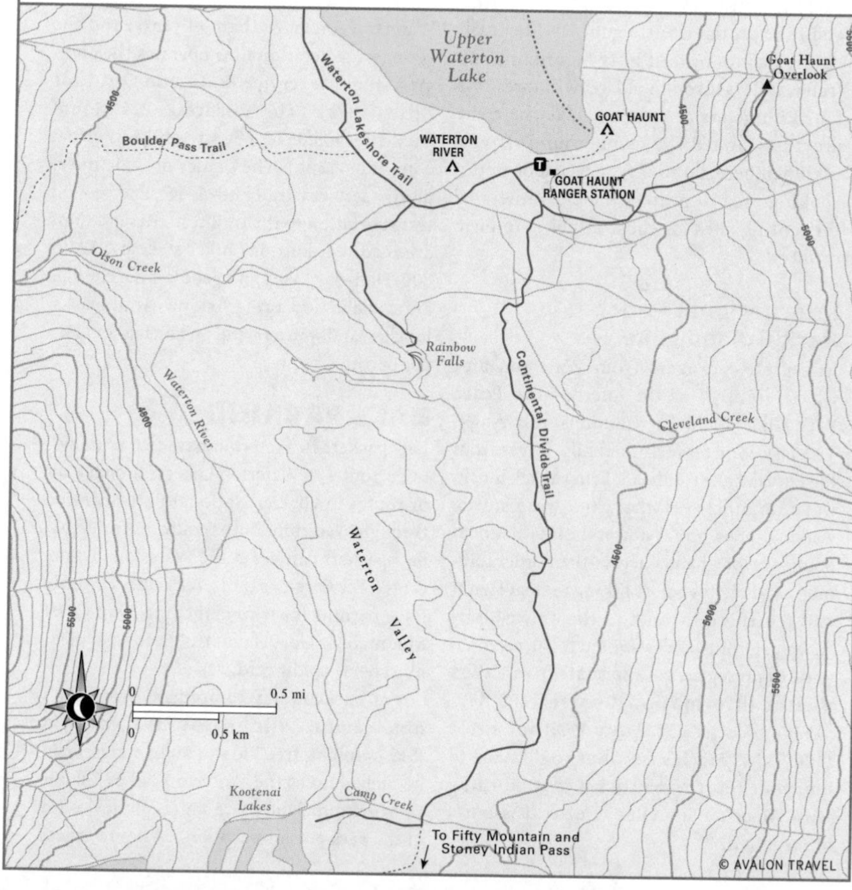

© AVALON TRAVEL

Kootenai Lakes

Distance: 9 km (5.6 miles) round-trip
Duration: 3-3.5 hours
Elevation gain: minimal
Effort: easy
Trailhead: behind the ranger station at Goat Haunt in Glacier National Park (see map p. 247)

Kootenai Lakes attracts hikers for its often-seen moose and sometimes-seen nesting trumpeter swans. Access is via the tour boat. Catch one of the earlier Waterton Shoreline Cruises boats, and schedule your return boat with enough time to complete your hike. Take your passport to pass through immigration control in Goat Haunt.

At Goat Haunt, follow the paved trail past the first right-hand turn to a dirt trail and hike on the Continental Divide Trail, heading south toward Fifty Mountain. The trail wanders through old-growth forest. At four kilometers (2.5 miles), take the right junction toward the campground. If you eat lunch here, do so on the beach or in the cooking area to protect the cleanliness of the tenting sites for those sleeping in bear country.

International Peace Park Guided Hike

Interpretive rangers from Waterton and Glacier jointly lead the International Peace Park Hike (10am Tues. and Fri. July-Aug.). The 14-kilometer (8.7-mile) hike leaves from the Bertha Lake trailhead. Bring a sack lunch, water, and extra clothes, and wear sturdy walking shoes. You'll stop at the international boundary for a hands-across-the-border ceremony and photos before hiking to Goat Haunt and returning by boat to the Townsite by 6:30pm. Group size is limited to 30, so you'll need to preregister at the **Waterton Lakes Visitor Information Centre** (403/859-5133) or Glacier's **St. Mary Visitor Center** (406/732-7751). It's free, but you'll need to buy your return boat ticket that morning with Waterton Shoreline Cruises. Passports are required.

Guides

Parks Canada naturalists guide free hikes to several destinations, usually Wednesday-Monday in summer. Destinations include Crandell Lake, Bertha Falls, and Blakiston Falls, which are suitable hikes for families with children. Check at the visitors center for the current schedule or look online (www.pc.gc.ca/waterton). Solo hikers can also join the Meetup group through Pearl's Café (http://pearlscafe.ca). Interpretive rangers from Glacier lead free hikes from Goat Haunt to Kootenai Lakes, Lake Janet, and Rainbow Falls. Passports are required. Check online or in visitors centers for schedules in *Ranger-led Activity Guide* (www.nps.gov/glac).

The Baker family has been hiking in Waterton for more than 90 years, and the youngest generation now operates the commercial guide service **Waterton Outdoor Adventures** (The Tamarack, 214 Mount View Rd., 403/859-2379, www.hikewaterton.com, June-Sept.). The guides provide interpretive services, trail knowledge, and ground transportation to the trailhead. Reservations are required. Full-day hikes start at C$240-300. Half-day hikes and paddle-hike combos are available, too. Bring your own trail snacks, lunches, and water, or add on lunches for C$15 per person.

BACKPACKING

Backpackers in Waterton have two route options: routes in Waterton Lakes National Park or routes in Glacier National Park accessed through Waterton. Both require permits that backpackers can get at the Waterton visitors center. For Glacier's trails, the center can only issue permits for trips launching from Chief Mountain or Goat Haunt trailheads; payment must be by credit card.

For backcountry camping at Waterton's nine camps, **Wilderness Use Permits** ($10 pp/night, free kids 16 and younger) can be picked up at the Waterton Lakes Visitor Information Centre (7.2 km/4.5 miles south of the park entrance station) 24 hours or less before your trip. Make advance reservations ($12) up to 90 days prior to the trip, starting April 1, by calling the visitors center (403/859-5133). For kids, the easiest backpack trip is the Waterton Lakeshore Trail, camping at Bertha Bay or Boundary Creek.

Goat Haunt provides a launch for outstanding backpacking in Glacier.

Tamarack Trail
39 KILOMETERS (24 MI)

A few lakes in a larch forest tuck under the Continental Divide on the boundary of Waterton and Alberta. Launch from the Red Rock Canyon trailhead, hiking west along Bauerman Creek to Twin Lakes for the first night. Then go south to Lone Lake for the second night. The final day climbs over the knife-edged Lineham Ridge to round through a glacier-scoured cirque before descending Rowe Creek to the exit at Rowe Lakes trailhead. Set up shuttles for the three-day trip through **Waterton Outdoor Adventures** (403/859-2379, www.hikewaterton.com).

Stoney Indian Pass
47 KILOMETERS (29 MI)

Hiking the Waterton Lakeshore Trail launches this four- to six-day backpacking trip over Stoney Indian Pass in Glacier National Park. Lop off walking down Waterton Lake to Goat Haunt by hopping the boat run by **Waterton Shoreline Cruises** (403/859-2362, www.watertoncruise.com). After going through customs at Goat Haunt, spend the first night at Kootenai Lakes (KOO) watching moose. Then climb to Stoney Indian Pass (STO) for the second night tucked below the Stoney Indian parapets. Split your remaining nights in campsites at lakes in the Mokowanis Valley: Mokowanis Lake (MOL), Glenns Lake Head (GLH) or Foot (GLF), Cosley Lake (COS), and Gable (GAB). Exit at Chief Mountain Customs. Take your passport, and make reservations for the shuttle from **Waterton Outdoor Adventures** (403/859-2379, www.hikewaterton.com) to return to Waterton.

BIKING

All roadways in Waterton offer good cycling, but be ready to ride with cars at your elbows on narrow-cornered roads with minimal shoulders on Akamina and Red Rock Parkways. Be prepared to encounter bears on both roads. Red Rock Parkway offers a unique cycling opportunity in spring and fall, when it is closed to vehicles. The seven-kilometer (4.3-mile) paved **Kootenai Brown Trail** connects

WATERTON
RECREATION

biker on the Kootenai Brown Trail

the park entrance with Waterton Townsite, offering the best family-friendly bicycling option. For campers traveling by bicycle, both the Townsite and Crandell Mountain Campgrounds have bear-resistant food storage facilities.

Parks Canada levies heavy fines of up to C$2,000 for riding on sidewalks, grass, or trails designated for hiking only. Alberta law requires children under age 18 to wear a helmet while bicycling. Given the narrow roads and the fact that most drivers are gaping at the scenery or looking for bears, and that winds can gust riders off bikes, it's a wise idea for riders of all ages to wear helmets.

Mountain Bike Trails

Four unpaved trails in Waterton permit bikes. For these, mountain bikes are best at handling the trail rubble, roots, and terrain. For current trail conditions, check with the visitors center.

Near the end of Akamina Parkway, **Akamina Pass Trail** climbs a stiff, steep 1.3 kilometers (0.8 mile) on a forested trail to the Continental Divide, which is the boundary of Waterton National Park, Akamina-Kishinena Provincial Park, Alberta, and British Columbia. From there, it rambles to Wall Lake (10.4 km/6.4 miles round-trip).

At the end of Red Rock Parkway, the **Snowshoe Trail** is 16.4 kilometers (10.2 miles) round-trip along Bauerman Creek to the Snowshoe Warden Cabin. An abandoned fire road with a fairly wide berth, the trail has some steep sections and creek fords for spice. Savvy hikers do biking-hiking trips: they bicycle to the Snowshoe Cabin, then hike to Lost or Twin Lakes.

Leaving Chief Mountain Highway less than one kilometer (0.6 mile) from the Highway 5 junction, the 21-kilometer (13-mile) round-trip **Wishbone Trail** rolls on an old wagon road through aspen parklands before narrowing in brush and fording a creek to traverse above Lower Waterton Lake.

The 21-kilometer (13-mile) **Crandell Mountain Loop** offers the most challenging ride, with rough terrain and washouts, to circle the massive mountain. You can start at three different trailheads: Crandell Lake trailhead six kilometers (3.7 miles) up Akamina Parkway, six kilometers (3.7 miles) up Red Rock Parkway on the Crandell Campground turnoff, or at Waterton Townsite.

Rentals

Pat's Gas Station (224 Mount View Rd., 403/859-2266, www.patswaterton.com) rents full-suspension mountain bikes (C$15/hour) and tandem bikes (C$25/hour). Helmets come free with rentals. You'll see Pat's famous two-person four-wheel surrey bikes tootling around the Townsite (C$30/hour); they're fun for a spin on the flat Townsite roads, but hills are difficult with only one gear.

HORSEBACK RIDING

Waterton's open grassland prairies flanking the mountains make a big view backdrop for trail rides with **Alpine Stables** (on the park entrance road opposite the golf course, 403/859-2462 or 403/653-2449, www.alpinestables.com, 9am-5pm daily May-Sept., C$40-185). With small saddles, the stables can take kids as young as four years old. You can either reserve a spot or simply show up about 20 minutes ahead. Wear long pants and sturdy shoes or boots. One-hour rides depart on the hour for meadow and lakeshore tours, with 1.5- and 2-hour versions offered less frequently. Three-hour rides head to the Bison Paddock or Bertha Falls, and longer rides tour trails for 4-8 hours. Those traveling with their own equines can board horses. Kids can get 15-minute pony rides for C$10.

BOATING

Motorized boats are permitted on two lakes: **Upper and Middle Waterton Lakes.** Jet Skis are not allowed. You can launch boats on ramps at Linnet Lake Picnic Area (1.1 km/0.7 mile north of the Townsite) on Middle Waterton Lake or the marina on Upper Waterton Lake. The marina sells gas and also has overnight mooring services operated by **Waterton Shoreline Cruises** be aware that whitecaps are common, with an average wind speed of 20 mph on Waterton Lake. A free permit is required for boats; you can pick one up at the visitors center.

★ Cameron Lake

Cameron Lake is the ideal spot for kayaking, canoeing, and rowing. Winds are often less cantankerous than at Waterton Lakes, and the views are tantalizing, especially with glassy water reflecting the mountains on the border of Canada and the United States. Avoid beaching at the southern half of the lake to protect the prime grizzly bear habitat there. **Cameron Lake Boat Rental** (403/859-2396, www.cameronlakeboatrentals.com, 8am-6:30pm daily mid-June-mid-Sept., shorter hours in shoulder seasons, C$30-40/hour) rents canoes, kayaks, paddleboats, rowboats, and paddleboards. Rates include life jackets and paddles.

Waterton Lakes

A few paddlers tackle Upper Waterton Lake, hugging shorelines because of the wind or paddling only when waters are calm. More kayakers and canoers opt for Middle Waterton Lake, the Dardanelles (the waterway connecting the two lakes), and Lower Waterton Lake for exceptional wildlife-watching, birding, and less-hefty gales. Hay Barn and Marquis Picnic Areas offer good put-ins for paddling these sections.

Rent canoes, kayaks, and standup paddleboards from **Blakiston and Company** (Crandell Mountain Lodge Garage, 800/456-0772, www.blakistonandcompany.com, C$30 one hour, C$50 two hours, C$85 half day, double kayaks and canoes $10-15 additional). The company also guides short watersport adventures.

FISHING

Fish are no longer stocked in Waterton Lakes National Park; however, introduced species still populate the waterways: arctic grayling, British Columbia and Yellowstone cutthroat, and rainbow, eastern brook, and brown trout.

marina in Waterton Townsite

(403/859-2362, www.watertoncruise.com). Free permits, available at the entrance station and visitors center, are required for launching. To prevent invasive species from entering the lakes, clean and dry your boat before arriving.

Three Upper Waterton Lake campsites are accessible by boat: Bertha Bay and Boundary Creek in Waterton, and Goat Haunt in Glacier. Boaters are not allowed to camp in their watercraft. Get required permits and reservations at the **Waterton Lakes Visitor Information Centre** (403/859-5133) or Waterton's **Parks Canada office** (403/859-5140) for Bertha Bay and Boundary Creek (adults C$10 pp/night, ages 16 and under free, $12 advance reservation) and for Goat Haunt (adults $7 pp/night, $40 advance reservation). All three campsites have docks, but secure boats due to high winds.

PADDLING

Canoeing, kayaking, rowing, and paddleboarding are perfect activities for many of Waterton's road-accessible lakes. However,

Conscientious anglers practice catch-and-release, especially to protect 17 species of native fish, including bull trout, ling, lake chub, deepwater sculpin, northern pike, pygmy whitefish, and spottail shiner.

In **Waterton Lake,** home to rainbow trout, whitefish, and pike, fish feed on the tiny opossum shrimp, a crustacean that is a relic of pre-ice age days. The record lake trout caught in Waterton Lake was 51 pounds. Some hiking destinations, like **Goat Lake,** offer decent rainbow trout fishing. At **Cameron Lake** (Cameron Lake Boat Rentals, 403/859-2396, www.cameronlakeboatrentals.com, C$12 half day), anglers can rent fishing poles and buy licenses.

Season

The general fishing season runs July-October, but anglers may fish Upper and Middle Waterton Lakes, Crandell Lake, Cameron Lake and Creek, and Akamina Lake mid-May-early September. Waters closed year-round include Maskinonge Lake and inlet, plus several creeks: Blakiston, Bauerman, Sofa, Dungarvan, and the North Fork of the Belly River.

Licenses and Regulations

Waterton Park requires a fishing permit (daily C$10, annual C$35) to fish within park boundaries. Purchase one at the visitors center, Parks Canada office, campground kiosks, Cameron Lake boat rentals, or Pat's Gas Station. The license is valid in all Canadian mountain parks. Kids under age 16 can either purchase their own permit to catch a full limit or share limits with an adult. Check for species limits when you purchase fishing licenses. Anglers planning to fish Wall and Forum Lakes in Akamina-Kishinena Provincial Park need British Columbia provincial fishing licenses.

Regulations on catch-and-release of native fish and limits of nonnative fish may be changed due to concerns with the aquatic ecosystems. Check for current limits at the visitors center as well as rules on hooks and

rentals at Cameron Lake

lead weights. Bull trout are a protected species. Follow the adage "No black, put it back."

WATERSKIING

Waterskiing is permitted only on **Upper and Middle Waterton Lakes;** however, most water-skiers gravitate to the middle lake. It's more sheltered and less windy than its upper sister. You'll find boat ramps at Linnet Lake Picnic Area (1.1 km/0.7 mile north of the Townsite) on Middle Waterton Lake or the marina on Upper Waterton Lake. Because the water is extremely cold, water-skiers wear dry suits or full wetsuits. Floating logs, sticks, and branches are common; keep your eyes open for these hazards. Waterton has no water-ski boat or ski rental service. Boats must pick up a free permit at the visitors center before launching.

SAILBOARDING

It's a rare day when Waterton doesn't see wind. Winds don't just blow, they rage. That's why traveling sailboarders head to Upper

Waterton Lake. Bring your own gear, as no rentals are available. The glacier-fed lake is freezing cold, so wear a dry suit or wetsuit to prevent hypothermia. To sailboard here, you should know how to water-start and self-rescue; it's not a place for beginners. For the best launching on the upper lake, head to **Windsurfer Beach** on Waterton Avenue, one block west of Vimy Avenue. For safety, check the current weather report at the Waterton Lakes Visitor Information Centre before launching into a big wind.

SCUBA DIVING

Scuba divers go after a spot in Emerald Bay where a sunken circa-1900 paddle steamer, *The Gertrude,* provides exploration at a depth of 20 meters (66 feet). For the clearest waters, early spring and fall are best for diving. Just remember that historic artifacts, which include anything on the wreck, are protected by the park; leave everything where you find it. Bring your own gear, as the nearest scuba shop for rentals and repairs is 130 kilometers (81 miles) east in Lethbridge.

SWIMMING

Beaches at Waterton Lake attract swimmers, but the water is chilly, and winds can howl. The indoor **Waterton Health Club and Recreation Centre** (Waterton Lakes Lodge, 101 Clematis Ave., 403/859-2150 or 888/985-6343, 7am-10pm daily, shorter hours in winter, C$7) includes a hot tub, 18-meter swimming pool, sauna, and fitness equipment. Pay for entry at the front desk at Waterton Lakes Lodge Resort. For kids, the outdoor community playground on Cameron Falls Drive and Windflower Avenue has fun water-spray features.

GOLF

Focusing on your putting can be difficult with huge scenery. Not only are sand traps a hazard, but sometimes grizzly bears, too. Located three kilometers (1.8 miles) north of the Townsite, the 18-hole **Waterton Golf Course** (403/859-2114, www.golfwaterton.com,

dawn-dusk May-Oct., C$49 18 holes, C$35 twilight) is an original Stanley Thompson design like the Banff Springs and Jasper courses. Aspens border the rolling fairways. The pro shop rents golf carts (C$33) and clubs, and a licensed clubhouse keeps guests fed and watered on its patio, which has outstanding views. Many of Waterton's hotels offer golf packages in May and after mid-September.

TENNIS

There are four hard-surface outdoor public tennis courts (Cameron Falls Dr. and Harebell Dr.). **Pat's Gas Station** (224 Mount View Rd., 403/859-2266, www.patswaterton.com, $3/hr.) rents tennis rackets. The free unlit courts, which are snow-covered in winter, are available on a first-come, first-served basis.

SPA

Part of the Bayshore Inn, **Serenity Spa** (111 Waterton Ave., 403/859-2404, www.bayshore-inn.com, C$20-280) offers day spa services. Relax with massages, manicures, pedicures, facials, and body wraps.

CROSS-COUNTRY SKIING AND SNOWSHOEING

In winter, when heavy snows render many of the roads impassable by vehicle, the parkways become ideal cross-country ski trails. Skiers can also glide down Waterton Lake after it freezes. Rent cross-country ski and snowshoe gear through **Waterton Lakes Lodge** (101 Clematis Ave., 403/859-2150 or 888/985-6343, C$15-20). With no snowmobiles allowed, a quiet backcountry experience is guaranteed on the park's ski trails.

Waterton is a land of winter extremes. It records the highest precipitation levels in Alberta, much of it as snowfall. It also records winter winds over 60 mph, which can plummet windchills. With winter chinooks, the park is also one of Alberta's warmest areas, with an average of 28 days above freezing in winter. With this diversity, snow varies from dry light powder to heavy wet glop.

Conditions can change within an hour. Most cross-country skiers sacrifice speed for reliable glide by using waxless skis.

Two designated ski trails are marked: **Cameron** and **Dipper Ski Trails,** both off Akamina Parkway, which is plowed to the trailheads at Little Prairie. Other trails such as Crandell Lake, Rowe Trail, and Akamina Pass offer more options, but be prepared with avalanche gear. Popular snowshoe trails lead to Bertha Falls and Crandell Lake. Contact the Waterton **Parks Canada office** (403/859-2224, www.pc.gc.ca) for details and avalanche conditions.

Entertainment and Shopping

ENTERTAINMENT

Parks Canada offers evening slide shows and indoor interpretive programs (8pm daily summer, free) at the **Falls Theater** (across Evergreen Ave. from Cameron Falls) and Crandell Mountain Campground. Programs cover wildlife, ecology, and geology. Call 403/859-2445 for a current schedule, which is also posted in the visitors center and campgrounds.

Re-opening in 2016 as a movie theater again, **Waterton Lakes Opera House** (309 Windflower Ave., 403/859-2466) has its vintage seats back, but new digital projection. **Waterton Teenie Weenie Theatre** (209 Fountain Ave., 877/999-9898, www.watertontwt.com, July-late Aug., adults $15, kids $10, free ages 0-2) stages family shows in repertory Monday-Saturday during the afternoons and evenings. Discounts are available for three or more siblings. It also offers daily drama workshops for kids.

EVENTS

Waterton celebrates festivals. For 10 days in late June, the **Waterton Wildflower Festival** (800/215-2395, www.watertonwildflowers.com) pulls together hikes, art shows, photography courses, watercolor painting workshops, drawing classes, slide shows, and free evening lectures in a tribute to the park's rare and diverse wildflowers. Some events are single-day programs lasting two hours; others are multiday. All are taught by

Waterton Townsite is loaded with shops.

regional experts. Course fees range C$10-300, but several are free. You can register online. The **Blackfoot Arts and Heritage Festival** stages exhibition powwows for several days in mid-August. In late September, when the elk bugle and animals congregate on Blakiston, the town celebrates the **Waterton Wildlife Festival** (800/215-2395, www.watertonwildlife.com), which includes the International Wildlife Film Festival and special excursions for wildlife-watching and photography.

SHOPPING

Shopping in Waterton features souvenirs that are decidedly Canadian, with moose and red maple-leaf T-shirts. Most shops are open daily May-September but close in winter. During shoulder seasons, hours are shorter, often

10am-5pm daily, but in midsummer shops stay open until 7pm-8pm. Many stores and restaurants sell specialty Cuban cigars, unavailable in the United States; check on restrictions, but many can be taken back over the U.S. border now.

If you need outdoor gear, **The Tamarack** (214 Mount View Rd., 403/859-2378, http://shopthetam.com, early May-Sept.) can outfit you from head to toe with hiking, backpacking, camping, and fishing gear. The shop carries good reputable brands at reasonable prices as well as topographic maps for hiking. Chocoholics and kids revel in **Welch's Chocolate Shop** (401 Windflower Ave., 403/859-2363), a sister shop to one in Banff. It stocks international chocolates and makes its own candy.

Accommodations

In Waterton, all hotels sit within walking distance in the compact town. No matter where you stay, you can walk to restaurants, shopping, boat tours, or hiking. (Staying at Prince of Wales Hotel requires a 15-minute walk to town; all others are within a block or two of restaurants.) All hotels have wireless Internet access. Six hotels (except Prince of Wales and Northland Lodge) outfit rooms with televisions, but channels are limited to just a handful. Waterton hotels are all smoke-free, and reservations are absolutely mandatory for midsummer. Minimal services remain open in winter. Only two hotels have views of Waterton Lake: Prince of Wales and Bayshore Inn.

All accommodations have the 5 percent GST and the 4 percent tourism tax added to the rates; together they add up. Rates are highest in July and August. Many of the hotels offer golf, seasonal activity packages, and shoulder season specials; ask or check their websites for current deals. You'll get better deals in Waterton in the off-season (May-early June, late Sept.-Oct., and winter), when most lodging properties drop their

rates substantially, making travel cheaper at a crowd-free time. Waterton lodging is at a premium in midsummer during the big visitor season. If you don't want to pay the high rates, drive 35 minutes north to Pincher Creek for less-expensive chain motels.

INSIDE THE PARK
Lodges
PRINCE OF WALES HOTEL

Located on a bluff above Waterton Lake, historic ★ **Prince of Wales Hotel** (across from the visitors center, 7.6 km/4.7 miles south of the park entrance station, 406/892-2525 from US or 403/236-3400 from Canada, front desk 403/859-2231, www.glacierparkinc.com, early June-mid-Sept., C$190-800) is a five-story wonder named for the prince who later became King Edward VIII. Kilted bellhops greet visitors, and high tea is served in the afternoon. Its lobby, with floor-to-ceiling windows, swings with a huge rustic chandelier. Lakeview rooms allow you to shower while looking into Glacier National Park, and mountain-view guest rooms let you spy on bighorn sheep. But despite its grand facade, the building is old, creaky, and thin-walled, and the upper stories seem to sway in high winds. Be prepared for tiny sinks and small baths, many installed in what were once closets. The guest rooms have phones but no other amenities. A cantankerous elevator accesses upper floors but requires a bellhop to run, rendering it unavailable at all hours. Top-floor lodgers get a workout climbing the stairs. A restaurant, a gift shop selling English bone china and Waterford crystal, and a lounge surround the lobby. You can reach town via a 5-minute drive or a 15-minute walk down a trail.

WATERTON LAKES LODGE RESORT

With mountain views from many of the rooms, the **Waterton Lakes Lodge Resort** (101 Clematis Ave., 403/859-2150 or 888/985-6343, www.watertonlakeslodge.com, C$200-320 summer, $100-220 winter) has 80 modern, air-conditioned guest rooms. Some include kitchenettes, suites, fireplaces, jet tubs, or are pet-friendly. The pleasant accommodations are in 11 two-story chalets. For 2nd-floor units, you'll need to climb the stairs, but some upstairs rooms include skylights and vault ceilings. Guests get free use of the on-site Waterton Health Club and Recreation Centre pool, hot tub, and workout room. The resort also has a restaurant and bar.

CRANDELL MOUNTAIN LODGE

The 17-room **Crandell Mountain Lodge** (102 Mount View Rd., 403/859-2288 or 866/859-2288, www.crandellmountainlodge.com, mid-Apr.-mid-Oct., C$100-290) is tucked beneath its namesake peak. The two-story circa-1940 inn has a variety of country-themed guest rooms, from standard rooms up to three-room suites with full kitchens and fireplaces. In a private garden area, a huge deck with a barbecue and lounge chairs begs for afternoon relaxation.

Motels
THE BAYSHORE INN

One of only two hotels on Waterton Lake, ★ **The Bayshore Inn** (Mount View Rd. and Waterton Ave., summer 403/859-2211 or 888/527-9555, www.bayshoreinn.com, May-early Oct., C$145-370) offers lakefront guest rooms with prime views from private balconies. Family rooms, deluxe suites, and pet-friendly rooms are available, along with less-pricey guest rooms with mountain views. The complex has a lounge, a saloon,

The Prince of Wales Hotel sits on a bluff overlooking Waterton Lake.

Bear Mountain Motel

restaurants, a hot tub, a gift shop, satellite Internet access, an ice cream shop, and the Serenity Spa. Located adjacent to the marina, it sits on the Townsite's main block that houses most of the shopping. Lakeside rooms overlook the Townsite Loop trail, lawn, trees, and the lake.

WATERTON GLACIER SUITES

With mountain views and large rooms, ★ Waterton Glacier Suites (107 Windflower Ave., 403/859-2004 or 866/621-3330, www.watertonsuites.com, C$155-325 summer, C$125-175 winter) has 26 units with private balconies for enjoying the mountain scenery. Room amenities include fridges, microwaves, air-conditioning, and whirlpool tubs. Some guest rooms have gas fireplaces, and 2nd-floor units require walking stairs.

ASPEN VILLAGE INN

Sporting red metal roofs (you won't get lost looking for these), the aging Aspen Village Inn (111 Windflower Ave., 403/859-2255 or 888/859-8669, www.aspenvillageinn.com, May-early Oct., C$112-330) combines a two-story motel with 16 cottages that accommodate 2-8 people. Some are pet-friendly or come with kitchens. The units surround mowed lawns, a playground, and an outdoor barbecue picnic area. Complimentary access to the Waterton Health Club and Recreation Centre is included.

BEAR MOUNTAIN MOTEL

New owners took over the ★ Bear Mountain Motel (208 Mount View Rd., 403/859-2366, www.bearmountainmotel. com, mid-May-early Oct., C$115-260) in late 2015. The 1960s wood-and-masonry motel has 36 small one- and two-bedroom units, several of which have tiny kitchenettes and living rooms with hide-a-beds. Expect clean, basic guest rooms with no frills; these are the most affordable rooms in town. Pay phones are available near the office. A shared patio has a microwave, two grills, and picnic tables.

Bed-and-Breakfast
NORTHLAND LODGE

For park-history buffs, the quiet Northland Lodge (408 Evergreen Ave., 403/859-2353, www.northlandlodgecanada.com, mid-May-early Oct., C$145-220, two-night minimum in summer) holds appeal. Louis Hill, builder of the Prince of Wales Hotel and many of Glacier National Park's historic hotels, constructed the Swiss-style lodge as his private residence circa 1948, although he never lived here. Two of the lodge's nine guest rooms share a bath, and the rest have private baths; guest rooms are split among three levels. A large balcony is great for soaking up the views with coffee and homemade muffins with Saskatoon-berry jam in the morning. A 10-minute walk leads to shopping and restaurants via the scenic Townsite Loop trail, just across the street. Some interiors were spritzed up in 2016.

Camping

INSIDE THE PARK

Waterton Lakes National Park campgrounds have flush toilets, drinking water, kitchen shelters, and bear-resistant food storage lockers. With the exception of the Townsite campground, some sites have fire rings, and firewood is supplied, but you pay C$9 per site for a burning permit in addition to the campground fee. Trailheads are adjacent to all campgrounds.

Waterton Townsite Camground

Smack in the heart of town, the ★ **Waterton Townsite Campground** (403/859-2224, www.pc.gc.ca, early May-early Oct., unserviced sites C$23-28, electrical or full hookups C$33-39) is citified with a mowed lawn, but it sits on prime real estate with gorgeous views. The 238-site campground borders the Townsite Loop trail and the beach. A few trees shade some sites, but most are open, offering little privacy. Go for the most scenic spots in the G loop (sites 26-46) but be prepared for winds. For more sheltered scenery, go for the Cameron Creek E loop sites (even numbers 2-16). Fires are only permitted in the kitchen shelters, but the campground includes hot showers, dishwashing stations, a dump station, and five new restroom buildings in 2016 that replaced older facilities. The campground also received electrical and sewer upgrades in 2016. In midsummer, the campground fills early; plan on arriving by noon to claim a site, or make reservations (C$12) starting in January through the **Parks Canada Campground Reservation Service** (877/737-3783, www.pccamping.ca). Early or late in the season, you'll have your pick of sites without a reservation; in the shoulder seasons (May-early June and mid-Sept.-early Oct.), the campground is virtually empty.

Crandell Mountain Campground

On the opposite side of Crandell Mountain from the Townsite and 6.8 kilometers (4.2 miles) up the Red Rock Parkway, **Crandell Mountain Campground** (403/859-2224, www.pc.gc.ca, mid-May-early Sept., C$22) is nestled along Blakiston Creek. With half of the sites deep in the trees, the campground has a remote feel, with greenery providing privacy between sites. Sometimes you can see bears and moose around Blakiston Creek. The 129 sites offer no hookups, but a dump station is available. The campground takes no reservations, so plan on claiming your site by midday in July-August. A, B, C, and D loops are in thicker trees; E, F, G, and H loops are open, with views of surrounding peaks. Five **tepees** (reservations 403/859-5133 or at the visitors center, C$55,

Waterton Townsite Campground

reservation fee C$12) are available for rent. Tight loops squeeze large RVs, so 30 feet or less is recommended. From the campground, you can hike 2 kilometers (1.2 miles) to Crandell Lake.

Belly River Campground

On Chief Mountain Highway and 26 kilometers (16 miles) from Waterton Townsite, the **Belly River Campground** (403/859-2224, www.pc.gc.ca, mid-May-early Sept., C$16) has 24 pleasant sites for small RVs and tents in aspen groves with hand-pumped well water and both pit and flush toilets. Some sites are shaded, and some are in meadows. It is a good location for watching wildlife and birding, and it is the closest campground to the Chief Mountain border crossing for those who want to scamper across the boundary first thing in the morning.

Pass Creek Winter Campground

In winter, when all other campsites have closed, free sites are available at **Pass Creek Winter Campground** (403/859-2224, www.pc.gc.ca, mid-Oct.-mid-Apr.). Located on the entrance road five kilometers (3.1 miles) from the Townsite, the eight sites offer primitive camping with only a pit toilet and a woodstove in the kitchen shelter.

Water from the creek may be boiled or purified for use.

OUTSIDE THE PARK

Just outside the park boundary, two private campgrounds can handle the overload when the park campgrounds are full. Be prepared for wind at both. GST will be added to your camping fees. On Highway 6 to Pincher Creek, **Waterton Springs Campground** (2.5 km/1.5 miles north of the park entrance road, 403/859-2247, www.watertonspringscamping.com, May-Sept., $27-30 tents, C$34-40 hookups, $5/adult after two) has 70 full-hookup sites in an open, dusty, parking lot-type setting that fit big rigs, along with 75 electricity-only sites. Tent and unserviced sites surround small ponds and a creek in a brushy aspen parkland. Amenities include token-operated showers ($1 for four minutes), laundry, flush toilets, picnic tables, a camp store, a playground, fire rings, and a one kilometer (0.6-mile) Nature Conservancy interpretive trail.

Crooked Creek Campground (6 km/3.7 miles east of the park entrance road, 403/653-1100, May-Sept., C$22 tents, C$30-33 hookups) has 79 sites adjacent to the highway. Amenities include flush toilets, showers, Wi-Fi, a dump station, a cook shack, laundry, ice, fire rings, and firewood.

Food

In this remote resort oasis in a national park, food prices can be exorbitant. Plus, the 5 percent GST gets slapped on every bill. But an influx of less-expensive eateries have moved into town in recent years. If you're camping or backpacking, consider bringing supplies with you, as groceries are limited. In late summer, blackflies descend for several weeks on the Townsite, even in restaurants. Just think of them as small wildlife.

With a few exceptions, restaurants in the Townsite cluster mostly in one block along Waterton and Windflower Avenues. The two streets have a European feel with patio and sidewalk dining. For a Canadian specialty, look for *poutine:* french fries smothered in cheese curds and gravy. Only Vimy's stays open year-round; all other restaurants are open daily May-September. In spring and fall, some restaurants often shorten their hours or days. For the trail, many restaurants sell hiker lunches at C$14-15. For adults, the **Thirsty**

Bear Saloon (111 Waterton Ave., 403/859-2211), the town's only nightclub, usually rolls out discounted beer jugs on Mondays.

INSIDE THE PARK
Fine Dining

Fine dining options are available in Waterton, but no dressing up is required; casual clothes, including hiking attire, are acceptable.

WATERTON LAKES LODGE RESORT

At Waterton Lakes Lodge Resort, ★ **Vimy's Lounge and Grill** (101 Clematis Ave., 403/859-2150 or 888/985-6343, www.vimys.com, 7am-10pm daily, shorter hours in winter) offers four dining options in summer: a lounge downstairs, upstairs dining with a view of Mount Cleveland, outside upper deck dining, and a patio. Breakfast (C$12-23) includes multiple variations on eggs Benedict, while lunch (C$17-24) has burgers, sandwiches, and salads. Try the Canadian classic poutine: homemade french fries drowning in cheese curds and gravy. The lunch menu continues through dinner but adds on entrées (C$25-40) starting at 5pm. Dinner entrées rotate seasonally with steaks and fish, which can be accompanied by international and Canadian wines.

PRINCE OF WALES HOTEL

The historic **Prince of Wales Hotel** (406/892-2525 or 403/236-3400, front desk 403/859-2231, www.glacierparkinc.com, daily early June-mid-Sept.) puts on a regal view of Waterton Lake from massive floor-to-ceiling windows in the **Royal Stewart Dining Room.** Breakfast (6:30am-10am, C$12-16) specializes in eggs Benedict and omelets, while the lunch (11:30am-2pm, C$12-16) and dinner (5pm-9:30pm, C$18-30) menus introduce classics from Great Britain such as bangers and mash plus traditional Canadian fare. Reservations are recommended in midsummer. Hikers can get bag lunches to go (C$15). The British atmosphere goes into full swing with **afternoon tea** (1pm-5pm daily, adults C$30, kids C$16) in the hotel lobby overlooking Waterton Lake. It's a full meal of finger sandwiches and a sugar-fest of desserts: pastries, fruits, and berries. Pour your tea from signature porcelain servers. It's a unique experience, but mostly about the atmosphere. Reservations with prepayment are recommended. You can also enjoy the hotel views down-lake with a lighter meal and cocktail from the **Windsor Lounge** (11:30am-10pm).

BAYSHORE INN

Located in the Bayshore Inn, the ★ **Lakeside Chophouse** (111 Waterton Ave., 403/859-2211 or 888/527-9555, www.lakeshorechophouse.com, 7am-10pm daily) packages up scenery with fine dining. It is the only restaurant with outdoor patio seating on Waterton Lake, with service for breakfast, lunch, dinner, and cocktails. The inside dining room has lake views, too. Breakfast (C$10-18) brings on eggs Benedict and a daily buffet. Lunch and dinner (C$13-30) feature burgers, sandwiches, salads, and an eclectic global cuisine. The after-5pm menu also adds on grilled aged AAA Alberta beef and bison steaks (C$30-42). Be sure to save room for Saskatoon berry pie. Combine dinner with beer, cocktails, or international wines. Reservations are recommended. The adjoining **Fireside Lounge** (noon-1am daily) also serves pizza, burgers, sandwiches, salads, and pastas.

Pizza

Two pizza restaurants, which sit next to each other on Windflower, offer seating indoors or outdoors. They also make to-go pizzas for your motel, beach, or campsite. A new kid on the block, ★ **49 Degrees North** (303 Windflower Ave., 403/859-3000, www.49degreesnorthpizza.com, noon-10pm Mon.-Thurs. 8am-11pm Fri.-Sun. C$12-28) makes its pizza and calzone dough fresh daily, including gluten-free, and bakes its pizzas in a stone-deck-fired oven. It also serves soup, salads, and appetizers, plus weekend breakfasts. Next door, the longtime Waterton staple **Pizza of Waterton** (305 Windflower Ave.,

the Taco Bar

(301 Windflower Ave., 403/859-0007, www. wienersofwaterton.com, 7am-9pm daily, C$5-12) knows how to pile large, high-end hot dogs with choose-your-own fresh toppings on homemade buns. Launched by brothers Jon and Max Low, the pair imports dogs from New York and local butchers with choices including a smokie, falafel dog, and kid-sized. Dip sweet-potato fries in tasty homemade sauces; pickles get an extra crunch from their deep-fried crust. The breakfast sausage dog and fresh-squeezed orange juice works for a grab-and-go start to the day. Those who get there first thing in the morning will find fresh-baked cinnamon buns and scones.

With the scent of sweet waffles wafting out into the street, ★ **Waffleton** (301 Windflower Ave., 403/859-2131, 8am-10pm, C$6-10) tops fresh-baked buttermilk and Belgian liege waffles with fruits, whipped cream, ice cream, frozen Greek yogurt, Nutella, or multiple other toppings. It also serves espresso and blends up smoothies.

The **Glacier Bistro Starbucks** (111 Waterton Ave., 403/859-2211, 7am-11pm daily, C$8-19) serves light meals for breakfast, lunch, and dinner: croissants and baked goods, wraps, sandwiches, and soups, plus a selection of dessert goodies, espresso, and hiker lunches.

Casual Dining

Two family restaurants are open 8am-9pm daily and anchor the opposite ends of the same block. Their appeal comes from large, diverse menus with broad Canadian choices, indoor or shaded outdoor sidewalk dining, and beer, wine, and cocktails. To decide between them, browse their outdoor menus and assess waiting lines. Both serve up classic breakfasts including omelets, sandwiches, salads, burgers, kids' meals, gluten-free and vegetarian options, and lighter or heavier meals. With slightly lower prices for family appeal, **Zums Eatery** (116 Waterton Ave., 403/859-2388, C$6-25) specializes in crispy fried chicken, pub-style fish-and-chips, and baby back ribs in its house Guinness

403/859-2660, www.pizzaofwaterton.com, 7am-9pm daily, C$12-28) serves handcrafted pizzas and calzones, lasagna, salad, beer, wine, and cocktails. For breakfast, it serves stuffed French toast, plus easily portable bagels, wraps, or paninis to carry out the door and eat on the way to the trailhead. Lunch features sandwiches and wraps.

Mexican

In a tiny, graffiti-walled café, the **Taco Bar** (310 Windflower Ave., 403/859-2150, http://watertontacos.wix.com/thetacobar, 11:30am-9:30pm daily, shorter hours spring and fall, C$8-12, cash only) brings the flavors of Mexico to Canada with burritos, tacos, and bowls filled with choices of meats, beans and cheese or veggies, gluten free, and kid-sized options. Crisp citrus slaw and fresh-made salsas add zing.

Cafés

A local to-go favorite with outdoor picnic tables for seating, ★ **Wieners of Waterton** barbecue sauce. The signature dessert is a tasty wildberry pie, a combination of raspberries, blueberries, blackberries, rhubarb, and apple. In addition to lighter meals, **Trappers Mountain Grill** (106 Waterton Ave., 403/859-2445, C$9-50) serves up high-end Alberta beefsteaks in a process that finishes with broiling. It also has lamb chops, smoked ribs, and fish entrées.

Coffee and Ice Cream

Espresso and ice cream outlets are ubiquitous in Waterton. You can linger over your favorite cappuccino or latte or get it to go at multiple locations on Waterton and Windflower Avenues. **Pearl's Café** (305 Windflower Ave., 403/859-2498, http://pearlscafe.ca, 7am-10pm daily) is the locals' fave for a sit-down coffee shop with Internet access. With a park vibe and a staff that talks hiking, you can yak about trails while chowing down on a gooey cinnamon bun, sipping espresso, and connecting with wireless Internet to catch up on email. Hikers can grab to-go fresh-baked goods and lunches to hit the trail.

The number of ice cream shops comes in a close second behind espresso outlets. For the biggest flavor selections, house-made waffle cones, and fruit-filled frozen yogurts, go to **Big Scoop Ice Cream Parlor** (114 Waterton Ave., 10am-10pm daily).

Groceries

While several outlets in town carry convenience foods, only the **Rocky Mountain Food Mart** (307 Windflower Ave., 403/859-2121, 8am-8pm daily May-Sept.) stocks fresh produce, meats, dairy, and deli and baked goods. It's tiny, so expect limited selection, and prices can be high. It also carries ice, firewood, and camping supplies. Off-season, find the closest grocery stores in Pincher Creek. Go to **Mountain Spirits Liquor Store** (504 Cameron Falls Dr., 403/859-2015, 11am-10:30pm Mon.-Thurs., 10am-11pm Fri.-Sat., 1pm-10:30pm Sun.) for beer, wine, and liquor.

Picnic Areas

Waterton has **14 picnic areas.** Those on Waterton Lake have shelters, which offer a place to hunker away from raging winds. Find six along the park entrance road and several located on the lakes. Red Rock Parkway and Akamina Parkway each have three picnic areas. In the Townsite on Waterton Lake, two picnic shelters are located near the end of Waterton Avenue and one at the end of Evergreen Avenue.

Wieners of Waterton serves up New York and Alberta dogs with homemade toppings.

Transportation and Services

DRIVING AND PARKING

Waterton roads are all two laners. Highway 5 and 6 are **open year-round,** as is the main road into Waterton Townsite. But Chief Mountain International Highway, Akamina Parkway, and Red Rock Parkway **close for the winter.** For **road conditions,** call 511 in Alberta or 855/391-9743 from outside the province.

In Waterton Townsite, find public parking lots at the marina, visitors center, streetside, picnic areas, trailheads, and Cameron Falls. Large public lots sit at the ends of Akamina Parkway and Red Rock Parkway. Rent mopeds from **Pat's Gas Station** (224 Mount View Rd., 403/859-2266, www.patswaterton.com, $45/hour, $180/day).

SERVICES

The Townsite has a coin-op **launderette** (302 Windflower Ave., 7am-9pm daily May-Oct.). Showers (C$7) are available at the **Waterton Health Club and Recreation Centre** (101 Clematis Ave., 403/859-2150 or 888/985-6343).

The Townsite has a **post office** (102 Windflower Ave., 8am-4:30pm Mon.-Fri. year-round). Remember to use Canadian postage stamps rather than U.S. stamps to send mail from Canada.

To get Canadian currency, **ATMs** are located at Pat's Gas Station, The Tamarack, Rocky Mountain Food Mart, Mountain Spirits Liquor Store, Bayshore Inn, and the Prince of Wales Hotel. Most businesses, including restaurants, shops, and lodges, will accept **U.S. currency;** however, return change will be given in Canadian currency. For conversions, most businesses use the bank exchange rate, but some have their own policies. For the best exchange rates, use a credit card as much as possible. Waterton has **no banks;** the nearest banking services are in Cardston and Pincher Creek.

The official travel planning website run by the **Waterton Chamber of Commerce** (http://mywaterton.ca) offers more information on lodging, activities, dining, events, services, shopping, and the community.

Gas and Repairs

Pat's Gas Station (224 Mount View Rd., 403/859-2266, www.patswaterton.com) is much more than a place to gas up or buy propane for the RV. Pat can magically perform minor car repairs, but go to Pincher Creek for serious vehicle repairs.

Cell Phone and Internet Access

Telus, Bell, and some Verizon cell phones can get service in the Townsite, but not on the internal parkway roads or at Goat Haunt. **Waterton Wi-Fi** services restaurants, motels, and the campground with two options. The **free service** offers limited speeds and intermittently cuts out, but it's enough to get a few emails and look up the weather; the **fee service** has faster speeds and is more dependable.

Newspapers/Magazines

The *Calgary Herald* carries regional, national, and international news. The *Lethbridge Herald* covers local and regional news.

Emergencies

For emergencies, dial 911 or contact the **Royal Canadian Mounted Police** (RCMP, 202 Waterton Ave., 403/859-2244 or 403/627-2113) during summer months or **Parks Canada Wardens** (215 Mount View Rd., 403/859-2224) year-round. The nearest hospitals are 50 kilometers (31 miles) away: **Pincher Creek Hospital** (1222 Bev McLachin Dr., Pincher Creek, 403/627-1234) and **Cardston Health Centre** (144 2nd St. W., Cardston, 403/653-5234). To contact the park's emergency ambulance, call 403/859-2636.

Tips for Waterton Travel

- **GST:** Everywhere in Canada, a 5 percent **Goods and Services Tax** (GST) is applied to some purchases and services. In most cases, it is added onto your bill, not already included. In general, groceries, prescription drugs, health care, and medical devices are not taxed. But you will pay GST on motels, campground fees, restaurant bills, souvenirs, clothing, gas, recreation rentals, and tours.

- **Gas:** Gas up before you head north across the border as gas in Canada is usually $0.50-0.80 per gallon more expensive than in the United States. Also, be aware that gas is sold by the liter in Canada, so the price on the pump will look pretty darn good. To convert the price, remember 3.8 liters equals one U.S. gallon.

- **Coins:** Canada has $1 Loonies, named for the loons on the coins, and $2 Toonies, named for its two-dollar value and to match the Loonie.

- **Tips:** Tipping in Canada is comparable to the United States. Tip 15-20 percent in restaurants, $2 per bag for bellhops, $2-5 per day for housekeeping, and 15-20 percent for guides.

- **Kids:** Ice cream, short trails, family theater, renting surrey bikes, and a play park with water-spray features attract families with kids.

- **Credit Cards:** For the best exchange rate, use credit cards rather than cash.

- **ATMs:** Remember that ATMs will give you Canadian dollars. Only withdraw as much as you will use.

Flathead Valley

Look for ★ to find recommended
sights, activities, dining, and lodging.

Highlights

★ **Whitefish:** Romp through this train town turned resort town for shopping, art galleries, restaurants, and a nightlife bar-hopping scene (page 269).

★ **Bigfork:** In summer, this resort town bustles with restaurants, shopping, and theater, and serves as a launchpad for whitewater kayaking (page 269).

★ **Flathead Lake:** Sail the blue waters or drive around the perimeter of the largest freshwater lake west of the Mississippi (page 270).

★ **Whitefish Lake:** On hot summer days this lake is hopping with water-skiers, boaters, paddlers, anglers, and swimmers (page 271).

★ **Whitefish Mountain Resort:** Ski or snowboard this winter wonderland, or find summer adventures: mountain biking, zipline tours, an aerial park, an alpine slide, or scenic chairlift rides (page 271).

★ **Mount Aeneas:** Hike the short trail up the highest peak in Jewel Basin. From the summit are views into the Great Bear Wilderness, down onto Flathead Lake, and north to Glacier (page 272).

★ **Danny On Trail:** Ride a chairlift to the top of Big Mountain to hike down the most popular trail in the Flathead. It's a romp through mounds of wildflowers with panoramic views (page 273).

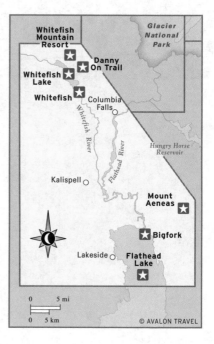

S urrounded by mountain ranges and abundant lakes, the Flathead Valley is an outdoor recreation paradise offering fishing, skiing, hiking, hunting, biking, and boating options.

With 2.5 million acres of wilderness and national parklands, there's no shortage of space to get away from it all. One of the country's largest national forests fringes the valley floor, which is dotted with lakes, including the largest freshwater lake west of the Mississippi. Summer brings flat-water kayaking and river floating. Anglers drop lines from drift boats, golfers hit the links, and hikers climb to wildflower-strewn heights with huge views of the vast valley.

Strip-mall culture has made some inroads into the valley, paving once pastoral farmlands. Housing developments sprout between towns, blending the borders of one with another. People who want to create another Aspen have thrown up multimillion-dollar mansions on the hillsides. But an underlying culture remains: Ripped Carhartts and a duct-taped jacket rank as fashion. Rather than hit the nine-to-five office hours, lots of folks work seasonally in Glacier or Flathead National Forest and at ski areas.

When snow falls, logging roads and golf courses become ski and snowshoe trails, while two alpine ski areas rack up the vertical for skiers and snowboarders. Many in the valley adhere to the six-inch rule: If six inches or more of snow falls, call in late for work.

HISTORY

Originally the home of the Flathead, Salish, and Kootenai people, the Flathead Valley saw in 1809 its first person of European descent, the famed explorer David Thompson. Within 40 years, trappers, homesteaders, and ranchers edged their way into the valley. By the end of the 19th century, the Great Northern Railway had laid tracks through the Flathead, prompting Kalispell to be plotted for township in 1890, in theory to become the next St. Paul.

Growing with ranchers, farmers, and timber harvesters, the Flathead soon sprouted other towns clustered around its lakes and rivers. In 1901 the Great Northern Railway rerouted its tracks through Whitefish to access Canadian coal, transforming the tiny lakefront community of Whitefish into a

Previous: gondola at Whitefish Mountain Resort; hiking at Picnic Lakes in Jewel Basin.
Above: Whitefish Trailhead.

Flathead Valley

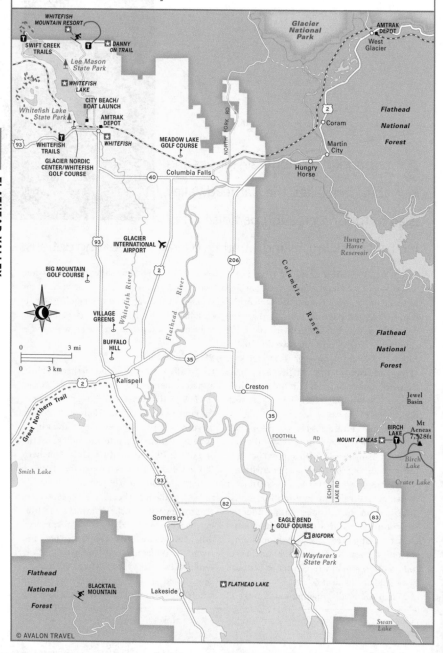

WHITEFISH MOUNTAIN RESORT

SWIFT CREEK TRAILS

DANNY ON TRAIL

Lee Mason State Park

WHITEFISH LAKE

CITY BEACH/ BOAT LAUNCH

Whitefish Lake State Park

AMTRAK DEPOT

WHITEFISH

WHITEFISH TRAILS

GLACIER NORDIC CENTER/WHITEFISH GOLF COURSE

MEADOW LAKE GOLF COURSE

Columbia Falls

BIG MOUNTAIN GOLF COURSE

GLACIER INTERNATIONAL AIRPORT

Whitefish River

Flathead River

VILLAGE GREENS

BUFFALO HILL

Kalispell

Creston

Somers

Lakeside

BLACKTAIL MOUNTAIN

EAGLE BEND GOLF COURSE

BIGFORK

Wayfarer's State Park

FLATHEAD LAKE

Smith Lake

Flathead National Forest

Great Northern Trail

FOOTHILL RD

ECHO LAKE RD

MOUNT AENEAS

BIRCH LAKE

Mt Aeneas 7,528ft

Jewel Basin

Birch Lake

Crater Lake

Swan Lake

Glacier National Park

AMTRAK DEPOT

West Glacier

Coram

Martin City

Hungry Horse

NORTH FORK RD

Flathead National Forest

Hungry Horse Reservoir

Columbia Range

Flathead National Forest

0   3 mi

0   3 km

© AVALON TRAVEL

railroad town. The mid-1900s saw tremendous change in the Flathead, with the construction of the Hungry Horse dam spawning an aluminum plant, the Plum Creek Timber Company, and the Whitefish Mountain Ski Resort. Today, while valley ranching, farming, and timber still support many families, part of the Flathead economy for its 90,000 residents comes from technology industries and tourism.

Exploring Flathead Valley

Flathead Valley centers around four main towns, each with its own draw of seasonal recreation. Outside the main towns, small burgs dot Flathead Lake's shoreline. Lakeside buzzes with summer water fun and serves as the launching point to reach Blacktail Mountain ski area in winter. Somers is a blink-and-miss-it town but is popular for its marina.

Flathead Valley is a casual place. Don't bother with a suit and tie or fancy dinner dress, even in the priciest restaurants. Recreational clothing is suitable everywhere.

Kalispell

The nucleus of Flathead Valley, with three golf courses, restaurants, and shopping, the area's largest town has moved beyond its cow-town past. In historic downtown Kalispell, you can tour the pre-1900s Conrad Mansion and unique art spots. In August, catch the Northwest Montana Fair and Rodeo, and in October, join in the Glacier Jazz Stampede.

★ Whitefish

The year-round cultural and recreation capital of Flathead Valley, downtown Whitefish fits compactly into several blocks connected to the Amtrak station. A railroad town transformed into a resort town, Whitefish boasts shops, boutiques, restaurants, bars, art galleries, and theaters. In the summer, downtown streets crowd with shopping tourists, especially during the Tuesday evening farmers market and craft fair. In winter, its ski town heritage emerges in early February with the Winter Carnival. The town also serves as a springboard for boating, paddling, golfing, hiking, mountain biking, and skiing.

Columbia Falls

The gateway to Glacier, Columbia Falls never had a waterfall of its own until the town built one. Recently, the town has boomed with restaurants in its downtown area, upgrading the quality of its dining. Besides its rebuilt public outdoor swimming pool, Columbia Falls is home to Big Sky Waterslides.

★ Bigfork

A summer resort town, Bigfork is a small yet charming cultural and recreation hub. Bigfork Summer Playhouse dominates the town, packing restaurants before nightly shows. Quaint gift shops and art galleries fill its several-block-long village, and its historic one-lane steel bridge crosses the Swan River. Recreation combines easy access to the Swan Mountains, golfing, and boating on Flathead Lake. In early June, the town hops with the Bigfork Whitewater Festival, when kayakers shoot the Swan's Wild Mile.

VISITORS CENTERS

Flathead Valley has six visitor information centers: **Flathead Valley Convention and Visitors Bureau** (406/756-9091 or 800/543-3105, www.fcvb.org), **Kalispell Chamber of Commerce** (406/758-2800, www.kalispellchamber.com), **Whitefish Convention and Visitors Bureau** (307 Spokane Ave., 877/862-3548, www.explorewhitefish.com), **Columbia Falls Chamber of Commerce** (406/892-2072, www.columbiafallschamber.com), **Bigfork Chamber of Commerce** (406/837-5888, www.bigfork.org), and **Lakeside Chamber of Commerce** (406/844-3715, www.lakesidechamber.com).

The Flathead National Forest surrounds the Flathead Valley, so you can pick up maps, current trail and camping information, forest and ski conditions, and regulations in several national forest offices and ranger stations, including **Flathead National Forest and Talley Lake Ranger Station** (650 Wolfpack Way, Kalispell, 406/758-5200) and **Swan Lake Ranger Station** (200 Ranger Station Rd., Bigfork, 406/837-7500).

SHUTTLES

By reservation, **Glacier Charters** (406/892-3390 or 800/829-7039, www.glaciertransportation.com, $40-75 one-way) operates shuttles between Glacier Park International Airport and Whitefish, Whitefish Mountain Resort, Columbia Falls, Kalispell, and Bigfork.

Whitefish shuttles (406/892-3390, http://bigmtncommercial.org, July-early Sept. and early Dec.-early Apr., free) go between the town of Whitefish and Whitefish Mountain Resort. The **Glacier Express** (adults $10, kids half price) goes several times daily to Apgar Visitor Center in Glacier National Park; buy tickets with cash only in advance at Whitefish outlets. Schedules for both shuttles are online.

Sights

★ FLATHEAD LAKE

Stretching 28 miles long and 15 miles wide, Flathead Lake is the largest freshwater lake west of the Mississippi. Its 188 square miles, six state parks, islands, deep fishing waters, and wildlife refuges make it a summer play land. Highways circle the lake with public access at 13 different points. The southern half of the lake is in the Flathead Indian Reservation. Paddlers and boaters can explore **Wild Horse Island State Park,** home to wild horses, bighorn sheep, and big views of Flathead Lake.

From Bigfork, **Flathead Lake Sailing Charters** (150 Flathead Lake Lodge, 406/837-5569, www.flatheadlakesailing.com, daily

Boaters and paddlers can visit Wild Horse Island State Park in Flathead Lake during the day.

mid-June-Aug.) launch from Flathead Lake Lodge's dock. Two 51-foot 1928-1929 Q-class sloops each carry 12 passengers. On the beautifully restored boats, there are regular 90-minute tours (1:30pm and 3pm, $40-45) and the 2-hour sunset cruise (6:30pm, $60), which includes beer, wine, champagne, and appetizers. From Lakeside, **Far West Boat Tours** (7135 U.S. 93 S., 406/844-2628, www.flatheadlakeboattour.com, late June-early Sept., 1pm daily, 7pm Sun.-Wed., $10-22) launches a 23-foot cabin cruiser. Sit upstairs in the sun for bigger views.

★ WHITEFISH LAKE

The 3,315-acre lake in Whitefish buzzes in summer. Anglers hit the lake in early morning and evening, while midday is a frenzy of water-skiers, Jet Skiers, party barges, kayakers, and canoers. Swimmers cool off at Whitefish State Park, City Beach, and Les Mason State Park. In winter, when ice covers the lake, hockey players make their own rinks, and anglers ice fish.

FLATHEAD RIVER

In Hungry Horse, the South, Middle, and North Forks of the Flathead River converge. The Flathead River then snakes 55 miles across the valley to Flathead Lake. Seven river access points allow anglers, canoers, and floaters to get onto its meandering pace. Toward Flathead Lake, the river takes several sharp S-turns in sloughs and estuaries, bird habitat for ospreys and waterfowl.

★ WHITEFISH MOUNTAIN RESORT

Skiers and snowboarders head to **Whitefish Mountain Resort** (end of Big Mountain Rd., 406/862-2900, www.skiwhitefish.com) for 3,000 acres of skiing in winter. Twelve lifts access an average 300 inches of snow per year. Snow ghosts, or ice-encrusted bent firs, compete with the view of Glacier National Park from the mountain's 6,817-foot summit. During summer, the **resort scenic lift rides** (10am-5:30pm daily mid-June-Labor Day and Fri.-Sun. Sept., $10-15) whisks riders via gondolas or open chairs to the summit of Big Mountain for views of Flathead Valley and Glacier National Park. Other summer activities include hiking, mountain biking, ziplines, an aerial park, an alpine slide, and treetop tours.

MUSEUMS

In Kalispell, the historic Victorian **Conrad Mansion** (330 Woodland Ave., 406/755-2166,

Lifeguards watch swimmers at City Beach on Whitefish Lake.

www.conradmansion.com, Tues.-Sun. mid-May-mid-Oct., $6-12) preserves 26 rooms with their original 1895 furniture, clothing, and toys. Drop in for docent-led tours that go on the hour 10am-4pm.

Also in Kalispell, the **Hockaday Museum of Art** (302 2nd Ave. E., 406/755-5268, www.hockadayartmuseum.org, 10am-5pm Tues.-Sat., adults $2-5, kids free) features Montana pottery, jewelry, and paintings, particularly by Native American and Glacier National Park artists.

Atop Big Mountain at Whitefish Mountain Resort, the **Forest Service Summit Nature Center** (406/862-2900, www.skiwhitefish.com, 10am-5pm daily mid-June-Labor Day, free) requires a hike or a lift ride ($10-15 round-trip) to reach its hands-on exhibits. Guides lead free walks 11am and 3pm July-August, and kids can do a Junior Ranger program.

Recreation

The Flathead Valley is a four-season recreation mecca. Lakes draw summertime boaters, paddlers, and swimmers, fall lures hunters, ski resorts cater to powder hounds, and spring explodes with hikers and mountain bikers.

DAY HIKES

Since Flathead National Forest surrounds Flathead Valley, hikers have no shortage of trails within spitting distance of the back porch. Most trails are multiuse, permitting mountain bikes and motorcycles in addition to hikers. But a few trails limit user groups.

Located north and west of Whitefish, the **Whitefish Trail** (www.whitefishlegacy.org) has more than 36 miles of paths and 10 trailheads. The multiuse trails allow hikers, mountain bikers, equestrians, and skiers. Pick up maps in various locations downtown, or download maps and get directions online.

In the Swan Mountains above Bigfork, **Jewel Basin** has 50 miles of hiking paths. Accessible late June-October, depending on snow, the 15,349-acre hiker-only area is called the "Jewel" for the 27 alpine fishing lakes that sparkle in its basins. Paths tromp across huckleberry meadows and high ridges with top-of-the-world views and huckleberry picking. Fido can go if he's on a leash. Holiday weekends can see 200 people per day at the Camp Misery trailhead. Trail signage is scanty, so find maps in local sports shops or contact **Flathead National Forest** (406/758-5208, www.fs.fed.us/r1/flathead) or **Swan Lake Ranger Station** (200 Ranger Station Rd., Bigfork, 406/837-7500).

★ Mount Aeneas
Distance: 5.9-mile loop
Duration: 3-4 hours
Elevation gain: 1,779 feet
Effort: moderate-strenuous
Trailhead: Camp Misery trailhead in Jewel Basin

Mount Aeneas, at 7,528 feet, is the highest peak in the Jewel and offers big views for little work, but don't expect solitude at the summit. From the top, you'll see Flathead Lake, Glacier National Park, the Bob Marshall Wilderness Complex, and the Swan Mountains. It yields a lot of scenery for a short hike.

Combined with Picnic Lakes, the trail loops on a ridge and through a lake basin. Begin hiking up Trail 717, a wide roadbed. In 1.5 miles, the trail reaches a four-way junction. Stay on 717, heading uphill. After a few switchbacks, you'll pass an ugly microwave tower before waltzing with the mountain goats along an arête to the summit. From the summit, drop down through the Picnic Lakes Basin. At the lakes, take Trail 392, then turn right onto Trail 68, and left onto Trail 8. At 1.7 miles from Camp Misery, Picnic Lakes makes a good little-kid destination; just reverse the route.

Flathead Valley Hikes

Trail	Effort	Distance	
Mount Aeneas	moderate-strenuous	5.9-mi loop	
Birch Lake	moderate	6 mi rt	3
Danny On Trail	moderate	4 mi one-way	2 h

Point for a 5.6- junction, tv before ' at '

Birch Lake

Distance: 6 miles round-trip
Duration: 3 hours
Elevation gain: 800 feet
Effort: moderate
Trailhead: Camp Misery trailhead in Jewel Basin

A short hop over a ridge along with a skip down a trail puts hikers on the shore of Birch Lake, a great destination for kids. Swim in the lake's west end, but don't expect balmy waters. This clear snowmelt pond retains its chill even in August. For those with more gumption,

Trails in Jewel Basin tour meadows of wildflowers.

another 2.5 miles puts you on the boulder shoreline of Crater Lake.

Begin hiking up the broad roadway of Trail 717 to the four-way junction. Take the right fork onto Trail 7. The trail curves around the lower flanks of Mount Aeneas as it descends to Birch Lake; you'll have to hike up this on the way out. A trail circles the lake, but the best place to stop is on its clearly visible peninsula.

★ Danny On Trail

Distance: 4 miles one-way
Duration: 2 hours
Elevation gain: 2,400 feet
Effort: moderate
Trailhead: next to the Chalet at Whitefish Mountain Resort
Directions: Drive seven miles north of Whitefish, following signs.

The Danny On Trail hosts over 14,000 hikers annually. At Big Mountain's summit, the Forest Service Summit Nature Center provides interpretive resources for the trail. Catch the chairlift up to hike down or hike up and then ride down (daily mid-June-Labor Day and Fri.-Sun. Sept., $8 pp one-way). While you can hike with a leashed pooch, dogs may not ride up or down the chairlift. Even without the chair ride, you can hike this trail through October.

After beginning in Whitefish Mountain Resort Village, the trail switchbacks up through a forested slope and crosses ski runs as it sweeps around the mountain. Snow hangs in the upper back slopes through June; valerian and penstemon bloom in July; huckleberries scent the air in August. Junctions are marked: Stay left at both to go directly to the top. You can also loop through Flower ile hike. At the East Rim left for a gentle, scenic loop he final steep ascent. Panoramas e top span Glacier National Park to Flathead Lake.

BIKING

Oodles of two-lane highways and paved country lanes make long loops around Flathead Lake or short farmland tours for roadies, and there are many single-track and dirt-road choices for mountain bikers. For the best list of itineraries to suit your interests and abilities, check **Glacier Cyclery's website** (www.glaciercyclery.com) for popular area routes. The shop also maintains a ride board with recent trail updates.

In Kalispell, the **Great Northern Historical Trail** (www.railstotrailsofnwmt.com) runs 12 miles of paved bike trail from Meridian Street to Smith Lake in Kila. Another 12-mile segment links Meridian with Somers for those who want to enjoy Flathead Lake. Find trailhead parking for both at Meridian Road and Derns Road.

In Whitefish, the expanding **Whitefish Trail** (www.whitefishlegacy.org) at more than 36 miles provides a curvy, multiuse dirt single-track trail with fun terrain for mountain

bikers. Current maps to trailheads can be found online. For single-track lift-served mountain biking, **Whitefish Mountain Resort** (end of Big Mountain Rd., Whitefish, 406/862-2900, www.skiwhitefish.com, 10am-5:30pm daily mid-June-Labor Day and Fri.-Sun. Sept., $21-36 depending on age and duration) hauls bikes and riders up two chairlifts. Twenty-two downhill routes descend the mountain in three zones for different abilities. New lower-mountain trails allow for skill building, while the Kashmir Flow Trail works for intermediates. Others drop on steep, hair-raising downhill descents with natural obstacles for advanced riders. The resort also has 10 miles of cross-country trails. The resort rents bikes ($20-85) and downhill protective gear ($15-30). Learn to downhill in beginner programs ($99) on Mondays, Wednesdays, and Fridays.

Rentals and Repairs

Flathead Valley also has multiple bike shops that rent, sell, and repair bikes. Bike rentals usually run $35-55 per day. In Whitefish, **Glacier Cyclery** (326 E. 2nd St., 406/862-6446, www.glaciercyclery.com) rents touring bikes, roadies, hybrids, and mountain bikes, plus car racks, utility trailers, and Burleys. In

The Danny On Trail climbs to the top of Big Mountain.

Kalispell, closest to the rail trails, **Sportsman** (145 Hutton Ranch Rd., 406/755-6484, www.sportsmanskihaus.com) rents mountain and road bikes. In Bigfork, rent mountain bikes at **Base Camp Bigfork** (8525 MT 35, 406/871-9733, www.basecampbigfork.com). All three shops include helmets with rentals, offer weekly rates, and do repairs.

Mountain Bike Center

Tucked in the woods north of Whitefish, the **Whitefish Bike Retreat** (855 Beaver Lake Rd., 406/260-0274, www.whitefishbikeretreat.com, year-round) is a unique trailside biker haven operated by Cricket Butler, a Great Divide record holder. Day passes ($15) let you access the skills park, flow and berm trails, pump track, disc golf, and two bike-washing stations. Trails connect to the Whitefish Trail system near the Beaver Lake trailhead. The camp store rents bikes (adults $35-45, kids $25) and paddleboards ($35-55). It also sells snacks and bike packing supplies. Lodging is in the large bunkhouse with repurposed bicycle parts as fixtures and railings. It has private rooms ($95-135) or shared bunkrooms ($41-45 pp), a large furnished kitchen, shared bathrooms with showers, an outdoor patio with fire pit,

laundry, and a workroom and secure storage for bikes. Campers can tent in the eight campsites ($30) with picnic tables, bear-resistant food storage, a dishwashing station, flush toilets, and showers. Shuttles run to the airport and train ($30-45) or to Glacier Cyclery (free).

HORSEBACK RIDING

Hop in the saddle for horseback adventures. In Bigfork, Averill's Flathead Lake Lodge (Flathead Lake Lodge Rd., 406/837-4391, www.flatheadlakelodge.com, daily mid-June-Aug., $50-150) leads one- and two-hour rides for views of Flathead Lake. The three-hour ride is on a private elk reserve. Reservations are recommended.

BOATING

Popular boating lakes dot Flathead Valley; the two largest are Flathead and Whitefish Lakes. Both have several launch sites, and rentals are available. Expect to pay hourly rates for Jet Skis ($70-85), water-ski boats ($85-125), and pontoon fishing boats and party barges ($85-120). In addition to your rental fee, you'll need to pay for the gas you use. Hand-propelled craft like canoes, kayaks, paddleboards, and rowboats rent for $15-30 per hour.

Whitefish Mountain Resort has lift-served mountain bike trails.

Flathead Lake

On Flathead Lake's north end, Bigfork, Somers, and Lakeside serve boaters with marinas and boat launches open May-October. The lake also has 13 public access points, six of which are state parks maintained by **Montana Fish, Wildlife, and Parks** (406/752-5501, http://stateparks.mt.gov, $5/ day). Boat rentals are available at **Wild Wave** (7220 U.S. 93 S., Lakeside, and 180 Vista Ln., Bigfork, 406/844-2400 or 406/257-2627, www. wildwaverentals.com).

Whitefish Lake

For launching boats ($5-10), find public ramps at **Whitefish Lake State Park** and **City Beach.** For rentals, mooring, and fuel service, **Whitefish Lake Lodge Marina** (1390 Wisconsin Ave., 406/863-4020, mid-May-Sept.) is the only option.

WATERSKIING

Most vacationers don't come to the Flathead solely for waterskiing since glacial-fed lakes are downright cold. Wetsuits are advised for those used to warm water. Water-skiers hit Whitefish Lake and Flathead Lake as well as smaller valley lakes. The marinas rent waterskiing boats and gear ($85-125/hour plus gas).

PADDLING

Sea kayakers, canoers, and paddleboarders have multiple places to launch. **Flathead** and **Whitefish Lakes** provide flat water, although Flathead can kick up with big winds. The most popular Flathead Lake paddling destination is **Wild Horse Island,** launching from the public beach in Dayton. Ambling portions of the **Flathead, Whitefish,** and **Swan Rivers** also flow slowly enough for flatwater paddling and adept paddleboarders.

White-water kayakers wearing dry suits gravitate to the freezing cold water of the Swan River outside Bigfork. For Class IV-V rapids, the **Swan River Wild Mile,** a short 1.25-mile stretch that drops 100 feet below Bigfork Dam, sees its best water May-July,

especially Wednesday nights when the dam releases flows.

Rentals

Rentals usually run $30-65 per day. Life jackets and paddles are included in the rates. Find them at marinas on Whitefish and Flathead Lakes. In addition, **Sportsman** (145 Hutton Ranch Rd., Kalispell, 406/755-6484, and Mountain Mall, Whitefish, 406/862-3111, www.sportsmanskihaus.com) rents canoes, kayaks, tandem kayaks, and paddleboards. In Bigfork, rent canoes, single and tandem kayaks, and paddleboards from **Base Camp Bigfork** (8525 MT 35, 406/871-9733, www. basecampbigfork.com). In Whitefish, rent paddleboards from **Paddlefish Sports** (105 Wisconsin Ave., 406/260-7733).

FISHING

Lakes, estuaries, and rivers abound for fishing. Flathead Valley is home to the **Flathead River,** a giant highway for migrating fish. Because of dam control and the cold glacial water, do not expect blue-ribbon trout fishing. It carries many nonnative species, especially northern pike lurking in larger southern sloughs. Seven river access points offer places to fish or launch boats downstream: Blankenship Bridge, the U.S. 2 bridge at Hungry Horse, a spur road at Bad Rock Canyon's west end, Kokanee Bend, Pressentine Bar, the Old Steel Bridge, and the Stillwater mouth. Most anglers hit the stretch between Columbia Falls and the Old Steel Bridge in Kalispell.

Flathead Lake teems with cutthroat, giant trophy lake trout, mountain and lake whitefish, largemouth bass, bull trout, and yellow perch. It's good for all types of fishing: bait, lure, fly-fishing, and trolling. Montana fishing licenses are only valid on the north half of the lake due to the Flathead Reservation on the south end.

Whitefish Lake draws anglers for its lake trout and whitefish. During winter, some anglers ice fish. Northern pike, lake trout, and kokanee are common, and it is regularly stocked with westslope cutthroat trout.

Huckleberry Mania

The huckleberry is a small, dark-purple fruit about the size of the tip of your little finger. It resembles a blueberry but is much sweeter and more flavorful. It grows only in the wild on low deciduous bushes with leaves that turn red in fall. Growing mostly at elevations above 4,000 feet, the berries ripen late July-September.

The berry has yet to be successfully cultivated. In Flathead Valley, you'll find berry stands selling hucks that have been picked by commercial permit in national forests or on private lands. Expect to pay near $50 per gallon for the precious purple gems (now you know why huckleberry pie is so expensive). Be cautious when purchasing berries in early summer, as you may be buying frozen berries from last year rather than freshly picked ones. The frozen berries are still yummy but are a little softer when they thaw. Fresh ones start hitting the stands in late July.

You can pick your own huckleberries to eat; no permit is needed. You'll find them on many trails in Glacier National Park and Flathead National Forest. While locals don't usually divulge their prized secret stashes, you can usually find good huckleberry picking on Big Mountain at Whitefish Mountain Resort. Glacier National Park rules permit plucking a few berries to eat, but not commercial harvesting.

Two mammals crave the berries: bears and humans. High in vitamin C, the berries are healthy and low in fat. They enliven any pastry, pie, sauce, or fruit concoction. They're tasty in smoothies and delightful on pancakes.

You'll find huckleberries in everything from ice cream to beer; syrup, jam, and jelly top everyone's favorites. Hucks also flavor and scent chocolate, honey, cocoa, barbecue sauce, tea, salad dressing, ice cream toppings, a daiquiri mix, lotion, lip balm, bubble bath, shampoo, soap, and more.

One word of advice: Avoid using huckleberry shampoo before hiking in bear country.

Licenses

Montana fishing licenses (Montana residents: $8-18 season, $13 adults for 2 days, free ages 1-11; nonresidents: $25 for 2 days, $44 for 10 days, $60 season; kids ages 1-14 free with adult with license for shared limit or $8 for own license) are required. Purchase them at fly shops and outdoor gear stores.

Fly Shops and Guides

Hit up fly-fishing shops in the Flathead for locally made, hand-tied flies and tackle as well as advice on where the fish are biting. Most of the following shops also offer guide services ($450-550 for two people/day). Rates do not include Montana fishing licenses.

Lakestream Flyshop (669 Spokane Ave., Whitefish, 406/862-1298, www.lakestream. com) guides fly-fishing trips on the main Flathead River plus all three tributaries. **Stumptown Anglers** (5790 U.S. 93 S., Whitefish, 877/906-9949, www.stumptown-angler.com) guides trips on the Flathead plus several regional rivers. For guided fishing on the Swan or Flathead Rivers, head to **Bigfork Anglers** (405 Bridge St., Bigfork, 406/837-3675, www.bigforkanglers.com).

Montana has no shortage of independent fly-fishing guide services operating unattached to shops; you can find them in business listings and on the Internet. Be sure the guide service is licensed with the state before hiring one.

Charter Fishing

Charter fishing services on Flathead Lake operate June-September and when ice permits December-March. From two locations, **Howe's Fishing** (688 Lakeside Blvd., Lakeside, and Marina Cay, Bigfork, 406/257-5214, www.aablefishing.com, $200-700 for 1-2 people) launches fishing trips by reservation.

swimming zones ...te parks (http:// ...ana residents free, ...nts). The best state ...s at the north end of ...ayfarers (8600 MT ...v.). **Whitefish Lake** ...Les Mason (2650 E. ...-Nov., summer rentals: paddleb... kayaks, canoes) and **Whitefish Lake** (1615 W. Lakeshore, year-round). **City Beach** on Whitefish Lake (406/863-2475, free) is a kid favorite due to sand imported decades ago and a snack stand that sells ice cream and hot dogs.

Two seasonal outdoor pools attract families at $3-8 per person. The **Pinewood Family Aquatic Center** (925 4th Ave. W., Columbia Falls, 406/892-3500, Mon.-Sat. mid-June-late Aug.) has a bromine 25-meter pool and kids' play pool. In Kalispell, the outdoor pool at **Woodland Park** (Woodland Park Dr. and Shady Glen Dr., 406/758-7812, daily June-Aug.) has slides, a current stream, and diving pools.

Big Sky Waterslides (7211 U.S. 2 E., Columbia Falls, 406/892-5025, www.big-skywp.com, 11am-7pm daily mid-June-Labor Day, $18-28) is a great place to take the kids to unwind after a hot day and a long drive. The park has 10 big and little slides along with a wading pool, hot pool, mini golf, and bumper cars. After 3pm, rates drop slightly.

Flathead Valley has two large physical-fitness complexes that include weights, cardio machines, indoor swimming pools, and hot tubs. Drop-in rates are available per day: adults $12, children $5-10. **The Summit** (205 Sunnyview Ln., Kalispell, 406/751-4100, www.krh.org/summit) also has a climbing wall. **The Wave** (1250 Baker Ave., Whitefish, 406/862-2444, www.whitefishwave.com) has a fun kids' pool with a slide and a water fountain. Call for current hours.

HUNTING

With Flathead Valley surrounded by Flathead National Forest, it is popular for hunting big game and birds. Get hunting regulations, seasons, and license info from Montana Fish, Wildlife, and Parks (406/752-5501, www.fwp.mt.gov).

GOLF

Golf Digest rated Flathead Valley one of the world's 50 greatest golf destinations. The recognition is due to the scenery, reasonable prices, and nine championship courses. With daylight lasting 16 hours in June, courses are open dawn-dusk, adjusting tee times as daylight hours wane. Depending on snow, most courses are open April-October. All of the Flathead courses have rentals, pro shops, instruction, driving ranges, restaurants, and lounges.

Flathead Valley summer greens fees run $50-115, depending on the course, but you can get cheaper greens fees in spring, fall, and

Whitefish Lake Golf Course driving range

ski tracks at Whitefish Mountain Resort

Whitefish, 406/862-4000, www.golfwhitefish. com) is Montana's only 36-hole course and has the most rounds played in the state. The north course tours through large cedars and firs; the south course runs past Lost Loon Lake. Both have mountain views. **Meadow Lake Golf Course** (490 St. Andrews Dr., Columbia Falls, 406/892-2111, www.meadowlakegolf.com) has 18 holes among woods, with some tight fairways and lots of adjacent houses. A couple of ponds and a creek separate the fairways, and some trees shade the course. **Big Mountain Golf Course** (3230 U.S. 93 N., Kalispell, 406/751-1950 or 800/255-5641, www.golfmt. com) is a Scottish links-style course. Since its 18 holes sit mid-valley, with few trees, views open up to Big Mountain and Glacier National Park. The Stillwater River runs adjacent to the back nine. **Buffalo Hill** (1176 N. Main St., Kalispell, 406/756-4530 or 888/342-6319, www.golfbuffalohill.com) combines an older course with a newer course for 27 holes. The older Cameron Nine abuts the highway; the newer 18-hole course is moderately difficult with a lot of terrain variety.

With the least expensive greens fees, **Village Greens** (500 Palmer Dr., Kalispell, 406/752-4666, www.montanagolf.com) surrounds its bent-grass greens with a few trees, ponds, and houses. The 18 holes afford a pleasant place to play on one of the easier courses.

DOWNHILL SKIING

Located seven miles north of Whitefish, **Whitefish Mountain Resort** (end of Big Mountain Rd., 406/862-2900, www.ski-whitefish.com, early Dec.-early Apr., $39-76) lives up to its former name of Big Mountain with 3,000 acres of skiing terrain, 2,353 feet of vertical drop, 14 lifts, five terrain parks, and 105 named runs. Big bowls, glades, and long cruisers head off the summit in every direction, and views from the summit on sunny days yield the entire panorama of Glacier's peaks. You can even find good tree skiing in the mountain's famous fog. The

daily after 3pm. Club rentals range $10-50 and carts $16-40.

One-stop tee time reservations are available through **Northwest Montana Golf Association** (www.golfmontana.net, 800/392-9795), with stats for most of the local courses. Call or book online for advance reservations and golf packages.

Courses

With the highest greens fees, **Eagle Bend Golf Course** (279 Eagle Bend Dr., Bigfork, 406/837-7310 or 800/255-5641, www.eagle-bendgolfclub.com) is ranked among the top 50 public courses in the country. The challenging 27-hole course is a Jack Nicklaus design with big variety in its fairway layouts. From different tees, you can see Flathead Lake, the Swan Mountains, and Glacier National Park; ospreys fly overhead.

Four courses offer summer greens fees in the $60-75 range. The city-owned **Whitefish Lake Golf Course** (1200 U.S. 93 N., resort's village contains restaurants, shops, rental gear, a ski school, day care, and lodging from economy to upscale condos.

Sitting above Flathead Lake, **Blacktail Mountain** (end of Blacktail Mountain Rd., Lakeside, 406/844-0999, Wed.-Sun. and holidays mid-Dec.-early Apr., $20-40) attracts families for its smaller 1,000 acres, four lifts, and family-friendly pricing.

CROSS-COUNTRY SKIING

Several small cross-country ski areas dot Flathead Valley, with trails groomed for classic and skate skiing mid-December-early March. **Glacier Nordic Shop and Center** (406-862-9498, www.glaciernordicclub.com, shop 9am-5:30pm daily, $5-10 trail fee, $8-20 rentals, $35-75 lessons) grooms 12 kilometers on Whitefish Lake Golf Course and 8 kilometers at Whitefish Mountain Resort. The club's website has grooming updates and information on other Flathead Valley ski trails, such as Round Meadows, Heron Park, Blacktail, and Bigfork. **Sportsman** (145 Hutton Ranch Rd., Kalispell, 406/755-6484, and Mountain Mall, Whitefish, 406/862-3111, www.sportsmanskihaus.com) also rents skis for skate, classic, or touring in Glacier.

SNOWMOBILING

The Flathead Valley is surrounded by 200 miles of groomed snowmobile trails open December-mid-April, but some trails close April 1. **Flathead Valley Snowmobile Association** (www.flatheadsnowmobiler. com) maintains the grooming on nine popular trails near Whitefish, Columbia Falls, and Bigfork. For those striking out on their own, check conditions with **Flathead Avalanche Center** (406/257-8402, www.flatheadavalanche.org).

Rentals are available at **Extreme Motorsports** (6191 U.S. 93 S., Whitefish, 406/862-8594, www.wfmextrememotorsports. com) and **J & L Rentals** (830 1st Ave. W., Columbia Falls, 406/892-7666, www.jandlsnowmobile.com). Expect to pay $200 per day for renting a snowmobile, helmets included; snowmobile suits, boots, and gloves are extra. Guided tours are available, too.

THRILL SPORTS AND FAMILY FUN

Whitefish Mountain Resort (end of Big Mountain Rd., 406/862-2900, www.skiwhitefish.com, daily mid-June-Labor Day and Sat.-Sun. Sept.) beefed up its summer adventure programs. **Zipline Tours** ($70-80) lets you

You can fly through the air on ziplines at Whitefish Mountain Resort.

sail through the air 20-300 feet above the ground on a five-line or seven-line tour. The AdrenaLine stretches the longest at 1,900 feet. **Walk in the Treetops** ($50) is a boardwalk tour through the tree canopy at 70 feet in the air. Guides lead the tours with participants clipped in with a safety harness. Reservations are a must for both ziplining and Walk in the Treetops. Multiple trips go out each day.

The **Alpine Slide** ($8/ride) offers speed thrills sledding down a track. Even little kids can ride with adults. For a physical challenge, tackle the new **Aerial Adventure Park** ($35-47) to traverse bridges, cables, ziplines, and more suspended 10-50 feet above the ground in courses of varied difficulty. Safety comes from being clipped in with a harness.

SPAS

Whitefish is hom
Remedies Day
406/863-9493,
makes all their
and wraps fr
found in the !
ture kitchen
whipped cr
rock foot rub, scrub.,
massages. In an upscale, quiet la..
the **Spa at Whitefish Lake** (1380 Wiscon...
Ave., 406/863-4050, www.lodgeatwhitefish-
lake.com) offers traditional spa facials, waxing, massage, scrubs, wraps, manicures, and pedicures. Their hot riverstone therapy aims for deep muscle relaxation.

Entertainment and Shopping

ENTERTAINMENT

In Bigfork, the **Bigfork Summer Playhouse** (526 Electric Ave., 406/837-4886, www.bigforksummerplayhouse.com, mid-May-Aug.) presents five shows in repertory during each summer, from Broadway musical favorites to comedies. In Whitefish, **Whitefish Theatre Company** (1 Central Ave., 406/862-5371, www.whitefishtheatreco.org) sponsors plays, concerts, speakers, and art films in the O'Shaughnessey Center. Broadway veterans formed the acclaimed **Alpine Theatre Project** (Whitefish, 406/862-7469, www.atpwhitefish.org), which produces plays during the summer at Whitefish Performing Arts Center (600 E. 2nd St.). Beloved musicals, classic comedies, and plays highlight its summer schedule with actors imported from Broadway.

You can catch a just-released blockbuster movie in the Flathead, but don't expect a hotbed of foreign, independent, or avant-garde films. Whitefish has one movie theater, **Mountain Cinema** (Mountain Mall, U.S. 93, 406/862-3130). In Kalispell, you'll find 14

movies showing at **Stadium 14** (185 Hutton Ranch Rd., 406/752-7804, www.signaturetheatres.com).

EVENTS

The annual **Glacier Jazz Stampede** (406/892-2115, www.glacierjazzstampede.com) is for those who love traditional jazz, swing, ragtime, Dixieland, and big-band sounds. The multiday October event crams with more than a dozen bands and performers from across the United States and Canada, pounding out nearly nonstop music in different Kalispell venues. Bands, schedules, and ticket prices vary yearly for each event or all-event entry. In August, the annual seven-day **Festival Amadeus** (406/257-3241, www.gscmusic.org) celebrates Mozart's music with guest artists, chamber concerts, and orchestra productions, with nightly performances in Whitefish or Bigfork.

Attracting hundreds of spectators even in soggy weather, the **Bigfork Whitewater Festival** (www.bigforkwhitewaterfestival.com) runs kayakers down the Class IV nt local souvenirs to take home? Look for the blue "Made in Montana" logo. Only arts, crafts, ood, and other products made by Montana residents and grown or produced within the state can use the label. More than 2,600 businesses, including single-item production, use the distinctive marker.

Find the "Made in Montana" logo on foods like coffee, jams and jellies, preserves, teas, pasta, salad dressings, barbecue sauces, herbs, cheese, jerky, and cookies. There are also personal health-care products ranging from soaps and shampoos to lotions and oils. Toys, games, pet goodies, furniture, and clothing also may sport the logo, as can arts and crafts like photography, music, lithographs, paintings, candles, and more.

For a Made in Montana product fix after you get home, check www.madeinmontanausa.com for companies that sell Made in Montana products online.

While in Montana, look for two other labels that identify Montana-made. The "Grown in Montana" label is used on fresh produce, eggs, honey, meats, grains, and other products. The "Native American Made in Montana" includes handicrafts, jewelry, art, beadwork, and apparel made by Native Americans on one of Montana's reservations.

Wild Mile of the Swan River at the peak of spring runoff. Traditionally held for two days over Memorial Day weekend, competitions run from slalom to boater-cross. Local pubs and restaurants party with nightly entertainment.

In the doldrums of winter, Whitefish celebrates its wacky **Winter Carnival** (406/862-3501, http://whitefishwintercarnival.com), a three-day spree of ski races, ice hockey, the penguin plunge, figure skating, a torchlight parade, fireworks, the rail jam, and skijoring, held the first weekend in February. Hundreds of people line the few blocks of downtown Whitefish for an old-fashioned "drive the old tractor down main street" parade disrupted by raucous yetis and Viking women kissing onlookers.

Art events abound in the Flathead. Whitefish hosts its **Gallery Nights** (www.whitefishgallerynights.org) on the first Thursday of each month May-October and three-day **Huckleberry Days art festival** (www.whitefishchamber.org) in mid-August in Credit Union Park. Kalispell celebrates its three-day **Arts in the Park** (www.discoverkalispell.com) in late July in Depot Park and a late November **Art Walk** (www.discoverkalispell.com) in downtown galleries.

The **Bigfork Festival of the Arts** (www.bigforkfestivalofthearts.com) takes place in early August on the town's main street.

Two farmers markets have grown into weekly outdoor fairs with fresh local produce, food vendors, music, plus arts and craft stalls 5pm-7:30pm late May-late September. On Tuesdays, find the **Whitefish Farmers Market** (www.whitefishfarmersmarket.org) in Depot Park and Main Street in front of O'Shaughnessey Center. On Thursdays, the outdoor venue at O'Brien's Liquor Store hosts the **Columbia Falls Community Market** (830 1st Ave. W., www.cfcommunitymarket.com) with bands, dancing, a beer garden, and kids' attractions such as puppet shows, climbing walls, magicians, and dance performances. On Saturday mornings, the more traditional **Kalispell Farmer's Market** (777 Grandview Dr., www.kalispellfarmersmarket.org, 9am-12:30pm early May-mid-Oct.), which has local produce and crafts, takes place at the Flathead Valley Community College.

RODEOS AND FAIRS

Located mid-valley between Whitefish and Kalispell, **Majestic Valley Arena** (3630 U.S. 93 N., 406/755-5366, www.

com), **Casey's Bar** (101 Central Ave., 406/862-8150, www.caseyswhitefish.com), and **The Craggy Range Bar & Grill** (10 Central Ave., 406/862-7550, www.thecraggyrange.com).

SHOPPING

While Flathead Valley thankfully has no Mall of America clone or factory outlet mall, it does have its share of strip malls and chain stores, mostly located on U.S. 93 north of Kalispell. However, if you can, head to the few strikingly different shops worth browsing: art galleries, jewelry stores, and eclectic gift shops. Most of the one-of-a-kind locally owned stores cluster in the few blocks of downtown Whitefish, Bigfork, and Kalispell.

For classy high-quality, inventive, classic, and educational toys, stop in **Imagination Station** (221 Central Ave., Whitefish, 406/862-5668, and 132 Main St., Kalispell, 406/755-5668, 9:30am-6pm Mon.-Sat., 11am-5pm Sun.). The store will even ship your toys home for you so you don't have to haul everything on the airplane. In Kalispell, visit **Sassafras** (120 Main St., 406/752-2433, http://sassafrasartcoop.com, 10am-5pm Mon.-Sat.), an artists and antiques co-op, featuring the works of 30-40 local northwest Montana artists. Pieces range from watercolors and cards to pottery, jewelry, clothing, furniture, and sculptures. In Whitefish, pick up handmade soaps at **Sage and Cedar** (214 Central Ave., 406/862-9411, www.sageandcedar.com, 10am-6pm Mon.-Fri., shorter hours weekends) and visit **Stumptown Marketplace** (12 Spokane Ave., www.stumptownmarket.com, 8am-5pm Mon.-Sat.) for locally made products and artisan foods.

Outdoor Gear

For outdoor gear, such as camping, backpacking, skiing, snowboarding, and fishing gear, several shops carry good brand-name selections and know how to fit equipment to individual people. **Rocky Mountain Outfitter** (135 Main St., Kalispell, 406/752-2446, www.

Rocky Mountain Outfitter in Kalispell

majesticvalleyarena.com) is the hub for events: concerts, rodeos, equestrian competitions, and trade shows. For cowpoke wannabes, the annual **Northwest Montana Fair** opens in mid-August at the Flathead County Fairgrounds (265 N. Meridian, Kalispell, 406/758-5810, www.nwmtfair.com).

CASINOS AND BARS

While gambling is legal in Montana, casinos haven't rocketed to Las Vegas style. Most Flathead bars have a few slot machines squirreled away in a corner; some even run a card table or two. In a twist to the usual gas station-convenience mart, some gas chains add small, dark, and smoky casinos featuring gaming machines and poker tables.

The best place for anything approximating nightclubbing is old-fashioned bar hopping in downtown Whitefish. Friday and Saturday nights usually feature dancing and live bands at **Great Northern** (27 Central Ave., 406/862-2816, www.greatnorthernbar.

rockymountainoutfitter.com) specializes in hiking, backpacking, climbing, and skiing. Don Scharfe, the owner, is well known for first ascents on several of Glacier's peaks.

The crew at **The White Room** (119 Central Ave., Whitefish, 406/862-7666, www.whiteroomshop.com) are the local ski experts, especially for telemark and backcountry, but in summer, the shop outfits hikers, backpackers, and climbers with gear and clothing. With two stores, **Sportsman** (145 Hutton Ranch Rd., Kalispell, 406/755-6484, and 6475 U.S. 93, Whitefish, 406/862-3111, www.sportsmanskihaus.com) carries gear and clothing for skiers, snowboarders, hikers, backpackers, anglers, hunters, campers, tennis players, and cyclists. In two locations, **Stumptown Snowboards** (128 Central Ave., Whitefish, 406/862-0955, and Whitefish Mountain Resort, Whitefish, 406/862-5828) are the local experts in snowboarding and skateboarding, with full equipment and clothing lines.

Maps and Books

To stock up on good topographic maps of Glacier and Flathead National Forest, you'll find the widest selection at **Rocky Mountain Outfitter** (135 Main St., Kalispell, 406/752-2446, www.rockymountainoutfitter.com) or **Sportsman** (145 Hutton Ranch Rd., Kalispell, 406/755-6484, and 6475 U.S. 93, Whitefish, 406/862-3111, www.sportsmanskihaus.com). Likewise, both shops carry guidebooks for hiking, fishing, and cross-country skiing in the area along with a few field guides. You can also find guidebooks and books on natural history, Lewis and Clark, Montana history, and field guides for flowers, birds, and animals at **Bookworks** (244 Spokane Ave., Whitefish, 406/862-4980). **Glacier National Park Conservancy** (402 9th St. W., Columbia Falls, 406/892-3250, http://glacier.org) has an outlet on U.S. 2 that carries books on Glacier.

Bigfork Lodging, Camping, and Food

Bigfork's location on Flathead Lake attracts scads of visitors to the resort town in summer. Lake and river activities are big, along with hiking, golf, and the playhouse. In the off-season, you may have the town nearly to yourself. Of the four major towns in Flathead Valley, Bigfork is the farthest from Glacier (65 minutes) and Glacier Park International Airport (35 minutes).

ACCOMMODATIONS

You can find a full list of Bigfork lodging options at www.bigfork.org. Locate lake, river, or golf vacation homes to rent through **Eagle Bend Flathead Vacation Rentals** (406/837-4942 or 800/239-9933, www.mtvacationrentals.com). Reservations are mandatory in summer, which also has the highest rates. Lodging rates are lowest in late fall, winter, and early spring. Properties will add on the 7 percent state bed tax. Contrary to Glacier, most lodging has air-conditioning, mini-fridges, microwaves, wireless Internet, and TVs.

Motel and Cottages

The town's most reasonably priced lodging is **Timbers Motel** (8540 Hwy. 35 S., 406/837-6200 or 800/821-4546, https://timbersmotel.com, mid-May-Oct., $65-170), located within a five-minute drive of Eagle Bend Golf Course and a couple of minutes from the Bigfork Summer Playhouse. It sits on a small knoll above the highway and has a heated pool, hot tub, and sauna.

In downtown Bigfork adjacent to the historic steel bridge over the Swan River, ★ **Bridge Street Cottages** (309 Bridge St., 406/837-2785 or 888/264-4974, www.bridgestreetcottages.com, $125-350) offers higher-end lodging. Four of the units overlook the river. Surrounded by small perennial gardens, these well-furnished, well-kept

Local Coffee and Ice Cream

Espresso stands and ice cream are virtually everywhere. But locally roasted coffee beans and locally made ice creams go beyond the norm. You'll find these coffee and ice creams served in restaurants across the valley. But here's where to find their eateries:

MONTANA COFFEE TRADERS

This local coffee roaster has coffeehouses and cafés throughout Flathead Valley. Since its birth in 1981, Montana Coffee Traders (www.coffeetraders.com) has been roasting beans in an old farmhouse south of Whitefish. Today, that roasting house has coffee sales and an espresso bar (5810 Hwy. 93 S., 406/862-7627, 7am-5:30pm Mon.-Fri., 9am-5pm Sat.). Montana Coffee Traders' cafés serve food and all types of espresso in three locations:

- Columbia Falls (30 9th St. W., 406/892-7696, 7am-2pm daily) has breakfast and lunch. Huge breakfast omelets, muffins, scones, salads, wraps, and deli sandwiches top the menu, with plenty of vegetarian options.

- Kalispell (328 W. Center St., 406/756-2326, 7am-3pm Mon.-Sat.) offers breakfast and lunch.

- Whitefish (110 Central Ave., 406/862-7667, 7am-6pm Mon.-Sat., 8am-4pm Sun.) has pastries, desserts, *bocadillos* (Spanish sandwiches), soups, and quiches.

SWEET PEAKS ICE CREAM

Starting as a mobile ice cream shop, Sweet Peaks Ice Cream (www.sweetpeaksicecream.com) has expanded to shops across Flathead Valley. Its specialty is eclectic flavors based on locally sourced ingredients. Sweet Peaks makes ice cream, frozen yogurts, and sorbets. Look for Sweet Peaks at three locations:

- Whitefish (419 3rd St., 406/862-4668, 11:30am-11pm daily, hours shorten Oct.-May)

- Bigfork (604 Electric Ave., 406/257-0841, 11:30am-9:30pm daily mid-June-Labor Day)

- Kalispell (343 Main St., 406/257-1102, 11:30am-10:30pm daily, hours shorten Oct.-May)

---

one-bedroom cottages come with fully equipped kitchens and fireplaces. Suites are smaller, with just a fridge and a microwave. Walk to restaurants and the playhouse.

Bed-and-Breakfast

A short 3.5 miles south of Bigfork puts you at **Candlewycke Inn Bed & Breakfast** (311 Aero Ln., 406/837-6406 or 844/617-9216, www.candlewyckeinn.com, $115-190, two-night minimum). On 10 acres, the cedar-and-log inn, serving a seasonal breakfast in the morning, has five folk-art-themed guest rooms with pillow-top beds and private baths, some with jetted tubs. Walk on trails around the property, cross-country ski in winter, or lounge on the massive decks or in the outdoor hot tub.

Resorts

★ **Averill's Flathead Lake Lodge** (Flathead Lake Lodge Rd., Bigfork, 406/837-4391, www.flatheadlakelodge.com, mid-June-Aug.) is a family-owned working dude ranch on 2,000 acres. Lodging, meals, and activities are all included in one big price for seven days: rates run around $3,850 per week for adults, with rates for children less depending on age. With horseback riding, fishing, swimming, waterskiing, tennis, and sailing, the ranch centers around the classy log lodge and cabins with 1-3 bedrooms. You can park the car and dive into vacation mode for several days, as the ranch coordinates all the activities.

At the Swan River mouth to Flathead Lake, **Marina Cay Resort** (180 Vista Ln., Bigfork, 406/837-5861 or 800/433-6516, www.

marinacay.com, $110-500) has courtyard suites, waterfront suites, and 2-3-bedroom condos, all individually themed. New owners took over in 2015 and have been revamping the complex, which includes restaurants, a summer tiki bar, a seasonal outdoor pool and hot tub, and a marina with boat rentals.

CAMPING

Located on Flathead Lake, **Wayfarer's State Park** (8600 MT Hwy. 35, 855/922-6768, http:// stateparks.mt.gov, mid-Mar.-mid-Nov., $18-28) is great for boating, fishing, and sunsets. The park is one of the lake's largest campgrounds, with 40 sites on 67 acres, a boat ramp, a swimming area, and 1.5 miles of hiking trails. Ten shared campsites are reserved for hikers and bikers ($6-12). Pets are allowed on a leash. Campground amenities include firewood, a fire grill, flush and vault toilets, showers, picnic tables, drinking water (May-Sept. only), and RV dump station. Maximum length for RVs is 40 feet. Four other state parks also rim the lake. Reservations are available online.

FOOD

For a tiny town, Bigfork packs in the tasty restaurants, most of which sit downtown within two blocks' walking distance of the theater. On performance nights, you won't get a table before the show unless you make reservations.

Cafés

In downtown Bigfork, the **Pocketstone Café** (444 Electric Ave., 406/837-7223, www.pocketstonecafe.com, 6am-3pm daily, $7-15) serves espresso and inventive twists on café staples from home-baked goods to omelets and sandwiches. The huckleberry jalapeño burger is a house specialty, and the Rueben tops the charts with its house-made sauerkraut, rye bread, corned beef, and sauce. Locals heading to Jewel Basin for hiking always fuel up at **Echo Lake Café** (1195 MT Hwy. 83, 406/837-4252, www.echolakecafe.com, 6:30am-2:30pm daily, $9-15), where breakfast and lunch are served all day.

Burgers

In the local dive **Garden Bar and Grill** (451 Electric Ave., 406/837-9914, 11am-2am daily, $7-12, cash only), you can eat burgers inside or out back in the funky garden, with live music on summer weekend evenings. The bar has 20 microbrews on tap.

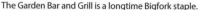

The Garden Bar and Grill is a longtime Bigfork staple.

Fine Dining

Known for exceptional food at modest prices, ★ **Showthyme!** (548 Electric Ave., 406/837-0707, www.showthyme.com, 5pm-9pm Tues.-Sat., $19-30) dishes up fresh fish, meats, and vegetarian entrées with an international wine list. Dishes rely on local and regional ingredients that get turned into inventive taste sensations, especially the nightly three-course dinner. The cozy, old two-story brick bank building adjacent to the theater has outside seating in summer.

★ **Moroldo's Fine Italian Restaurant** (7951 MT Hwy. 35, 406/837-2720, 5:30pm-9pm Mon. and Wed.-Sat.) tucks hidden off the highway, but serves up caprese, bruschetta, pasta, gnocchi, and meat entrées ($19-30), including veal, designed by Fabrizio Moroldo. Leave room for tiramisu, and enjoy the Italian ambience.

Sushi

Located upstairs in Twin Burch Square, **SakeTome Sushi** (459 Electric Ave., 406/837-1128, www.saketomesushi.com, 5pm-10pm Mon.-Sat., shorter hours off-season) garners a loyal following. The restaurant, expanded in 2016, includes a bar, indoor seating, and deck seating. Find *sashimi, nigiri* and *maki* rolls ($7-12), and specialty rolls ($14-20) with fun twists on spicy crab or ahi.

Ice Cream

Bigfork's outpost of **Sweet Peaks Ice Cream** (604 Electric Ave., 406/257-0841, 11:30am-9:30pm daily mid-June-Labor Day) offers the local brand's usual lineup of unusual ice cream, frozen yogurt, and sorbet flavors.

Columbia Falls Lodging, Camping, and Food

Columbia Falls is the closest town to Glacier and Glacier Park International Airport, but they are in opposite directions. The town is 18 minutes from West Glacier and 12 minutes from the airport. Rather than a tourist town, it's a working-class lumber-mill town and sprawls along the highway.

ACCOMMODATIONS

Good for those on a budget, the town has a Super 8 chain motel plus two small independent motels, all located on U.S. 2 near the waterslide and the Flathead River. Surrounding Columbia Falls, cabins and vacation homes are scattered in the woods and along the Flathead River. Locate properties rented by their owners via **VRBO** (www.vrbo.com). Summer rates are highest, but you can find lower rates and deals during the rest of the year. Contrary to Glacier,

Wi-Fi is common in Columbia Falls lodging. Lodging is year-round, and properties will add 7 percent bed tax to lodging and camping.

Hotel

Built in 2016 and owned by Xanterra, which runs the Glacier National Park lodges, the geothermally heated and cooled ★ **Cedar Creek Lodge** (930 Second Ave. W., reservations 855/733-4522, front desk 406/897-7070, www.cedarcreeklodgehotel.com, $120-330) has environmentally friendly elements while tipping its hat to Glacier with cedars and park artwork in the lobby. In three floors with elevator access, it has 64 rooms (king, queens, and family suites), an indoor pool, and a fitness center. It is within walking distance to restaurants. Rates include a complimentary hot breakfast buffet.

Cabins

Located partway between Whitefish and Columbia Falls, **North Forty Resort** (3765 Hwy. 40 W., 406/862-7740 or 800/775-1740, www.northfortyresort.com, $130-370) clusters 22 log cabins under tall evergreens with community hot tubs and saunas. Sleeping 5-8 people, the cabins have log furnishings, kitchens, barbecues, and picnic tables. Summer stays require two nights.

Bed-and-Breakfast

On 10 quiet acres 10 minutes from town, **Bad Rock Bed and Breakfast** (480 Bad Rock Dr., 406/892-2829 or 888/892-2829, www.badrock.com, $125-230) has four log cabins surrounding a river-rock and log-frame house. Cabin guest rooms have handcrafted log furniture, while the three main guest rooms in the house are decorated in different styles. Some rooms and cabins require a two-night minimum stay in summer. All have private baths. Breakfast is a large Montana-style affair, sometimes featuring Belgian waffles heaped with fruit.

Resort

Outside Columbia Falls, among big trees and quiet, **Meadow Lake Resort** (100 St. Andrews Dr., 406/892-8700 or 800/321-4653, www.meadowlake.com, $90-600) is on an 18-hole golf course, with a restaurant, indoor and outdoor swimming pools, a spa, and tennis courts. The resort has 24 hotel rooms and studios, condos with 1-3 bedrooms, and vacation homes. In winter, a ski shuttle runs to Whitefish Mountain Resort.

CAMPING

Two private campgrounds are on U.S. 2 and Highway 40, with Glacier National Park about 20 minutes away. Be prepared for road noise with the highway locations. Both have hookups for electricity, sewer, and water and can accommodate big rigs with slideouts. Other amenities include flush toilets, hot showers, dump stations, wireless Internet access, cable TV, and laundries. Rates run $35-55 for hookups and $26-30 for tents for two people.

Right in town in a manicured grass setting surrounded by trees, the 71 campsites of **Columbia Falls RV Park** (103 U.S. 2 E., 406/892-1122 or 888/401-7268, www.columbiafallsrvpark.com, Apr.-mid-Oct.) are the closest to Glacier and one mile from the waterslides, an outdoor community swimming pool, and grocery stores. A few blocks' walk puts you at the restaurants in town. **Glacier Peaks RV Park** (3185 Hwy. 40, 406/892-2133 or 800/268-4849, www.glacierpeaksrvpark.com, year-round) is easy to spot with its flower-painted VW bug and trailer as a sign. Sixty grassy full-hookup sites sprawl under partial shade. With its location at the junction of Highway 40 and U.S. 2, driving access is quick to Columbia Falls, Whitefish, and Kalispell.

FOOD
Bakery

Columbia Falls has never been known as a dining mecca until recently. New restaurateurs have ushered in new tastes, catapulting the cuisine beyond the fast-food enterprises along the highway. Several new dining options opened in 2016, including **Uptown Hearth Bakery** (619 Nucleus Ave., 406/871-6791, 7:30am-4pm Tues.-Fri. summer, $4-8), with fresh breads and French pastries baked by two different microbakers in the shared space. More eateries are slated to open in 2017.

Café

Frequently crowded, **Montana Coffee Traders' Columbia Falls Cafe** (30 9th St. W., 406/892-7696, 7am-2pm daily, $6-11) serves huge breakfast omelets, muffins, scones, salads, wraps, and deli sandwiches, with plenty of vegetarian options and espresso.

Pizza

Opening in 2016, **North Fork Pizza** (605 Nucleus Ave., 406/897-5000, www.

than packing in the crowds, ★ **Three Forks Grille** (729 Nucleus Ave., 406/892-2900, www.threeforksgrille.com, 5pm-10pm daily, $10-25) sprinkles the menu with burgers, salads, and Italian flavors: gnocchi appetizers, seafood risotto, and cannoli. The grilled Tuscan flatiron steak comes with a Montana twist from local free-range, antibiotic-free beef. Make reservations for the two-floor restaurant for weekends and in summer. The adjacent deli (11am-5pm Mon.-Sat.) makes sandwiches for lunch.

When locals crave greasy barbecue, they head for **The Back Room Restaurant** (522 9th St. W., 406/892-3131, www.niteowlbackroom.com, 4pm-9pm daily, $10-22). The restaurant serves old-time gooey ribs and broasted chicken. A gigantic combo plate accompanied by homemade sauces lets you try all its rib styles. Fry bread with honey, coleslaw, and homemade french fries overflow the plate. A server may call you "hon" as she delivers a roll of paper towels instead of napkins to handle the colossal mess.

Three Forks Grille in Columbia Falls

northforkpizza.com, 3pm-9pm Tues.-Sun., $4-24) serves pizza by the slice, calzones, build your own, and specialty pies. Delivery is available, too.

Casual Dining

With attention to atmosphere and taste rather

Groceries

Columbia Falls has two large groceries. For organic foods, stop in at **Sundrop Health Foods** (639 9th St. W., Columbia Falls, 406/892-9295, 9:30am-6:30pm daily).

Kalispell Lodging, Camping, and Food

Kalispell, which lacks the resort atmosphere of Bigfork and Whitefish, has a variety of hotels and a changing array of restaurants downtown, along the access highways, and near strip malls. Most of the hotels and restaurants are located 15 minutes south of Glacier Park International Airport (on U.S. 2), the opposite direction from Glacier National Park and almost one hour from West Glacier.

ACCOMMODATIONS

Kalispell has several chain hotels sprawled on the outskirts of downtown, including hotels around the mall and strip mall areas (one new Marriott SpringHill Suites was added in 2016). You can find them online (www.kalispellchamber.com). Other than chain hotels, the pickings are slim. Rates will be highest in summer, with lower prices fall, winter, and spring. Add 7 percent tax to lodging and camping.

Hostel

Downtown above Wheaton's Cycle, the **Kalispell Hostel** (214 1st Ave. W., 406/270-1653, www.kalispellhostel.com, $40-80) has the historical ambience of the 1918 bike shop. Three private bedrooms have a queen or set of bunks. Amenities include a living room with fireplace, a kitchen, Wi-Fi, a shared bathroom with shower, and laundry.

Hotel

Right in downtown Kalispell's shopping district, the historic **Kalispell Grand Hotel** (100 Main St., 406/755-8100 or 800/858-7422, www.kalispellgrand.com, $80-185) feels like it's a century back in time. The lobby still has a tin ceiling, an ornate pump organ, and the original wide oak-banister stairway. Renovated guest rooms have smaller baths with showers rather than tubs. Although the ambience harks back to 1912, when the hotel opened with room rates at $2, its modern amenities now include an elevator, high-speed Internet access, air-conditioning, TVs, and a continental breakfast. In the afternoon, pick up home-baked cookies in the lobby.

CAMPING

Year-round commercial campgrounds scatter around Kalispell, all within 30-40 minutes of Glacier and 15-20 minutes to Flathead Lake or golf courses. Standard amenities include hookups, flush toilets, hot showers, dump stations, laundries, playgrounds, cable TV, Wi-Fi, fire rings, and picnic tables. Rates run $35-55 for RV hookups for two people.

The nearest to Glacier, **Rocky Mountain "Hi" RV Park and Campground** (825 Helena Flats, 406/755-9573 or 800/968-5637, www.glaciercamping.com) is adjacent to a spring-fed creek with 98 grassy sites tucked between large fir trees; a few have Swan Mountain views. The setback from the highway reduces road noise. With swimming, fishing, and canoeing in a wide creek, it's a good campground for kids. Tent sites cost $25.

Nearer to Kalispell, **Glacier Pines RV Park** (1850 Hwy. 35, 406/752-2760 or 800/533-4029, www.glacierpines.com) has a seasonal outdoor heated swimming pool and sites shaded by large trees for RVs only.

FOOD

Kalispell has common national chain restaurants along U.S. 93, but not in the few blocks of the downtown area. For a 1950s soda fountain throwback with huge scoops of ice cream, candy racks, and hot dogs, drop in at **Norm's News** (34 Main St., 406/756-5466, 9am-7pm Tues.-Sat.). Stop by **Ceres Bakery** (318 Main St., 406/755-8552, 8am-3pm Mon.-Fri.) for an espresso with a sticky sweet potato roll or croissant.

Cafés

The small **Bonelli's Bistro** (38 1st Ave. E., 406/755-7577, www.bonellisbistro.com, 8am-3pm Mon.-Sat., $7-14) dishes up Mediterranean breakfasts and lunches with fresh local ingredients, many organic. Sit indoors or outdoors to feast on Greek and Italian scrambles, quiche, paninis, salads, wraps, subs, and house specialties of lasagna and eggplant Parmigiana. Many menu items come with gluten-free, dairy-free, egg-free, and low-calorie variations, and the kitchen will accommodate allergies. It's also worth a mid-morning stop for espresso and homemade dessert. **Montana Coffee Traders' Kalispell Cafe** (328 W. Center St., 406/756-2326, 7am-3pm Mon.-Sat.) also has breakfast and lunch options.

Pizza

For old-style Montana atmosphere, visit **Moose's Saloon** (173 N. Main St., 406/257-8669, www.moosessaloon.com, 11am-1:30am daily, $6-24), where peanut shells and sawdust cover the floor in this funky old-time bar that has been a valley staple since 1957. It will be just what you imagine a Montana bar to be: dark and loud. But the pizza crust ranks highly with locals, and beer prices are cheap.

Burgers

A chef-owned restaurant, ★ **Hop's Downtown Grill** (121 Main St., 406/755-7687, www.hopsmontana.com, 5pm-10pm Mon.-Sat., $10-30) is a local favorite. Dinner features gourmet Kobe beef burgers with homemade buns and house-made potato chips. You can also get wild boar, bison, or yak burgers. An extensive beer and wine collection complements the menu.

Ice Cream

Kalispell has an outpost of **Sweet Peaks Ice Cream** (343 Main St., 406/257-1102, 11:30am-10:30pm daily, hours shorten Oct.-May), which uses locally sourced ingredients for its eclectic flavors.

Groceries

Kalispell has many large grocery markets. For organic and healthy foods, go to **Withey's Health Foods** (1231 S. Main St., Kalispell, 406/755-5260, http://witheyshealthfoods.tflmag.com, 9am-6pm Mon.-Sat.) or **Natural Grocers** (2395 Hwy. 93, Kalispell, 406/755-5300, www.naturalgrocers.com, 8am-9:04pm Mon.-Sat, 8am-7:35pm Sun.).

Whitefish Lodging, Camping, and Food

Bustling with summer lake fun and winter skiing, Whitefish is a resort town loaded with lodging and restaurants. It sits 15-20 minutes west of Glacier Park International Airport (on U.S. 2) and 45 minutes west of Glacier National Park.

ACCOMMODATIONS

Whitefish is the only Flathead Valley town that offers luxury lodging, but it also has a myriad of less-pricey options, including chains (one new Hampton Inn in 2016) and independent hotels. Find a full listing at www.explorewhitefish.com. You can also locate vacation homes and cabins to rent through **Lakeshore Rentals** (406/863-9337 or 877/312-8017, www.lakeshorerentals.us) or from individual owners through **VRBO** (www.vrbo.com) or **Airbnb** (www.airbnb.com).

Reservations downtown are mandatory in summer, but when town books out, rooms are usually still available at Whitefish Mountain Resort. In town, summer has the highest rates with the second-highest rates in winter; Whitefish Mountain Resort has its highest rates in winter. Find off-season deals in spring and fall. Taxes in Whitefish are higher than other towns in the area, so you will see an extra 11 percent tacked onto your bill.

Hotels

With a two-story lobby draped with a giant wrought-iron chandelier and a river-rock fireplace, ★ **The Lodge at Whitefish Lake** (1380 Wisconsin Ave., 406/863-4000 or 877/887-4026, www.lodgeatwhitefishlake.com, $115-1,200) is the only hotel on the lake. The premier, upscale guest rooms overlook the lake, facing the sunset; upstairs north guest rooms have mountain views. Viking Lodge rooms are across the street adjacent to the parking lot. The lodge also has spacious 2-3-bedroom suites and condos. Varying in size, they have balconies, fireplaces, slate floors, granite countertops, fridges, and tubs and walk-in showers. The lodge has a private beachfront on Whitefish Lake, indoor hot pool fed by a waterfall, indoor hot tub, summer outdoor pool and year-round outdoor hot tub, full-service marina, boat rentals, day spa, several restaurants, and a lounge. A walking trail tours the neighboring Viking Creek, and luxury cabins, which are really full homes, have a five-day minimum.

Built in 2016, the downtown ★ **Firebrand**

Flathead Breweries and Distilleries

Flathead Valley has seen new craft breweries and distilleries pop up. Here's the best for libations and dining:

- **Bonsai Brewing** (549 Wisconsin Ave., Whitefish, 406/730-1717, 1pm-8pm Tues.-Sun., $8-14): This Kickstarter-funded project has become a Whitefish institution. With five regular and five rotator beers on tap, you may have trouble deciding on a brew. Order a flight of four to taste a variety, or go nitro with a creamy Sheriff. A grill offers a small menu: gumbo, kabobs, burgers, rice bowls, and salads.

- **Whitefish Handcrafted Spirits** (204 Wisconsin Ave., Whitefish, 406/730-2282, http://whitefishspirits.com, noon-8pm daily, $7-15): Rums, whiskey, and gin come plain or in brisk flavors. Taste a flight of straights or signature essences, or dive into artisan cocktails. Tapas vary on a seasonal menu. House-made bar nuts sail with brown sugar, cayenne, rosemary, and bacon. Lounge indoors amid vintage chandeliers and restoration hardware in a cozy dining room with fireplace or cigar room (smoke outside) with pool table. The outdoor patio has large fire pits and gazebos.

- **Backslope Brewing** (1107 9th St. W., Columbia Falls, 406/897-2850, www.backslopebrewing.com, 11am-8pm Mon.-Sat., $10-14): Teaming up with the former owners of the Palette Café, this brewery serves up locally sourced burgers, bowls, fresh salads, and small plates. The Aussie burger stacks up huge! The taps pour four crafted beers plus rotators; taste four choices in a flight.

- **Flathead Lake Brewing Co. Pubhouse** (116 Holt Dr., Bigfork, 406/837-2004, http://flatheadlakebrewing.com, 11am-10pm daily): This Bigfork brewery with an accompanying pubhouse named its headliner Two Rivers Pale after the Flathead and Swan Rivers, and its Wild Mile Wheat, an unfiltered summer wheat beer, after the town's famous white water. With a deck with a fireplace overlooking Flathead Lake, it serves seafood specialties, burgers, sandwiches, fish-and-chips, and salads ($11-22) in a scenic pub atmosphere. Add on a nitro cold-frothed 369' Stout, named for the depth of the lake, or one of the seasonal brews.

- **Tamarack Brewing** (105 Blacktail Rd., Ste. #1, Lakeside, 406/844-0244, www.tamarackbrewing.com, 11am-10pm daily, $9-25): The Lakeside brewery puts out about a dozen beers, including the light golden Bear Bottom Blonde and robust amber Yard Sale Ale (named after ski lingo for someone who crashes hard, littering the hill with skis and poles). It also has a smooth Switchback Stout topping the tastes. Pair with a big menu of pub food, including pizza. Inside seating can be noisy; outside patio seating abuts the creek.

Flathead Valley also has tasting rooms. No food, just the drinks:

- **Great Northern Brewing** (2 Central Ave., Whitefish, 406/863-1000, www.greatnorthernbrewing.com, 11am-11pm daily) is a longtime staple whose beers honor local skiing and Whitefish.

- **Spotted Bear Spirits** (503 Railway St. Whitefish, 406/730-2436, www.spottedbearspirits.com, noon-8pm daily, $6-12): Spotted Bear Spirits inhabits a downtown location prime for popping in on farmers market nights and conveniently close to Great Northern Brewing. Fresh, lively, organic ingredients are distilled into vodka and gin for artsy cocktails.

- **Kalispell Brewing Company** (412 Main St., Kalispell, 406/756-2739, www.kalispellbrewing.com, noon-8pm Mon.-Sat.) serves up German-style lagers and ales in a building that once served as a car dealership. It has an upper deck for outside seating.

- **Whistling Andy** (8541 MT Hwy. 35, Bigfork, noon-8pm Mon.-Sat., 11am-6pm Sun.) sources local botanicals, grains, and cherries for spirits.

Hotel (650 E. 3rd St., 406/863-4055 or 844/863-1900, www.firebrandhotel.com, $120-370) has 81 rooms and five suites with queen or king beds, spa and concierge services, and a fitness center. Rooms have large windows that open for fresh air, mini-fridges, USB charging ports, and accents from burnished steel, reclaimed wood, and tile. For families, some rooms adjoin. Elevators access all floors. The two-story lobby has floor-to-ceiling windows to take in views, as well as a rooftop patio with a hot tub overlooking town and Big Mountain. The restaurant serves a breakfast buffet, grab-and-go lunches, coffee, and tapas and small plates in the evening.

Located one mile from downtown restaurants and nightlife, **Grouse Mountain Lodge** (2 Fairway Dr., 406/892-2525 from US or 403/236-3400 from Canada, front desk 406/862-3000, www.grousemountainlodge.com, $115-325) sits on the golf course, which turns into a groomed Nordic ski center in winter. It has an indoor pool, outdoor hot tubs, and restaurant. Its 143 guest rooms come in six configurations, including basic hotel rooms and upscale suites with oversize showers containing multiple showerheads. A complimentary shuttle accesses the town, airport, and ski resort.

Bed-and-Breakfasts

A three-minute drive from downtown and 10 minutes from the ski resort, Woody and Betsy Cox's spacious ★ **Good Medicine Lodge** (537 Wisconsin Ave., 406/862-5488 or 888/860-5488, www.goodmedicinelodge.com, $130-320) provides six rooms and three suites with private baths. Two of the suites sleep four people. The gourmet breakfast consists of three or four courses, including a hot entrée, often with local ingredients, and a buffet of cereals, breads, and yogurts. Light hors d'oeuvres and wine are served in the evening. Amenities include an outdoor hot tub, a ski storage room, outdoor seating patios, several restful common areas, and cookies.

With modern log architecture, **Hidden Moose Lodge** (1735 E. Lakeshore Dr., 406/862-6516 or 888/733-6667, hiddenmooselodge.com, starts at $100) centers around a spacious great room and an outdoor sitting deck overlooking gardens and woods. Both have river-rock fireplaces. Montana-themed rooms have a queen or king bed and large bathrooms, some with Jacuzzi tubs. Amenities include breakfasts, complimentary evening drinks, outdoor hot tub, and nearby SNOW bus to the ski resort.

The Lodge at Whitefish Lake offers luxury accommodations.

Next to downtown Whitefish, the circa-1920 **Garden Wall Inn** (504 Spokane Ave., 406/862-3440 or 888/530-1700, www.gardenwallinn.com, $155-270, suite $295-370) is furnished with antiques, historical photos of Glacier, and warmth from a real log-burning fireplace in the living room. Five guest rooms have private baths, some with oversize clawfoot tubs. In the morning, awake to room delivery of a coffee tray followed by breakfast downstairs.

Resort

Located six miles above town, ★ **Whitefish Mountain Resort** (406/862-2900 or 800/858-5439, www.skiwhitefish.com) has a broad range of options from budget to luxury, motels and condos ($75-670), and vacation homes ($200-1,370). Winter sees the highest room rates when restaurants, shops, and lifts open for the ski season. July-August run a close second with hiking, chairlift sightseeing, ziplining, mountain biking, and summer activities. Fall and spring are very inexpensive, but lodging options are limited, and no lifts, shops, or restaurants are open. For upscale condos, go for Morning Eagle, and for budget rooms, stay in the Hibernation House.

Guest Ranch

The **Bar W Guest Ranch** (2875 U.S. 93 W., 409/863-9099 or 866/828-2900, www.thebarw.com) houses guests in a 6,200-square-foot Western lodge and cabin suites adjacent to a small lake and Spencer Mountain. Ranch activities pile on trail rides, rodeos, cookouts, boating, archery, hiking, fishing, and campfires. Three- and six-night packages include meals, lodging, and ranch activities ($800-3,300 pp). November-April, the lodge serves as a bed-and-breakfast ($140-250).

Hostel

Two sisters opened the **Whitefish Hostel** (28 Lupfer Ave., 409/863-9450, www.whitefishhostel.com, May-Oct., $33-45) and café in 2013 in a small house two blocks from the town's bars, shops, restaurants, and train depot. Two dorm rooms have 10 beds. Shared bathrooms and showers are downstairs. Rates include sheets, comforter, towel, lockers (bring lock), bike racks, ski storage, and Wi-Fi.

CAMPING

Set in the woods right on Whitefish Lake, **Whitefish Lake State Park** (U.S. 93, one mile west of Whitefish, then one mile north following signs, 406/862-3991, http://stateparks.mt.gov, year-round, $18-28) is perfect for swimming and launching boats but not for sleeping, as trains frequently rumble on the tracks crossing the park. With a good set of earplugs, you can survive the night. Amenities include flush toilets, showers, picnic tables, fire rings with grills, firewood, running water, bear-resistant storage lockers, and a shared biker-hiker site ($6-12 pp). Water is only turned on May-September.

Two miles south of town, **Whitefish KOA** (5121 U.S. 93 S., 406/862-4242 or 800/562-8734, www.glacierparkkoa.com, mid-Apr.-mid-Oct., tents $43-55, RV hookups $58-90, $8-10 pp for more than two campers) sits on 33 acres shielded from the highway by thick forest. The outdoor pool attracts kids, while oldsters gravitate to the adults-only hot tub. Amenities include flush toilets, showers, picnic tables, fire rings, cabins, hookups, laundry, a dump station, a camp store, wireless Internet access, free mini golf, and a restaurant.

FOOD

As a resort town, Whitefish is overloaded with outstanding restaurants. Because of the crowds, make reservations to avoid long waits in summer or winter. In spring and fall, a few restaurants alter their hours or close for a month on a whim to vacation; call ahead to be sure they are open.

Whitefish is the party town. For cheap burgers and beers, head to the **Bulldog Saloon** (144 Central Ave., 406/862-5601), but keep the kids out of the X-rated-decorated bathroom stalls. The downtown bar-hopping scene heats up with locals dropping in after work, dining, and dancing to weekend bands at **Great Northern** (27 Central Ave., 406/862-2816, www.greatnorthernbar.com). **Casey's Bar** (101 Central Ave., 406/862-8150, www.caseyswhitefish.com) mixes together the works in three stories: a restaurant, bar, casino, dance hall, and summer rooftop dining for the best view in downtown Whitefish.

With outside seating in summer, **The Craggy Range Bar & Grill** (10 Central Ave., 406/862-7550, www.thecraggyrange.com) renovated its dining area, added a frost bar to the lounge, and improved the stage for live music. Although located outside downtown, **Montana Tap House** (845 Wisconsin Ave., 406/862-6006, www.montanatap.com) has 58 taps pumping out mostly Montana beers, but also Pacific Northwest brews, wine, and specialty sodas.

Cafés

Two cafés share the back of **Stumptown Marketplace** (12 Spokane Ave., 8am-4pm Mon.-Sat., $6-13). **Zucca Marketplace Bistro** (406/862-4646, www.zuccamarketplacebistro.com) has attracted a loyal clientele due to its organic foods with a Mediterranean flair. Espresso, croissants, salads, and paninis taste ultra-fresh. **Pig and Olive** (406/862-7444, http://pigandolive.com) does a twist on the traditional deli with locally grown ingredients. It features fried potatoes, salads, house-made sauces, sausage, and bagels, as well as an international lineup of sandwiches: fried pork belly, falafel, barbecue pulled pork, and *banh mi.*

Local faves attract families for the food, prices ($7-22), broad menus, beer, and wine. You might have to arm wrestle a local's claim to a daily seat at **The Buffalo Café** (514 E. 3rd St., 406/862-2833, www.buffalocafewhitefish.com, 7am-2pm and 5pm-9pm Mon.-Sat., 8am-2pm Sun.). Start the day with Buffalo Pie; hash browns piled with eggs and goodies. Finish the day with fish tacos or a Hot Date burger topped with dates, bacon, and blue cheese. **Loula's Café** (300 2nd St. E., 406/862-5614, www.

whitefishrestaurant.com, 7am-3pm Mon.-Wed., 7am-3pm and 5pm-9:30pm Thurs.-Sun.) starts the day with lemon-stuffed french toast followed by fresh salads and home-style entrées. Top your meal with one of Mary Lou and Laura's trademark fresh-baked fruit pies, or buy one to go.

Montana Coffee Traders' Whitefish Coffeehouse (110 Central Ave., 406/862-7667, 7am-6pm Mon.-Sat., 8am-4pm Sun.) offers pastries and desserts as well as *bocadillos* (Spanish sandwiches), soups, and quiches, in addition to a full-service espresso bar.

Italian

Lilting to tunes of Frank Sinatra and Andrea Bocelli, **Ciao Mambo** (234 E. 2nd St., 406/863-9600, www.ciaomambo.com, 5pm-9pm Mon.-Thurs., 5pm-10pm Fri.-Sat., $12-32) transports diners beyond the Flathead to Italy in a cramped, noisy dining room with an open kitchen. Start with Tootsie Roll appetizers of ricotta-cheese-stuffed phyllo on marinara, choose from multiple homemade pastas for entrées, and finish with tiramisu, spumoni, or cannoli. The wine list contains plenty of Italian options.

For pizza, Montana's homegrown chain **MacKenzie River Pizza** (9 Central Ave., 406/862-6601, www.mackenzieriverpizza.com, 11am-10pm daily, $10-22) is a family-friendly restaurant with traditional and eclectic (chicken fajita, Thai) pizzas with sourdough, natural-grain, or gluten-free crusts. Local microbrews are on tap.

Sushi

Although most people don't see sushi and Montana as going together, ★ **Wasabi Sushi Bar and Ginger Grill** (419 2nd St., 406/863-9283, www.wasabimt.com, 5pm-10pm daily, $5-22/roll) packs with crowds. Fusion rolls, *nigiri, sashimi,* sake, and grilled Asian specialties are served in a relaxed, bright atmosphere surrounded by wasabi-green walls. Large mirrors reflect the deft fingers of the sushi chefs in action as they make your rolls.

Cajun and Creole

At ★ **Tupelo Grille** (17 Central Ave., 406/862-6136, www.tupelogrille.com, 5pm-10pm daily, $16-38), the flavors come from New Orleans with gumbo, Andouille sausage, and shrimp and grits. The Zydeco Combo combines a crawfish-shrimp cake, fried catfish, crawfish étouffée, and jambalaya. The eatery also serves grilled steaks, and nightly specials usually include fish. Don't leave without dessert: The bread pudding is scrumptious without being overly sweet.

Mexican

More than a cute variation on the name of Whitefish, **Pescado Blanco** (235 1st St., 406/862-3290, www.pescadoblancorestaurant.com, 5pm-10pm daily, $11-24) excels at mountain Mexican cuisine: bison enchiladas, halibut tacos, and house elk chorizo. Salsas and tortillas are hand-made. Many dishes come from locally sourced, often organic ingredients, but fresh seafood is flown in a couple times each week. Signature margaritas are made with fresh lime and a 14 percent distilled agave wine, and the menu serves a full range of south-of-the-border beers and wines.

Fine Dining

Whitefish has more than its share of fine restaurants that specialize in Montana game, fish, and steaks accompanied by extensive wine lists. At Whitefish Lake Golf Course, **Whitefish Lake Restaurant** (1200 U.S. 93 N., 406/862-5285, www.whitefishlakerestaurant.com, daily year-round) offers historical ambience in a renovated 1937 log building. Lunch (11am-5pm during golf season, $11-20)

is served on the deck or in the clubhouse. Dinner (5:30pm-10pm, $19-48) is served in the dining room. The New Zealand mussels appetizer can lead into the halibut baked in filo with feta, roasted garlic, and spinach. House specialties include roasted rack of lamb and prime rib. Smaller-portioned plates are available, too.

Only one restaurant overlooks Whitefish Lake. Settle in for the romance of watching the sunset across the water at ★ **The Lodge at Whitefish Lake Boat Club** (1380 Wisconsin Ave., 406/863-4040, www.lodgeatwhitefishlake.com, daily year-round). Dinner (5pm-10pm, $28-59) is served in the dining room or on the deck with specialties of fish, prime rib, and Allen Brothers steaks that take on seasonal tastes. The restaurant also serves an à la carte breakfast (7am-11am, $8-16). The adjacent bar with an outdoor deck serves lunch and dinner (11am-9pm, $10-32). Summer adds a pool and lakeside Tiki Bar, and the grill in the Viking Lodge serves food and drinks on weekends and in summer.

Ice Cream

Sweet Peaks Ice Cream (419 3rd St., 406/862-4668, 11:30am-11pm daily, hours shorten Oct.-May), local purveyor of ice cream, sorbets, and frozen yogurts in eclectic flavors, has an outpost in Whitefish.

Groceries

Whitefish has two large grocery stores, several small groceries, plus convenience marts. Find organic, healthy, and local foods at **Third Street Market** (3rd St. and Spokane Ave., 406/862-5054, www.thirdstreetmarket.com, 8:30am-7pm Mon.-Sat.).

Transportation and Services

DRIVING AND PARKING

Most roads in Flathead Valley are two-laners, with four-lane portions of main arteries such as U.S. 2 and 93. To bypass the many Kalispell stop lights on U.S. 93 when heading toward Whitefish, take the new **Kalispell Bypass** (U.S. 93 Alternate), turning west near United Drive south of Kalispell and ending at West Reserve Drive north of Kalispell.

In Flathead Valley towns, most parking is streetside or in small lots for businesses. Large RVs can find parking at **Kalispell Center Mall** (20 N. Main St.) and **Whitefish Mountain Mall** (6475 U.S. 93 S.). Whitefish is erecting a new public parking garage on 2nd and Baker Streets, which is expected to open in 2017. Additional public parking lots in Whitefish are located at First Street and Spokane Avenue as well as Depot Street and Spokane Avenue.

BUSES

Eagle Transit (https://flathead.mt.gov/eagle, $1-2) runs daily bus routes between Kalispell, Whitefish, and Columbia Falls. Additional runs go to Bigfork and Lakeside a few days per week. **Flathead Transit** (406/275-2877 ext. 1352) runs one bus daily between Missoula, Kalispell, and Whitefish ($32 one-way) as part of the Greyhound Connect program (www.greyhound.com). It leaves Missoula at 11:30am, arriving at 3:10pm in Whitefish. The return trip departs Whitefish at 4pm to arrive in Missoula at 7:30pm.

The **SNOW Bus** (www.bigmtncommercial.org) in Whitefish operates several seasonal routes. Free summer (July-early Sept.) and winter (early Dec.-early Apr.) buses run between Whitefish and Whitefish Mountain Resort multiple times daily. The **Glacier Park Express** (www.glacierparkexpress.com, daily July-early Sept., adults $10, child $5) links Whitefish with the Apgar Visitor Center shuttle stop in Glacier National Park several times per day. Purchase tickets for the Glacier Park Express in advance online or at cash-only outlets (Whitefish Chamber of Commerce, Sportsman, Montana Coffee Traders, Whitefish Mountain Resort, and the Glacier Conservancy bookstore in Apgar Visitor Center). Park entrance fees are not included in the bus fare.

SERVICES
Post Offices

Each major town in Flathead Valley has at least one post office. Locations are in Bigfork (265 Holt Dr., 406/837-4479), Columbia Falls (65 1st Ave. E., 406/892-7621), Kalispell (350 N. Meridian Rd., 406/755-6450, and 248 1st Ave. W., 406/755-0187), Whitefish (424 Baker Ave., 406/862-2151), Somers (150 Somers Rd., 406/857-3330), and Lakeside (7196 U.S. 93 S., 406/844-3224).

Banks

Banks and ATMs are common in Flathead Valley, but several banks have branches in more than one town. Find **Glacier Bank** (www.glacierbank.com) in Kalispell (202 Main St., 406/756-4200), Bigfork (Old Town Center, 406/837-5980), Columbia Falls (822 Nucleus Ave., 406/892-7100), and Whitefish (319 E. 2nd St., 406/863-6300). **First Interstate Bank** (www.firstinterstate.com) is located in Kalispell (2 Main St., 406/756-5200, and 100 Hutton Ranch Rd., 406/756-5222), Bigfork (8111 Hwy. 35, 406/837-7200), and Whitefish (306 Spokane Ave., 406/863-8888).

Cell Phone and Internet Access

Contrary to Glacier's sketchy cell and Internet service, Flathead Valley has ubiquitous coverage, although most of the towers are Verizon, sometimes booting non-Verizon customers off during peak usage. Most motels have added wireless and DSL Internet services.

You can also get online in the local county **public libraries** on their computers for a limited amount of time in Kalispell (247 1st Ave. E., 406/758-5820), Columbia Falls (130 6th St. W., 406/892-5919), Bigfork (525 Electric Ave., 406/837-6976), and Whitefish (9 Spokane Ave., 406/862-6657). Each library has its own access policies; call for hours (mostly Mon.-Sat.).

A few cafés have wireless Internet access available for patrons: **Montana Coffee Traders Cafés** (110 Central Ave., Whitefish, 406/862-7667; 30 9th St. W., Columbia Falls, 406/892-7696; 328 W. Center St., Kalispell, 406/756-2326, www.coffeetraders.com) as well as **Colter Coffee** (424 Main St., Kalispell, 406/755-1319, www.coltercoffee.com).

Newspapers/Magazines

The local valley daily news comes in the *Daily Interlake* and the weekly news in the free *Flathead Beacon,* with the daily updated online version at www.flatheadbeacon.com. You'll also find other northwestern Montana newspapers around, such as the *Great Falls Tribune* and the *Missoulian.* Community weeklies, which cover everything from local events to politics, include Columbia Falls's *Hungry Horse News,* the *Whitefish Pilot,* and the *Bigfork Eagle.*

Emergencies

For medical, fire, or police emergencies in Flathead Valley, call 911. For medical emergencies in Whitefish and Columbia Falls, the new **North Valley Hospital** (1600 Hospital Way, Whitefish, 406/863-3500) is closest. For emergencies in Kalispell, Bigfork, and Lakeside, the upgraded **Kalispell Regional Medical Center** (310 Sunny View Ln., Kalispell, 406/752-5111) is closest.

City police stations have jurisdictions inside city limits only; much of Flathead Valley is covered by the county sheriff's department. In an emergency, when you dial 911, you don't have to think about whether you are inside city boundaries or not; your emergency will be relayed to the appropriate jurisdiction. But just in case, here are the police and sheriff contacts you may need: **Flathead County Sheriff** (920 S. Main St., Kalispell, 406/758-5585), **Columbia Falls Police** (130 6th St. W., 406/892-3234), **Kalispell Police** (312 1st Ave. E., 406/758-7780), and **Whitefish Police** (2nd St. and U.S. 93, 406/863-2420).

Background

The Landscape

GEOLOGY

Glacier's mountains tell a story of approximately 1.6 billion years of geologic history. During that time, three geologic events sculpted the scenery into its colorful, jagged parapets with swooping valleys: First, sediments layered on top of each other in an ancient sea; then, mountains moved; and, most recently, an ice age gouged vertical formations. Since then, relentless erosion has continued to shape the landscape. Wind and water chip away at peaks. Freeze-melt cycles wreak havoc on cliffs, prying off slabs of rock. And weather leaves its mark on the land.

Ancient Belt Sea

Approximately 1.6 billion-800 million years ago, a shallow lake covered parts of what is now Washington, Idaho, Montana, and British Columbia. The lake, known as the Belt Sea, accumulated sands washing down from adjacent highlands. Through pressure and heat, cake-like layers of dolomites, limestone, argillites, siltites, and quartzites piled one on top of the other. Over eons, the layers built up thousands of feet thick.

You can see these layers today in the mountains of Glacier. In a geologic feat found in very few places in North America, Glacier retained its **sedimentary rock** instead of seeing it metamorphose. Find these colorful layers in the mountainsides around Logan Pass, where multihued sediments stripe Mount Clements. You can also find layering on trails to Iceberg Lake, Grinnell Glacier, Gunsight Pass, and Cobalt Lake. The north entrance to Ptarmigan Tunnel has striking red and white layering. Most of Glacier's lakes and rivers collect a rainbow of rocks from higher elevations, compliments of the Belt Sea layers.

Uplift of Mountains

Between 150 and 60 million years ago, major tectonic movement along massive faults created the northern Rocky Mountains. The Pacific and Continental Plates pushed against each other until the ancient Precambrian rocks of the Pacific Plate slid atop the much younger dinosaur-age rock of the Continental Plate. During this uplift, a several-mile-thick Belt Sea chunk sidled 50 miles east and higher in elevation, where it is exposed today for visitors to see. This movement is known as the **Lewis Overthrust Fault.** Look for its evidence where geologists originally discovered the fault in 1890: on the side of Summit Mountain north of Marias Pass on U.S. 2.

During the uplift, rock heated and became pliable like bread dough. Sometimes it simply folded due to the pressure and heat. Find folds on Waterton Lake's east shore, above the Ptarmigan Tunnel trail, and between Lake Josephine and Bullhead Lake on the Swiftcurrent Trail.

Glaciation

More recently, glaciers carved the landscape. Two million years ago, the **Pleistocene ice age** engraved the park's topography via huge advancing and retreating glaciers. Only the tops of Glacier's highest peaks poked out as nunataks, summits completely surrounded by ice. Glaciers thousands of feet deep gouged out huge valleys, leaving a 5,000-foot variation in elevations from valley floors to peaks.

These ancient ice rivers bit into the landscape. Long, fingerlike lakes sit where large glaciers once filled valleys such as St. Mary and Lake McDonald. In other valleys, such as Swiftcurrent, the large glacier receded in a series of melts, leaving a series of smaller

---

Previous: backpacking Boulder Pass; meadows at Logan Pass.

lakes instead of one large one. These huge rivers of ice also left U-shaped drainages, such as the broad Two Medicine Valley. These rounded valley floors stand in contrast to V-shaped river-carved valleys such as the Grand Canyon.

Glaciers are what molded the rugged peaks in the park. When three or more glaciers gnawed away on a peak, a horn resulted, such as Mount Reynolds or Triple Divide. Sometimes two glaciers chewed ridges paper thin into arêtes (French for "fish bone"), such as the ragged Iceberg-Ptarmigan Wall or the Garden Wall on the Continental Divide. The upper ends of glaciers often carved out cirques, steep-walled round basins such as Avalanche Lake basin.

As glaciers retreated, they left large piles of debris in the form of moraines, where rocks, sand, and gravel collected like dirty laundry. Large moraines, such as Howe and Snyder Ridges flanking Lake McDonald, remain from Pleistocene ice, whereas smaller rubble piles in the Grinnell or Sperry Glacier basins date to the last century.

While ancient Pleistocene ice melted in Glacier about 12,000 years ago, several miniature ice ages since then have shaped the land. The glaciers currently in the park are products of the last 8,000 years. During the **Little Ice Age** (1500-1850), most glaciers grew. Park tree-ring studies and moraines show evidence that there were more than 150 glaciers in the early 1900s. These are the smaller alpine glaciers in the upper basins of peaks. Some of these glaciers plummeted off cliffs, forming hanging valleys: The 492-foot Bird Woman Falls dives from a hanging valley suspended between Mount Oberlin and Mount Cannon that was once home to a glacier.

Less than 17 percent of those alpine glaciers remain today, the largest of which is Harrison Glacier, at 0.7 square mile. The 25 glaciers that remain in 2016 are expected to melt around 2030. Waterton no longer has any active glaciers. At Cameron Lake, you can look across the border to the icy remnants of Herbst Glacier, now too small to be classified as an active glacier.

So where can you get close to a glacier? Grinnell has the shortest trail, whereas Sperry requires a 20-mile round-trip one-day hike or a multiday backpack or chalet trip. Either way, avoid the hazards of walking on a glacier.

Glaciers and Snowfields

It's often hard to tell the difference between a glacier and a snowfield. In early summer,

Glacier National Park only has small alpine glaciers left.

Ancient Rocks

Glacier contains some of the oldest exposed rock in North America.

ARGILLITES

Of Glacier's colorful rock formations, the most striking is the argillite, an iron-rich mudstone formed in layers on the floor of the shallow ancient Belt Sea 800 million-1.6 billion years ago. Its blue-green and purple-red hues leap off mountainsides and intensify under water. This clay and silt contains iron, which changes to red hematite when exposed to oxygen, thus giving Grinnell argillite its burgundy color. The Appekunney argillite did not oxidize, remaining green. Spot the red colors on **Red Eagle Mountain** when driving down the east side of Going-to-the-Sun Road. Find both argillites on the **Grinnell Glacier Trail,** the **Iceberg Lake Trail,** at **Red Rocks Falls,** and while rafting on the **Middle Fork of the Flathead.**

RIPPLE ROCK AND MUD CRACKS

Raindrop impressions, water ripples, and mud cracks remain etched in stone, evidence of their origins in ancient seas. Ripple rocks, found most often in red, blue, or beige layers, look like sands on a beach where waves left their marks. As the sea dried up, sediments compacted and cracked, similar to a mud puddle drying up in a driveway. Large blocks show webs of cracks filled in with other sediments, an effect that looks like dull maroon or turquoise tiles. Look for slabs with ripple marks and mud cracks on **Hidden Lake Overlook Trail** and along **Many Glacier Valley** trails.

MAGMA INTRUSIONS

Don't be fooled: Yes, Granite Park and its namesake chalet are dubbed for the igneous rock; however, Glacier has no granite. When early prospectors found rounded blue-gray formations of Purcell lava, or pillow lava, they mistakenly called it granite. This lava intruded up through sediment layers, billowing out in ropey coils and bubbles. See this lava on the **Highline Trail** between Granite Park Chalet and Ahern Pass.

they look the same, covered with fresh snow from winter. But they are distinctly different. It's simple math: When more snow adds than melts annually, glaciers form. The snow transforms into icy grains through freeze-thaw cycles. Snow builds up on the upper end of glaciers and pushes down, compressing ice crystals. Over years, the ice compacts in layers, mounting into a huge mass with a rigid surface and a supple base.

Glaciers are **slow-moving ice.** Aided by gravity, the ice presses down, forming a thin elastic barrier that carries the mass toward the glacier's toe, where it may calve off in chunks. When the ice travels over convex ground features, its surface cracks, forming crevasses sometimes hundreds of feet thick. Hidden crevasses make glaciers deadly for travel, so do not walk out on them without appropriate rescue gear.

For a glacier to move, a certain amount of ice is needed—usually a surface of at least 25 acres and a minimum depth of 100 feet. Less than that and the ice becomes a static, permanent snowfield. Moving glaciers behave similarly to a bulldozer, gouging out troughs and picking up rocks from the surrounding mountain. Once the winter season's snow melts, you can recognize glaciers by their telltale debris bands of rock piles lining up on the surface.

Glacier After the Glaciers Melt

Locals often joke about Glacier National Park's name: What should the park be called after its glaciers all melt? Of course, the name will remain the same. Despite the disappearance of the glaciers in the next two decades, evidence of the large ice-age glaciers and smaller alpine glaciers will remain. The U-shaped valleys, horns, arêtes, hanging

One of the most visible magma intrusions is the diorite, or Purcell, sill. It appears from a distance as a 100-foot-thick horizontal black line sandwiched between thinner whitish layers. When magma boiled up between limestone layers 800 million years ago, it superheated the limestone, turning it white. You can see the diorite sill from **Many Glacier Road,** visible as a thick dark line on Mount Gould and Mount Wilbur. Hikers see it as black jagged teeth above **Iceberg Lake** or the solid line above **Grinnell Glacier.** The **Highline Trail** passes through the sill approximately one mile beyond Haystack Saddle. Look for a crystallized green sheen covering deep black. When the footing changes from broken scree beds to solid, blocky, volcanic rock, it's the sill.

round stromatolites

STROMATOLITES

The Belt Sea became habitat for blue-green algae. Six species of this petite primitive life-form lived in the sea, doing what algae does best: It removes carbon dioxide from the water and gives off oxygen. During this process, calcium carbonate formed into stromatolites, a round formation 6-15 inches in diameter that looks like Van Gogh's *Starry Night* swirls. They grew in colonies that made 30-foot columns up to three miles wide and solidified into rocks. Find stromatolites along **Going-to-the-Sun Road,** the **Highline Trail,** and **Piegan Pass Trail.** The presence of these algal forms in the Belt Sea produced an oxygen-rich atmosphere that allowed other life-forms to develop, including humans.

valleys, and moraines retain their formations thanks to glaciers. Smaller evidence of glaciers will remain, too. On the Avalanche Lake or Hidden Lake Trails, look for glacial striations, or large scratches, on rocks where ice abraded the surface. Also, on the Avalanche Trail, large boulders called erratics are strewn about from receding ice.

CLIMATE

Glacier and Waterton live on a collision course for both **arctic continental** and **Pacific maritime** weather. Wet weather races in from the Pacific with moderate temperatures. Near West Glacier, precipitation results in an annual average 29 inches of rainfall and 157 inches of snow. Waterton also sees more precipitation than the rest of Alberta.

Although the east side of the Continental Divide equals the west in terms of precipitation, east-slope winds produce more extremes. Winter winds blow snow from slopes, providing forage for ungulates. Winds also blow trains off their tracks. Several east-side high passes are notorious for raging unpredictable winds causing hikers to crawl on all fours. **Chinook winds,** warm winds with speeds that can exceed 90 mph, occur any time of year, but mostly in winter. Native Americans called them "snow eaters" for the snow they rapidly melted. When a Chinook descends the Continental Divide's east side, it blows warm and dry, fooling trees into thinking it's spring and catapulting their cells into spring water absorption. When temperatures plummet again, the cold freezes the water in their cells, killing the trees. This "winter kill" accounts for the number of dead silver trunks dotting east-side forests, especially visible in Two Medicine and Waterton.

Exploring the Ecosystem

One of the best ways to become intimate with Glacier's wildlife, geology, birds, and cultural history is to join the regionally and nationally recognized experts from the **Glacier Institute** (406/756-1211, www.glacierinstitute.org). Offered year-round, the courses blend in-the-field experiences with hands-on learning at Big Creek Camp in the North Fork or Glacier Field Camp near Apgar. You can learn to bird, watch bears, track animals on snowshoes, photograph wildlife, find herbs and mushrooms, and identify wildflowers. College credit is available for some of the workshops and classes. Adult seminars include wilderness first aid, art, photography, science, and ecology. Youth camps for ages 7-16 emphasize outdoor science. Most single-day courses cost $50-75; most multiple-day courses range $125-725, including lodging and meals.

For an intimate experience in Glacier, **Glacier National Park Volunteer Associates** (406/888-7800, gnpva.org) looks for volunteers each summer for backcountry and front-country projects. Some tasks restore historic log structures, reconstruct damaged trails and campsites, and transplant seedlings from the park's native-plant nursery. Past projects have included work at Sperry Chalet and backcountry patrol cabins. Volunteers also staff the Apgar Nature Center and help at visitors centers and permit offices. Work projects are led by a backcountry ranger intern. No special skills are required, just a desire to help.

For those itching to contribute to scientific research in Glacier, the **Crown of the Continent Research Learning Center** (406/888-7800, www.crownscience.org) conducts citizen science projects every summer. Since 2008, they have contributed to field studies on common loons, invasive weeds, and high-country species of concern such as mountain goats and pikas. Some training is necessary but is available through the center.

Glacier is a land of weather extremes. Its maximum high hit 99°F, while its low was -36°F. Elevation makes a huge difference too: While Lake McDonald beckons swimmers to sunny beaches, frigid winds can rage across Logan Pass. Sometimes you'll experience four seasons in one day, so always dress in layers and carry extra clothing, no matter what the weather looks like in the morning. Rains move in fast, and snow can fall any month of the year.

Spring

While March-May are appealing off-season months to travel, in Glacier they are wet and cold, still clinging to winter. Snow buries the high country and some of the lowlands. May is moody, alternating between warm days and rainstorms or frequent late snows that can cause avalanches in the high country.

Summer

During summer months, June habitually monsoons, but July-August usher in warmer, drier skies. Higher elevations are often substantially cooler—up 15 degrees chillier than valley floors. While cool breezes are welcome on baking summer days, they can also bring snows in August.

Fall

Autumn begets lovely bug-free warm days and cool nights. While aspen and larch trees turn gold, temperatures bounce through extremes, from highs of 75-80°F during the day to below freezing at night. The weather is seemingly schizophrenic as rains and snows descend for a few days, followed by clearing and warming trends.

Winter

Winter temperatures in Glacier vary depending on elevation, but mostly hang in the 10-25°F range, and snowfall is voluminous. Logan Pass is buried under 350-700 inches of snow per year. Temperatures can spike above freezing, with accompanying rain, or below 0°F with an arctic front. Because Chinooks visit Waterton more than the rest of Alberta, it is one of the warmest places in the province in winter. While the Canadian prairies suffer below-freezing temperatures, Waterton may be reveling in 30-50°F temperatures.

Daylight

Given Glacier's latitude and placement on the western edge of the Mountain Time zone, hours of daylight fluctuate wildly during the year. In June, about 18 hours of daylight leaves lots of time to play outdoors. First light appears around 5am, and dark doesn't descend until almost 11pm. By late August, dark comes at 9pm, with daylight hours shortening through autumn. At the winter solstice, the sun rises at 8am and sets at 4:30pm.

Plants and Animals

PLANTS

Glacier and Waterton Lakes National Parks have rich floral diversity. That's one of the reasons the parks are UNESCO Biosphere Reserves. Forests, prairies, and peaks have different vegetation specific to elevation, habitat, and weather. Five different floral habitats flank the park's mountains, yielding a rich, broad spectrum of plant life that goes from rainforest to arid alpine tundra.

Glacier is home to 46 rare Montana plants; four are found only in the park. The flora includes 1,150 vascular plants, 400 mosses, and 275 lichens. Many species are at the edges of their distribution: Great Plains flowers to arctic bulbs. The Lake McDonald Valley has nearly 100 Pacific Coast species.

For a small park, Waterton has a lot of rare plants: 30 grow only within its borders, including the rarest plant, the Waterton moonwort. Waterton can also boast a total of 970 vascular plants, 190 mosses, and 220 lichens, ironically chalking up more diversity than its much larger northern national park siblings, Banff and Jasper.

Grasslands

More than 100 grass species proliferate across the Glacier-Waterton prairies. These prairies poke into valley drainages on the Continental Divide's east side and have been preserved by natural fires in the North Fork Valley. Waterton has 13 square miles of prairie. It's one of two prairie lands in the Canadian national park system and one of North America's last places where grizzly bears range into their historic grassland habitat. Grassland prairies sprout wildflowers that adapt to dry, shadeless, windy, and warm conditions.

Aspen Parklands

Aspens dominate east-side valleys of Many Glacier, Belly River, Two Medicine, St. Mary, and Waterton where they harbor elk herds in winter. Broken by wildflower meadows of **arrowleaf balsamroot** and **sticky geranium,** groves of quaking aspen shake their leaves in the slightest breeze, hence their name. They mark the transition between grasslands and coniferous forests. Flowers such as **mountain death camas, paintbrush, pasqueflower, lupine, stonecrop,** and **horsemint** thrive in these parklands.

Montane Forests

In low to mid-elevations, dense forests mix poplars and firs. Species vary substantially depending on moisture and winds. **Cedar-hemlock** and **birch** forests dominate wetter western valleys, while drier slopes yield **limber pine, Douglas fir, white spruce,** and **lodgepole pine.** The **western larch,** a conifer that loses its needles each winter, also inhabits lower-elevation forests. Below the shade-producing canopy, six-petaled queen's cup wildflowers hide for protection from the sun's drying rays, along with fragile twinflower, foamflower, and orchids. Juniper,

Spectacular Wildflower Spots

Wildflowers do not bloom park-wide all at once. When spring hits lower elevations, popping open buds around Lake McDonald and St. Mary, big Logan Pass alpine meadows cower under snow. As summer progresses, like a mist lifting, higher and higher habitats spread out floral displays. To identify wildflowers, pick up a field guide from the **Glacier National Park Conservancy** (406/892-3250, http://glacier.org) in the St. Mary Visitor Center.

Here are some top places to see Glacier's wildflowers on display:

FROM THE CAR

- **Many Glacier Road:** Late May-early June brings tiny pink shooting stars, followed in July by hot-pink sticky geraniums, purple lupine, and tall light pink hollyhock.

- **Chief Mountain International Highway:** In June, meadows pop with pink shooting stars. In early July, the few miles between the Waterton Overlook and Highway 5 are lined with tiger lilies.

- **Two Medicine Road:** Blue camas blooms in early July.

- **Going-to-the-Sun Road:** Lower elevations bloom with huge white cow parsnip heads in early July. In late July-early August, wildflowers along the road's alpine section bloom with orange paintbrush, purple shrubby penstemon, and yellow columbine. In some years, high meadows' slopes will look snow-covered in mid-July when three-foot-tall creamy bear grass blooms prolifically. July also brings on the big sunflower-like arrowleaf balsamroots and dusty pink prairie smoke in Two Dog Flats on the east side of the road along St. Mary Lake.

- **Logan Pass:** Yellow glacier lilies bloom as the snow melts in early July, but they give way to pink alpine laurel, pale yellow paintbrush, and fuchsia monkeyflower by early August.

Pacific yew, thimbleberry, and serviceberry proliferate in the forests.

Subalpine Zone

Between 5,000 and 7,000 feet in elevation, stately forests surrender to **subalpine firs,** dwarfed and gnarled in their struggle to survive in a short growing season, brutal winds, frigid temperatures, and heavy snows. Trees often develop a bent, stunted krummholz, forming a protective mat rather than growing upright. **Whitebark pine** and **Engelmann spruce** also sneak into the subalpine. Between tree islands, lush mountain meadows bloom with a colorful array of **columbine, bog gentian, valerian, fleabane,** and **bear grass.** Flowers must do their business so fast in the subalpine zone that yellow **glacier lilies** and **spring beauties** force their blooms through the snow.

Alpine Tundra

Nearly 25 percent of Glacier and Waterton is alpine tundra. Above the tree line, the land appears to be barren rock, but a host of miniature plants adapt to the harsh conditions of high winds, drying altitude, short summers, cold temperatures, and rocky soil that lacks organic matter. The miniature wildflowers survive by hugging the ground, blooming during a short few-week season. Hairy leaves provide protection from winds and the sun's high-elevation intensity. Mats of pink **moss campion,** delicate **spotted saxifrage,** purple **butterwort,** and **Jones' columbine** fling their energy into tiny flowers.

Huckleberries

Of all Glacier's flora, the huckleberry draws the most attention. While several varieties

ON THE TRAIL

- **Quartz Lakes:** In the North Fork, find fairy-slipper orchids in the rich forest duff in late June.

- **Scenic Point:** In early July, see several-hundred-year-old mats of pink moss campion, small bluebells, and red king's crown, the miniature plants of the alpine tundra.

- **Preston Park:** Hikers on the **Piegan Pass** and **Siyeh Pass Trails** revel in the show of purple fleabane, fuchsia paintbrush, and fuzzy-headed western anemones spread thick across meadows. In early July, rare Jones' columbine blooms on the switchbacks between Preston Park and Siyeh Pass.

- **Fifty Mountain:** Meadows that stretch about 1.5 miles yield big floral displays, starting with yellow glacier lilies and white spring beauties in early July. Late July-early August brings on a rich palette of wildflowers.

paintbrush, fleabane, and yarrow

- **Hidden Lake Overlook:** In late July, tall bear grass, fuchsia monkeyflower, and several varieties of paintbrush flank the trail.

- **Highline Trail:** Color bursts everywhere along the Garden Wall in late July-early August with yellow arnica, deep blue gentians, creamy death camas, white valerian, and fuchsia monkeyflowers. More than 30 varieties of wildflowers speckle meadows.

grow throughout the park, from lowlands to subalpine, they all have one thing in common: a sweet berry. Look for a low-growing shrub with small green to reddish leaves. About the size of a small blueberry, huckleberries ripen into a rich dark purple-blue. Find lowland berries in late July, but mid-August-early September is known as huck season. Grizzly bears carbo-load on hucks to survive winter.

Wildflowers

Glacier's wildflowers peak late June-early August, depending on snowmelt and elevation. Early summer brings on fields of yellow **glacier lilies** and white **spring beauties** poking buds through the snowpack. At lower elevations, the large white heads of **cow parsnip** bloom alongside roads and continue into higher elevations as summer progresses. Some years, **bear grass** blooms so thickly in July that subalpine hillsides look snow-covered. **Paintbrush** spews across fields in yellow, red, fuchsia, white, salmon, and orange. Just a reminder: Picking flowers in national parks is prohibited. Use your camera instead.

Poisonous Plants

Very few plants in Glacier are poisonous. Several can be toxic if eaten, so avoid eating plants or mushrooms. Most of Glacier is inhospitable for poison ivy, poison oak, and poison sumac, but watch for **stinging nettles:** Although not poisonous, they leave an obnoxious itchy residue on contact. A few people have allergic reactions to **cow parsnip.** If you have sensitive skin, wear long sleeves and long pants to avoid contact with irritating plants.

ANIMALS

Glacier and Waterton teem with wildlife: 24 fish species, 63 mammals, and 272 birds. The diversity of animal life is one reason the parks have been designated Biosphere Reserves by UNESCO. The Crown of the Continent remains a North American bastion of an intact ecosystem, with many animals present that were here before the massive impact of human activity over the past 150 years. Wolves, eliminated in federally funded programs, migrated from Canada in the late 1980s, adding more original members to Glacier's wildlife family. Only mountain bison and woodland caribou remain extirpated.

Bears

Two bear species roam Glacier's mountains: the **black bear** and the **grizzly bear.** Omnivores and opportunistic feeders, bears will eat anything that is easy pickings. Intent on eating to gain 100-150 pounds before winter, Glacier's bears feed on a diet heavy in plant matter: bulbs, roots, berries, shoots, and flowers. Ants, insects, carrion, and ground squirrels fill in proteins. Contrary to popular opinion, humans are not on their menu of favorite foods.

Because bears learn fast, they adapt quickly to new food sources, be it a pack dropped by the side of the trail or dog food left out in a campground. For this reason, Glacier imposes strict rules for handling food and garbage in picnic sites, campgrounds, and backcountry areas. All garbage cans and dumpsters are bear resistant. Bears that eat human foods and garbage find themselves moved to a new habitat, or worse, destroyed.

Because grizzly and black bears are integral to Glacier's ecosystem, the National Park Service employs several bear rangers whose jobs entail monitoring and deterring bears from trouble. For bruins that linger near roadways and front-country campgrounds, the bear team uses hazing methods, such as loud noises, gunshots, pellet beanbags, and sometimes Karelian bear dogs, in an attempt to teach bears to stay away. Nuisance bears

Bear grass blooms on three-foot-tall stalks.

are transplanted to remote park drainages or destroyed if their offenses warrant. "A fed bear is a dead bear," the truism goes. A bear that dabbles in human food often aggressively seeks more.

Bears are one of the least fertile mammals, giving birth once every two or three years. While black bears have a gestation of 220 days, for grizzlies spring mating season is followed by delayed implantation, in which the fertilized eggs are simply stored until winter. Pending the sow's health, the egg or eggs implant, resulting in 1-3 cubs born during winter's deep sleep. If her health is severely threatened, she may abort the egg instead.

Bears don't actually hibernate, as their respiration and pulse remain close to normal. Instead, they enter a deep sleep in which the body temperature drops slightly. Before crawling into their dens, they scarf down mountain ash berries, rough grasses, and twigs to form an anal plug, which inhibits eating, urinating, or defecating during winter. Bears emerge in the spring ravenously hungry, heading straight for avalanche chutes to rummage for snow-buried carcasses.

Other Megafauna

Megafauna, the big animals that everyone wants to see, populate Glacier and Waterton. They include three elusive members of the cat family: **mountain lions, bobcats,** and **Canada lynx.** Quiet hunters and mostly nocturnal, cats may see you while you have no idea that they linger nearby. For mountain lions, deer tops the menu, while lynx favor snowshoe hares. Both cat populations rise and fall with their prey populations. With keen eyesight and hearing, these three cats stalk their prey, the lynx with the help of large snowshoe-shaped feet.

Gray wolf packs inhabit fairly large ranges of 100-300 square miles, so chances of seeing a wolf are fairly rare despite their relatively high reproductive potential of 4-7 pups per year. **Coyotes, foxes, wolverines,** and **badgers** round out the list of large carnivores. Although wolverines are the most elusive creatures, Glacier provides prime habitat for them with remote terrain, snowfields, and plentiful ground squirrels. Many hikers spot them along the Highline Trail.

Ungulates crowd Glacier's high and low country. **Moose** feed in streambeds and lakes. Find them in Swiftcurrent Valley, especially around bogs and willow thickets. **Elk, mule deer,** and **white-tailed deer** live throughout the park at the tree line and below, while **mountain goats** and **bighorn sheep** cling to rocky alpine slopes. During late spring, goats congregate at the Goat Lick on U.S. 2, seeking minerals for their depleted systems. They are also a regal staple at Logan Pass.

In Waterton, a small **bison** herd grazes in a paddock, a tiny remnant of what once roamed the prairies by the thousands. Visitors may drive the viewing road and hike a short overlook trail to see the bison.

Small Mammals

Members of the weasel family such as **fishers, pine martens, minks,** and **weasels** inhabit forests and waterways. The short-tailed weasel changes color in winter: Its fur becomes white, except for the small black tip of its tail. Snowshoe hares also change to white in winter, their large feet providing extra flotation on snow. In subalpine country, a chorus of eeks, screams, and squeaks bounce through rockfalls. The noisemakers are **pikas,** which look like tailless mice, and the ubiquitous **Columbian ground squirrel,** recognized

Bighorn sheep feed in high alpine meadows.

Bear Country

GRIZZLY BEARS VERSUS BLACK BEARS

Even though colors are used to name the bears, black and grizzly bears display a variety of fur hues. For instance, a reddish-black bear can give birth to three cubs of different colors: blond, black, and brown. Grizzly bears, while their name evokes silver hair, appear in all colors of the spectrum. Don't be fooled by color; look instead for body size and shape.

Grizzlies are bigger than black bears, standing on all fours at 3-4 feet tall and weighing in at 300-600 pounds. Black bears average 12-18 inches shorter on all fours. Adult females weigh around 140 pounds, while males bulk up to 220 pounds.

In profile, the grizzly has one notable feature: a hump on its shoulders. The solid muscle mass provides the grizzly's forelegs with power for digging and running. Black bears lack this hump. Their face profiles are also different. On the grizzly, look for a scooped or dished forehead-to-nose silhouette; the black bear's nose will appear straighter in line with its forehead. Note the ears, as the grizzly's will look a little too small for its head while a black bear's ears seem big, standing straight up. Paw prints in mud reveal a difference in their claws and foot structure. Grizzly claws are four inches long with pads in a relatively straight line, while black bear claws are 1.5 inches long with pads arced across the top of the foot.

Although both bears have mediocre vision, they are fast runners. In three seconds, a grizzly bear can cover 180 feet.

HIKING IN BEAR COUNTRY

With a few precautions, you can eliminate the scares.

- **Make noise.** To avoid surprising a bear, use your voice. Sing loudly, hoot, or holler. Clap your hands. Bears tend to recognize human sounds as ones to avoid; they'll usually wander off if they hear people approaching. Make loud noise in thick brushy areas, around blind corners, near babbling streams, and against the wind.

- **Hike with other people.** Avoid hiking alone. Keep children near. Very few bear attacks happen to groups of four or more.

- **Avoid bear feeding areas.** If you stumble across an animal carcass, leave the area immediately and notify a ranger. Toward summer's end, huckleberry patches provide high sugars for bears.

- **Hike in broad daylight.** Avoid early morning, late evening, and night.

- **Never approach a bear.** Head swaying, teeth clacking, laid-back ears, a lowered head, and huffing or woofing are signs of agitation: Clear out slowly.

- **If you do surprise a bear, back away.** Contrary to all inclinations, do not run. Instead, back away slowly, talking quietly and turning sideways or bending your knees to appear smaller

by its reddish tint. Looking like fat house cat-size fur balls, **hoary marmots** splay on rocks, sunning themselves. Scampering between high alpine rocks, **golden-mantled ground squirrels** look like oversize chipmunks with their telltale gold stripes.

Fish

With 750 lakes and 1,500 miles of streams, Glacier provides abundant habitat for native and nonnative species of fish. **Bull trout, westslope cutthroat trout,** and **whitefish** are among the 17 native species. To promote recreational fishing, lakes were once stocked with nonnative fish such as rainbow trout, arctic grayling, and kokanee salmon. Introduced species flourished, threatening native fish, whose populations are now

Bears are integral to Glacier's ecosystem.

and nonthreatening. Avoid direct eye contact. Leave your pack on; it can protect you if the bear attacks.

- **Use pepper spray.** If you surprise a bear that attacks in defense, aim pepper spray at the bear's eyes and nose. Watch wind direction, as it may affect the spray's ability to reach the bear.

- **Play dead.** Should a bear attack, protect yourself and your vulnerable parts by assuming a fetal position on the ground with your hands around the back of your neck. Play dead. Move again only when you are sure the bear has vacated the area.

- **If a bear stalks you as food, or attacks at night, fight back.** Bears stalking humans as prey is extremely rare. Use any means at hand, including pepper spray, shouting, waving sticks, or throwing rocks, to tell the bear you are not an easy food source. Try to escape up something, like a building or a tree.

- **Pay attention to trail signage.** Special bear signage is used at trailheads to inform hikers of concerns. Yellow **bear warning** signs indicate bears are frequenting the trail; use extra caution and make noise. Orange **bear closure** signs indicate a trail is closed, usually because one has been aggressive or is defending a carcass.

- Two books have accurate information on bears: Bill Schneider's *Bear Aware* and Stephen Herrero's *Bear Attacks: Their Causes and Avoidance.*

waning. Since the 1970s fish are no longer stocked in Glacier or Waterton.

Fish in Waterton Lakes feed on a tiny crustacean, the opossum shrimp. It's a relic species that inhabited the area prior to the Pleistocene ice age. As glaciers melted, the tiny shrimp returned through the Missouri-Mississippi watersheds. Spending its entire life in darkness, it lingers on the lake bottom during the day, surfacing only at night.

Birds

More than 200 species of birds mean every park visitor can see wildlife. Bird checklists are available at visitors centers in both parks to assist with identification. In summer, trees teem with songbirds: **cedar waxwings,** thrushes, chickadees, vireos, sparrows, dark-eyed juncos, and finches. Brilliant-colored western tanagers and striking mountain bluebirds flit between treetops. Sightings of rufous and calliope hummingbirds are common. Woodpeckers, including the large redcapped pileated woodpecker, pound at bark in search of bugs. Ground birds such as the chicken-size grouse surprise hikers on trails, while smaller ptarmigans, whose plumage turns white in winter, blend with summer coloration into rocks. Steller's jays and Clark's nutcrackers add to the cacophony.

Because of Glacier's profuse rivers, streams, and lakes, waterfowl find plentiful habitat. Loons, grebes, mergansers, and goldeneyes fill almost every lake, while harlequin ducks migrate to rapidly flowing streams in spring for nesting. Tundra swans use Glacier's lakes as a stopping place during their annual migration to and from their arctic breeding grounds. American dippers, or water ouzels, nest near waterfalls: The dark bird's obvious bobbing action is a dead giveaway of the species.

Raptors

Nothing is more dramatic than sighting a golden eagle soaring along the Continental Divide. Commonly nesting in remote spots, goldens often return yearly to the same location. Glacier also boasts about 10 nesting pairs of bald eagles, seen along waterways yearround. Above lakes, ospreys dive for fish from impressive heights, while red-tailed hawks and American kestrels hover over field mice. Listen carefully, for nights are haunted by the small pygmy owl's "whew" call and the great horned owl's six deep hoots.

Snakes and Spiders

For the most part, Glacier and Waterton are devoid of poisonous snakes and spiders. The climate is too harsh for rattlesnakes. However, you will find garter and bull snakes on some trails. Due to colder conditions, native spiders are small, although a bite may produce swelling or an allergic reaction.

ENVIRONMENTAL ISSUES
Climate Change

The current increase in global temperatures affects Glacier like nowhere else. Changes seem to be happening faster here than elsewhere, which is why Glacier serves as a living laboratory for studying climate change. While glaciers have shrunk since 1850, the park's namesakes will all have melted around 2030. Melting produces not just a loss of ice but a shift in flora and fauna. As temperatures warm, the tree line advances upward in elevation, encroaching on alpine zones. Glacier's tree line was once 3,200 feet lower than it is today; how far up it will climb is unknown.

A rising tree line will cause basins scoured clean by ice and blooming with wildflower meadows to succumb to heavy forests of spruce, fir, pines, shrubs, and bushes. Photographs have already recorded significant changes in vegetation in some locations in the park. Plants at the fringes of their distribution may disappear entirely.

Shifts in floral habitat may force wildlife to change elevation or latitude in search of food sources. Species such as the heatintolerant pika may suffer extinction. Animals adapted to cold winters, waters, or snow, such as mountain goats, bighorn sheep, bull trout, westslope cutthroat trout, ptarmigan, short-tailed weasels, showshoe hares, and wolverines may suffer if they can't adapt. Climate change poses a threat to alpine species that rely on cooler temperatures. In the past several years, citizen science programs have aided Glacier National Park in collecting population data on several species that may be threatened by climate change. Gathering baseline population counts and following up with monitoring will track how these animals respond.

Because of Glacier's easily accessed alpine

areas, scientists are monitoring melt rates of Grinnell and Sperry Glaciers to help predict future impacts on the park's biodiversity. The **Northern Rocky Mountain Science Center** (https://www.usgs.gov/centers/norock/) has produced a series of repeat photography collections showing changes in glaciers and forest growth, comparing photographs from the last century to the present day. Find these online and at Many Glacier Hotel.

Endangered Species

In the 1800s, more than 100,000 **grizzly bears** roamed grasslands and foothills in the Lower 48. Today, in less than 1 percent of their historic range, fewer than 1,500 grizzlies forage for food. Greater Glacier's grizzly bears are currently listed as threatened on the Endangered Species List, but due to bear management efforts assisting their recovery, that may not be for long.

In an effort to count the grizzly population, the U.S. Geological Survey conducted two major studies around Glacier and continues with monitoring today. Collecting scat and bear hair via barbwire stapled to rub trees and surrounding scent lures, scientists used tweezers to bag the hairs for DNA genotyping of species, sex, and individual. You may find barbwire on trees along trails where biologists still gather samples. The study documented a rebounding population of grizzlies across eight million acres in northwest Montana. Today, the population is estimated at 1,000. Glacier houses the densest number. A continuing Montana Fish, Wildlife, and Parks study radio-collars female grizzlies to track reproduction and mortality. It found that the grizzly population in the Northern Continental Divide Ecosystem, which includes Glacier, is growing at 3 percent per year. Both studies revealed that grizzlies have exceeded federal recovery targets, so government machinery now churns toward delisting the grizzly bear.

Grizzlies require a large range; many travel outside the park and across international boundaries. Human pressures from road and house building, agriculture and livestock, timber harvesting, and mineral, oil, and gas mining impact their habitat. Just outside Waterton, legal Canadian hunting and predator-control programs subject bears to high mortality rates. In northwest Montana, poaching, management actions, and private landowners account for the deaths of 20-30 grizzlies per year. While bad berry crops and encroaching rural development contribute to bears getting into trouble, inappropriate attractants such as garbage, livestock grain, pet food, and bird feeders lead to many of the deaths.

Recorded sightings of the **Canada lynx** have declined substantially in the past 40 years, prompting it to be listed as threatened in 2000. In coniferous forests, the lynx follows its primary prey, the snowshoe hare; the cat's population rises and falls with hare numbers. Park studies have followed tracks in the snow to ascertain the lynx's status.

Two indigenous trout descended from ice age lakes that formed as the glaciers retreated: **westslope cutthroat trout** and **bull trout.** Glacier provides a stronghold for these fish. Bull trout populations have declined 90 percent, forcing it to be listed as an endangered species in 1998, but pure westslope cutthroat have yet to be placed on the list. While habitat degradation and overfishing contributed to the demise, another menace came from nonnative lake trout stocked for recreational fishing, turning bull trout into easy prey. But the biggest threat comes from hybridization with other trout such as rainbows. The park uses fishing regulations and fish kill programs to protect pure populations.

Other species not officially listed as endangered also suffer threats to their survival. Of all the ungulates, **bighorn sheep** face the greatest risk. Once widely scattered across most western mountain ranges, the sheep today live in fragmented pockets. Hunting, disease, agriculture, mining, competition for food, fire-suppression policies, and habitat destruction forced this grassland forager into the more rugged fringes of its historic range. Today, 400-600 bighorn sheep graze in Glacier, with an additional population in Waterton. Recent studies used GPS radio collars to track the sheep, and DNA samples revealed two genetically different populations in northern and southern Glacier.

Current research is also monitoring other species of concern. Annual counts of waterbirds, such as **loons** and **harlequin ducks,** are keeping tabs on these small populations. A winter-hair snag study is tracking the number of **wolverines,** as Glacier appears to be one of the few strongholds in the Lower 48 for the gluttonous weasel.

While other animals are in danger, **gray wolves** have seen a recovery. Once ranging throughout most of North America, gray wolves disappeared from Glacier-Waterton by 1920 due to predator-control programs. In the 1970s they were placed on the Endangered Species List. In 1986, following the natural migration of the Magic Pack from Canada, Glacier saw its first litter of pups born in over 50 years. By 2009, numbers in the Northern Rockies rebounded to the point where the federal government delisted the wolf. Outside the park, Montana permits hunting and trapping wolves.

North Fork in the United States and Canada

Currently, Glacier's northern boundary is twice as long as the joint boundary with Waterton. The area is one ecosystem, but it lacks protection for its contiguous boundary. Threats include proposed mining operations that could alter the unique North Fork ecology. A coalition of U.S. and Canadian organizations has joined forces to lobby for **Akamina-Kishinena Provincial Park** in British Columbia to become a national park wilderness area in order to protect the North Fork of the Flathead River. That change would match the two national park boundaries in

mountain goat with radio-tracking collar

length, offering more protection for the shared watershed, wildlife, and air. Find more information at www.flathead.ca.

Going-to-the-Sun Road Corridor

In 2016, Glacier National Park wrapped up a **three-year study** to assess how to manage future visitation on the Sun Road. It addressed dilemmas such as an aging shuttle fleet crowded to capacity, lack of funding for shuttle replacements, nonnative noxious weeds proliferating via vehicles, parking lots crammed full by 8:30am, human-wildlife interactions, overcrowded trails, and increased shoulder season bicycling. Simply adding more parking spots is not a viable solution to crowding, as the repercussions spin off in excessive traffic on trails. Damage (widening, trampled vegetation) is already visible on trails, such as the Hidden Lake Overlook, Avalanche Lake, Highline, and St. Mary Falls. Some trails have seen a 250 percent increase in traffic. Recent years have broken visitor records: 2014 and 2015 saw 2.4 million visitors each, while 2016 visitation smashed July and August records by 18 percent and the year overall totaled nearly 3 million visitors. Starting in 2017, study results may change how visitors are allowed to tour the Sun Road and hike on some of the more popular trails.

Part of the study focused on mountain goats at Logan Pass. The goats frequently slurp antifreeze from the pavement, lick railings and urination spots for salts, and approach humans. In 2016, the park launched a pilot "Bark Ranger" program, where a trained border collie herded sheep and goats from the parking lot into adjacent meadows for safety.

Biologists also collared 25 mountain goats with radio and GPS transmitters to follow their movements. They discovered the goats hang around humans rather than cliffs for protection from predators.

Historical Protection

Glacier has many cultural and historical resources, but protecting archaeological and historic assets is difficult. At 50 years old, artifacts including garbage dumps are considered historic, according to federal law. To date, Glacier has identified 429 archaeological sites, and Waterton has 358. But many have not been cataloged. More funding is needed for adequate protection.

History

Human use of the Crown of the Continent dates back at least 10,000 years. Evidence shows that the native people living near Glacier and Waterton today have ancestral roots fishing in Upper Waterton Lake and driving bison across the Blakiston Valley prairies.

NATIVE AMERICANS

Spanning what became the U.S.-Canadian border, the **Blackfeet,** or Niitsitapi ("original people"), included three nomadic groups who based much of their livelihood on hunting bison in the vast prairies on the Continental Divide's east side. The most northerly group, the Siksika, or Blackfoot, were the first to meet European traders. (To refer to the group, *Blackfoot* is used in Canada, and *Blackfeet* is used in the United States.) The Blood (or Kainai) and Piegan (or Piikani) make up the southern groups. For thousands of years, according to the Blackfeet, their lands were between the Saskatchewan and Yellowstone Rivers.

During the summer, Blackfeet groups convened for the sun dance, a ceremony held on the plains. During the rest of the spring and summer, efforts focused individually on stocking food: hunting, digging roots, and collecting berries. As bison moved northwest to their wintering ranges, groups met again, often at buffalo jumps, where hunters funneled bison over a cliff to slaughter them for food, hides, and bones. Afterward, they returned to their winter camps, sheltered in deep mountain forests.

For the Blackfeet, the Glacier National Park area was known as the "Backbone of the World." Used for spiritual sanctuary, the mountains provided places for prayer and sacred ceremonies. They were a place to gather guidance, holy plants, and roots used for their healing properties. Some of Glacier's peaks, lakes, and rivers still use Blackfeet names today: Going-to-the-Sun Mountain, Two Medicine Lake, Pitamakin Pass, and Running Eagle Falls.

On the Continental Divide's west side, the **Salish** and **Kootenai** hunted, trapped, and fished. They ventured east over the mountains on annual bison hunts. Known as the Ktunaxa, the Kootenai (in Canada *Kootenay*) comprised seven bands spanning the western Rockies from southern Alberta to Missoula, Montana. The Kootenai typically used mountain passes like Marias, Cut Bank, Red Eagle, and Brown to cross through Glacier and Waterton to hunt, and the Blackfeet used the same passes for raiding parties. For the Kootenai, the Lake McDonald area was a place for sacred dances, hence its original name of Sacred Dancing Waters.

Two other nations lived in the Glacier-Waterton vicinity: the Assiniboines, or Stoney people, and the Gros Ventre. Both of these groups find namesakes in the park, with a lake, a pass, and three peaks named for the Stoney. In the park's northeast corner, the Gros Ventres, which means "big belly," left their name on the Belly River and Mokowanis drainages with Gros Ventre Falls. Little evidence remains in the park of the presence of the Flathead and Kalispel people.

As westward expansion brought more non-natives, Native Americans were moved into government-planned reservation boundaries: The Siksika were settled near Calgary, the Blood were moved onto a reserve adjacent to Waterton, and the Piegans, the largest of the three Blackfeet groups, split in two, with the North Piikani settling near Pincher Creek in Alberta and the South Piikani in Montana. Their reservation included Glacier's eastern slopes up to the Continental Divide. The Salish and Kootenai were moved to the Flathead Reservation southwest of Glacier. Smallpox and social problems took their toll on all of these indigenous groups.

EXPLORERS, TRAPPERS, AND MINERS

In 1803, when **Lewis and Clark** came west, they bypassed Glacier. At Camp Disappointment, located today on the Blackfeet Reservation, they came within 25 miles of Marias Pass, one of the lowest passes through the treacherous Rocky Mountains. But they never found it.

Soon, French, Spanish, and English fur

Glacier was sacred to Native Americans.

trappers entered the Glacier-Waterton area, but the land between the Continental Divide and the plains belonged to the Blackfeet. In 1895 the federal government negotiated a settlement with the Blackfeet to purchase the portion of their reservation that makes up Glacier's eastern slopes today. Starving and in dire need of money, the Blackfeet agreed to the terms of the sale, and Glacier became a public **forest reserve.**

Miners arrived, looking for copper and gold. At the turn of the 20th century, mining boomed in Many Glacier and Rising Sun. Oil wells spewed: western Canada's first in Waterton, and Montana's first at Kintla Lake. Neither oil nor mining paid off, both supplanted by burgeoning tourism.

BUILDING A PARK

Pressure to find rail passages through the northern Rockies began in the mid-1800s. When the Great Northern Railway finally succeeded in 1891 to lay track over the Continental Divide, the face of Glacier changed. The railroad company needed a destination to lure wealthy passengers. The railroad's economic needs and preservationists spawned the idea of **Glacier National Park,** which became a reality on May 11, 1910.

William Logan, for whom Logan Pass is named, took the reins as the first superintendent of the nation's 10th park. Charged with building a headquarters, hiring rangers, constructing trails, and surveying for a road through the park's interior, Logan did little his first year but put out fires. Literally. More than 10 percent of the park flamed during one of the West's biggest fire seasons. His second summer finally saw steps toward readying Glacier for visitors.

In order to provide travelers with places to stay and go, the **Great Northern Railway** created many of the park's facilities: hotels, tent camps, chalets, roads, trails, and boats. Competing for travel time and dollars from wealthy Americans taking steamships to Europe, the railroad pitched the slogan "See America First" to lure vacationers to Glacier, which became known as "America's Switzerland." Large hotels such as Many Glacier and Glacier Park Lodge were built to impress. They touted high-end amenities of the era, such as steam heat.

Horse concessionaires operating from every hotel and chalet in the park merged into the Park Saddle Horse Company. By the mid-1920s, the way to see the park was on horseback. At its peak, the Park Saddle Horse Company operated more than 1,000 horses and led more than 10,000 visitors through the park each summer.

As the country's infatuation with the automobile grew, the demand for a road bisecting Glacier's interior increased, and the **Transmountain Highway,** named later after Going-to-the-Sun Mountain, altered how visitors toured the park. Although building the western portion of the Sun Road began in 1919, the 50-mile project was not completed until 1932. The opening of Going-to-the-Sun

Road ushered in a new era of park visitation. A fleet of red buses hit Glacier's roads for touring. With increased motorized travel, camping gained in popularity, and the Great Northern Railway added budget motor inns to its property collection. With the popularity of Going-to-the-Sun Road, saddle trips and the pricey chalets began to meet their demise.

During the Great Depression and World War II, travel restrictions and fuel conservation made park visitation plummet, forcing hotels and chalets to close. Several chalets fell into disrepair and had to be razed. As bus-tour business usurped rail travel and private car travel grew, the Park Saddle Horse Company folded. The railroad's hotel business suffered, losing $500,000 annually. Finally, in 1954, the Great Northern Railway sold Many Glacier Hotel and Lake McDonald Lodge to the National Park Service and unloaded the two remaining chalets for $1. In 1957 the railroad sold the hotel concession business and remaining Glacier Park Lodge and Prince of Wales Hotel to a Minneapolis corporation, which subsequently sold three years later to Glacier Park, Inc., current owner of the two hotels.

Of the remaining park lodges and chalets, six are listed as **National Historic Landmarks.** Going-to-the-Sun Road was recognized as the first road in the United States to become a National Historic Landmark. It also is the only road in the country to be a National Historic Landmark and a National Civil Engineering Landmark.

SAVING PARK ATTRIBUTES

In the past two decades, ailing park facilities have received facelifts and rehabilitation. The Sperry and Granite backcountry chalets saw restoration after they were both closed in the 1990s. Today, they offer rustic places for hikers to overnight, much like they did in their heyday. Glacier's red jammer buses were also sidelined in the 1990s, but Glacier Park, Inc., the National Park Fund, and Ford Motor

Company collaborated on getting them back on the road.

Two major rehabilitation projects will see completion in 2017. A 10-year, $270 million reconstruction of Going-to-the-Sun Road has shored up the road against vehicle wear and tear, torrential rains, mudslides, and avalanches. Many Glacier Hotel has undergone a multiyear $30 million reconstruction to fix structural issues without damaging the historical appearance.

INTERNATIONAL PEACE PARK

In 1932, Glacier and Waterton made front-page headlines as the world's first **International Peace Park.** The brainchild and work of Rotary International chapters from Alberta and Montana, their lobbying efforts paid off as the Canadian Parliament and U.S. Congress officially recognized the continuity of the parks. With credit to the longest undefended border in the world, the U.S. and Canadian governments dedicated the parks together as **Waterton-Glacier International Peace Park.**

BIOSPHERE RESERVE

In 1976, the United Nations Educational, Scientific, and Cultural Organization (UNESCO) designated Glacier National Park a **Biosphere Reserve.** Three years later, Waterton Lakes received the same recognition. As Biosphere Reserves, the parks are recognized for their huge diversity of wildlife and plants. Part of the designation is also due to the parks functioning as living laboratories for significant scientific research into fire ecology and climate change.

WORLD HERITAGE SITE

In 1995 UNESCO declared Waterton and Glacier a **World Heritage Site.** This designation was assigned for the parks' natural beauty and unique geological features. Their beauty is attributed to the dramatic topography created by sedimentation in the Belt Sea, the Lewis Overthrust, and glaciation. Those three actions exposed some of the oldest sedimentary rock in North America and created unique geological features, such as Triple Divide Peak, from which water flows to the Pacific, the Gulf of Mexico, and Hudson Bay.

Glacier has been designated a World Heritage Site due to its rugged topography.

INTERNATIONAL DARK SKY PARK

In 2016, Waterton-Glacier garnered a provisional designation as the world's first **International Transboundary Dark Sky Preserve.** It is one of the dwindling places in the world to see the Milky Way due to minimal light pollution. Astronomy programs at Logan Pass, Apgar Visitor Center, and St. Mary Visitor Center provide constellation tours and telescopic views of daytime solar phenomena and nighttime viewing of planets, star clusters, nebulae, and galaxies.

Essentials

Getting There

ORIENTATION

Getting your bearings in Glacier is not difficult; the park is split along the Continental Divide into the east side and west side, each with several entrances to valley drainages. Two Medicine, St. Mary, and Many Glacier are on the east, while Lake McDonald and the North Fork cover the west. Although U.S. 2 passes briefly through the park's southern tip between East Glacier and West Glacier, southern entrances into the park's core are via foot or on horseback trails. On the north side, Waterton Lakes National Park provides access via boat or on foot across the Canadian-U.S. border into Glacier's interior.

Only one route bisects the entire park: Going-to-the-Sun Road. Rush hour on this road is 8am-5pm seven days a week July-August.

Most summer visitors love the park's expansive east-side views. On a clear day, not much obstructs the view of mountains. By autumn, not many services remain open to take the Rocky Mountain Front's brutal winds.

The park's heavily forested west side balances remote corners of the North Fork with the busy hub of West Glacier. Mountain snows feed large rivers that drain into Flathead Lake. Mixed with farmland, rural pockets, and resort towns, the fast-growing Flathead Valley, anchored in winter by recreational skiing, is a year-round enclave for close to 90,000 people.

SUGGESTED DRIVING ROUTES
From Western Montana

From I-90 just west of Missoula, take exit 96 onto U.S. 93 north, which leads 103 miles to Flathead Valley. This scenic route passes

below the craggy Mission Mountains and along Flathead Lake, the largest freshwater lake west of the Mississippi.

Drivers from Spokane can cut off miles by exiting I-90 at St. Regis and following the signs to Glacier National Park (northeast on Highway 135, northwest on Highway 200, and

ESSENTIALS
GETTING THERE

Suggested Routes

© AVALON TRAVEL

Previous: backpacking Dawson-Pitamakin Loop Trail; motorcycles and red buses at Logan Pass.

Top Sightseeing en Route to Glacier

- **National Bison Range** (Dixon, Montana): One of the oldest national wildlife refuges and home to preserving the American bison (406/644-2211, www.fws.gov/bisonrange).

- **First Peoples Buffalo Jump State Park** (Ulm, Montana): The National Historic Landmark is one of the largest buffalo jumps in the country (406/866-2217, http://stateparks.mt.gov/first-peoples-buffalo-jump).

- **Lewis and Clark Caverns State Park** (Whitehall, Montana): A limestone cave of fantastical shapes with guided tours (406/287-3541, http://stateparks.mt.gov/lewis-and-clark-caverns).

- **Lewis and Clark National Historic Trail Interpretive Center** (Great Falls, Montana): A museum with historical displays, live demonstrations, hands-on activities, and multimedia shows (406/727-8733, www.fs.usda.gov/main/lcnf/learning).

- **C. M. Russell Museum** (Great Falls, Montana): Museum celebrates the work of the famous Western painter Charlie Russell (1864-1926), who summered in his cabin on Glacier's Lake McDonald (406/727-8787, http://cmrussell.org).

- **Frank Slide** (Blairmore, Alberta): Interpretive center that commemorates a 1903 rockslide that buried a mining town (403/562-7388, www.frankslide.com).

- **Head-Smashed-In Buffalo Jump** (Fort Macleod, Alberta): A World Heritage Site and museum that shares the early life of indigenous Blackfoot peoples (403/553-2731, www.head-smashed-in.com).

- **Ice Age Floods National Geologic Trail** (Montana, Idaho, Washington, Oregon): The first national geologic trail in the United States that shows the results of massive ice-age floods that originated in northwest Montana (http://iafi.org/floods-features-map).

---

northeast on Highway 28). The route passes the funky little towns of Paradise and Hot Springs, before joining U.S. 93 heading north at Flathead Lake. Spokane to West Glacier (271 miles) is a five-hour drive.

In Kalispell, a confusing highway maze jogs through Flathead Valley. Follow signs to the park or West Glacier. In downtown Kalispell, turn east onto U.S. 2 (East Idaho Street). Travel for two miles and turn left with U.S. 2, going north 12 miles toward Columbia Falls. At the intersection with Highway 40, turn right; follow the highway through Columbia Falls, continuing another 16 miles on U.S. 2 to West Glacier. The total mileage from I-90 to West Glacier is 145 miles; driving time on the two-lane highway is usually less than three hours, but it can be four hours or more with heavy traffic, snow, or road-construction delays.

From Eastern Montana or Yellowstone

This long but scenic approach follows the Rocky Mountain Front, a highway for golden eagle migrations and buttress for the Bob Marshall Wilderness. Stitching together a Yellowstone National Park and Glacier vacation requires an entire day (7-10 hours) to drive from one park to the other. From I-90 in **Butte,** turn north toward Helena onto I-15 (exit 129/227) and drive 101 miles to exit 228, two miles north of Wolf Creek. Turn north onto U.S. 287.

Along U.S. 287, strong side winds can slow travel with gusts that rock RVs and trailers. Follow the narrow two-lane U.S. 287 north 66 miles through Augusta to Choteau (SHOW-toe), the epitome of a Rocky Mountain Front town, with 1,700 residents, grain elevators, and hunting. In

Choteau, the road turns left onto U.S. 89 (Main St.). From Choteau, head north 72 miles to Browning. Again, narrow curves slow driving time, but Glacier's peaks soon jut up from the plains. Just before Browning, join U.S. 2. At Browning's west end, turn left as U.S. 2 leaves town. It leads 13 miles to East Glacier. Total driving time for the 253 miles from I-90 to East Glacier is about five hours. High winds and traffic may slow travel, but the scenery is worth the drive.

From **Great Falls,** two routes lead to East Glacier, both with spectacular views of the Rocky Mountain Front as it pops above the plains. For easy interstate and highway driving, take I-15 heading north to Shelby and then U.S. 2 west to East Glacier (143 miles). This quicker route takes 2.5 hours.

A much more interesting 139-mile approach strikes off through small, rural Rocky Mountain Front towns. From Great Falls, head 10 miles north on I-15 to catch U.S. 89 north toward Browning. The route travels past Freezeout Lake, known for its snow goose migration. Connect with the Butte route in Choteau. While shorter, the narrow road makes for slower driving, taking 2.75 hours to reach East Glacier, or longer with explorations.

From the Canadian Rockies

Many travelers link Glacier-Waterton with the national parks of the Canadian Rockies: Jasper, Banff, Yoho, and Kootenay. The Flathead Valley connects directly to Banff and the Canadian Rockies via U.S. 93 and British Columbia Highway 93. To get to Glacier, travel south on Highway 93 through British Columbia toward Cranbrook. Six kilometers (3.7 miles) before Cranbrook, merge with Highway 3 heading 58 kilometers (36 miles) east toward Elko, where roads go east to Waterton and Glacier's east side or south toward West Glacier.

To head to Waterton, stay on Highway 3 for 96 kilometers (60 miles) through Crowsnest Pass and turn south onto Highway 6 at Pincher Creek. Drive 32 kilometers (20 miles) to Waterton Lakes National Park, where the seasonal Chief Mountain Highway connects with Glacier National Park's east side.

To head to West Glacier, take Highway 93 south at Elko for 39 kilometers (24 miles) toward Roosville on the Canadian-U.S. border. After crossing, continue south 63 miles on U.S. 93 through Eureka to Whitefish. Drive with caution: Deer frequent the road between Eureka and Whitefish, earning it the nickname "Deer Alley." In downtown Whitefish, U.S. 93 turns south again at the third stoplight. Drive two miles to the junction with Highway 40 with signs for Glacier. Turn left toward Columbia Falls. En route, Highway 40 becomes U.S. 2, goes through several small burgs and reaches West Glacier. Expect 6.5 hours driving time from Banff.

From Calgary

From Calgary, head south for 181 kilometers (113 miles) on Highway 2 toward Fort Macleod. For Waterton Lakes National Park, turn west onto Highway 3 and drive 27 kilometers (17 miles) to Pincher Creek. At Pincher Creek, turn south onto Highway 6 for 32 kilometers (20 miles) to the park entrance. From Calgary to Waterton is 240 kilometers (149 miles) via Pincher Creek. The distance can be covered in three hours.

To head straight to Glacier from Calgary, continue from Fort Macleod south through Cardston to the Carway-Piegan border crossing. The 266 kilometers (165 miles) from Calgary to the border at Carway should take about three hours. As a general rule, speed limits in Alberta tend to be a little lower than in Montana, especially compared to Montana's narrow, two-lane rural highways, which can be posted at 70 mph. Speed limits in Canada are posted in kilometers; 80 km/h is 50 mph. From Carway, cross the Canadian-U.S. border onto U.S. 89. Drive 19 miles to St. Mary for Going-to-the-Sun Road's east entrance, 25 minutes from the border. To enter the park at Many Glacier instead, turn right at Babb, 10 miles south of the border, and drive 12 miles to Many Glacier Hotel and Swiftcurrent (40 minutes).

TRAIN ROUTES

In the United States, Glacier is one of the rare national parks serviced by train. In fact, much of the park's development came from the Great Northern Railway, and Amtrak offers an updated way to reach the park on a historic rail line.

Amtrak

Amtrak's daily *Empire Builder* (800/872-7245, www.amtrak.com) stops at several locations at Glacier National Park. Between Seattle and Shelby, Montana, National Park Service guides offer educational services on board. High summer travel volumes make reservations imperative, and riders may need to contend with delays. Heavy freight traffic, spring flooding, and winter avalanches can cause delays, but the addition of double tracks in 2015 improved on-time performance to almost 90 percent in 2016. Trains that run late can lag by several hours or more.

Three stops are year-round in the Glacier environs: Essex, West Glacier, and Whitefish. East Glacier is a summer-only stop. Check with Amtrak for schedules.

The westbound route originates in Chicago, stopping at Milwaukee, St. Paul-Minneapolis, and Fargo, plus smaller towns on its way to Glacier. The ride from Chicago to East Glacier takes about 30 hours or more. From Chicago, westbound trains arrive in the evening at East Glacier, Essex, West Glacier, and Whitefish.

Eastbound trains starting in Seattle and Portland join in Spokane and stop in Whitefish before reaching West Glacier in a little more than 15 hours. From West Glacier, the train skirts the southern edge of Glacier, stopping in Essex and East Glacier. The eastbound train lands riders in the Glacier environs in early morning.

Check for special deals on Amtrak's website. Kids ages 2-12 pay half price. Seniors,

Amtrak stop

veterans, AAA and NARP members, military personnel, and students can get discounts.

VIA Rail Canada

Travelers across Canada by **VIA Rail** (800/842-7245, www.viarail.ca) struggle to get to Waterton and Glacier. Between Winnipeg and Vancouver, the route jogs far north to Edmonton, 534 kilometers (332 miles) away from Waterton. It even bypasses Calgary, the nearest metropolitan city. Most train travelers switch to air or bus travel to reach Calgary and then rent a car.

TRAVEL HUB: FLATHEAD VALLEY

Flathead Valley is the closest, easiest access to Glacier National Park. Flights arriving before evening can put you via shuttle at Lake McDonald in time to catch the sunset in the park. Because Glacier Park International Airport has no lodging in its immediate vicinity, if you arrive on a late flight or want to explore Flathead Valley, you will need to stay in one of four towns. Columbia Falls is closest, between the airport and Glacier, but Whitefish is more attractive, with its resort-town atmosphere. Kalispell and Bigfork are farthest from Glacier.

Airport

Nonstop flights from Minneapolis, Chicago, Atlanta, Denver, Salt Lake City, Las Vegas, Los Angeles, Oakland, Portland, and Seattle via Alaska/Horizon, Allegiant, Delta/SkyWest, and United service the closest airport to Glacier National Park, **Glacier Park International Airport** (FCA, www.iflyglacier.com). Some routes are winter or summer only. Even though the airport has an international designation, the connections are Canadian charter flights. The tiny airport has only three gates. Baggage claim and car rental desks sit just a few hundred feet from the gates. Prearranged shuttles are right outside.

Although the airport is within Kalispell city limits, many visitors are surprised to find Kalispell hotels 15 minutes away in the opposite direction of the park. In fact, the airport is almost equidistant between downtown Kalispell, Whitefish, and Columbia Falls. Because the airport is only 25 miles from West Glacier, you can maximize your park time by sitting on the beach at Lake McDonald the day you arrive.

Although Spokane is an alternative airport, it requires a five-hour drive to reach the park.

Train

Amtrak's *Empire Builder* (800/872-7245, www.amtrak.com) stops in Whitefish twice daily, once eastbound in early morning and once westbound in late evening. Reservations are a must in summer.

Bus

Flathead Transit (406/275-2877 ext. 1352, www.greyhound.com, $32 one-way) runs one bus daily between Missoula and Whitefish as part of the Greyhound Connect program. It leaves Missoula at 11:30am, arriving at 3:10pm in Whitefish. From Whitefish, buses connect to **Whitefish Mountain Resort** (SNOW Bus, www.bigmtncommercial.org, July-early Sept. and early Dec.-early Apr., free) and Apgar Visitor Center (Glacier Park Express, www.glacierparkexpress.com, daily July-early Sept., adults $10, child $5).

Taxi and Shuttle

Glacier Charters (406/892-3390 or 800/

shuttle bus tours

829-7039, www.glaciertransportation.com) provides shuttles to all lodges in Glacier, Flathead Lake environs, and Whitefish Mountain Resort. Drivers will meet any flight or pick you up at any park lodge, trailhead, or surrounding town to transport you back to the airport. They even accommodate the early morning and late night flights.

For visitors staying in Flathead Valley, several hotels have airport shuttles. For those that don't, call **Glacier Taxi** (406/250-3603, glaciertaxi.com) to reach hotels in Bigfork, Whitefish, Columbia Falls, and Kalispell.

Car Rental

The Glacier Park International Airport terminal has four car-rental agencies with desks in the airport: **Hertz** (406/758-2220 or 800/654-3131, www.hertz.com), **National-Alamo** (406/257-7144 or 800/227-7368, www.nationalcar.com), **Avis** (406/257-2727 or 800/230-4898, www.avis.com), and **Budget** (406/755-7500 or 800/527-0700, www.budget.com). Kalispell and Whitefish also have car-rental agencies (check www.iflyglacier.com); they will deliver a car to the airport or pick you up.

RV Rental

Although somewhat expensive ($200-350/day), RVing is an easy way to tour Glacier with the good parts of camping minus the hassle of tents. Be aware, however, of Going-to-the-Sun Road's vehicle length restrictions (21 feet). You may need to use shuttles or bus tours to see the historic road, or rent a car. **Gardner RV** (3100 US 93 S., Kalispell, 406/752-7683, www.gardnerrv.com) carries a few rental RVs. With prior arrangement, the company will pick you up at the airport. **Bigfork Outdoor Rental** (275 Hwy. 83, Bigfork, 406/837-2498, www.bigforkoutdoorrentals.com) rents 23-28-foot trailers.

Equipment Rental

Flathead Valley does not have equipment rentals for camping. But West Glacier has multiple equipment rental locations.

Accommodations and Food

Because Glacier is so close to Glacier Park International Airport, many travelers go directly into the park the day they arrive; likewise with flying out. However, Flathead Valley lodging varies from dirt-cheap to high-end, and many hotels offer complimentary airport shuttles. There is no lodging or dining in the immediate vicinity of the airport; find the closest options in Columbia Falls, downtown Kalispell, and Whitefish.

TRAVEL HUB: GREAT FALLS

Straddling the mighty Missouri River, Great Falls, Montana, is an east-side gateway to Glacier. But the additional distance to Glacier and lack of easy connections with Amtrak and buses make renting a car preferable to drive to the park. With a flight arriving by late afternoon, you can be in East Glacier to watch the sunset that same day.

Airport

Alaska/Horizon, Allegiant, Delta/Sky West, and United airlines service **Great Falls International Airport** (GTF, 406/727-3404, www.gtfairport.com) with nonstop flights from Denver, Salt Lake City, Minneapolis, Las Vegas, Phoenix, Chicago, and Seattle. The airport's international label comes from a couple of Canadian charter flights. Located outside town, the airport is convenient for picking up on-site rental cars but requires hotel shuttles or taxis to reach lodging and restaurants in town, 10 minutes away.

Train and Bus

Greyhound (www.greyhound.com) reaches Great Falls, but not farther to Glacier. The closest westbound **Amtrak** depot is Shelby, 87 miles north. A free county van with **Golden Triangle Transit** (406/873-2207 or 406/470-0727, www.toolecountymt.gov) runs between Great Falls and Shelby on Thursdays, but not in time to prevent spending a night in Shelby. You're better off renting a car to drive to Glacier.

Taxi

Some hotels provide airport shuttle service. Otherwise, call **Diamond Cab** (406/453-3241).

Car Rental

Great Falls has most national car-rental chains. The airport terminal contains **Alamo** (406/727-0273 or 800/462-5266, www.alamo. com), **Hertz** (406/761-6641 or 800/654-3131, www.hertz.com), **Enterprise** (406/216-5001 or 800/325-8007, www.enterprise.com), **National** (406/453-4386 or 800/227-7368, www.nationalcar.com), and **Avis** (406/761-7610 or 800/230-4898, www.avis.com).

RV Rental

Gardner RV (4035 10th Ave. S., Great Falls, 406/454-0777, www.gardnerrv.com) carries a few rental RV motorhomes ($200-300/day). Be aware of Going-to-the-Sun Road's vehicle length restrictions (21 feet). You will need to use shuttles or bus tours to see the historic road, or rent a car.

Accommodations and Food

Great Falls has hotels and motels ranging from low-end to moderately priced accommodations, but nothing upscale. Most national hotel chains are downtown. For hotels offering airport shuttles, check with the **Great Falls Airport** (www.gtfairport.com) or the **Great Falls Convention and Visitors Bureau** (800/735-8535, www.genuinemontana.com).

For a filling meal at a reasonable price and a view overlooking the Missouri River, head for **MacKenzie River Pizza Company** (500 River Dr. S., 406/761-0085, daily 11am-10pm, $8-22), Montana's creative answer to pizza chains. The restaurant serves cowboy nachos, giant salads and sandwiches, eclectic pizzas, and Montana microbrews.

TRAVEL HUB: CALGARY

Calgary is the closest metropolitan city to Glacier. If coming in mid-July, you can take in the **Calgary Stampede** (403/269-9822 or 800/661-1767, www.calgarystampede. com), one of the biggest rodeos in the world. However, travel from Calgary to Glacier or Waterton can be a challenge. No train connection is available. No bus route goes all the way to Waterton or Glacier. Most visitors traveling from Calgary rent a vehicle. With an early afternoon flight arrival, you can be walking the beach at Waterton Lake in the evening.

Airport

Calgary International Airport (YYC, 403/735-1200, www.calgaryairport.com) bustles with flights from Tokyo, London, and Frankfurt. It has restaurants, shopping, and service from more than 25 airlines. Airport shuttles connect with downtown, hotels, car-rental agencies, and the Greyhound bus terminal. Because Calgary is still 240 kilometers (149 miles) from Waterton, most visitors heading to the park rent a car. Others chop off part of the distance by flying south to **Lethbridge** (YQL, www.lethbridgecountyairport.com) via **Air Canada** (888/247-2262, www.aircanada. com), where they rent a car to drive the 140 kilometers (87 miles) to Waterton.

Bus, Taxi, and Shuttle

You cannot reach Waterton or Glacier traveling by **Greyhound Canada** (403/265-9111 or 800/661-8747, www.greyhound.ca). Daily buses run from Calgary International Airport to Pincher Creek, but no farther: From Pincher Creek, hire a taxi with **Pincher Creek Taxi** (403/632-9738 or 406/632-9420, www.pinchercreektaxi.com, C$75-80 one-way) to get the 50 kilometers (31 miles) to Waterton. Reservations are advised.

The **Airport Shuttle Express** (403/509-4799, www.airportshuttleexpress.com, C$620-785) runs charter vans and ride-shares from the Calgary airport to Waterton. A charter van can be economical for small groups to split the fare and the tip for the driver.

Car Rental

Most major car-rental chains have desks inside the Calgary Airport terminals or within a shuttle ride down the road. Book vehicles from home through American sister companies: **Alamo** (800/462-5266, www.alamo.com), **Hertz** (800/654-3131, www.hertz.com), **Dollar** (800/800-4000, www.dollar.com), **National** (800/227-7368, www.nationalcar.com), **Budget** (800/472-3325, www.budget.com), and **Avis** (800/230-4898, www.avis.com).

RV Rental

Two RV-rental companies are within three kilometers (1.8 miles) of the Calgary Airport: **Canada RV Rentals** (250/999-2734 or 866/672-3572, www.canada-rv-rentals.com) and **CanaDream** (403/291-1000 or 800/461-7368, www.canadream.com). Motorhome RVs start at C$400-600 per day. Be aware of Going-to-the-Sun Road's vehicle-length restrictions (21 feet). You may have to supplement your RV tour with shuttles or red bus tours to see the historic landmark.

Equipment Rental

If you need outdoor gear, **Calgary Outdoor Centre** (2500 University Dr. NW, 403/220-5038, www.calgaryoutdoorcentre.ca) rents equipment for camping, backpacking, boating, bicycling, fishing, snowshoeing, climbing, and skiing. Per-day rates ($4-25/item) are charged for tents, backpacks, GPS units, stoves, sleeping bags, clothing, hiking boots, climbing gear, and rain gear. It also rents rafts, kayaks, skis, canoes, mountain bikes, and car racks. Find the complete list of rental gear and rates online. Call to reserve equipment ahead of time, a must during midsummer; a nonrefundable credit card deposit is required.

When picking up gear, try it on to be sure it fits, and have the staff demonstrate how to use unfamiliar equipment. You'll need a driver's license or photo ID to rent gear.

Accommodations and Food

The airport terminal houses the extremely convenient **Delta Calgary Airport Hotel** (403/250-8722 or 877/814-7706, www.marriott.com, C$145-400). Within a few miles of the airport, major chain hotels start at C$120; some offer airport shuttles. Find them via the **airport** (http://calgary.airporthotelguide.com) or contact **Tourism Calgary** (403/263-8510, www.tourismcalgary.com).

Budget-minded travelers may want to head for a hostel. The revamped **HI-Calgary City Centre Hostel** (403/269-8239 or 866/762-4122, www.hihostels.ca, C$35) has dorm beds. If your travels include staying in hostels across Canada, purchase a Hostelling International membership ($35).

For dining, Canadian cuisine has a few Alberta specialties meriting a taste. Calgary is in the heart of cattle country; grass-fed Alberta beef graces menus in all forms, as does bison. At the high end, it's tender and sweet; at the lower end, it's still decent. The doctored-up Canadian french-fry dish called *poutine* comes with a variety of toppings, but the traditional version includes cheese curds and gravy. Contrary to many towns east of the Rocky Mountains where steak-and-potato fare reigns, Calgary is much more cosmopolitan, with a good share of international restaurants. Canada's 5 percent Goods and Services Tax (GST) will be added to lodging and food bills.

Getting Around

DRIVING

Driving in Glacier National Park is not easy. Narrow roads built for cars in the 1930s barely fit today's SUVs, much less RVs and trailers. With no shoulders and sharp curves, roads require reduced speeds and shifting into second gear on extended descents to avoid burning brakes. Two roads cross the Continental Divide: Going-to-the-Sun Road bisects the park, while U.S. 2 hugs Glacier's southern border. Both are two-lane roads; however, the seasonal Going-to-the-Sun Road (mid-June–mid-Oct.) is the more difficult drive, climbing 1,500 feet higher on a skinnier, snakier road than year-round U.S. 2. Going-to-the-Sun Road's decade of reconstruction wraps up in 2017. It does not permit RVs or trailer-combos over 21 feet long.

Paved two-lane roads also lead to Two Medicine, St. Mary, Many Glacier, and Waterton. But don't be deluded: Just because roads are paved doesn't mean that they are smooth. Frost heaves and sinkholes pockmark them, bouncing passengers and slowing travel. Montana is also the land of dusty, potholed dirt roads: On the west side, two notoriously narrow, bumpy roads lead up the North Fork Valley; on the east side, a dirt road leads into the Cut Bank Valley. In some places they are as bad as they can be without requiring a 4WD vehicle. Larger RVs and those with trailers will not be comfortable on these dirt roads.

Gas

Gas up before you go: Service stations are not on every corner. Find gas in West Glacier, East Glacier, St. Mary, Babb, and Waterton, but few of the stations can repair severely broken-down vehicles. For big vehicle work, hit Browning or Flathead Valley in Montana or Pincher Creek in Canada.

SHUTTLES
Bus Shuttles

Inside Glacier, the National Park Service runs **free Going-to-the-Sun Road shuttles** July–Labor Day. These are shuttles, not guided tours. Between Apgar and St. Mary, they stop at 17 points, including Logan Pass

Going-to-the-Sun Road is cut into high cliffs.

Driving Times

Mileage is an inaccurate way to plan for trips around Glacier, as narrow, curvy, two-lane mountain roads take more time to drive than regular highways do. For example, Going-to-the-Sun Road is only 50 miles long but takes two hours to drive without stops during midday traffic. Logan Pass driving times are the most variable and depend on conditions.

Instead of using miles to plan your trip, use driving times that reflect the real road conditions around Glacier. From the following hubs, add up the times between each of the hubs for your chosen route. Plan to add more time for photo stops, sightseeing, traffic delays, entrance station lineups, border crossings, or construction.

FROM WEST GLACIER TO:

- Apgar: 0:08
- Polebridge via Outside North Fork Road: 1
- Polebridge via Inside North Fork Road: closed
- Essex: 0:35
- East Glacier: 1:10
- Logan Pass: 1-1:30
- St. Mary: 1:15-2

FROM POLEBRIDGE TO:

- Bowman Lake: 0:30
- Kintla Lake: 1:10

FROM EAST GLACIER TO:

- Essex: 0:35
- West Glacier: 1:10
- Two Medicine: 0:25
- Browning: 0:15
- St. Mary via Highway 49 and U.S. 89: 0:50
- St. Mary via Browning and Duck Lake Road: 1:05

and trailheads. Get on or off at any of the stops denoted by interpretive signs. No tickets are needed, and no reservations are taken. Departing every 15-30 minutes, these extremely popular shuttles enable point-to-point hiking on some of Glacier's most spectacular trails. Routes begin uphill service at 7am daily, with the last departures from Logan Pass at 7pm. On the west side, confirm your destination when you board, as some shuttles only run between certain locations.

Two companies operate fee-based shuttles. For hikers and backpackers, these aid in doing point-to-point trails, and for travelers without vehicles, they help connect east-side locations. Find schedules online; make reservations to

FROM ST. MARY TO:

- East Glacier via U.S. 89 and Highway 49: 0:50
- East Glacier via Duck Lake Road: 1:05
- Browning via U.S. 89: 0:40
- Browning via Duck Lake Road: 0:45
- Logan Pass: 0:35
- Many Glacier: 0:35
- Chief Mountain border crossing: 0:35
- Waterton: 0:75

FROM MANY GLACIER TO:

- St. Mary: 0:35
- Waterton: 1:30

TO WEST GLACIER FROM:

- Columbia Falls: 0:25
- Glacier Park Airport in Kalispell: 0:40
- Whitefish: 0:45
- Kalispell: 0:50
- Bigfork: 1:10

FROM GREAT FALLS TO:

- East Glacier: 2:30

FROM CALGARY TO:

- Waterton: 3:20
- St. Mary: 3:30
- Many Glacier: 3:45

ensure seats. **Glacier Park, Inc.** (406/892-2525, www.glacierparkinc.com) runs van service daily early June-late September north-south on the park's east side. It links East Glacier, Two Medicine, Cut Bank Creek, St. Mary, Many Glacier, Chief Mountain Customs, and Waterton. **Xanterra** (855/733-4522, www.glaciernationalparklodges.com) operates shuttles July-Labor Day from Many Glacier to St. Mary to accommodate hikers on the Highline-Swiftcurrent and Piegan Trails.

Running shuttles year-round by reservation, **Flathead-Glacier Transportation** (406/892-3390 or 800/829-7039, www.glaciertransportation.com) picks up travelers and backpackers at Glacier Park International

Airport and transports them to the Chief Mountain border crossing, Many Glacier, St. Mary, Two Medicine, East Glacier, Essex, West Glacier, Apgar, Lake McDonald Lodge, Polebridge, and U.S. 2 trailheads. It also runs shuttles to Flathead Valley towns: Whitefish, Columbia Falls, Kalispell, and Bigfork.

In Waterton, **Waterton Outdoor Adventures** (The Tamarack, 214 Mount View Rd., 403/859-2378, www.hikewaterton. com) shuttles hikers in summer to the popular Carthew-Alderson trailhead or Chief Mountain border crossing to catch Glacier Park, Inc.'s east-side shuttle.

Boat Shuttles

Hikers and backpackers also use tour boats as hiking shuttles to reduce foot miles. In Glacier, **Glacier Park Boat Company** (406/257-2426, www.glacierparkboats.com, June-Sept.) carts hikers across Two Medicine Lake and in Many Glacier across Swiftcurrent Lake and Lake Josephine. Both add early morning Hiker Express shuttles in July-August. Get advance reservations (one day for Two Medicine, three days for Many Glacier) for round-trip shuttles only. No reservations are necessary to catch a return boat; pay cash for a half-price fare upon boarding. Return shuttles run until all hikers are accommodated.

In Waterton, **Waterton Shoreline Cruises** (403/859-2362, www.watertoncruise. com) runs boat shuttles to the Crypt Lake trailhead late May-early October, and the tour boat to Goat Haunt functions as a hiker shuttle June-mid-September for round-trip or one-way rides. Reservations are advised.

TOURS
Bus Tours

Two bus-tour companies operate in Glacier National Park, both traveling the scenic Going-to-the-Sun Road. You'll get the "inside story" on the park from both companies' guides. Neither include park entrance fees, meals, or guide gratuities.

Departing from East Glacier, Browning, St. Mary, and West Glacier, **Sun Tours** (406/226-9220 or 800/786-9220, www.glaciersuntours.com) leads four- and seven-hour tours daily mid-June-mid-September over Going-to-the-Sun Road in 25-passenger air-conditioned buses with huge windows. Interpretation is steeped in Blackfeet cultural history and park lore.

The **red jammer buses** with rollback canvas tops are operated by **Xanterra** (855/733-4522, www.glaciernationalparklodges.com). Late May-September, daily tours depart from all the park lodges for Going-to-the-Sun Road, Waterton, and other park destinations.

Boat Tours

Five glacier-carved lakes in Waterton-Glacier International Peace Park have scenic boat tours. Tour boats run daily with multiple departures. Buy tickets at the docks or prepay by phone. In Glacier, **Glacier Park Boat Company** (406/257-2426, www.glacierparkboats.com) operates June-September boat tours on Lake McDonald, Two Medicine Lake, St. Mary Lake, and in Many Glacier on Swiftcurrent Lake and Lake Josephine. In Waterton, **Waterton Shoreline Cruises** (403/859-2362, www.watertoncruise.com) travel down Waterton Lake across the international border May-early October. The boats stop at Goat Haunt, USA, late May-mid-September.

TRAVELING BY RV

RVing is a great way to travel, but in Glacier it has its limitations. Roads are narrow, curvy, and shoulderless, and some campsites cannot fit larger RVs.

Road Restrictions

Going-to-the-Sun Road restricts RVs and trailers. From bumper to bumper, vehicles must be 21 feet or shorter to drive the road over Logan Pass between Avalanche Campground on the west and Rising Sun on the east. A truck-trailer or car-trailer combination must also be under 21 feet. The maximum width allowed, including mirrors, is 8 feet; maximum height is 10 feet. Despite meeting width and height requirements, small RV drivers will still feel pinched as they navigate the skinny lanes hemmed in by a 1,000-foot vertical wall and oncoming traffic inches away.

RVers shouldn't lose heart. You can still see the famed Going-to-the-Sun Road via Xanterra's red bus tours, Sun Tours, and free park shuttles, or rent a car in West Glacier, East Glacier, or St. Mary.

Camping

Not all campgrounds in Glacier can accommodate large RVs. Apgar can handle up to 40 footers. Fish Creek, Many Glacier, and St. Mary can fit RVs up to 35 feet. Two Medicine can accommodate RVs up to 32 feet. Only the shorter RVs can fit into sites at Rising Sun (up to 25 feet), Avalanche (up to 26 feet), and Sprague Creek (up to 21 feet, but no towed units). Large units are not recommended at Bowman Lake, Cut Bank, Kintla Lake, Logging Creek, and Quartz Creek.

Campgrounds inside the park do not have hookups, nor do adjacent national forest campgrounds. For hookups, head outside the park to commercial campgrounds in West Glacier, East Glacier, St. Mary, Flathead Valley, outside Waterton Park, and along

U.S. 2. In Waterton Lakes National Park, the Townsite Campground has hookups.

Generator use is restricted in campgrounds inside Glacier by hours and campsite location. Find details on generator hours and permitted locations online (www.nps.gov/glac).

Disposal Stations

Six campgrounds inside Glacier have disposal stations: Apgar, Fish Creek, Many Glacier, Rising Sun, St. Mary, and Two Medicine. Many private campgrounds at West Glacier, St. Mary, and East Glacier have disposal stations, too, but the North Fork has none. In Waterton, find dump stations at Townsite and Crandell Mountain Campgrounds and commercial campgrounds outside the park.

Repairs

Should you need repair services, drive to **Pierce RV Supercenter** (3138 U.S. 2, Kalispell, 406/752-8050 or 888/896-0889, www.piercerv.com) in Flathead Valley. Call ahead for an appointment; its summer schedule fills. If unable to drive, **Mike's Mobile RV Services** (406/261-7684) can come to you. He can repair many things where you are, but you'll pay handsomely for him to come to Glacier. In Waterton, **Pat's Gas Station** (224

Bikers relish touring Going-to-the-Sun Road.

Mount View Rd., 403/859-2266, www.patswaterton.com) can do minor repairs.

TRAVELING BY BICYCLE

Glacier is a tough place to cycle. There are no shoulders, roads are narrow and curvy, and drivers gawk at scenery instead of the road, all putting cyclists in precarious positions. With that caveat, for a dedicated cyclist, nothing compares with bicycling Going-to-the-Sun Road, one of the country's premier routes. Other roads surrounding Glacier also make good rides, particularly the 142-mile loop linking Going-to-the-Sun Road and U.S. 89, Highway 49, and U.S. 2. Roadies loop them in one day; tourers ride the loop in 2-3 days. Riders need to be prepared for large trucks and RVs whizzing by their elbows.

Find rental bikes at several locations in Flathead Valley. If you fly in, you can ship your bike to **Glacier Cyclery** (406/862-6446, www.glaciercyclery.com) in Whitefish for storage until you arrive, reassembly, and return shipping.

Bike Trails

Designated bike trails are few and far between in Waterton-Glacier. In fact, Glacier has only two trails, one paved and one dirt in the Apgar area. No bicycles are allowed on any other backcountry trails in Glacier. In Waterton, a paved bike trail and four backcountry paths permit bicycles. Outside Glacier, the 10-mile **Gateway to Glacier Trail** (www.gatewaytoglaciertrail.com) is a paved pathway paralleling U.S. 2 from Hungry Horse to West Glacier.

Campsites

Glacier's campgrounds designate campsites for cyclists and hikers at Apgar, Fish Creek, Sprague Creek, Avalanche, Rising Sun, St. Mary, Many Glacier, and Two Medicine. Held until 9pm, the sites are shared, holding up to eight people, who pay $5-8 per person. If these sites are full, you must find a regular unoccupied tent site, which is impossible in midsummer or late at night. Hiker-biker sites have special bear-resistant food storage containers.

Safety

Because of the narrow shoulderless roads, cyclists should have some riding ability before hitting Glacier's roads. Drainage grates, ice, and debris can quickly throw bikes off balance, adding to the challenge. Although cyclists on Going-to-the-Sun Road are fairly common, many drivers are so agog at the view that they may not be fully aware of your presence. That's a good reason to wear a helmet and bright colors. Skinny shoulderless roads demand riding in single file. For added protection, be sure your bike has reflectors on both ends, and use lights in fog and at dawn, dusk, or at night.

Restrictions

Because of high traffic volume and narrow lanes, Glacier enforces bicycling restrictions on Going-to-the-Sun Road's west side. Two sections of the road are closed 11am-4pm daily June 15-Labor Day: between Apgar Loop Road and Sprague Creek Campground, and eastbound (uphill) from Logan Creek to Logan Pass. The ride from Sprague to Logan Creek takes about 45 minutes; the climb from Logan Creek to Logan Pass usually takes at least three hours.

Repairs

Bring spare tubes and brake pads, a pump, and equipment to make minor repairs yourself. The park doesn't have any bike shops to bail you out. For major repairs, head to the bike shops in Flathead Valley.

TRAVELING BY MOTORCYCLE

Motorcyclists relish riding Going-to-the-Sun Road. On sunny days, the ride is unparalleled; on inclement days, it's bone-chilling. The alpine wonderland attracts scads of decked-out Harleys, Goldwings, and motorcycle clubs who come just to tour Going-to-the-Sun Road. Between East Glacier and U.S. 89, Highway 49 is posted for motorcycle warnings due to severe uneven pavement and gravel sections.

Many motorcyclists gravitate to Montana because the state requires helmets only for those under age 18. However, since most drivers on Going-to-the-Sun Road find their attention severely divided between the scenery and the road, you may want to consider head protection. In Waterton, helmets are required.

Missoula has the closest motorcycle rentals at **Grizzly Harley-Davidson** (406/721-2154, www.grizzlyhd.com). If you need repairs, the Flathead Valley has several motorcycle shops that specialize in one brand over another. Check business listings to pick the appropriate service for your machine.

TRAVELING WITH BOATS, CANOES, KAYAKS, AND PADDLEBOARDS

Glacier poses unique issues for those traveling with boats. Trailers are not allowed over Going-to-the-Sun Road, so those towing boats are required to drive U.S. 2 to get from one side of the park to the other. Due to overhangs on the Sun Road, rigs also can be no higher than 10 feet, so truck-camper combinations with kayaks, canoes, or rafts on top may be too tall.

Regulations in both Glacier and Waterton require all boats, including kayaks and canoes, to obtain permits. Boats must be cleaned, drained, and dried to avoid infesting the pristine park lakes with aquatic invasive species. In Glacier, get permits at park headquarters in West Glacier, St. Mary Visitor Center, Two Medicine and Many Glacier Ranger Stations, plus the Polebridge entrance station. For Waterton, get permits at the park entrance and visitors center. Pick up park boating regulations at all locations;

some lakes ban motorboats. Outside Glacier, you may pass boat inspection stations, where all watercraft are required to stop.

Outside Glacier, out-of-state boats over 12 feet in length must have a home-state registration, but they can be used in Montana for up to 90 consecutive days. In-state boats must have Montana registration and decals on the boat. For a complete list of Montana boating regulations, see www.fwp.mt.gov. For boating on Blackfeet Reservation lakes, get a conservation permit in St. Mary, Browning, or East Glacier.

Motorboaters head most often to **Lake McDonald,** as it sees less-gusty winds than St. Mary Lake. Smaller **Bowman Lake** and Two Medicine Lake are also fun. Most larger boats and water-skiers prefer Flathead Valley's warmer lakes.

Canoers and kayakers paddle Glacier's lakes for the stunning scenery and quiet ambience. While paddlers can tour any lake that offers a launch spot, some adventures rank more highly. In **Many Glacier,** paddle across **Swiftcurrent Lake** and up the slow-moving **Cataract Creek** to **Lake Josephine** for bear-watching and views of the Continental Divide. In the **North Fork,** take in the remoteness of **Kintla Lake** and **Bowman Lake** with an overnight trip.

River rafters and kayakers gravitate to the **Middle Fork** and **North Fork of the Flathead River,** which form Glacier's west and south boundaries. Designated Wild and Scenic Rivers, they bounce between float sections and white water. Check with the Flathead National Forest's **Hungry Horse Ranger Station** (406/387-3800, www.fs.fed.us/r1/flathead) for regulations, float guides, and flow levels.

Recreation

DAY HIKING
Trail Status

Conditions on Glacier's trails vary significantly depending on the season, elevation, recent severe weather, and bear closures. Swinging and plank bridges across rivers and creeks are installed in late May-June. Some years, bridges are installed and then removed a few weeks later to wait for rivers swollen with runoff to subside. Most years, higher passes are snowbound until mid-July. Steep snowfields often inhibit hiking on the Highline Trail until mid-July or so. Ptarmigan Tunnel's doors are usually open mid-July-early October. Several backcountry campsites are snowbound until August. To find out about trail conditions before hiking, stop at ranger stations or visitors centers for updates or consult trail status reports June-September on the park's website (www.nps.gov/glac). Bear closures are also listed online.

Signage

All park trailheads and junctions have excellent signage. Be prepared to convert kilometers to miles in your head to understand distances. Some signs show both kilometers and miles, others simply kilometers. This is, after all, the International Peace Park, and kilometers are more international. In Waterton, all trail sign distances use kilometers. Pull out your math skills: To convert kilometers to miles, multiply the kilometers listed by 0.6 (example: 3 km x 0.6 = 1.8 miles). To convert miles to kilometers, multiply the miles by 1.6 (example: 2 miles x 1.6 = 3.2 km). These calculations are simple, easy approximations for the trail. For more precise conversions, multiply by 0.62 to convert kilometers to miles; to convert miles to kilometers, multiply by 1.61. Some hikers enjoy kilometers: the number is always higher, so the accomplishment feels greater.

Trailheads may also display **yellow warning** or **orange closure** signs to alert hikers to bear or mountain lion activity. Obey the closures! They can mean an animal is guarding prey.

Heavily trampled areas may have a **footprint with a red slash** in fragile alpine meadows and areas of abuse replanted with native vegetation. It means "don't walk here."

Guides

National Park Service naturalists guide free hikes during summer in Glacier and snowshoe excursions in winter. Consult schedules in the current *Ranger-led Activity Guide* online (www.nps.gov/glac) or in visitors centers. Parks Canada naturalists guide free summer hikes in Waterton; find current schedules in the visitors center or online (www.pc.gc.ca). Naturalists from both parks lead the

Glacier trail sign with kilometers and miles

Hiking Essentials

Hiking in Glacier demands preparedness. Unpredictable, fast-changing weather can mutate a warm summer day into wintry conditions in hours. Different elevations vary in temperature, wind, and visibility: Sun on the shore of Two Medicine Lake may hide knock-over winds barreling over Dawson Pass six miles away. Hot valley temperatures may give way at Grinnell Lake to chilly breezes blowing down from the Continental Divide across the ice. To be prepared in Glacier's backcountry, take the following:

- **Extra Clothing:** Rain pants and jackets can double as wind protection, while gloves and a lightweight warm hat will save fingers and ears. Carry at least one extra water-wicking layer for warmth. Avoid cotton fabrics, which stay soggy and fail to retain body heat.

- **Extra Food and Water:** Depending on the hike's length, take a lunch and snacks, like compact high-energy food bars. Low-odor foods will not attract animals. Always carry extra water: Heat, wind, and elevation lead quickly to dehydration, and most visitors find they drink more than they do at home. Avoid drinking directly from streams or lakes. Due to the possibility of giardia and illness-inducing bacteria, always filter or treat water sources before drinking.

- **Map and Compass or GPS Device:** Although Glacier's trails are extremely well signed, a map can be handy for ascertaining distance traveled and location. A compass or GPS device will also help, but only if you know how to use it. In deep, heavily forested valleys, a GPS receiver may not pick up the satellites.

- **Flashlight:** Carry a small flashlight or headlamp for after-dark emergencies. Take extra batteries, too.

- **First-Aid Kit:** Two bandages may not be enough. Carry a fully equipped standard first-aid kit with blister remedies. Many outdoor stores sell suitably prepared kits for hiking. Don't forget to add personal items like bee-sting kits and allergy medications.

- **Sun Protection:** Altitude, snow, ice, and lakes all increase ultraviolet radiation. Protect yourself with SPF 30 sunscreen, sunglasses, and a sun hat or baseball cap.

- **Emergency Toilet Supplies:** Not every hike conveniently places a pit toilet at its destination. To accommodate an alfresco toilet stop, carry a small trowel, plastic baggies, and toilet paper, and move at least 200 feet away from water sources. For urinating, aim for a durable surface, such as rocks, logs, gravel, or snow. "Watering" fragile plants, campsites, or trails attracts mineral-starved animals that dig up the area. Bury feces 6-8 inches deep in soil. Do not bury toilet paper; use a baggie to pack it out.

- **Feminine Hygiene:** Carry heavy-duty zippered baggies and pack out tampons, pads, and everything else.

- **Insect Repellent:** Summer can be abuzz at any elevation with mosquitoes and blackflies. Insect repellents that contain 50 percent DEET work best. Purchase applications that rub or spray at close range rather than aerosols that go airborne onto other people, plants, and animals.

- **Pepper Spray:** If you want to carry pepper spray, purchase an eight-ounce can, as nothing smaller will be effective; however, do not bother unless you know how to use it and what influences its effectiveness. Do not use it like bug repellent.

- **Miscellaneous:** A knife may come in handy, as can a few feet of nylon cord and a bit of duct tape (wrap a few feet around something small like a flashlight handle or water bottle). Many hikers have repaired boots and packs with duct tape and a little ingenuity.

International Peace Park Hike twice weekly in July-August.

One company in Glacier and one company in Waterton provide guide services, with reservations required. **Glacier Guides** (406/387-5555 or 800/521-7238, www.glacierguides.com) leads day hikes, chalet overnights, and backpacking trips. One of the most popular trips hikes to both backcountry chalets for two nights each. **Waterton Outdoor Adventures** (The Tamarack, 214 Mount View Rd., 403/859-2379, www.hikewaterton.com) leads day hikes in Waterton Lakes National Park.

BACKPACKING

Glacier National Park's backpacking is unrivaled, with miles of well-marked scenic trails. Sixty-six designated backcountry campgrounds spread campers out to avoid crowds, and the permit system guarantees solitude. Go for popular trails such as Gunsight Pass, or head for something remote, like the Nyack-Coal Loop or Boulder Pass. Long-distance trekkers can tackle more than 100 miles of Continental Divide Trail in 7-10 days. Find backpacking information, permit applications, advance reservations, trail status reports, and backcountry campsite availability online (www.nps.gov/glac). To speak with someone in person regarding conditions and routes, call the permit offices. Use hiker shuttles to create easy point-to-point routes.

Each backcountry campground has 2-7 sites, with four people allowed per site. All backcountry campgrounds have pit toilets (some with great views), community cook sites, and separate tent sites. No food, garbage, toiletries, or cookware should be kept in the tent sites. A bear pole, hanging bar, or bearproof food storage boxes are in or near every cooking site. Many backcountry campsites do not allow fires; carry a lightweight stove for cooking. Take low-odor foods to avoid attracting bears, and practice Leave No Trace principles religiously.

Bring **backpacking gear** (tent, sleeping bag, pad, clothing, rain gear, topographic maps, compass or GPS device, first-aid kit, insect repellent, sunscreen, fuel, cooking gear, and stove) plus a 25-foot rope for hanging food, a small screen or strainer for sifting food particles out of gray water, a one-micron or smaller filter for purifying water (tablets and boiling can also do the job), and a small trowel for emergency human waste disposal when a pit toilet is unavailable.

backpacking Pitamakin Pass

Permits

Permits are required (adults $7 pp/ night). Starting mid-March, the park service accepts online requests for **advance reservations** ($40 extra). You'll still need to pick up the physical permit the day before your trip and pay the per person fees. If you don't have an advance reservation, you can still nab a permit in person 24 hours prior to a trip. Current availability is updated frequently online (www.nps. gov/glac). **If you have your heart set on a specific route in July-August, be in line by 6am** at the **Apgar Backcountry Permit Office** (406/888-7859 May-Oct., 406/888-7800 Nov.-Apr., 7am-4:30pm daily May-Sept., 8am-4pm daily Oct.) or **St. Mary Visitor Center** (406/732-7751, daily late May-early Oct., backcountry permit desk 7am-4:30pm). You can also get permits at **Many Glacier Ranger Station** (406/732-7740), **Two Medicine Ranger Station** (406/226-4484), and **Polebridge Ranger Station** (406/888-7742). During winter, permits are available at park headquarters by appointment (406/888-7800, Nov.-Apr.).

Guides

For guided backpacking, **Glacier Guides** (406/387-5555 or 800/521-7238, www.glacierguides.com) leads group trips that depart weekly for three, four, and six days. To avoid schlepping your own gear, hire a sherpa. The custom trips are the best option for families with kids.

CLIMBING

Glacier's peaks and off-trail scrambles are irresistible, but the park's crumbly sedimentary rock makes climbing risky. Loose handholds, wobbly footholds, rockfall, and unstable scree and talus slopes are hazardous. Each year, accidents and sometimes fatalities occur from falling while climbing. Only venture off-trail for climbing if you know the terrain and inherent risks. Do not attempt climbing in Glacier alone or without experience. Most ascents are actually scrambles, but still not for the inexperienced. For routes, J. Gordon Edwards's *A Climber's Guide to Glacier National Park* has been the bible, but Blake Passmore's several volumes of *Climb Glacier National Park* gives more detailed information for peak ascents, especially around Logan Pass.

Begin all off-trail adventures by registering at a ranger station or visitors center, and go prepared. Be aware of closures for bears and fragile vegetation, especially around Logan Pass. Check with visitors centers or ranger stations for the status, or call 406/888-7800. Always practice Leave No Trace principles. For emergencies, carry a cell phone along, but don't depend on its ability to work everywhere in the park. Be ready to self-rescue.

No commercial guiding outfitters operate climbing trips in Glacier. To hook up with climbers, **Glacier Mountaineering Society** (www.glaciermountaineers.com) offers volunteer-led climbs for members, usually on weekends, and each summer the club packs one week in July full of climbs for Mountaineering Week. Annual memberships cost $30.

Travel Tips

INTERNATIONAL BORDERS

Glacier National Park in the United States and Waterton Lakes National Park in Canada share an international boundary and combined designation as the world's first International Peace Park. For that reason, those who want to explore all parts of the joint park need to have appropriate travel documents.

Entering the United States

International travelers entering the United States must have passports. One exception applies to travelers from Canada and countries in the Western Hemisphere Travel Initiative, who may use a U.S. passport card, enhanced driver's license, or NEXUS card instead. Visas may also be required for some countries; check www.state.travel.gov for countries with visa waivers and visa applications. Except Canadians, international travelers entering the United States must have a current I-94 form ($6).

Entering Canada

International travelers entering Canada must have passports. The one exception is travelers from the United States and Western Hemisphere Travel Initiative countries, who may use U.S. passport cards, enhanced driver's licenses, or NEXUS cards instead. Visas are not required for visitors from about 50 countries, including the United States. All others must apply for visas. Find the list of visa-exempt countries and visa requirements at www.cic.gc.ca.

Road Ports of Entry

A seasonal port of entry on Chief Mountain International Highway, **Chief Mountain border crossing** is only open daily mid-May-September (7am-10pm June-Labor Day, 9am-6pm May and Sept. after Labor Day). When it is closed, the daily year-round port of entry on Waterton-Glacier's east side is **Piegan-Carway** (7am-11pm) on U.S. 89 and Alberta Highway 2. Due to flood damage in the North Fork Valley in Canada, the only west-side daily year-round port of entry is **Roosville** (open 24 hours) on U.S. 93 between Montana and British Columbia. It's 90 miles from West Glacier, but on the direct route to Banff.

Goat Haunt, USA

A small summer-season port of entry at the south end of Waterton Lake, Goat Haunt is accessible only by boat or on foot across the mid-lake boundary. Because of the International Peace Park status, special regulations are in effect. For visitors in Canada traveling down Waterton Lake in private boats or on the tour boat, clearing U.S. immigration is not required, even though you cross the Canadian-U.S. border. At Goat Haunt, you can debark and freely wander around the International Peace Park Pavilion and the walkway along the beach without going through immigration control. However, hikers going beyond Goat Haunt must show appropriate border crossing documentation at the immigration office (11am-5:30pm daily June-mid-Sept.). Visitors from countries other than Canada and the United States must have a current I-94 form or I-94W status to hike beyond Goat Haunt; these forms ($6) must be previously acquired at the Chief Mountain, Piegan-Carway, or Roosville border crossings. For further information on crossing from Canada into the United States, call the **Roosville Port of Entry** (406/889-3865).

For day hikers returning to Canada, immigration inspection is not required; however, backpackers hiking into Canada must phone the **Canada Border Services Agency** (403/653-3535) when they reach the Waterton Townsite. You can also phone the agency for information in advance of your trip. Backpackers taking the Waterton boat will be given immigration forms to fill out.

Customs

In general, Canada and the United States have similar customs laws: no plants, drugs, firewood, or live bait can cross the border. Some fresh meats, poultry products, fruits, and vegetables are restricted, as are firearms in Canada. Pets are permitted to cross the border with a certificate of rabies vaccination dated within 30 days prior to crossing. Bear sprays are considered firearms in Canada; they must have a U.S. Environmental Protection Agency-approved label to go across the border. For clarification, call the **Roosville Canadian customs office** (250/887-3413).

Travel Green in Glacier

Montana may not be up to par with big cities for recycling infrastructure, but Glacier is making advances. Because the park is located at the apex of three continental watersheds, it is a prime place to practice green habits.

CUTTING EMISSIONS

· Park your car to take shuttles. Free shuttles run July-Labor Day on Going-to-the-Sun Road, and other paid shuttles link points on Glacier's east side, including Waterton.

· Get out and hike rather than spending more time driving in the car.

· Consider a guided tour. The historic red bus fleet converted to a dual-fuel system that allows the buses to run on propane as well as gasoline.

· Many park restaurant menus now include local wine, beer, meats, and veggies to reduce excessive transportation.

RECYCLING

· All campgrounds, picnic areas, and visitors centers are equipped with recycling bins adjacent to bear-resistant garbage cans. Please recycle aluminum and plastic. Operators of most of the park lodges provide blue containers for recycling collection in the guest rooms of each hotel.

· Glass is problematic in Montana, as the state has no recycling infrastructure for it yet. If you are driving, consider carrying your glass containers home with you to recycle.

· If purchasing water in plastic bottles, please consider refilling the same bottle rather than disposing of it and buying another. Water refill stations are in many lodges.

Money and Currency Exchange

Traveling to Waterton for a day or two doesn't require exchanging money. Waterton has no bank, but **The Tamarack** (214 Mount View Rd., 403/859-2378, www.hikewaterton.com, May-mid-Oct.) does offer money-exchange services for Canadian and U.S. currency only. Most stores and businesses in Waterton accept U.S. currency but give Canadian currency as change. Exchange rates vary by store; to receive the best exchange rates, use credit or debit cards.

For Canadians visiting Glacier or Flathead Valley, some businesses accept Canadian currency. They are used to converting it, but credit and debit cards will receive the most accurate exchange rate. On Glacier's east side, the Native American Bank is in Browning.

For both Canada and the United States,

smaller denominations ($20 and under) work best for short trips on either side of the border. International travelers should exchange currency at their major port of entry (Seattle, Vancouver, or Calgary).

TRAVELING SOLO

Plenty of people travel solo to Glacier, but hiking alone is not recommended due to bears and mountain lions. Nevertheless, some hikers still venture into the backcountry alone. If you're one of them, make lots of noise while hiking and brush up on your bear skills. Solo travelers looking for trail companions can join park naturalist hikes. For times and dates, check the *Ranger-led Activity Guide* (www.nps.gov/glac). Solo travelers can also join guided group day hikes and backpacking trips with **Glacier Guides** (406/387-5555 or 800/521-7238, www.glacierguides.com) for a fee.

TRAVELING WITH CHILDREN

Children can find plenty of fun in Glacier and Waterton. The lakes, albeit chilly, offer lots of water play, and both parks have child-friendly trails. In Glacier, when the snow melts, Logan Pass has special interpretive signs with hand-cranked speakers geared toward kids, and in Waterton, the Townsite children's park has water-spray features.

Families with babies can rent gear such as cribs, day packs, car seats, and strollers from **Glacier Baby Outfitters** (406/261-9363, www.glacierbabyoutfitters.com). The company delivers equipment to Flathead Valley locations and West Glacier, but you can travel with it throughout the park. **Glacier Outfitters** (196 Apgar Loop Rd., 406/219-7466, www.goglacieroutfitters.com, 9am-8pm daily mid-May-late Sept., shorter hours in shoulder seasons) rents baby backpacks and bicycle trailers from its yurt in Apgar.

Junior Ranger Program

In Glacier, kids can earn a Junior Ranger badge by completing self-guided activities in the *Junior Ranger Activity Guide,* available at all visitors centers. Most activities target ages 6-12 and coincide with a trip over Going-to-the-Sun Road. When kids return the completed newspaper to a visitors center, they are sworn in as Junior Rangers and receive Glacier National Park badges. Waterton has a comparable program with the *Parks Canada Xplorers Program.*

Interpretive Programs

The **Apgar Nature Center** in Apgar serves up educational kid fun during summer. Interpretive rangers lead hands-on activities, including talks and walks, to teach children about wildlife, geology, and habitats. Elsewhere in select locations, rangers lead special children's interpretive programs; consult the *Ranger-led Activity Guide* (www.nps.gov/glac) for schedules. Waterton offers family geocaching activities (www.pc.gc.ca).

Hikes

For young kids, short hikes of 2-4 miles round-trip work best; always pack water and snacks. On Going-to-the-Sun Road, go for **Avalanche Lake, Hidden Lake Overlook,** and **St. Mary and Virginia Falls.** In Many Glacier, hike to **Red Rock Lake** or take the boat across Swiftcurrent Lake and Lake Josephine to hike to **Grinnell Lake.** In Two Medicine, take the boat up-lake to hike to **Twin Falls** or **Upper Two Medicine Lake.** In Waterton, climb the **Bear's Hump** or walk around **Red Rock Canyon.**

TRAVELING WITH PETS

Pets are allowed in Glacier National Park, but only in limited areas: campgrounds, parking lots, and roadsides. They are not allowed on trails, beaches, off-trail in the backcountry, or at any park lodges or motor inns. When outside a vehicle or in a campground, pets must be on a leash or caged. Be kind enough to avoid leaving them unattended in a car anywhere. Be considerate of wildlife and other visitors by keeping your pet under control and disposing of waste in garbage cans.

Protection of fragile vegetation and prevention of conflicts with wildlife are two main reasons pets are not allowed on Glacier National Park trails; bears provide their own class of reasons. For pooch-walking purposes, you can head to the paved two-mile Apgar Bike Trail, which allows pedestrians as well as pets (on leashes), or the surrounding Flathead National Forest, where pets are permitted. Contrary to Glacier, Waterton permits dogs on leashes on its trails.

Find overnight kenneling in Flathead Valley. **Columbia Mountain Kennels** (531 Windy Acres Dr., Columbia Falls, 406/897-7197, www.columbiamountainkennels.com) is the closest. More choices are in Kalispell, Whitefish, and Bigfork.

SENIOR TRAVELERS

National parks, as well as lands run by the U.S. Fish and Wildlife Service, U.S. Forest Service, and Bureau of Land Management, offer a bargain for U.S. citizens or permanent residents over age 61: $10 buys the National Parks and Federal Recreational Lands Pass, valid for life; however, the rate is set to increase in 2017 to $80. To purchase one, bring proof of age (state driver's license, birth certificate, or passport) in person to any national park entrance station. In a private vehicle, the card admits four adults in the vehicle, plus all children under age 16. This pass is not valid in Waterton, but seniors can get into the Canadian national park at a special rate.

The lifetime park pass also grants 50 percent discounts on fees for federally run tours and campgrounds; however, discounts do not apply to park concessionaire services like hotels, boat tours, and bus tours. Glacier's historic hotels do not give discounts to seniors, but some private lodging establishments surrounding the park do; ask to be sure.

ACCESS FOR TRAVELERS WITH DISABILITIES

Visitors with special needs should pick up an *Accessible Facilities and Services* brochure to see a list of services and accessible facilities. Get these at visitors centers and online (www. nps.gov/glac). The **Disabled Traveler's Companion** (www.tdtcompanion.com) gives comprehensive information for traveling in Glacier. Call 406/888-7806 for information by TDD. Special programs and sign-language interpretation may be available with two weeks' notice; call 406/888-7930 to set it up.

Park Passes

Blind or permanently disabled U.S. citizens or permanent residents can get a free lifetime National Parks and Federal Recreational Lands Access Pass for access to all national parks and other federal sites. The pass admits the pass holder plus three other adults in the same vehicle; children under age 16 are free. Pass holders also get 50 percent discounts on federally run tours and campgrounds. Get

these passes in person at entrance stations with proof of medical disability or eligibility for receiving federal benefits.

Park Facilities

Five campgrounds in Glacier reserve 1-2 sites each for wheelchair needs: Apgar, Fish Creek, Rising Sun, Sprague Creek, and Two Medicine. Picnic areas at Apgar, Rising Sun, and Sun Point also have wheelchair access, as do all lodges within the park boundaries, although they have a limited number of guest rooms that conform to Americans with Disabilities Act Accessibility Guidelines. Other wheelchair-accessible sites include boat docks at Lake McDonald, Many Glacier, and Two Medicine as well as evening naturalist programs in Apgar Amphitheater, Lake McDonald Lodge Auditorium, Many Glacier Hotel Auditorium, Rising Sun Campground, and Two Medicine Campground. Most parking lots offer designated parking.

Park Trails

In Glacier, the Apgar Bike Trail, Trail of the Cedars at Avalanche, Running Eagle Falls Nature Trail in Two Medicine, Goat Lick Overlook, Oberlin Bend Trail, the International Peace Park Pavilion at Goat Haunt, and the Many Glacier Trail from the picnic area are wheelchair accessible, although some surfaces are rough in places. In Waterton, wheelchairs can access Linnet Lake Trail, Waterton Townsite Trail, and Cameron Lake Day Use Area.

While pet dogs are not permitted on Glacier's backcountry trails, service dogs are allowed. But due to bears, they are discouraged. With service dogs, be safe by sticking to well-traveled trails during midday.

MAPS AND PLANNERS

Get park maps that include Glacier and Waterton at entrance stations, visitors centers, ranger stations, and online (www.nps. gov/glac). These maps are perfect for driving tours and perhaps a short walk or two. For hiking trails, small-area brochure-type

Cell Phone and Internet Access

FAQS: CELL PHONES

- **Where can I find service?** St. Mary, East Glacier, West Glacier, Apgar, Waterton, and Flathead Valley.

- **Where will I NOT find service?** Going-to-the-Sun Road, Logan Pass, U.S. 2, North Fork, Goat Haunt, Many Glacier, Two Medicine, and most trails in Glacier National Park.

- **Why did my call get dropped?** With only a few cell towers and service companies, alternate services get bumped during heavy use times.

- **How do I use an old-fashioned landline?** Pick up the phone and dial using a phone card. Phone cards are sold in camp stores inside the park.

- **What do I do if I get a flat tire and can't call AAA?** Flag down help and ask them to go to the nearest pay phone, ranger station, or visitors center.

- **What about an emergency while hiking or backpacking?** Be prepared to deal with emergencies yourself and self-rescue. If you can't, send someone for help to the nearest trailhead or ranger station.

Cell Phone Etiquette

- Turn off ringers. Phone noise catapults park visitors from a natural experience back into the hubbub of modern life.

- If you must make a call, move away from campsites, beaches, and other visitors to avoid disrupting their experience. At backcountry chalets, go outside and away from people.

- On trails, refrain from using phones in the presence of other hikers. Be considerate of other people in the backcountry and their desire to get away from it all.

FAQS: INTERNET ACCESS

- **Why don't Glacier or Waterton park services offer public Internet access?** National park visitors centers, ranger stations, and campgrounds do not have Wi-Fi. Get over it. We'd rather see them spend their tight resources on wildlife research and needed facilities.

- **Where can I hook up to wireless Internet?** Inside park lodges offer limited Wi-Fi for overnight guests. Some private campgrounds and hotels in West Glacier, Apgar, East Glacier, St. Mary, and Waterton have wireless Internet for guests. At least one coffee shop or restaurant in West Glacier, East Glacier, Polebridge, and Waterton has public Internet access available. Contrary to Glacier National Park environs, Internet is widely available in Flathead Valley at hotels, campgrounds, cafés, and libraries.

maps (Many Glacier, Lake McDonald, Two Medicine, Logan Pass, and St. Mary) are available free at ranger stations, visitors centers, and online. These do not have as much detail as topographic maps but can work in a pinch for day hikes on well-signed trails. Each year the National Park Service updates its *Glacier Vacation Planner,* a newspaper listing current information on campgrounds, roads, the park,

visitors centers, border crossings, trails, and safety. The current edition is online.

For those heading into the backcountry on day hikes and backpacking trips, pick up a topographic map through **Glacier National Park Conservancy** (406/892-3250, http://glacier.org, $10-12). Order these ahead online or purchase them in Glacier at conservancy bookstores. Three **Trails Illustrated maps** are sold: the large Glacier map that includes Waterton, and the more detailed North Fork and Two Medicine maps. The **Day Hikes of Glacier National Park** map guide combines a topographic map with trail descriptions. The conservancy also sells the **Going-to-the-Sun Road Driving Guide** map that includes stops and interpretive details.

For more detailed maps, USGS maps are sold in the 7.5-minute series at Flathead Valley sporting goods stores or through the **U.S. Geological Survey** (888/275-8747, http://store.usgs.gov). These maps do not include Waterton. You can also download and print them free from **National Geographic** (www.natgeomaps.com).

For hiking Waterton, find the Gem Trek topographic map at the **Waterton Lakes Visitor Information Centre** (403/859-5133) or order online (www.gemtrek.com, C$14). The map shows roads, trails, and bike routes, and it adds trail descriptions for easy, moderate, and strenuous hikes. It also includes the eastern end of Akamina-Kishinena Provincial Park and the Goat Haunt area of Glacier.

River floaters can find river maps in the *Three Forks of the Flathead Float Guide* ($13 or download free online) at **Hungry Horse Ranger Station** (Flathead National Forest, 10 Hungry Horse Dr., Hungry Horse, 406/387-3800, www.fs.fed.us/r1/flathead). For maps and information about national forests and the Bob Marshall Wilderness Complex adjacent to the park, contact the **Hungry Horse Ranger Station**. For Lewis and Clark National Forest, call the **Rocky Mountain Ranger Station** (1102 Main Ave. NW, Choteau, 406/466-5341, www.fs.fed.us/r1/lewisclark).

COMMUNICATIONS

Cell-phone service and Internet connectivity surrounding Glacier is limited. High mountains block reception on remote trails and many of the roads surrounding the park. Sometimes you can't even get a GPS signal with peaks blocking reception. In general, plan to be out of reach while you travel inside the park, where service is unavailable on many roads, trails, campgrounds, picnic areas, and lodges. Internet is equally limited. Glacier offers a chance to sever the technological chain and sink into utter beauty. Only then can you notice the ascending trill of a Swainson's thrush and catch the alpenglow on the peaks.

PACKING FOR GLACIER COUNTRY

Northwest Montanans have a saying: "Wait five minutes . . . the weather will change." Weather can fluctuate wildly within two days. Because snow can fall in August, **dress in layers.** Lightweight wicking synthetics, fleeces, and breathable waterproof or water-resistant fabrics are best. Bring gloves, a warm hat, and rain gear for cold snaps and a hat, sunscreen, and sunglasses for sun. Sturdy **walking shoes** or **hiking boots** work best on the rugged trails.

In Montana, dressing for dinner means putting on a clean shirt. **Casual attire** is the restaurant norm, as are hiking boots and river sandals. Cool weather brings out fleece rather than cashmere. Despite the Wild West heritage, cowboy hats and boots are only for wranglers.

Health and Safety

BEARS

Glacier has the highest density of grizzly bears in the Lower 48, and black bears find likable habitat here, too. Food is the biggest bear attractant. Proper use, storage, and handling of food and garbage prevents bears from being conditioned and turning aggressive. With strict food and garbage rules, Glacier has minimized aggressive bear encounters, attacks, and both human and bear deaths.

Bears are dangerous around food, be it a carcass in the woods, a pack on a trail, or a cooler in a campsite. Protecting bears and protecting yourself starts with being conscious of food, including wrappers and crumbs. Gorp tidbits dropped along the trail attract wildlife, as do "biodegradable" apple cores chucked into the forest. Pick up what you drop and pack out all your garbage; don't leave a Hansel-and-Gretel trail for the bears.

Camp safely: Use low-odor foods, keep food and cooking gear out of sleeping sites in the backcountry, and store them inside your vehicle in front-country campgrounds. Every picnic table in the park has detailed explanations of how to camp safely in bear country stapled to them. For information on camping in bear country, pick up the *Waterton-Glacier Guide* and Glacier's *Backcountry Guide* at entrance stations, visitors centers, ranger stations, permit offices, or online (www.nps. gov/glac).

Hike safely: On trails, you'll hear jingle bells, sold in gift shops as **bear bells.** Locals call them "dinner bells," and many hikers hate them. While making noise best prevents surprising a bear, bells fail to carry sound the way a human voice does. To check their minimal effectiveness, see how close you get to hikers before you hear the ringing. Bear bells are best as a souvenir, not as a substitute for human noise on the trail in the form of talking, singing, hooting, and hollering. You may feel silly at first, but everyone does it.

As of 2010, federal law allows people that can legally carry **firearms** under federal, state, and local laws to bring their guns into Glacier. However, federal law prohibits firearms in government offices, visitors centers, ranger stations, fee-collection buildings, and maintenance facilities. Those places are marked with signs at all public entrances. Discharging firearms in the park is illegal except when presented with "imminent danger."

Most hikers carry **pepper spray.** Its capsicum derivative deters bear attacks without injuring the bears or humans. Unlike insect repellents, do not use bear sprays on your body, in tents, or on gear; it is to be sprayed directly into a bear's face, aiming for the eyes and nose. Wind and rain may reduce its effectiveness. Small purse-size pepper sprays are too small to deter bears; buy an eight-ounce can. Practice how to use it, but still make noise on the trail. Carry it on the front of your pack where it is easily reached. If confronted with a bear, you won't have time to dig it out of your pack. Pepper spray is not allowed on airplanes unless it's in checked luggage, and only brands with U.S. Environmental Protection Agency labels can be carried into Canada.

MOUNTAIN LION ENCOUNTERS

These large cats rarely prey on humans, but they can, especially small kids. Making noise for bears will also help you avoid surprising a lion. Hike with others, and keep kids close. If you stumble on a lion, above all, do not run. Be calm, and group together to appear bigger. Look at the cat with peripheral vision rather than staring straight on, and back away picnic areas has been treated; you'll taste the chlorine.

DEHYDRATION

Many first-time hikers to Glacier are surprised to find they drink more water than at home. Glacier's winds, altitude, and lower humidity can add up to a fast case of dehydration. It manifests first as a headache. While hiking, drink lots of water, even more than you normally would. With children, monitor their fluid intake.

ALTITUDE

Some visitors from sea level locales feel the effects of altitude at high elevations like Logan Pass. Watch for lightheadedness, headaches, or shortness of breath. To acclimatize, slow down the pace of hiking and drink lots of fluids. If symptoms spike, descend in elevation as soon as possible. Altitude also increases UV radiation exposure: To prevent sunburn, use a strong sunscreen and wear sunglasses and a hat.

ICE AND SNOW

While glacial ice often looks solid to step on, it harbors unseen caverns beneath. Buried crevasses (large vertical cracks) are difficult to see, and snow bridges can collapse as a person crosses. Be safe by staying off the ice; even Glacier's tiny ice fields have caused fatalities. Steep-angled snowfields also pose a danger from falling. Use an ice ax and caution, or stay off them. If you want to slide on the snow for fun, slide only where you have a safe run out away from rocks and trees.

HYPOTHERMIA

Insidious and subtle, exhausted and physically unprepared hikers are at risk for hypothermia. The body's inner core loses heat, reducing mental and physical functions. Watch for uncontrolled shivering, incoherence, poor judgment, fumbling, mumbling, and slurred speech. Avoid becoming hypothermic by staying dry. Don rain gear and

Ensure kids drink lots of water while hiking.

slowly. If the lion attacks, fight back with everything: rocks, sticks, or kicking.

WATER HAZARDS

Contrary to popular belief, bears are not the number-one cause of death in Glacier; rather it is drowning from falling. Be extremely cautious around lakes, fast-moving streams, and waterfalls, where slick moss and algae cover the rocks. Waters are swift, frigid, clogged with submerged obstacles, unforgiving, and sometimes lethal.

GIARDIA

Lakes and streams can carry parasites like *Giardia lamblia*. If ingested, it causes cramping, nausea, and severe diarrhea for up to six weeks. Avoid giardia by boiling water (for one minute, plus one minute for each 1,000 feet of elevation above sea level) or using a one-micron filter. Bleach also works (add two drops per quart and wait 30 minutes). Tap water in campgrounds, hotels, and warm moisture-wicking layers, rather than cottons that won't dry and fail to retain heat. Get hypothermic hikers into dry clothing and shelter. Give warm nonalcoholic and noncaffeinated liquids. If the victim cannot regain body heat, get into a sleeping bag with the victim, both stripped for skin-to-skin contact.

BLISTERS

Incorrect socks and ill-fitting shoes cause most blisters. Cotton socks absorb water from the feet while you're hiking and hold onto it, providing a surface for friction. Synthetic or wool-blend socks wick water away from the skin. To prevent blisters, recognize "hot spots" or rubs, applying moleskin or New-Skin to sensitive areas. In a pinch, slap duct tape on trouble spots. Once a blister occurs, apply blister bandages or Second Skin, a product developed for burns that cools blisters and cushions them. Cover Second Skin with moleskin to absorb future rubbing and secure the Second Skin.

HANTAVIRUS

Hantavirus infection, with flu-like symptoms, is contracted by inhaling dust from deer mice droppings. Avoid burrows and woodpiles thick with rodents. Store all food in rodent-proof containers. If you find rodent dust in your gear, disinfect it with water and bleach (1.5 cups bleach to one gallon water). If you contract the virus, get immediate medical attention.

MOSQUITOES AND TICKS

Bugs can carry diseases such as West Nile virus and Rocky Mountain spotted fever. Protect yourself by wearing long sleeves and pants as well as using insect repellent in spring-summer, when mosquitoes and ticks are common. If you are bitten by a tick, remove it, disinfect the bite, and see a doctor if lesions or a rash appears.

HOSPITALS AND EMERGENCIES

For emergencies inside the park, call 406/888-7800. For emergencies outside the park, call 911. On Glacier's west side, the nearest hospitals are in Flathead Valley. **Kalispell Regional Medical Center** (310 Sunny View Ln., Kalispell, 406/752-5111) and the **North Valley Hospital** (1600 Hospital Way, Whitefish, 406/863-3500) are 35 minutes from West Glacier and can be up to 90 minutes from Logan Pass, depending on traffic. On Glacier's east side, **Blackfeet Community Hospital** (760 Government Sq., Browning, 406/338-6100) is 20 minutes from East Glacier and one hour from St. Mary.

Resources

Suggested Reading

DRIVING GUIDES

Guthrie, C. W., Martha Cheney, and Diane Krage. *Glacier National Park Legends and Lore: Along Going-to-the-Sun Road.* Helena, MT: Farcountry Press, 2002. An 88-page mile-by-mile tour of the historic road with Native American tales from Hugh Monroe, known as Rising Wolf of the Blackfeet.

Schmidt, Thomas. *National Geographic Road Guide to Glacier and Waterton Lakes National Park.* Washington DC: National Geographic, 2004. A handy 93-page guide to driving the park's roads. Each section is complete with a map, nature notes, landscape features, and stops.

GEOLOGY

Ahlenslager, Kathleen. *Glacier: The Story Behind the Scenery.* Wickenburg, AZ: KC Publications, 1988. Color photos and text in this 48-page book tell the natural history of Glacier with an emphasis on geology.

Alt, David, and Donald W. Hyndman. *Roadside Geology of Montana.* Missoula, MT: Mountain Press, 1986. Although Glacier's roads are treated minimally, the diagrams and descriptions are useful even to non-geologists. It is the best resource for geology on roads outside the park.

Raup, Omar B., Robert L. Earhart, James W. Whipple, and Paul E. Carrara. *Geology Along Going-to-the-Sun Road.* West Glacier, MT: Glacier Natural History Association,

1983. An easy-to-read 63-page geology guide for folks with no science background. Maps, 21 stops, and diagrams describe the geologic phenomena on the historic highway, along with great photos showing rock formations.

GRIZZLY BEARS

Chadwick, Doug. *True Griz.* San Francisco: Sierra Club Books, 2003. True stories of four grizzly bears—their survival and deaths. Chadwick is a reputable bear biologist.

Herrero, Stephen. *Bear Attacks: Their Causes and Avoidance.* Guilford, CT: The Lyons Press, 2002. Somewhat sensationalized with attention to gory detail, Herrero's book paints a picture of the myriad reasons for bear attacks while also covering safety and how to avoid attacks. Not for light sleepers who plan to go into the backcountry. Herrero is one of the leading authorities on bear research.

McMillion, Scott. *Mark of the Grizzly.* Helena, MT: Falcon Press, 1998. McMillion tells the stories behind 18 different grizzly bear attacks. He doesn't shy away from the gore, nor does he become preachy or judgmental, but he does examine each attack in detail to determine what we can learn about bears.

Olsen, Jack. *Night of the Grizzlies.* Moose, WY: Homestead Publishing, 1996. A true story of one night in 1968 when grizzlies killed two women in two different locations in Glacier's backcountry. This event altered park policies regarding food and garbage as well as bear management practices.

Schneider, Bill. *Bear Aware.* Helena, MT: Falcon Press, 2004. This handy little 96-page book is packed with advice on how to hike safely in bear country. One section tackles bear myths, debunking them with facts.

WILDLIFE

Chadwick, Doug. *The Wolverine Way.* Ventura, CA: Patagonia Inc., 2010. Stories of the gluttonous creatures that epitomize wilderness, gleaned from research in Glacier.

Fisher, Chris. *Birds of the Rocky Mountains.* Edmonton, Alberta, Canada: Lone Pine Publishing, 1997. A Lone Pine Field Guide for birds found in the Rocky Mountains—every species from raptors to waterfowl, songbirds to woodpeckers. Large drawings help with identification, and descriptions include details on size, range, habitat, nesting, and feeding. Details point out differences between similar species.

Fisher, Chris, Don Pattie, and Tamara Hartson. *Mammals of the Rocky Mountains.* Edmonton, Alberta, Canada: Lone Pine Publishing, 2000. A Lone Pine Field Guide for 91 species of animals found in the Rocky Mountains—a breeze to use. Each animal has details on physical description, behavior, habitat, food, denning, range, and young. Similar species are described to point out differences for identification.

Harada, Sumio, and Karen Yale. *Mountain Goats of Glacier National Park.* Helena, MT: Farcountry Press, 2008. Harada has photographed mountain goats in Glacier for the past two decades; Yale chronicles their behavior.

Wilkinson, Todd, and Michael H. Francis. *Watching Glacier's Wildlife.* Helena, MT: Riverbend Publishing, 2002. A 96-page guide to when, where, and how to see Glacier's wildlife.

HISTORY

Djuff, Ray, and Chris Morrison. *Glacier's Historic Hotels and Chalets: View with a Room.* Helena, MT: Farcountry Press, 2001. Loaded with historical photos, this quasi-coffee-table book tells the story behind each of Glacier Park's lodges and chalets, including the chalets that no longer exist. A great background read for anyone who falls in love with Glacier's historic lodges.

Glacier Centennial Program Committee, ed. *A View Inside Glacier National Park.* Glacier National Park, 2010. This collection of 100 stories about Glacier's 100 years celebrated the park's centennial in 2010.

Guthrie, Carol. *All Aboard for Glacier: The Great Northern Railway and Glacier National Park.* Helena, MT: Farcountry Press, 2004. For train buffs, this is the history of the Great Northern Railway building up Glacier as a destination for its passengers.

Guthrie, C. W. *Glacier National Park: The First 100 Years.* Helena, MT: Farcountry Press, 2008. The official centennial book contains rich color and historical photos in its decade-by-decade waltz through Glacier's history.

Guthrie, C. W. *Going-to-the-Sun Road: Highway to the Sky.* Helena, MT: Farcountry Press, 2006. With historical photos and maps, Going-to-the-Sun Road takes shape in this chronicle of the 20-year building of the National Historic Landmark.

Holterman, Jack. *Place Names of Glacier National Park.* Helena, MT: Riverbend Publishing, 2006. A list of 663 park names—how peaks, passes, lakes, rivers, and valleys in Glacier acquired their monikers.

Lawrence, Tom. *Pictures, a Park, and a Pulitzer: Mel Ruder and the Hungry Horse News.* Helena, MT: Farcountry Press, 2000. Photos and stories from Lawrence, a Pulitzer Prize-winning journalist and editor for 32 years at the *Hungry Horse News*. Much of the history covers Glacier.

NATIVE AMERICANS

Grinnell, George Bird. *Blackfoot Lodge Tales.* Whitefish, MT: Kessinger Publishing, 2007. Grinnell, who negotiated the purchase of reservation land for the park, chronicles Blackfeet stories from his days in Glacier in the late 1800s.

Schultz, James Willard. *Blackfeet Tales of Glacier National Park.* Helena, MT: Riverbend Publishing, 1916. Original Blackfeet stories collected by Schultz in the late 1800s, including the history of Two Medicine, Cut Bank, St. Mary, Swiftcurrent, and Chief Mountain.

Thompson, Sally. *People Before the Park: The Kootenai and Blackfeet before Glacier National Park.* Helena, MT: Montana Historical Society Press, 2015. Thompson spent three decades working to construct Native American history in the Northern Rockies and then published their stories in this 220-page book.

NATURAL HISTORY

DeSanto, Jerry. *Logan Pass: Alpine Splendor.* Guilford, CT: Globe Pequot Press, 1995. Gorgeous photos and short, easy-to-read descriptions of the Logan Pass environment, including grizzly bears, red buses, hiking, climbing, winter, wildflowers, and geology.

Kershaw, Linda, Andy MacKinnon, and Jim Pojar. *Plants of the Rocky Mountains.* Edmonton, Alberta, Canada: Lone Pine Publishing, 1998. A Lone Pine Field Guide for eight types of flora found in the Rocky Mountains: trees, shrubs, wildflowers,

aquatics, grasses, ferns, mosses, and lichens. Although the pictures are small, the detailed descriptions of appearance, season, and habitat help in identification. Notes on each of the 1,300 species given include fun tidbits on the origin of names and Native American uses.

Kimball, Shannon Fitzpatrick, and Peter Lesica. *Wildflowers of Glacier National Park and Surrounding Areas.* Kalispell, MT: Trillium Press, 2005. One of the best regional flower guides. Flowers are categorized by color, with big sharp photos allowing easy identification. Includes entries for trees, ferns, and grasses.

Rockwell, David. *Exploring Glacier National Park: A Natural History Guide.* Helena, MT: Falcon Press, 2002. Contrary to the title, this is not a guidebook but a description of Glacier Park's natural history. Rockwell covers geology, glaciers, flora, fauna, fires, and human impact on the ecosystem in the best available in-depth natural history book on the park.

OUTDOOR RECREATION

Arthur, Jean. *Montana Winter Trails: The Best Cross-country Ski and Snowshoe Trails.* Guilford, CT: Globe Pequot Press, 2001. Trail descriptions include five detailed trips for Glacier and several more for Flathead Valley.

Duckworth, Carolyn, ed. *Hiker's Guide to Glacier National Park* and *Short Hikes and Strolls in Glacier National Park.* West Glacier, MT: Glacier Natural History Association, 1996. Two books covering Glacier only, not Waterton. The hiker's guide contains 110 pages describing popular trails. *Short Hikes* is a 46-page book covering 16 favorite 1-4-mile walks.

Edwards, J. Gordon. *A Climber's Guide to Glacier Park.* Helena, MT: Falcon Press, 1995. The definitive guide to mountaineering in

Glacier National Park. Edwards pioneered many of the routes up Glacier's peaks and is considered the park's patron saint of climbing. Routes cover technical climbs and off-trail scrambles.

Good, Stormy R. *Day Hikes Around the Flathead.* Whitefish, MT: Flathead Guidebooks, 2011. A self-published book covering 99 day hikes with maps, route descriptions, distances, difficulty, and special emphasis on identifying dog-friendly trails. Available only through local bookstores and outdoor shops.

Meador, Mike, and Lee Stanley. *Mountain Bike Rides of the Flathead Valley.* Whitefish, MT: self-published, 2005. A 60-page roundup of the Flathead's best fat-tire rides, with maps, directions, and elevation profiles. Available only at Glacier Cyclery in Whitefish.

Molvar, Erik. *Best Easy Day Hikes in Glacier and Waterton Lakes.* Helena, MT: Falcon Press, 2001. A roundup of day hikes in both Glacier and Waterton. At half the size of his hiking guidebook, this focuses only on day hikes, with emphasis on well-signed, less-strenuous trails.

Molvar, Erik. *Hiking Glacier and Waterton Lakes National Parks.* Helena, MT: Falcon Press, 2012. The most definitive trail guide for Glacier and Waterton Parks. Molvar gives detailed trail descriptions, including maps, for all the popular trails inside the parks. Routes cover day hikes, overnights, and extended backpacking trips. Hiker safety, campsite details, and fishing information are also included.

Molvar, Erik. *Hiking Montana's Bob Marshall Wilderness.* Helena, MT: Falcon Press, 2001. A detailed trail guide covering the Great Bear, Bob Marshall, and Scapegoat Wilderness areas. Trail descriptions include maps, elevation charts, and accurate information on how to find even the more difficult-to-locate trailheads.

Passmore, Blake. *Climb Glacier National Park,* vols. 1, 2, and 3. Stevensville, MT: Stoneydale Press, 2011-2013. These illustrated guides provide climbing routes for peaks in the Logan Pass, Two Medicine, and central Glacier area. Color photos, maps, and GPS points identify routes.

Schneider, Russ. *Fishing Glacier National Park.* Helena, MT: Falcon Press, 2002. The most definitive fishing guide to Glacier. Schneider explains what flies to use to catch certain fish, where you'll catch arctic grayling or westslope cutthroat trout, and where you'll find nothing.

Internet Resources

GLACIER
Glacier National Park
www.nps.gov/glac
The official website for Glacier National Park. It provides information on park conditions, roads, campsites, trails, history, and more. Six webcams are updated every few minutes. In addition to trip planning information, the site includes downloadable maps, publications, and backcountry permit applications as well as a Going-to-the-Sun Road status report, updated daily.

Glacier National Park Conservancy
www.glacierconservancy.org
The best resource for books, maps, posters,

and cards on Glacier Park. Proceeds from book sales are donated to the park to support education, preservation, and research.

Northern Rocky Mountain Research Center
www.usgs.gov/centers/norock
The research center works under the U.S. Geological Survey. The website contains current research in Glacier on grizzly bears, glaciers, climate change, bighorn sheep, avalanches, and amphibians.

The Glacier Institute
www.glacierinstitute.org
An educational nonprofit park partner, the Glacier Institute presents programs for kids and adults in field settings taught by expert instructors. Field classes take place in Glacier as well as surrounding ecosystems.

Glacier National Park Volunteer Associates
http://gnpva.org
This nonprofit assists with historic preservation, education, and trail work. The organization looks for volunteers to help on projects ranging from a few days to summer-long.

National Park Service Reservation Center
www.recreation.gov
Fish Creek, Many Glacier, and St. Mary Campgrounds take reservations using this service.

Trail photos, videos, and blogs
www.hike734.com
Jake Bramante documented all of Glacier's 734 miles of trail in 2011. You can look up specific trails by map to see photos, video, and blogs.

Glacier Park Chat Room
www.glacier.nationalparkschat.com/phpBB3
Locals moderate a chat room about hiking, camping, eating, lodging, climbing, and traveling in Glacier.

WATERTON

Waterton Lakes National Park
www.pc.gc.ca/waterton
The official website for Waterton. It contains basic park information on camping, hiking, and Parks Canada-operated services, but not the commercial services in Waterton Townsite.

National Park Service Reservation Center
www.pccamping.ca
Log on to make reservations at Waterton Townsite's campground.

Waterton Chamber of Commerce
www.mywaterton.ca
The official website for Waterton Townsite contains dining, lodging, recreation, visitor services, and camping information for Waterton. Some services adjacent to the park are also included.

FLATHEAD VALLEY

Flathead Valley Convention and Visitors Bureau
www.fcvb.org
The Flathead Valley's tourism board covers info on Kalispell, Columbia Falls, Whitefish, Bigfork, Lakeside, Flathead Lake, and ski resorts. It covers recreation, lodging, dining, and special events.

MONTANA TRAVEL

Glacier Country
www.glaciermt.com
The official state travel website for northwest Montana. You can find lodging, dining, and activity information, and it's easy to navigate by activity or location.

Montana Travel
www.visitmt.com
The official travel website for Montana. You'll find access to the state's activities, lodging, dining, and recreation by location or activity.

Montana Department of Transportation
www.mdt.mt.gov
Travel advisories and road conditions for Montana. Glacier's interior roads are not yet included on the website; information on Going-to-the-Sun Road is sporadic. Check the park's website for the most accurate information.

Lewis and Clark National Forest
www.fs.fed.us/r1/lewisclark
Information on campgrounds, trails, fishing, cabin rentals, and other recreation, particularly for the Bob Marshall Wilderness.

Flathead National Forest
www.fs.fed.us/r1/flathead
Information on campgrounds, fishing, rafting, wilderness areas, cabin rentals, ski areas, trails, and other recreation. However, the recreation section is limited to specifics for trails.

Montana Fish, Wildlife, and Parks
http://fwp.mt.gov
Up-to-date fishing and hunting information, licenses, state park, and wildlife refuge details for Montana.

CANADIAN TRAVEL

Travel Alberta Canada
www.travelalberta.com
The province's official portal to Alberta resorts, parks, ski areas, festivals, events, cities, outdoor recreation, and touring. It's easy to navigate by location or activity to find what you want.

Alberta Road Reports
www.ama.ab.ca/road-reports
Check this site for road construction, advisories, and closures from the Alberta Motor Association.

British Columbia Transportation
www.gov.bc.ca/tran
Road reports update travel information, closures, construction, and weather for British Columbia. Webcams give you a firsthand look.

Akamina-Kishinena Provincial Park
www.gov.bc.ca/bcparks
Information on recreation, camping, and hiking in Akamina-Kishinena Provincial Park, adjacent to Waterton and Glacier. Maps are also available.

Index

INDEX

List of Maps

Also Available

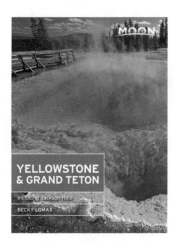

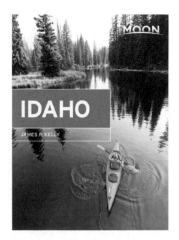

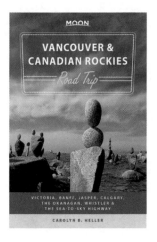